Every

NAME OF GOD

in the Bible

Every

NAME OF GOD

in the Bible

LARRY RICHARDS

Illustrated by
Dan Pegoda
and
Paul Gross

THOMAS NELSON PUBLISHERS
Nashville

VW TH EN VW MS

Published in Nashville, Tennessee, by Thomas Nelson, Inc.

Library of Congress Cataloging-in-Publication Data Available from Library of Congress

Richards, Larry, 1931-
   Every name of God in the Bible/Larry Richards; illustrated by Dan Pegoda and Paul Gross

ISBN 0-7852-0702-3

Printed in the United States of America

1 2 3 4 5 6 7 8— 06 05 04 03 02 01

CONTENTS

See Expository and Scripture Indexes for Complete Topical and Scripture Listings

INTRODUCTION

Welcome to *Every Name of God in the Bible*, the eighth in Nelson's "Everything in the Bible" series. Like other books in this series, this book is intended to serve as a resource for those studying God's Word. Yet this, as the other books, has also been written for your personal enrichment. This is especially true for this book, which explores God's revelation of Himself through names, titles, and images found in Scripture.

For those who want to know God better, there is hardly a richer approach than to explore the names, the titles, the similes, and the metaphors through which God has presented Himself to us in both testaments. These unveil the essence of who God is, they describe His qualities and character, and they depict His work both in this universe and in our lives.

For most of human history, names given the deity by pagans served to distance human beings from the one true God. And then God stepped in, to reveal Himself to His Old Testament people. Three chapters of this book trace God's revelation of His true self through the names, titles, and images found in the Old Testament. Another chapter examines the names and titles specifically ascribed to Jesus Christ in the Old Testament, while additional chapters focus on the names and titles given each person of the Trinity in the New Testament. How wonderfully each name and title opens a new window through which we can gaze on our Lord in awe and wonder, and respond with thanksgiving and love.

Three added features make this book especially valuable. The first is an Expository Index, which organizes names and titles alphabetically under several headings, and which guides you to pages where they are discussed.

The second feature, Appendix A, is a summary of what we know about God as He has revealed Himself to us. This appendix is in the form of a creed—a statement of what we can and do firmly believe about God based on His Word.

The third special feature is found in Appendix B, where a variety of special issues growing out of our study are discussed. For instance, the Scripture presents God as a loving and compassionate person, and yet we also see Him as a God who is angered by and will surely judge sin. How can a loving God also be a God of wrath? God is also said to be just and righteous. How can such a God freely forgive sin? And, God is said to be both good and all-powerful. How then can evil infect His universe? Such issues are explored in Appendix B in articles on God's wrath, on forgiveness, and on God's relationship to evil. In addition, mysteries like the Incarnation and the Trinity are explored here. And in each case, Scripture provides satisfying answers to supposed contradictions in the nature of the God who has revealed Himself so powerfully in the names, titles, similes, and metaphors found in the Bible.

What you read here then will show you fresh and exciting ways to deepen your understanding of God and your relationship with the Lord. What you read here will also confirm your certainty that God can be trusted, and that any supposed contradiction others may cite has a satisfying answer already revealed in the wonderful, reliable, and trustworthy Word of God.

WHAT'S IN A NAME?

ind a globe map of the world. Spin it, and let your finger fall at random. Any place your finger falls, in any era of history or prehistory, people who live there will speak about "god" or "gods."

Yet it would be a mistake to assume that what the peoples of Africa, China, South America, Europe, or the Ancient Middle East mean by "god" is what we mean when we use that word. The word "god" has had different meanings to peoples of differing times and places.

In this chapter we'll take a look at various peoples' idea of "god." And we'll suggest why so many notions about God have emerged in human history. This survey is extremely important, for only when we understand humankind's various conceptions of "god" can we grasp the significance of Scripture's revelation of the names and titles of God. Only when we see what humanity has done to distort the image of the deity will we grasp what knowing His names and titles can mean to us in our own personal relationship with the Lord.

RELIGION AND HUMANKIND

In his book *Religions of the World*, Lewis M. Hopfe notes that religion is a universal phenomenon. He writes,

Wherever people are found, there too religion resides. Occasionally religion is hard to find or pin down, but in the great metropolitan capitals and in the most primitive areas of the world, there are physical and cultural temples, pyramids, megaliths, and monuments that societies have raised at tremendous expense as an expression of their religion. Even when we explore the backwaters of time in prehistoric civilizations, we find altars, cave paintings, and special burials that point toward our religious nature.

Indeed, there is no other phenomenon so pervasive, so consistent from society to society, as the search for gods (p. 6).

But is the religious nature of human beings evidence of a "search for gods"? Or is it evidence of something else? In Romans 1 the apostle Paul offers a unique explanation for man's preoccupation with religion. Paul teaches that God has implanted awareness within the human spirit that there is a reality

Pagan worship, such as sun worship, is evidence of humanity's frantic effort to distance ourselves from Him.

beyond the material universe, and that a "god" or "gods" exist.

Paul's argument is stated succinctly. "What may be known of God is manifest in them, for God has shown it to them. For since the creation of the world His invisible attributes are clearly seen, being understood by the things that are made, even His eternal power and Godhead, so that they are without excuse" (Rom. 1:19, 20). On the one hand this argument is logical: the creation testifies to a Creator, who in order to create what now exists must be both personal and powerful. We might liken the created universe to a powerful radio station sending out a clear and unmistakable signal. This thought is reflected in Psalm 19:1-4,

The heavens declare the glory of God;
And the firmament shows His handiwork.
Day unto day utters speech,
And night unto night reveals knowledge.
There is no speech nor language
Where their voice is not heard.
Their line has gone out through all the earth,
And their words to the end of the world.

But there is an even more significant element here. Paul says that God has manifested Himself "in" people (Rom. 1:19). It is as if God implanted in human beings a radio receiver that He Himself tuned to the signal sent by creation. The message is not only sent; it is received! The very universality of religion and man's belief in a god or gods is clear evidence that Paul's insight is accurate and true.

But Paul has more to say about man's reaction to nature's message from God. While what may be known about God through natural revelation is plain, human beings "suppress the truth in unrighteousness" (v. 18). Paul writes that "although they knew God, they did not glorify God, nor were thankful, but became futile in their thoughts, and their foolish hearts were darkened. Professing to be wise, they became fools and changed the glory of the incorruptible God into an image made like corruptible man—and birds and four-footed animals and creeping things" (vv. 21-23).

The knowledge of God available to human beings from the beginning was rejected, suppressed, and corrupted. The word "god" was drained of its original meaning and perverted by humankind. And the "gods" of various peoples and places were not invented in a pious search *for* Him, but rather in a desperate attempt to escape *from* Him.

THEORIES ABOUT THE ORIGIN OF RELIGION

As it became more and more clear that religion is a universal phenomenon, students of comparative religion began to offer suggestions about where religion came from. Typical theories held today include the Animistic Theory, the Nature Worship theory, and what has been called the Original Monotheism theory.

The Animistic Theory. This theory was promoted in the book *Primitive Culture*, published in 1871 by Sir Edward Burnett Tylor. Tylor argued that primitive peoples had trouble distinguishing dreams and reality, and that their dreams about the dead led them to believe in spirits that exist after death. They extended this belief in spirits to a belief that animals, trees, and rocks possessed spirits too. As these spirits could be helpful or harmful, primitive peoples attempted to appease the harmful spirits and appeal to the beneficial. Out of this belief in spirits grew the multiple deities that characterize the more sophisticated religions found in the ancient world.

The Nature Worship Theory. Max Muller, who taught at Oxford in the 1880s, studied mythology and Indian religions. He suggested that human beings developed their religions by observing the forces of nature. To interact with the forces of nature, primitive peoples personalized them, giving names to the sun, the moon, storms, and so on. The stories [myths] that were invented to explain how these forces operate gradually developed into pantheons of deities, around whom religions developed.

The Original Monotheism Theory. It wasn't until the beginning of the twentieth century that a Jesuit priest entered the discussion with the proposal that the world's religions were corruptions of an original monotheism. He did not base his argument on Scripture, but on the observation that even in the most primitive areas in Africa or Australia, where religion was animistic or polytheistic, there was a persistent belief that once there was a single great god above all. While this god had

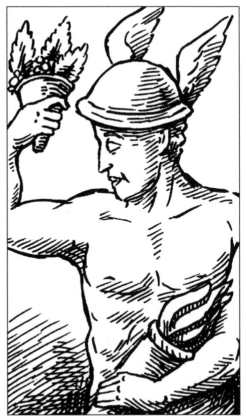

One strategy for suppressing knowledge of the true God has been to imagine gods in man's image.

lost contact with the world, or the world had lost contact with him, the belief that he existed was pervasive. The priest, Father Wilhelm Schmidt, argued that the later monotheistic religions had simply recovered the original belief of humankind. Father Schmidt's view was rejected out of hand, for an evolutionary assumption underlay the research of the scholars working in the field of comparative religion.

The Biblical Theory. The biblical theory of the origin of religions is clearly expressed by the apostle Paul, as discussed briefly earlier. In the beginning, God created the material universe and the first human beings. But Adam and Eve fell, and in introducing sin into our race corrupted every gift God had given human beings. Mind, heart, and will were twisted in the Fall, and the bond of love and obedience that had united God and man was broken.

While God did not abandon human beings, human beings abandoned Him. Yet human beings retained an innate awareness of the reality of the spiritual world. Knowledge of God might be suppressed, but the need for God could not be. So as generation succeeded generation, over the centuries and millenniums, human beings remained "religious animals." But strikingly, *humanity's religions reveal a drive not to find God but to distance themselves from Him.*

RELIGION AS A WAY OF DISTANCING FROM GOD

Data from all over the world suggests that human beings retain knowledge of God but have persistently sought to distance themselves from Him. This distancing takes several forms. One strategy is reflected in stories of a High God who is uninterested in His creation. God's existence is acknowledged, but He has become irrelevant.

Another strategy subordinates deities by assuming that the gods were themselves created. Typically the many gods in such systems are organized in hierarchies, and humankind is to deal with the lesser gods. A very common strategy for distancing from God is to envision deities in man's image. The basic strategy of eastern religions is to depersonalize Him. Perhaps the most significant strategy for distancing from God is seen in the religions of the ancient Middle East, the culture within which the Old Testament revelation was given.

Let's look at these strategies and how they have been used.

The first strategy: make God irrelevant. The literature on comparative religions contains many accounts of a high deity who has withdrawn. *The Eerdman's Handbook of the World's Religions* notes the following:

Many primal religions have a single supreme god above all other powers. Sometimes he is even thought of as a universal god for all peoples. For instance, North American Indians think of the Great Spirit, and the New Zealand Maoris of Io. This God is usually the creator of all things. Sometimes he is concerned that people live moral lives, and deals with them through the lesser gods. At other times he is believed to have been angry with mankind and to have withdrawn from the world, or else he is so high and mysterious that we cannot possibly reach him (p. 131).

In *Religions of the World*, Hopfe, writing about basic concepts in African religions, identifies

a belief that above all local deities there is one supreme High God who created the world and then withdrew from active participation in it. . . . Although most of the native religions of Africa are basically polytheistic in their day-to-day practice, there is an overriding belief that beyond all the minor gods, spirits, and ancestors, one High God exists (p. 27).

In volume 2 of Mircea Eliade's *History of Religious Ideas* the author notes the same phenomenon in Bronze Age China. The cult of the supreme celestial god, Ti, "shows a certain diminution of religious primacy. Ti is found to be distant and less active than the ancestors of the royal lineage" (pp. 7, 8).

In volume 3 Eliade quotes Helmond's study of the Slavic peoples. There Helmond notes that "Slavs do not dispute the existence of one god in the heavens, but consider that this god concerned himself only with celestial affairs, having abandoned the government of the world to inferior divinities whom he has procreated himself" (p. 30).

Robert S. Ellwood Jr., in *Many Peoples, Many Faiths*, states,

It is characteristic of many peoples to believe that the supreme god who created the earth is remote from our affairs, and that it is really the finite but far more involved ancestral or nature spirits with whom we have the most to deal. The Luguru of East Africa, for example, say that the earth was made by the high god Mulungu, but he is not normally concerned with human affairs. He is given no prayers or sacrifices; they are made rather to the *mitsimu*, or ancestral spirits.

In these and many other instances the existence of a supreme god is acknowledged, but *he becomes less and less relevant to the lives of ordinary people.* Whether he is angry with humankind and withdraws, or simply loses interest in his creation and wanders off, the high god becomes irrelevant to religion and to daily life. In Paul's words, "although they knew God, they did not glorify Him as God, nor were thankful" (Rom. 1:21). Knowledge of God has been suppressed by casting Him as more and more distant from the world He made.

The second strategy: subordinate "God." Many ancient religions present a variety of gods and goddesses. In Mesopotamia these deities were supposed to have been formed in a watery mass that preexisted the universe, and thus are subordinate beings. Eliade (Vol. 1, p. 88) notes the following:

> Like so many other traditions, the Egyptian cosmogony begins with the emergence of a mound in the primordial waters. The appearance of this "First Place" above the aquatic immensity signifies the emergence of the earth, but also the beginning of light, life, and consciousness (p. 58).

The Eerdman's handbook adds, "Different gods were thought to have somehow emerged from the hill or the water, and in various ways to have created other gods" (p. 87).

The Eerdman's handbook describes a similar belief held by the Aztecs of Central America.

The Aztecs believed that two primordial beings originated everything, including the gods. They were Ometecuhtli, 'Lord of Duality,' and Omeciuatl, 'Lady of the Duality.' They lived at the summit of the world in the thirteenth heaven. These two produced all the gods and also all mankind (p. 89).

These belief systems subordinate even the most powerful of the gods by making them creations emerging from preexisting matter, while the hierarchies of deities are an additional attempt to gain distance from the source of reality. The handbook adds that "by the time of the Spanish Conquest, the two primordial beings had largely been pushed into the background by a crowd of younger and more active gods."

EVOLUTION AS RELIGION

It is significant to note that the theory of evolution, which most people today unquestioningly accept, is essentially a religion. It utilizes a familiar strategy for distancing from God. Like the religions of the ancient Middle East, of Egypt, and of Greece, evolution assumes that the material universe always existed. While the ancients imagined that deities sprang from pre-existing matter to give the world its present shape, the evolutionist assumes that impersonal laws of nature and chance combined to spontaneously create life from non-living matter. The ancients sensed the reality of a spiritual realm, but peopled that reality with gods of their own invention. Moderns deny the existence of a spiritual realm, and stridently insist that what can be touched and tested is all there ever was. But the distancing strategy adopted by the superstitious priest of Mesopotamia 3,000 years before Christ and by the rationalist scientist of America 2,000 years after Christ is essentially the same. Both, by asserting the priority of the material universe, rule out *a priori* the God of Creation. Both make God subordinate to the material universe, and so deny their obligation to glorify Him or be thankful.

The third strategy: make gods in man's image. Most educated people are somewhat familiar with the pantheons of Greece and Rome. Here Zeus is held up as the father of the gods, in a literal sense. The mythology recorded in the works of Homer and others describes relationships between the gods in human family terms, with husbands and wives and offspring. While the gods are more powerful than human beings, their motives and passions, their lies and sexual liaisons, reflect what is worst in human society. While the gods may take an interest in human affairs, their interest is fleeting and their advocacy undependable, for feuds and intrigues within the family of the gods makes human beings vulnerable to becoming pawns in games played only for the deities' benefit. Moreover, these deities created in man's image are far from all-powerful. They, like human beings, are subject to fate and destiny, and they too came into existence after the material universe.

Later pagan philosophers, who expressed the opinion that there must be one god underlying reality, criticized the religion of Greece and Rome. But as one of the critics, Maximus of Tyre, wrote,

> God, the Father and Demiurge of what exists, older than the sun, older than the heavens, superior to time and the age of every transient nature, is anonymous for any legislator and ineffable to voice and invisible to the eyes. We have no means of ascertaining his nature (Oration 2).

It was as Paul described. Some cultures "changed the glory of the incorruptible God into an image made like corruptible man" (Rom. 1:23). In the process such cultures so perverted their knowledge of God that those who realized He must exist had no notion of how to find Him.

The fourth strategy: depersonalize God. Yet another strategy for distancing from God is seen in beliefs rooted in the Far East. There the very personality of God is denied, and several religions hold that whatever the ultimate reality may be, it cannot be comprehended by human beings.

In describing Taoism, a religion originating in China, Eliade (Vol. 2, p. 29) asserts that the Tao is "the ultimate, mysterious, and inapprehensible reality, *fons et origo* of all creation, foundation of all existence." Even a second Tao, contingent on the first, cannot be apprehended. Lao Tzu says, "I gaze and I see nothing. . . . I listen and I hear nothing. . . . I find only an undifferentiated Unity. . . . Indiscernible, it cannot be named" (ch. 14).

A classic expression of the nature of "god" is found in this stanza from the 25th chapter of *Tao Te Ching*:

> There was something undifferentiated and
>   yet complete,
> Which existed before heaven and earth.
> Soundless and formless, it depends on
>   nothing and does not change,
> It operates everywhere and is free from
>   danger.
> It may be considered the mother of the
>   universe.
> I do not know its name; I call it Tao.

In Hinduism the name given the "something," the unknowable Absolute, is the Brahman. Ward J. Fellows in *Religions East and West* notes that the Brahman "is one, is many, is personal, is impersonal, is everything, is nothing, is red, is green, is good, is bad, is the world, is emptiness" (p. 92).

Fellows adds, "The idea of an impersonal ultimate Being which is the source of becoming, or of the unchanging which remains when all else changes, is not peculiar to India, but the root idea has been more fully elaborated, and then incorporated more centrally, in philosophic Hinduism than anywhere else" (p. 93).

But here Hinduism goes even further. The doctrine of the Atman affirms that the human soul and the Brahman are fundamentally the same. Rather than see human beings as separate from and subordinate to God, the Hindu sees himself or herself as one with "god" and thus as "god" or as a part of "god."

It is especially striking to realize that in the practice of Hinduism there are many gods and goddesses who are not "god" in any biblical sense, yet are worshiped, prayed to, and relied on by the people. That the many gods and goddesses of the Hindu might co-exist with a philosophical system that utterly depersonalizes the true God is logically contradictory. Yet the notion that "gods" exist while the Brahman ["god"] is everything and nothing, unknown and unknowable but essentially part of ourselves, is a foundational feature of Eastern religions. Clearly this strategy for distancing from God has successfully entrapped untold millions, from China through India and Tibet.

Hindu mythology multiplies deities, while Hindu philosophy argues that "god" is indefinite, unknowable, and impersonal.

The fifth strategy: emasculate "God." Old Testament faith originated in the ancient Middle East, often called the cradle of civilization. Written records there go back some 3,000 years before Christ, and it is from this part of the world that we have our first written accounts of religion. It is especially fascinating to see how the peoples of Canaan developed a strategy for distancing themselves from the primary deity, whom they called El ("god").

In Syria-Palestine, El was the head of a pantheon of deities. His name simply meant "god" in the Semitic languages of the area. In the west, he was viewed as a personal God, and called "Powerful," the "Father of Gods and Men," and "King." According to myth, El formed the female, Asherah or Ashtoreth, and the two produced seventy divine sons.

However, despite El's primacy, he is increasingly depicted in myths as "physically weak, indecisive, senile, resigned" (Eliade, Vol. 1, p. 151). Gradually he is replaced by Baal, a forth generation deity. According to a rather mutilated text, Baal and some confederates attacked El in his palace on Mount Sapan. They wounded El, tied him up, and castrated him. In the ancient East this mutilation excluded a person from sovereignty. Baal then carried off El's wife. She became his consort, and as the Old Testament records, was worshiped with him by the Canaanites. El was forced to seek refuge at the end of the world.

While the myths suggest that El begged the help of his family and promised to make the god Yam his successor if he would drive Baal from the throne, El himself could now be dismissed. He had *literally* become an impotent deity!

What do we learn from this survey of salient elements of religions around the world? First, we see that human beings truly are "religious." Wherever human society is found, religion is a significant element. Second, we find clear evidence that religion cannot be characterized as a "search for god or gods." Features of all religions suggest that they "*devolved*," gradually withdrawing from original assumptions about the deity. Third, we find compelling evidence that the world's religions in essence are mechanisms for distancing human beings *from* God. Many of man's religions typically reveal an original knowledge of God, which has been actively suppressed and corrupted!

In this we see unmistakable evidence of the accuracy of Paul's account of fallen humanity's decline:

> Although they knew God, they did not glorify Him as God, nor were thankful, but became futile in their thoughts, and their foolish hearts were darkened. Professing to be wise, they became fools, and changed the glory of the incorruptible God into an image made like corruptible man—and birds and four-footed animals and creeping things. . . . [They] exchanged the truth of God for the lie, and worshiped and served the creature rather than the Creator, who is blessed forever. Amen (Rom. 1:21-23, 25).

THE CREATOR

Paul states it clearly. The central truth about God, a truth that has been continuously available to humankind, is that the word "God" can rightly be applied only to the Creator.

The Creator and natural revelation. While God Himself is invisible, and not accessible to our senses, the creation testifies to what Paul calls God's "eternal power and Godhead" (Rom. 1:20). This witness to God in the creation is often referred to as "natural revelation." What Paul is saying is that "what may be known of God" (v. 19)—His eternal power and Godhead—is both broadcast in

nature and is intuitively grasped by human beings.

The first phrase, "eternal power" (v. 20), indicates that both God and His power are eternal. The material universe is not self-existent; its existence is dependent on the exercise of God's power. Paul's choice of the Greek word *aidios* (which means "everlasting") here rather the more common term *aionios* (which means "eternal") indicates that God's power is also continuously at work in maintaining the universe. God brought the world into being, and the operations of what we sometimes call "natural laws" are in fact dependent on the continuous exercise of God's power.

The Greek word translated "Godhead" (v. 20; or in many other English versions, "deity" or "divine nature") is *theotes*. F. B. Meyers suggests that this term encompasses all the perfections of God. Rather than present a single quality, *theotes* indicates "the totality of that which God is as a being possessed of divine attributes." While the evidence available in the creation is not sufficient to reveal God's love and grace, it is more than enough to make it plain that a Being who is both Powerful and Personal is the source of all. It is this Person and this Person only who is "God."

A common argument for the existence of God illustrates this truth. An individual walking through a field finds a pocket watch. He picks it up, looks at it, and immediately realizes that this object didn't just happen, as might an outcropping of rock. The watch is too complex. The outside of the watch is polished metal. It has a glass face that seems intended to protect hands that move in a regular, consistent way. And there are numbers painted on the face of the watch to which the moving hands point. Within the watch are complex gears that seem designed to maintain the regular movement of the hands.

Upon further reflection, the finder realizes that the features of the watch that he has noted are interrelated. The removal of any one element would make it impossible for the rest to function as intended. No one finding such a watch would assume for an instant that it "just happened." Both the intuitive and the logical conclusion is that the watch had a maker, and that the maker was personal, intelligent, skilled, and had *designed* it.

And so, the argument insists, when we look at the creation we simply *must* assume a Creator. Creation is too complex to have simply just happened. The design of the universe—the multiple systems that keep our planet livable, each of them marked by interrelated mechanisms that must operate in concert—are far more complex than those of the watch. There simply must be a personal God to explain the existence of the material universe.

And what can we determine about this God? We know He existed before that which He made; He must predate His creation. We know He is a personal Being, for the design of the universe and its details shows intelligence and purpose. He clearly is great and powerful. He is intelligent, inventive, and imaginative. The final product even suggests that He is benevolent, for what He has designed sustains and enriches the experiences of living creatures. Yes, indeed. The invisible things of God, His "eternal power and *theotes*" are "clearly seen" in the things that are made (v. 20).

It is this that makes humankind's response to God so wrong. The appropriate response to a God who presents Himself to us as Creator is to glorify Him and be thankful. But rather than give God credit and worship Him, human beings suppress the truth about God in unrighteousness. Fallen human beings create religions in the name of God, which in reality serve to distance themselves from the Creator God and to deny Him His honor! In taking this course, human beings suppressed and distorted an original knowledge of God that went beyond even that available to all "since the creation of the world" (v. 20).

As the design of a watch testifies to the existence of a watchmaker, so the complex harmony of the universe demonstrates the existence of the Creator.

Original Knowledge of the Creator. Paul's argument from natural revelation makes it clear that God continuously makes Himself known to human beings of every time and place. Psalm 19:1-4, quoted earlier, states this truth very clearly:

> The heavens declare the glory of God;
> And the firmament shows His handiwork.
> Day unto day utters speech,
> And night unto night reveals knowledge.
> There is no speech nor language
> Where their voice is not heard.
> Their line has gone out through all the earth,
> And their words to the end of the world.

But we need to remember that in the beginning our race had a much more pure, much more complete knowledge of God. That knowledge is reflected in the Genesis

1—3 account of Creation. God, who made the universe and shaped earth as a home for humankind, stooped to fashion the first man. God breathed into Adam's body the breath of life, so sharing His own image-likeness.

BIBLE BACKGROUND:

THE IMAGE-LIKENESS OF GOD

Who are we? To some we are simply animals, evolved from single-cell ancestors. To others we are merely fallen creatures, with sinfulness being man's defining characteristic. But to the psalmist we are the focus of God's concern, "crowned . . . with glory and honor" (Ps. 8:5). The biblical view of humankind reflects the confidence that, with all our failings, we are special. We bear the "image" and "likeness" of God (Gen. 1:26). This is the place we must begin to understand the nature of humankind. The *Nelson Illustrated Bible Handbook* notes the following:

This phrase, "image and likeness," is best understood as a statement about personhood. We share with God capacities that only persons possess; we think, we feel, we value, we choose. It is because we are, like God, persons, that we have the capacity for fellowship with God and for meaningful relationships with each other.

Many have been troubled by man's capacity for hatred, brutality, and crime. Certainly sin has twisted us. But sin has not robbed us of personhood, or of the potential for fellowship with God. It is in the Bible's revelation of our origin in God's gift of personhood that we grasp the source of our capacity for love, self-sacrifice, appreciation for truth and beauty, creativity, worship, and moral sensibility. The good in humankind is adequately explained only by our origin at God's own hand.

The Bible, like our newspapers, testifies to the damage sin does in human experience. We carry God's likeness imperfectly. But the basic fact is that we human beings have the potential for restoration. God's image has not been eradicated (cf. Gen. 9; James 3:9). We are created in the image of God, and thus have infinite worth and value. Our respect for others, our acceptance of ourselves, and our sense of the worth of every individual, rest on this foundation (pp. 30, 31).

God placed Adam in a garden designed to give Adam every opportunity to use the copious gifts the Lord had bestowed in creating Adam in His own image-likeness. When Adam finally came to realize that his very nature required a companion who shared the image-likeness, God formed Eve. For an unknown time Adam and Eve lived together in Eden, often visited by God in the "cool of the day" (Gen. 3:8).

Even after Adam and Eve disobeyed God and sin warped and twisted the gifts God had given, God sought the first pair out. He came to them, not to punish, but to promise. In history's first sacrifice God clothed Adam and Eve in animal skins, and spoke about an offspring who would one day put down evil and restore humankind (vv. 9-21). Adam and Eve and their descendants have lived with the consequences of that initial rebellion against God, but throughout history God's pursuit of human beings has been intended to recapture human hearts and restore them to an intimate, loving relationship with Him (Rom. 5:12-21).

Humanity's original knowledge of God was far more complete than the knowledge of God available through natural revelation. God was known not only as Creator but also as friend. He was known not only intellectually but also personally, experienced and enjoyed face to face. And even in sin God was experienced as a person whose love and grace were available to forgive and to restore.

Yet as generation succeeded generation, this truth about God too was suppressed. As sin tightened its grip on the human heart, the

In the Scripture, God's reliable and relevant Word, He has revealed the truth that humankind suppressed.

God of creation seemed more threatening to a spiritually blinded humanity. Tradition bundled truth and falsehood, then spun it to give human beings greater distance from the God they did not wish to know. The "high God" of racial memory was pushed into the background, as stories about His indifference or anger were invented to explain why He might be safely ignored.

Paul's explanation of man's spiritual and moral condition, developed in Romans 1, conveys both existential and historic truth. Existentially human beings of each generation suppress truth about God readily available through the creation. Historically human beings gradually suppressed and twisted the original knowledge of God transmitted as tradition from Adam and Eve to succeeding generations. In the process, the word "god" lost its meaning, and new and different notions were incorporated in a des-perate effort to gain distance from the Creator, the one and the only true God.

RECOVERING GOD

What I've suggested so far is both simple and profound. Following the apostle Paul's teaching in Romans 1, I've argued that humankind's religions represent an effort to distance people from God. Religion does not function as a search for god or gods, but rather as a mechanism to suppress the knowledge of the true God available through creation and in the most ancient of traditions.

Religion adopts different strategies to distance people from God, but each of them involves *redefining* "god." Attributes and functions of deity are ascribed to someone, to many, or to some thing other than the Creator. In the process the meaning of the word "god" is radically altered, and human beings thus "suppress the truth in unrighteousness" (v. 18).

This presents a challenge for us. How do we recover the suppressed truth? How do we come to know God as He truly is? One answer is that we study the names and titles of God as revealed to us in Scripture. If we are to fill the term "God" with its true meaning, there is no better way than to trace in Scripture those words and phrases the Holy Spirit uses to identify and to describe the Lord!

We begin, of course, as Paul and all of Scripture begins, with the fact that the God about whom Scripture speaks is the Creator. Then we go on to look into Scripture and there to learn all we can about Him. We learn about Him from His names. We learn about Him from His titles. We learn about Him from similes and metaphors. And as we learn, a wonderful thing happens. As man's religions have distanced us from God by distorting our notions of who He is, so *revelation draws us closer to Him by helping us see Him more clearly.*

The more clearly we see God—the sharper and more vivid our grasp of who He is—the more wonderful He appears. As each name and title adds fresh dimensions of understanding, our hearts respond and we find ourselves praising and glorifying Him. And we find ourselves utterly thankful—not simply for His gifts, but also for Him.

THE PRIMARY NAMES
OF GOD

Imagine if you will two teenagers on a date. As they walk toward the movie theater his hand brushes against hers. Immediately, naturally, their fingers entwine, and they walk on together holding hands. Now imagine the same girl preparing for her date, using an iron to put the finishing touches on the garment she plans to wear. Her hand brushes the hot iron—and instinctively she jerks her hand away.

This is what has happened to the relationship between human beings and the true God. No wonder humankind has invented substitutes.

HUMANKIND'S RESPONSE TO THE TRUE GOD

In Romans 1 Paul argued that human beings have been provided with sufficient truth about God to recognize His existence and be moved to gratitude. But instead of responding to God's revelation of Himself in this way, humankind chose to suppress what they knew about Him. In this way humankind

"exchanged the truth of God for the lie" (Rom. 1:25). Paul has a simple point to make in presenting this argument. Humankind's reaction is unmistakable evidence of our lost condition.

What Paul is showing us is that when human beings brush up against the God who created and loves us, our instinctive response should be to draw closer, warmed and thankful for His touch. But what actually happens, in individuals and in history, is that human beings instinctively pull away! Again in Paul's words, "they did not like to retain God in their knowledge" (v. 28).

Humankind's invention of religions as a way to distance themselves from God and suppress the truth about Him shows that people truly are fallen creatures, in desperate need of redemption and of a righteousness that can only come as a gift from God.

NATURAL AND SPECIAL REVELATION

There is, of course, another problem with the knowledge of God to be gained through the

God does reveal Himself to all people in nature, but what can be known about Him through this source is limited.

creation, a source theologians call "natural revelation." There are definite limits to what even a person tuned to God might learn about Him from this source. We can both intuit and reason to His "eternal power and theotes." But more than this remains hidden, a mystery beyond penetration by mere human powers. The apostle Paul makes this point in 1 Corinthians 2:9 when he speaks about the limits of human wisdom:

Eye has not seen, nor ear heard,
Nor have entered into the heart of man
The things which God has prepared
for those who love him.

While many have taken this verse as a allusion to Isaiah 64:4 or 65:17, it is more likely Paul has in mind a passage in the writings of the fifth century B.C. philosopher Empedocles:

Weak and narrow are the powers implanted in the limbs of man; many the woes that fall on them and blunt the edges of thought; short is the measure of the life in death through which they toil. Then are they borne away; like smoke that vanished into the air; and what they dream they know is but the little that each hath stumbled upon in wandering about the world. Yet boast they all that they have learned the whole. Vain fools! For what that is, no eye hath seen, no ear hath heard, nor can it be conceived by the mind of man.

We know certain limited truths about God through nature. But we cannot even imagine what the whole might be. To know more about God would require a truly special revelation—a revelation by God in unmistakable word and deed.

❖

BIBLE BACKGROUND:

SPECIAL REVELATION

The Book of Hebrews begins, "In the past God spoke to our forefathers through the prophets at many times and in various ways, but in these last days he has spoken to us by his Son" (1:1-2). Special revelation has come through dreams, waking visions, and by "face-to-face" communication with God. This revelation has been shared in stories passed down verbally, expressed in ritual and sacrifice, and recorded in Scripture. Separate revelations, unfolding over the centuries, have been gathered into a harmonious whole, together giving us in our Scripture a clear portrait of God and his purposes.

What is so exciting about special revelation is that it does more than show us God from a distance. Special revelation takes us inside the heart and mind of God, showing us his deepest motives and purposes. In special revelation, the meaning of his actions in our world is explained. Why did God create? Who are human beings? What is God's attitude toward sin and sinners? Why did to God choose Israel as his people and miraculously free this people from slavery in Egypt? As God reveals more and more about himself and his purposes, we come to realize that all special revelation is gospel; all is good news, for all portrays a God who cares deeply about human beings and who reaches out to establish a personal relationship with any who will trust him. Through general revelation we know that God is. Through special revelation we know who he is and what he is like.

Special revelation takes us beyond the evidence that God exists to help us know God as a person. We trace his thoughts as they are unveiled in Scripture, and in Jesus we sense the fervor of his love and the depth of his commitment to us. As we come to know the God who unveils himself so fully, our fears dissolve, and we joyfully respond by trusting him with everything we have and are.

The Zondervan Dictionary of Christian Literacy, p. 309.

When we approach Scripture to study the names and titles of God, we enter the realm of special revelation. The words and phrases we find here are vastly different from the names and descriptions of "god" given in human religions. Scripture's names and titles are unveilings. Through the names and titles given, God unveils Himself, stripping off the layers of mystery, so that we might see Him as He really is.

While the names and titles will have little impact on those who dismiss the God of the Bible as yet another invention of the human spirit, for believers these names and titles are wonderful gifts. For we who know and love God delight to draw closer to Him. As a man or woman in love delights in the letters sent by the beloved, so we delight in every fresh insight into our Lord. And this is exactly what we have in His names and titles.

One of the things that amazes us as we look into Scripture is to see the vast number of names and titles that the Bible contains. At the same time we quickly become aware that the Old Testament revelation of God focuses on two names, each of which is unique to Scripture, and each of which frequently appears as the core of other compound names. In this chapter we'll look at these two foundational names of God, and then in the next chapters go on to look at the many names constructed on them.

'ELOHIM

"El" was both the word for "god" and the name of the original high god among the Semitic peoples of the ancient Middle East. In the Old Testament we find three closely related terms: 'el, 'eloah, and 'elohim.

EL: GOD, MIGHTY ONE, STRENGTH

The ancient name "El" was the most widely used term for the deity among the Semitic-speaking peoples of the ancient Middle East. It functioned both as a personal name for God and as a generic term. However, as we noted in Chapter 1, in the mythologies of the ancient world El was gradually but definitely emasculated. Overcome by the younger deity Baal, El was portrayed as castrated and powerless, huddling impotent at the end of the world.

It is not surprising then that in Scripture, El seldom stands alone as a name for the true God. Instead in the Bible, El is "almost always qualified by words or descriptions which further define the word" (*Theological Wordbook of the Old Testament,* p. 42). It is as if the writers of Scripture intend to make sure that the God about whom they speak is not the emasculated deity of the Semites, but a different God indeed. The God of Scripture is *ha'el haggadol,* "the great God." He is *'el hashashmayim,* "the God of heaven," and *'el 'olam,* "God of eternity." In the following chapters, we'll look at the many names and descriptions of God constructed in this way.

It is only in the Book of Job, the oldest book in the Old Testament, where Job and his friends use El as the common term for the true God, that El is used without further definition.

'ELOAH: GOD

The exact relationship of this name for God to El and Elohim is uncertain. It is an ancient name, found most often in the Book of Job. It occurs only 13 times outside of that book. While seldom found in the Old Testament, a similar term is constantly used in Aramaic.

'ELOHIM: GOD, GODS, JUDGES, ANGELS

The most striking thing about this towering Old Testament word for God is that it occurs only in Hebrew and in no other Semitic language, including biblical Aramaic. It is as if Elohim is carefully isolated from the El of other Semitic peoples, that He might be honored as truly unique. No one speaking about the God of the Hebrews and using this title could possibly confuse Him with the emasculated El of other traditions. Used in the general sense of deity some 2,570 times in the Old Testament, Elohim is a distinctive name for the God of the Bible.

BIBLE BACKGROUND:

UNCOMMON USES OF ELOHIM

Infrequently Elohim is used with some other purpose than to designate Scripture's God. The Old Testament speaks about the "gods" of Egypt (Ex. 12:12) and other nations (Deut. 6:14; 13:7, 8; Josh. 24:15; Judg. 6:10). The images of the pagans are also referred to generically as their gods (Ex. 20:23; Jer. 16:20). There are also irregular uses of Elohim, as in Psalm 82:6, where it has the sense of "judges," and 1 Samuel 28:13, where it simply means a "supernatural being." Most take the use of Elohim in Psalm 8:5 as a reference to angels, often called "mighty ones."

These uncommon uses of Elohim in no way diminish the significance of this majestic name of Scripture's God.

THE INTRODUCTION OF ELOHIM (GENESIS 1)

Elohim is introduced to us in the very first verse of the Old Testament: "In the beginning God created the heavens and the earth" (Gen. 1:1). The name is repeated 28 times in this chapter, each time describing what God did, said, or intended. This foundational chapter not only introduces Elohim but also identifies and defines Him as the Creator, the One glimpsed by all humankind through natural revelation.

"In the beginning God created" (Gen. 1:1). The text immediately asserts that there was a beginning to the cosmos. The material universe, the heavens and the earth, are not self-existent. They were created by Elohim.

The Hebrew word for created here is *bara'*. It is used in the Old Testament in a tense found here only of God's action. A similar word, *yasar*, means to fashion or shape an object. But *bara'* emphasizes initiation of something new. God did not just re-form existing matter when He made the universe; He brought something totally new into existence.

Thus we are immediately introduced to an eternal person who existed before the universe and who is Himself its origin. There is no confusion about the relationship between Elohim and the material universe, no doubt as to which has precedence, and no uncertainty about the power possessed by Israel's God.

God did not just re-form existing matter when He made the universe; He brought something totally new into existence.

"Then God said" (Gen. 2:3, 6, 9, 11, 14, 20). Psalm 148:1-5 picks up on this theme in awed wonder at the power of God. The psalmist says,

> Praise the LORD from the heavens;
> Praise Him in the heights!
> Praise Him, all His angels;
> Praise Him, all His hosts!
> Praise Him, sun and moon;
> Praise Him, all you stars of light!
> Praise Him, you heavens of heavens,
> And you waters above the heavens!
>
> Let them praise the name of the LORD,
> For He commanded and they were created.

It is not simply that Elohim created; it is the fact that He required no intermediary

means to create. What God's mind conceived, God simply spoke into existence.

God's power over the creation is utter and absolute.

Whether the sun and stars worshiped by pagans, the hills and mountains, or the living creatures that adorn the earth, these all exist because God chose to call them into being, and they persist at His pleasure.

The apostle Paul expresses his confidence that "neither death nor life, nor angels nor principalities nor powers, nor things present nor things to come, nor height nor depth, nor any other created thing, shall be able to separate us from the love of God which is in Christ Jesus our Lord" (Rom. 8:38, 39). That confidence is rooted in Genesis 1's revelation of God as being supreme over all creation. He is the source and the sustainer of all. What power indeed could thwart the purposes of a God, who by merely speaking a word could and did bring all things into being?

"Let us make man in Our image, according to Our likeness" (Gen. 1:26). This verse introduces several important themes. First, it introduces a peculiar feature of the term, Elohim. For in Hebrew Elohim is plural, not singular.

Hebrew scholars typically describe this as a "plural of majesty" rather than a true plural. That is, this plural does not suggest that there are several gods, but rather that the one God so indicated is to be exalted above all. In fact, the Hebrew noun Elohim is consistently used with singular verb forms, singular adjectives, and singular pronouns.

However, here in the very first chapter of Genesis, God speaks and says, "Let *Us* make man in *Our* own image" (v. 26; emphasis mine). And what is special about the plural Elohim is that in this word we have a term capable of communicating the unity of the one God while also allowing for a plurality of persons. While the nature of Scripture's one God as a trinity of persons was unveiled later in Scripture, here in the first chapter of Genesis God is identified by a plural name found in no other Semitic language!

No single name of God reveals all that may be known about Him. But the name Elohim identifies God as the Creator, and in its uniqueness sets the stage for future revelations of His nature and character.

THE ENRICHMENT OF ELOHIM

Earlier we noted that when used of Scripture's God, the word El is qualified by descriptive words and phrases. In the same way descriptive words are attached to the Hebrew noun Elohim, and so these become titles by which God's people know Him. In fact, Elohim is a favorite word used in God's titles.

We'll look at specific titles later in this book. But it is helpful now to note various categories of titles by which Elohim came to be known.

God the Creator. The title Elohim is itself a Creator name. But Scripture adds to His honor by calling Him "God, who formed the earth" (Is. 45:18) and "God of heaven, who made the sea and the dry land" (Jonah 1:9).

God the Sovereign One. A number of titles emphasize God's sovereignty. He is called "God . . . of all the kingdoms of the earth" (Is. 37:16), "the LORD, the God of heaven and the God of the earth" (Gen. 24:3), summed up in "God Most High" (Ps. 57:2).

God the Judge. One aspect of Elohim's sovereignty is seen in His role as "God who judges in the earth" (Ps. 58:11) and as "God of justice" (Is. 30:18).

God as Savior. A number of titles emphasize God's relationship to the human beings He has redeemed and called. Thus Elohim is "the God of your father Abraham" (Gen. 26:24), "the God of Abraham, the God of Isaac, and the God of Jacob" (Ex. 3:6). In fact, some 100 such titles are found in the Old Testament, including those that link God with Israel, as "God of the armies of Israel" (1 Sam. 17:45). In these titles God is represented as the Savior of His people, truly the "God of our salvation" (1 Chr. 16:35).

God of history. Other titles link God with His acts in history. Moses noted that the Israelites "heard His voice from the midst of the fire. . . . God speaks with man; yet He still lives" (Deut. 5:24). David declared that "God . . . went out before [His] people" and "marched through the wilderness" (Ps. 68:7).

God of relationships. There are also titles that convey a sense of God's intimacy with His own people. Elohim is "a God near at

In calling Himself the "God of Abraham" the Lord defined Himself as a Person who seeks a personal relationship with those who believe in Him.

hand" (Jer. 23:23) and "God in whom you trust" (2 Kin. 19:10). He is "my God of mercy" (Ps. 59:17) and "the God who has fed me all my life long to this day" (Gen. 48:15).

While our English translations frequently present such concepts as descriptions, it is clear from the Hebrew construction that they are titles. They are words and phrases that invite the faithful to look at Elohim in yet another fresh and new way, to come to know Him better, and to be captivated by the wonder of this Person who has called us to know and to worship Him.

YAHWEH

Elohim is the first name of God we meet in Scripture. Genesis 1 immediately establishes the fact that Elohim is the Creator, the one and only true God. He is the source of and sovereign over all that exists in the material and immaterial universe. From this information we see that Elohim is one of the primary names of God.

But there is another primary name of God found in the Old Testament. That name, Yahweh, occurs 5,311 times in the Old Testament, more than twice as often as Elohim. Yahweh also is found 50 times as the poetic abbreviation, Yah. This name is unique among all the names of God, for it is the one personal name of God found in the Old Testament. It's not necessary to know Hebrew to tell where this name occurs in the Old Testament text. This name is so significant that the translators of many English versions identify its every occurrence by printing it with a capital "L" followed by "ord" in small capitals: LORD.

Why is this name so significant, and what does it mean? The answers are found in the Book of Exodus, where a critical moment in sacred history is described.

A SHORT HISTORY OF ISRAEL

ABRAHAM (GENESIS 12—50; EXODUS 1)

Genesis tells us how God spoke to a man named Abram in the ancient Mesopotamian city of Ur. God gave Abram, who was later renamed Abraham, great and wonderful promises. God also told Abraham to leave Ur and travel to a land He would show him. That land was Canaan, which is modern Israel/Palestine. When Abraham arrived in Canaan, God promised Abraham that his descendants would surely inherit that land (Gen. 12:1-9).

Abraham lived out his life in Canaan. The promises God had made to him were transmitted to his son Isaac, his grandson Jacob, and to Jacob's twelve sons. When a terrible famine devastated Canaan, Jacob's family moved to Egypt and settled there. In Egypt the little family prospered and multiplied. Within a few hundred years there were so many of Abraham's descendants living in Egypt that the ruler of that land, Pharaoh, became concerned. At that time foreign enemies ethnically related to the Hebrews threatened Egypt. What if the all-too-numerous Hebrews inside Egypt should join forces with the foreign hordes (Ex. 1:1-10)?

Pharaoh's solution was to enslave the Hebrew people. He stripped them of their privileges and set them to hard labor under cruel overseers. But still the Hebrew people multiplied. Finally Pharaoh issued orders that every male child born to the Hebrews should be cast into the Nile River and drowned (vv. 11-22). He would reduce the threat by gradually eliminating the race!

❖

BIBLE BACKGROUND:

KEY EVENTS IN ISRAEL'S EARLY HISTORY

- c. 2167 B.C. Abraham is born in Ur of the Chaldees
- c. 2091 B.C. Abraham is called to set out for Canaan
- c. 2066 B.C. Isaac is born to Abraham and Sarah
- c. 2006 B.C. Jacob is born to Isaac and Rebekah

- c. 1991 B.C. Abraham dies in Canaan
- c. 1915 B.C. Joseph is born to Jacob and Rachel
- c. 1886 B.C. Isaac dies in Canaan
- c. 1876 B.C. Jacob and his family move to Egypt
- c. 1859 B.C. Jacob dies in Egypt
- c. 1805 B.C. Joseph dies in Egypt
- c. 1730 B.C. The Israelites are enslaved in Egypt
- c. 1527 B.C. Moses is born
- c. 1487 B.C. Moses flees Egypt for Midian
- c. 1447 B.C. Moses receives revelation of the name "Yahweh"
- c. 1446 B.C. Moses leads the Israelites out of Egypt
- c. 1445 B.C. God delivers the Law on Mount Sinai
- c. 1446-1406 B.C. Forty years of wilderness wandering
- c. 1406 B.C. Moses presents the Deuteronomic Law
- c. 1406 B.C. Moses dies
- c. 1405 B.C. Joshua succeeds Moses
- c. 1405 B.C. The conquest of Canaan begins
- c. 1405 B.C. The Israelites cross the Jordan into Canaan
- c. 1405-1400 B.C. The Israelites take Jericho and other cities
- c. 1398 B.C. Canaan is apportioned to the tribes
- c. 1380 B.C. Joshua dies
- c. 1375-1050 B.C. Judges rule in Israel
- c. 1105 B.C. Samuel is born
- c. 1050 B.C. Saul becomes king of Israel

MOSES (EXODUS 2)

The command to murder all the male Hebrew children was in force when Moses was born. At first his mother hid him in their home. But in time she determined to hide Moses in a basket-boat placed among the rushes of the very river that Pharaoh had intended to be Moses' grave (Ex. 2:1-3).

It was there, while Moses lay in a basket-boat woven from papyrus reeds, that an Egyptian princess found him, had compassion on him, and decided to raise him as her own. For the first few years of Moses' life, Pharaoh's daughter had his own mother nurse him. She undoubtedly took this opportunity to teach him the traditions of his people (vv. 4-10).

Although in his later years Moses was educated as an Egyptian prince, he identified himself with the Hebrews, and dreamed of delivering his people from slavery (Acts 7:20-25). One day when Moses was about forty years old, his zeal betrayed him and he killed an overseer who was brutalizing a Hebrew slave. When Moses realized that his act had become known, he fled to the Sinai Desert. There Moses spent the next forty years as a simple shepherd. And there Moses' dream of delivering his people apparently died (Ex. 2:11-22; Acts 7:26-29).

During the four decades Moses spent in the wilderness, the anguished cries of the Hebrews came up to a God known by them as Elohim. He was the God of their forefathers, Abraham, Isaac, and Jacob. This is the same God who had made promises to the patriarchs centuries earlier and who intended one day to fulfill them (Ex. 2:23-25).

YAHWEH (EXODUS 3—4)

When Moses was eighty years old, he saw a wonder in the desert. A flame burned brightly in a bush, but the bush was not consumed. When Moses approached the spot, God spoke to him from the burning bush. God then commissioned Moses. Moses was to return to Egypt. And Moses was to set God's people free (Ex. 3:1-10).

Forty years before, Moses would have leaped at the chance. But now, an old man, his pride perhaps burned from him by the desert heat, Moses could only say, "Who am

God first revealed the significance of the name Yahweh when He appeared to Moses in the Sinai wilderness.

I that I should go to Pharaoh, and that I should bring the Israelites out of Egypt?" (v. 11). Stripped of the self-confidence that had marked him in his youth, Moses saw no way that he could carry out the mission that long ago had been his dream.

God responded with a promise: "I will certainly be with you" (v. 12). But still Moses hesitated. And then Moses asked the question that led to the revelation of the Old Testament's most significant name of God. Moses said to God, "Indeed, when I come to the children of Israel and say to them, 'The God of your fathers has sent me to you,' and they say to me, 'What is His name?' what shall I say to them?" (v. 13).

In response God revealed to Moses the name Yahweh, "the LORD" (vv. 14, 15).

The meaning of Yahweh. Exodus 3:14 is the key verse in this passage. It states, "God said to Moses, 'I AM WHO I AM.' And He said, 'Thus you shall say to the children of Israel, "I AM has sent me to you."'"

Scholars have struggled over how best to translate "Yahweh." The name is composed of four Hebrew letters, Yod, Hey, Vav, and Hey. All agree that the name is constructed on consonants used in the Hebrew verb "to be." But just what aspect of the verb "to be" is emphasized?

Many settle for the simple phrase found in verse 14, "I AM," and let it go at that. Others suggest that God here is identifying Himself as the "Self-Existent One." Yet this rather abstract and philosophical rendering of the name fails to do justice to the context. In context, the revelation of the name "Yahweh" was to have unique significance to Moses, to the Israelites, and to succeeding generations.

BIBLE BACKGROUND:

YAHWEH OR JEHOVAH?

Why does a debate exist over how this special name of God should be pronounced? The reason is both simple and complex. Old Testament Hebrew was written using only consonants. There were no written vowels, and a reader was expected to add the appropriate vowel sounds. Thus, this special name of God was written YHWH. But by the time the name was translated into English, the original pronunciation had been lost.

The reason, however, for the confusion is more complicated. Around A.D.1100, a group of Jewish scholars produced what is known as the Massoretic text. In this document, the scholars added a series of vowels to the Hebrew text, the vowels being represented by various placements of dots.

The special name of God was so sacred that no observant Jew would pronounce it. Instead, when reading the Scripture, a person coming to that name would substitute an entirely different word. This is a technical rule known as *"kethive Kere."* This phrase means "written one way, to be read another." It directed readers of the sacred Hebrew text that when they came to the four consonants YHWH, they were to attach vowel signs indicating that in its place they should read the Hebrew word Adonai, which means "Lord." In this case, the scholars who produced the Massoretic text added the vowels "e," "o," and "a" to the consonants "Y," "H," "W," and "H" (in other words, "YeHoWaH").

The translators of the King James Version of the Bible followed this convention to translate YHWH as "Jehovah" (the sound of the consonant "Y" being represented by "J" and the sound of the consonant "W" by "V"). In other words, they used the vowels of the term to be pronounced (namely, Adonai) rather than the vowels associated with YHWH, which represented the correct pronunciation of this most sacred name of God. This explains how the name "Jehovah" was introduced into the English language Bible. And it is for this reason that the form "Jehovah" does not represent the correct way to pronounce the covenant name of God.

The majority of Hebrew scholars think the consonants YHWH were originally pronounced "Yahweh." A minority of others, however, remain unsure. Regardless of just exactly how the sacred name was pronounced in Bible times, its essential meaning shines through to enrich our understanding of God.

The significance of the name for Moses (Ex. 3:12). God had commissioned Moses to go to Egypt and free the Hebrew slaves. Moses responded by pleading his inadequacy: "Who am I?" (v. 11). God's next words to Moses were, "I will certainly be with you" (v. 12). Moses could not succeed on his own. But the God who spoke to Moses in the wilderness would be with Moses in

Pharaoh's court. Wherever Moses went, there God would be.

The significance of the name to the Israelites (Ex. 3:15-22). God told Moses to inform the elders of the Hebrew people that, as Yahweh, God was the God of their forefathers. This was the same God who had appeared to Moses. God explained to Moses that even as the Israelites suffered in slavery, He had watched over them. He had seen what was being done to them. God was now ready to free them from their misery in Egypt and bring them into Canaan—"a land flowing with milk and honey."

Notice the many points in time referred to in this brief section. When Abraham and the other forefathers lived, God was there. When the Israelites suffered as slaves, God was there. When Moses found the burning brush, God was there. Even in the future, when the Israelites would journey to Canaan, God would be there.

God is not merely self-existent. As Yahweh, He is ever present with His people! God was present with Abraham, present with the Israelites, and present with Moses. God would also be present in the future as He fulfilled the ancient promises!

In essence, the name "Yahweh" revealed God as the "One who is always present" with His people.

The significance of the name for future generations (Ex. 3:15b). The words that God spoke to Moses when the name "Yahweh" was revealed included this significant affirmation: "This is My Name forever, and this is My memorial to all generations." The NIV renders the verse, "This is my name forever, the name by which I am to be remembered from generation to generation."

The name "Yahweh" is central to our understanding of God. Each generation is to remember God as the "One who is always present."

The Hebrew word translated "remember" is significant in the Old Testament. It describes more than a mental act. To remember something is to recall and then to act accordingly. Thus when God says that all future generations are to remember Him as Yahweh, what God is saying is that from that point onward, all who know God are to see Him as being present with them, and to act accordingly.

Because God is present with us, we need not draw back as Moses did from any task to which God calls us, no matter how challenging it might be. Of course, because God is present with us, we do draw back from sin. We are aware that His eyes are upon us, and we are ever eager to please Him.

The person who lives in the awareness that God is present at every moment will live a very different life from the person who forgets and ignores God!

The immediate literary context of the revelation of God's name as "Yahweh," then, leads us to understand and to translate that name as "the One who is always present." Whenever we read the Old Testament and see the name "LORD" printed so distinctively, we are to remember who God is and how He wants us to know Him.

The significance of the name established in history. God's revelation of the name "Yahweh" took place in a distinct historical context. One of the rather interesting objections to the trustworthiness of Scripture has been raised by critics who point to Exodus 6:3. The verse quotes God as stating, "I appeared to Abraham, to Isaac, and to Jacob as God Almighty, but by my name LORD [Yahweh] I was not known to them."

The critics are quick to point out that the name "Yahweh" does occur earlier. For instance, Genesis 15:7 records God saying to Abraham, "I am the LORD [Yahweh], who brought you out of Ur." And verse 8 records Abraham's reply: "LORD [Yahweh] God." Not only did God speak of Himself as Yahweh to Abraham, but Abraham also used the name!

But before we follow the critics and jump to the conclusion that Exodus 6:3 is in

The Exodus plagues were a powerful demonstration of the significance of the name Yahweh: God proved to be present with His people indeed!

error, we need to note something important. This verse does not say that the name "Yahweh" was unknown. What it says is that God was not known by that name. It is one thing to have a label to pin on God. It is another thing entirely to understand the label's significance! The patriarchs may have used the name "Yahweh." But God had not unlocked its meaning for them.

While the Bible's account of creation immediately establishes the significance of Elohim, it was the events of the Exodus period that filled the name "Yahweh" with meaning. For immediately after God revealed Himself as Yahweh to Moses, the Lord sent Moses back to Egypt on a mission of redemption. In Egypt, God explained to Moses that Pharaoh would resist His demands. God told Moses to explain to the Israelites what would happen: "I will rescue you . . . and I will redeem you with an outstretched arm and with great judgments"

(v. 6). And God added, "then you shall know that I am the LORD your God" (v. 7).

Exodus describes the ten devastating plagues that followed. These plagues reduced the verdant land of Egypt to a wasteland, and stripped the nation of its wealth and power. These plagues, which came at Moses' command and left when he dismissed them, were unmistakably supernatural. They demonstrated God's unfettered ability to intervene in this world on His people's behalf. And the culminating event that followed Israel's release, the parting of the Red Sea, served to underscore the wonder of it all. In the plagues on Egypt God filled the name "Yahweh" with meaning, and displayed what it meant for His people to experience Him as the "One who is always present."

It was this experience of the meaning of the name "Yahweh" that the patriarchs lacked. And it was the experience of a slave people saved by the exercise of Yahweh's great power that filled the name with meaning for all time to come. No wonder God said "this is My name forever, and this is My memorial to all generations" (v. 15b). Whenever the name "Yahweh" came to mind, so did images of God's power unleashed on behalf of His people. The "One who is always present" is the powerful God of miracles. Because He is present, we can walk securely. And we can follow Him anywhere.

IMPLICATIONS OF THE NAME "YAHWEH" FOR TODAY

At times we may fall into the habit of thinking of God primarily in past or future tenses. As Christians, we memorialize the death and resurrection of God's Son, and we look forward to Jesus' return. This is good to do. But the name "Yahweh" reminds us that we are to know and experience our Lord as God of our present as well as our past and future. We are to walk with Him daily. We are to trust Him with our daily needs. We are to act on His Word, confident that He who is with us can and will intervene on our behalf.

When we understand and honor God as Yahweh, we will never be alone.

Perhaps Isaiah's exalted vision of a God who is both transcendent and wonderfully immanent best sums up the implications of the name "Yahweh" for us.

"To whom will you liken Me,
Or to whom shall I be equal?"
  says the Holy One.
Lift up your eyes on high,
And see who has created these
  things,
Who brings out their host by
  number;
He calls them all by name,
By the greatness of His might
And the strength of His power;
  Not one is missing. . . .

Have you not known?
Have you not heard?

The everlasting God, the Lord,
The Creator of the ends of the
  earth,
Neither faints nor is weary.
His understanding is unsearchable.
He gives power to the weak,
And to those who have no
  might He increases strength.
Even the youths shall faint and
  be weary,
And the young men shall
  utterly fall,
But those who wait on the
  Lord
Shall renew their strength;
They shall mount up with
  wings like eagles,
They shall run and not be
  weary,
They shall walk and not faint.
  Isaiah 40:25-26, 28-31

NAMES, MANY AND WONDERFUL

N ames were particularly important in the biblical world. The *New International Encyclopedia of Bible Words* reminds us that "in biblical cultures a name did more than identify; it communicated something of the essence, the character, or the reputation of the person or thing named" (p. 453). This fact helps us understand why the Bible is so filled with many and wonderful names of God. Each name reveals something about the essential nature and character of God. And no one name or title could possibly sum up who He is.

It's fascinating as we survey the Old Testament names of God to note that some names emphasize His power and excellence, others His relationship with human beings, and still other names are descriptive, providing special information about who He is. In this chapter we will look at the many Old Testament names of God, as distinct from titles and images for Him. In doing so we will not only learn about our God, but also meet Him. This is because God comes to us in such encounters, and He invites us to respond to Him with worship and praise.

BIBLE BACKGROUND:

BIBLE NAMES

In Bible times names were expected to express something important about the person or place named. Thus, Hannah, whose son Samuel was born in answer to prayer, chose a name for him that means "God hears." Likewise, in the New Testament, the name "Barnabas" means "Encourager." (Clearly, that was a major role played by this warm and caring first-century Christian.)

Names that are changed often have extra-special significance. The birth name of Abram meant "father," which must have seemed more than a little ironic to the childless patriarch we read about in Genesis. Nevertheless, when Abram believed God's promise that his offspring would be as uncountable as the stars of heaven, God

Job wrestled with God.

changed the patriarch's name to "Abraham," a name that means "exalted father" or "father of a multitude." We can sense how deep Abraham's faith was, for he risked taking that new name despite the disguised laughter that must have bubbled up in the herdsmen who worked for him.

The patriarch Jacob also experienced a name change. After a night of struggling to hold fast to the Angel of the Lord, God changed his name to "Israel," which means "he struggles with God."

The above information suggests that when we read Scripture, we should have a Bible dictionary handy. We can use it to check out the meaning of the names of the significant men and women we read about in the Word. Often the name will provide a vital clue to understanding their role in God's plan of redemption.

THE EXALTED NAMES OF GOD

The prophet Isaiah reports a vision in which he "saw the Lord sitting on a throne, high and lifted up, and the train of His robe filled the temple" (Is. 6:1). In Isaiah's vision, seraphim were positioned around the throne, together crying "Holy, holy, holy is the LORD of hosts; the whole earth is full of His glory!" (v. 3). Isaiah's reaction was one of awe and humility. Confronted by this revelation of God enthroned in heaven, the prophet cried, "Woe is me, for I am undone! Because I am a man of unclean lips, and I dwell in the midst of a people of unclean lips" (v. 5).

Through his vision, a stunned Isaiah suddenly became fully aware of the vast gap that exists between any human being and God. We are made in the image of God, yet God remains unimaginably different from and greater than us. What theologians speak of as the transcendence of God was impressed upon the prophet, and Isaiah was immediately aware of how far he fell short of God's glory (Rom. 3:23).

What I call here the "exalted names" of God are intended in Scripture to convey this same message. Our God is high and lifted up. He is a God of power and excellence. He is so far above us that we can never truly fathom His greatness and majesty. Yet, through certain names in Scripture, we are invited to glimpse His greatness, and like Isaiah we are called to bow down in wonder before Him. Here, then, are Scripture's exalted names of our God.

CREATOR AND MAKER

Genesis begins with an account of creation. Elohim, the one true God, has brought all that exists into being. The conviction that the Lord is the Creator and source of all things is foundational to the Bible's revelation of God.

The Hebrew verb translated "created" (1:1) is *bara'*. While often described as indicating the "making of something out of nothing," the biblical emphasis is actually on initiating an object or project. When used in the Qal stem of God's action, what is initiated is clearly beyond the ability of human beings. Only God could (1) launch the heavens and the earth, (2) fashion the human race, (3) call Israel into being as a distinct people of God, and (4) through forgiveness, create in sinners a cleansed and renewed heart. Ultimately, at history's end, God will create again, this time initiating a new heavens and a new earth.

Bara' occurs in the Old Testament in this special sense of initiation by God in Genesis 1:1, 21, 27; 2:3; 5:1, 2; 6:7; Numbers 16:30; Deuteronomy 4:32; Psalms 51:10; 89:12, 47; Ecclesiastes 12:1; Isaiah 4:5; 40:26, 28; 41:20; 42:5; 43:1, 7, 15; 45:7, 8, 12, 18; 54:16; 57:19; 65:17, 18; Jeremiah 31:22; Amos 4:13; and Malachi 2:10.

While a biblical understanding of God unquestionably begins with the affirmation that He is Creator, the name "Creator" or "Maker" is used infrequently in Scripture. When it is used, the tendency is to emphasize the fact that God is *our* Maker. Thus, Psalm 95:6 says,

> Oh come, let us worship and bow down;
> Let us kneel before the LORD our Maker.

And Isaiah presents the Lord as "the Holy One of Israel, and his Maker" (Is. 45:11).

While this language affirms a special relationship between God and an individual or God and Israel, references to God as Maker also emphasize God's transcendence. The God who made us has proven by His act of creation to be far above us. Compared to this God we are indeed insignificant. How foolish then it is to "forget the LORD your Maker, who stretched out the heavens and laid the foundations of the earth" (Is. 51:13). And as 45:9 says, "Woe to him who quarrels with his Maker,

to him who is but a potsherd among the potsherds on the ground" (NIV).

Despite the emphasis of the name "Creator" or "Maker" on God's greatness and transcendence, it is a comfort to know God as the One who is far above all that now exists. Isaiah reminds his readers,

> Have you not known?
> Have you not heard?
> The everlasting God, the LORD,
> The Creator of the ends of the earth,
> Neither faints nor is weary.
> Isaiah 40:28

It is because our Creator truly is all-powerful and unlimited that He is able to give strength to the weak and lift up those who fall.

LORD GOD

This exalted name of God is formed by combining the two primary names of God, Yahweh and Elohim. The combination occurs 595 times in the Hebrew Old Testament, and it is one of the most significant of the many and wonderful names of God.

This is the name used in the Genesis 1 account of God's creation of the universe, in the chapter 2 account of God's fashioning of Adam, and in the chapter 3 account of God's forming of Eve. It is the name Moses used when commanding Pharaoh to let God's people go (Ex. 7—10). "Lord GOD" is the name by which David addressed God after He had promised David that his offspring would be the Messiah, history's ultimate Ruler. David acknowledged the promise and affirmed his conviction that "O Lord GOD, You are God, and Your words are true, and You have promised this goodness to Your servant" (2 Sam. 7:28).

It was God our Lord who announced to the king of Judah, just before the Babylonians took Jerusalem in the days of the prophet Jeremiah, "I will bring calamity on this place" (2 Chr. 34:24). And it was to God our Lord that Jeremiah made an appeal, acknowledging in these powerful words God's sovereignty (Jer. 32:16-19):

> Ah, Lord God! Behold, You have made the heavens and the earth by Your great power and outstretched arm. There is nothing too hard for You. You show lovingkindness to thousands, and repay the iniquity of the fathers into the bosom of their children after them—the Great, the Mighty God, whose name is the Lord of hosts. You are great in counsel and mighty in work.

Many of the occurrences of "Lord God" are in direct address or in prayer, as God's people express their confidence in His sovereign authority over all. There is no God but Yahweh. Because He is all-powerful in whatever He wills, what He promises will surely come to pass.

It shouldn't surprise us then that "Lord God" is a name favored by the psalmists and others when speaking to the Lord. What a wonderful encouragement it is to know that the God to whom we appeal is perfectly able to answer us and grant our requests. With the psalmist we gladly cry out,

> You are my hope, O Lord God;
> You are my trust from my youth.
> Psalm 71:5

BIBLE BACKGROUND:
SOVEREIGN LORD

While the traditional and most accurate way of translating the Hebrew phrase *Yahweh Elohim* is the phrase "Lord God," the New International Version (NIV) and some other versions frequently render the Hebrew as "Sovereign Lord." This is because the NIV has adopted a translation philosophy known as "dynamic equivalency." The translators, rather than render the Hebrew or Greek word for word, seek to find the closest possible equivalent in contemporary English to what they believe the word or phrase meant to the Hebrew or Greek reader.

In this case the translators rightly agreed that as used in Scripture, the Hebrew phrase *Yahweh Elohim* emphasized the sovereign power and authority of God. Thus frequently where the New King James Version (NKJV) has "Lord God," the NIV will read "Sovereign Lord."

There are both advantages and disadvantages to this approach to translation, each of which is illustrated in the rendering of *Yahweh Elohim*. The advantage is that at times using a dynamic equivalent such as "Sovereign Lord" brings out a connotation of the original that the English reader might otherwise miss without a detailed study of each use of the phrase.

The disadvantage is illustrated in the fact that while *Yahweh Elohim* occurs 582 times in the Hebrew, and is consistently translated "Lord God" in the NKJV, the NIV translates this Hebrew phrase by "Sovereign Lord" only 293 times! This means that an English reader using the NIV would never know that the Hebrew text has *Yahweh Elohim* in an additional 289 verses! So anyone without access to a Hebrew concordance and wishing to do a word study would never know that he or she missed 289 uses of the words studied!

There is certainly nothing wrong in using the translation principle adopted by the NIV translators. Often this approach brings out meanings in the biblical text that might otherwise be missed. But for the serious student of Scripture, consistency in translation—in which the same word or phrase is rendered in the same way most times it occurs—is an important matter.

GOD ALMIGHTY

God is identified as "Almighty" 48 times in the Old Testament (31 times in Job). The Hebrew term rendered "almighty" is *sadday*. In 41 of the 48 occurrences, *sadday* stands alone. In the other seven occurrences, it is connected with *el*.

The Hebrew word *sadday* comes from a root meaning "mountain" and portrays God as One who is exalted far above all human authority. None can challenge God's control of His universe.

The first mention in the Bible of God as *el-sadday* is found in Genesis 17:1. God appeared to Abraham and identified Himself as "Almighty God." At the time Abraham was 99 years old, and Sarah was 89. Yet God promised that Abraham would become a father of many nations, and that he and Sarah would have a son whom they would name "Isaac." The next year, as God had promised, Sarah bore Abraham the promised son.

Humanly speaking, the birth of Isaac was impossible. Sarah was long past menopause, and her womb was long dormant. And yet what God promised came to pass, for our Lord truly is God Almighty.

While "Almighty" is one of the exalted names of God, it is also linked with God's ability to fulfill any promise He might make to humankind. It is because God truly is the Almighty One that we can count on His word to us, for that word is good and true.

GOD OF HOSTS

Some might wonder why the NKJV casts God as Almighty only 48 times, while the NIV has Almighty no less than 345 times. The answer is that the translators of the NIV chose "Almighty" to render two different Hebrew words. That other word is *saba'*, traditionally rendered as "hosts." In fact, what *saba'* means is "armies," and in half of the 486 occurrences of *saba'* in the Old Testament, the word is associated with Yahweh.

God demonstrated that His power is without limits by enabling Abraham and Sarah to have the son He had promised.

The *New International Encyclopedia of Bible Words* explains why this name of God is so significant.

First, the connection of this term with Yahweh is important. Yahweh identifies God as the living, active, ever-present Lord, who intervenes in history on behalf of his people. . . . It is significant that the word "armies" is linked with this particular name of God; this affirms his active presence in history.

Second, the concept of armies extends beyond massed human military forces. The forces of heaven as well as of earth are at God's command, and nature itself may be called into battle on behalf of God's people (Jos 5:13-14; 10:10-19). The conviction that "it was the Lord . . . God who fought for" Israel (Jos 23:3) was basic to the OT believers' understanding of Israel's relationship with God.

Third, the concept LORD of Armies (LORD of Hosts) affirms God's rule over every earthly power (p. 34).

God retains universal power over humankind. While His power may be masked now and denied by those who refuse to believe the truth, the day is coming when God will openly exercise His power as Lord of hosts and enforce His will on all. In the meantime, although that power may be masked, it continues to operate in our world.

It is interesting that while the Israelite armies that invaded Canaan under Joshua were identified as the Lord's hosts, or armies (Josh. 5:14, 15), the name "God of hosts" does not appear until 1 Samuel, near the end of the era of the Judges. In chapter 1 we read Hanna's desperate prayer in which she begs God for a son and expresses her willingness to give that son back to the Lord in service. Her appeal is addressed to God as "LORD of hosts" (v. 11), which expresses her conviction that if God chose to give her a son, He could surely do so.

It is significant that the psalmists also frequently address prayers to God. Psalm 80 illustrates this point. There the writer cries, "Restore us, O God of hosts" (v. 7), "Return, we beseech You, O God of hosts" (v. 14), and again "Restore us, O LORD God of hosts" (v. 19).

How appropriate it is to address prayers to God as the Lord of hosts. We should acknowledge Him as the One who, in exercising His unlimited power, is able to intervene on our behalf. It is because our God truly is exalted above the heavens that we can pray to Him, having total confidence in His ability to answer any and every prayer.

GOD MOST HIGH

Some 54 times in the NKJV God is presented to us as the Most High. At times the name stands alone. At other times He is spoken of as God Most High, the Most High God, or Lord Most High.

The first few occurrences of this name help us to see its significance. The name is reported first in Genesis 14. There Melchizedek is described as the priest of "God Most High" (v. 18). Melchizedek then proceeds to bless Abraham in the name of "God Most High" (vv. 19, 20). The next time the name is used, it is spoken by Abraham, who is addressing the king of Sodom. Abraham tells the king, "I have raised my hand to the LORD, God Most High, the Possessor of heaven and earth" (v. 22). The next time the name is used, it is uttered by Balaam the prophet, who claims that his visions and messages come from "God . . . Most High" (Num. 24:16).

In each of these passages the name "God Most High" is used to identify the supreme deity, in distinction from the false gods and goddesses venerated by the peoples among whom the speaker lived.

I noted earlier that one of the primary Hebrew names of God, *Elohim*, had no parallel in the other languages of the ancient Near East. Thus in Genesis when a Caananite spoke about God, or when one wished to speak to someone else about the true God, the name "Most High God" was used. The Most High God was no local or tribal deity, but in Abraham's words the "Possessor of heaven and earth" (Gen. 14:22). No idol worshiped by ancient peoples could make that claim.

The psalmists, who use an array of names for God in their effort to portray His excellencies, do speak of and address God as "Most High." But the uniqueness of the name is best seen in the Book of Daniel. There Nebuchadnezzar comes to realize that the Lord is God Most High, and that His decree rules in the kingdom of humanity. After a time of being disciplined, Nebuchadnezzar acknowledged the sovereignty of Daniel's God. Daniel 4:34 reports the great king's submission:

I, Nebuchadnezzar, lifted my eyes to heaven, and my understanding returned to me; and I blessed the Most High and praised and honored Him who lives forever:

For His dominion is an everlasting dominion,

And His kingdom is from generation to generation.

How significant the name "God Most High" is for us today. Throughout history people have quaked at the power of autocrats and mourned under the oppression of corrupt regimes. Yet through it all, our God is God Most High, Ruler of those who refuse to believe the truth, even as He rules in our lives. We need never fear the power of unbelief, for God Most High rules over all!

THE GREAT GOD

There is no doubt that this simple phrase—which is both a name and a description—sums up the exalted names of God. Moses reminded the Israelites, "The LORD your God is God of gods and Lord of lords, the great God, mighty and awesome" (Deut. 10:17). He is in fact "the great God who formed everything" (Prov. 26:10). He is exalted above everything that people worship or rely on. In the words of Isaiah 46:9, 10,

> Remember the former things of old,
> For I am God, and there is no other;
> I am God, and there is none like Me,
> Declaring the end from the beginning,
> And from ancient times things
>   that are not yet done,
> Saying, "My counsel shall stand,
> And I will do all My pleasure."

He truly is the great God!

THE RELATIONAL NAMES OF GOD

The exalted names of God emphasize His transcendence. God truly is high and lifted up, far beyond our capacity to understand, comprehend, or even imagine. Yet one of the most stunning truths revealed in the Bible is that the transcendent God is also immanent. He is totally involved in His creation and in the lives of believers.

This wonderful truth is expressed in what we might call the *relational* names of God. In other words, God identifies Himself

as the *God of* a particular person, place, or people. In effect, the Lord expects us to come to know Him by the company He keeps and by those with whom He has chosen to identify Himself. Among the relational names of God mentioned in the Old Testament are the following:

Place names
    God of Bethel
    God of Jerusalem
    God of the house of God
Personal names
    God of Shem
    God of Abraham
    God of Elijah
    God of Daniel
    God of your father Abraham
    God of his father David
    God of Isaac
    God of Jacob
    God of Nahor
    God of Shadrach, Meshach, and
        Abednego
People names
    God of the spirits of all humankind
    God, the God of Israel
    God of the Hebrews

Frequently personal names also function as people names, for in the Old Testament all the Hebrew people are frequently referred to as Jacob or Israel. These names reveal much about God, especially when we examine the link between the Lord and the place, person, or people names.

GOD OF PLACES

It was common for the peoples of the ancient world to identify God with places. The assumption was that the influence of a pagan deity (such as the idol of Moab; 1 Kin. 11:7) was limited to that land or the people who lived on it. Frequently wars between peoples were assumed to be settled on a divine battlefield. In other words, the winners

The Jerusalem temple was the visible symbol of God's presence with His Old Testament people.

in a war won because their deity was more powerful than the deity of the losers.

This narrow view is not reflected in biblical references to the Lord as the God of Jerusalem or the God of Israel. The reason is that from earliest times the Israelites, insofar as their Scriptures are concerned, recognized God as exercising His power universally. He was not simply the God of Jerusalem or the God of the land of Israel. Yahweh was the God who created all things. Yahweh was not only sovereign over His own people, but also was the "God of the spirits of all flesh" (Num. 16:22; 27:16).

Thus, when an enemy nation gained victory over Israel, it was not because that nation's idol was more powerful than the true God. Rather, it was because the Lord chose to use Israel's enemy to discipline His own people. Thus, God through Isaiah speaks of Assyria as "the rod of My anger and the staff in whose hand is My indignation" (Is. 10:5). In other words, God was emphatically promising to send Assyria against His own ungodly people.

What then is the emphasis when God identifies Himself with a place? While not limiting the Lord to sovereignty over that place alone, the names "God of Bethel," "God of Jerusalem," or "God of the house of God" identify these places as being set apart and holy to the Lord. In other words, these are places where God has done or will do great things.

Bethel is the place where Abraham erected an altar and first worshiped God in the Holy Land. Jerusalem is the capital city of God's people.

The temple became the symbol of God's presence with His people, and the one site where sin offerings might be made and to which the Israelites might turn for forgiveness and help.

BIBLE BACKGROUND:

BETHEL

The name "bethel" means "house [Hebrew, *beth*] of God [Hebrew, *el*]." Bethel is one of the most important sites in Bible history. From around 3500 B.C., the bare mountaintop there was a center where the Canaanite deity El was worshiped. Both Abraham (Gen. 12:8) and Jacob (28:19) worshiped the Lord there and allowed the spot to retain the name "Bethel."

After the conquest of Canaan by Joshua some five hundred years later (Josh. 8:9), the district was given to the tribe of Benjamin. For a time after the conquest, the ark of the covenant, which was the center of Israel's worship, was located at Bethel, which remained an important site through the era of the Judges. When the united Hebrew kingdom established by David and Solomon divided in 930 B.C., Jeroboam I (the ruler of the northern kingdom of Israel) established Bethel as a rival worship center to Jerusalem.

Throughout the existence of the independent northern kingdom, the temple erected at Bethel drew the hearts of the population away from authentic worship of the Lord at His Jerusalem temple. The Bethel temple was demolished when the northern kingdom was destroyed by the Assyrians in 722 . While people settled near Bethel after the Jews returned to their homeland following the Babylonian captivity, the city never again served as a worship center. The name "Bethel" is not found in the New Testament.

It was in Jerusalem, on what was then known as Mount Moriah, that Abraham displayed his faith and prepared to sacrifice Isaac in obedience to God's command. It was at Jerusalem that the temple was built as a symbol of God's presence with His people. It was to Jerusalem that the Savior would one day come to present Himself as Israel's King, only to be rejected and crucified by them (as well as by the Romans). And it is to Jerusalem that Jesus will return to set up God's kingdom on earth.

In identifying Himself with a particular place in the Old Testament, God also identified Himself with *what took place there*. When we examine the events at Bethel, at Jerusalem, and at the temple, we discover wonderful truths about our God and about His loving purposes for humankind. God, as the God of places, reveals Himself through the events that took place in these various locations.

GOD OF PERSONS

In identifying Himself with specific places in the Old Testament, God (unlike the idols prevalent in the ancient Near East) was not geographically limiting Himself. Instead, the Lord revealed Himself through the events that occurred in these various locations.

Similarly, in identifying Himself with particular individuals, God was not limiting Himself to those people. Instead, God used His involvement with them to further reveal who He is, and also to make known what is involved in developing and maintaining a personal relationship with Him.

God is immanent (that is, everywhere present). But God is uniquely present with Scripture's men and women of faith. It is not wrong to say that in identifying Himself as the God of Abraham, the God of Jacob, or the God of Shadrach, Meshach, and Abedego, the Lord was revealing Himself through the relationship He had with these (and other) people named in Scripture.

God of Abraham. The above principle is especially clear in the case of Abram, whom God later named Abraham. The Lord appeared to Abram and gave him several wonderful covenant promises (Gen. 12:1-3). Among them was the promise that his offspring would become a great nation, and that all the world would be blessed through his descendants. (For a thorough study of the covenant promises to Abraham and their significance throughout Scripture, see the companion volume in this series, *Every Promise in the Bible*.) God also told Abram to leave his home and journey to a land that God would show him.

Abram did as God said, and traveled to the land of Caanan (v. 4). There Abram was given another promise. The Lord pledged that his offspring would inherit the land (v. 7). But Abram had no son. How could God's promises be fulfilled?

Years passed, and finally, when Sarah was long past menopause and it was physically impossible (from a human perspective) for her to give birth, God promised that Abram's own son would be his heir and that his descendants would be as innumerable as the stars of heaven (15:5). The Bible tells us that the patriarch "believed in the LORD, and He accounted it to him for righteousness" (v. 6).

The New Testament picks up this theme and presents Abraham as the prototype person of faith. It is those who believe God's promise—however humanly impossible it may seem that what God says could ever come to pass—who are counted righteous by God. And it is the spiritual children of Abraham who, as Abraham did, trust completely in the Lord and His promises in Christ. They are the ones who have a personal relationship with God.

Thus, in identifying Himself as the "God of Abraham," the Lord clearly reveals Himself as One who will accept an individual's trust in Him in place of a righteousness God requires but which no human being possesses. In identifying Himself as the God of Abraham, the Lord reminds us that it is through faith—and faith alone—that we find forgiveness and become the children of almighty God.

God of Abraham, Isaac, and Jacob. The Old Testament revelation of the Lord as the God of Abraham, Isaac, and Jacob has additional significance. While the phrase "God of Abraham" reveals the Lord as One who seeks and who merits our trust, the phrases "God of Isaac" and "God of Jacob" add an extra dimension of truth. Isaac and Jacob were the son and grandson respectively of Abraham. More significantly, they were the offspring of the person who had inherited God's covenant promises. The covenant promises passed from Abraham to Isaac, and not to Isaac's half-brother Ishmael. The covenant promises then passed to Jacob, and not to his twin brother Esau. The Lord's identification of Himself as the God of these three individuals (namely, Abraham, Isaac, and Jacob) tells us much about Him.

In Romans 9, Paul notes that this transference of the covenant promises from one generation to another teaches us that God is both sovereign and free. God chooses whom He will for salvation, without being dependent on any human act to make His choices. God's choice is utterly gracious, flowing from His good will. It is not determined by any supposed good works we have done.

In addition, God's identification of Himself as the God of Abraham, Isaac, and Jacob reminds us that human history has direction and purpose. God has made covenant promises that express what He intends to do in history. Also, His continuing relationship with the patriarchs to whom the covenant promises passed is an implicit guarantee that history proceeds according to His plan.

God of Shadrach, Meshach, and Abednego. There is another dimension of the Lord's willingness to identify Himself as the "God of" individuals. God is not ashamed to be known as the God of men and women of courage as well as faith.

The account of Shadrach, Meshach, and Abednego is well known. These three Hebrews were administrators in Nebuchadnezzar's kingdom. The king commanded them to worship an idol he had constructed. When they refused, he gave them a second chance to conform. But the three Hebrews remained committed to God. They told the furious Nebuchadnezzar, "our God whom we serve is able to deliver us from the burning fiery furnace, and He will deliver us from your hand, O king. But if not, let it be known to you, O king, that we do not serve your gods, nor will we worship the gold image which you have set up" (Dan. 3:17, 18).

The outraged ruler immediately had the three cast into a roaring furnace. But rather than die, the three walked about in the flames, accompanied by a fourth person. When the three Hebrew men came out of the blazing fire, Nebuchadnezzar confessed "blessed be the God of Shadrach, Meshach, and Abednego" (v. 28). The king then issued a decree that no one speak anything against this God on pain of death (v. 29).

In this way the three Hebrews, who were ready to die rather than deny the Lord, brought honor and glory to God. And He is not ashamed to be called their God (Heb. 11:16).

We have considered what these very personal names of God teach us about our Lord. They remind us that He is ever present with us, not simply distant and removed. God's relationship with those persons whose names are linked with Him teaches us much about who He is. And the way in which such persons glorified God encourages us to honor Him by all we say and do, for the God of Abraham, Isaac, and Shadrach is our God, too. And we are channels through whose lives the Lord reveals Himself to others.

God does not hesitate to identify Himself with persons like Shadrach and his friends who were utterly committed to Him.

GOD OF PEOPLES

In the Old Testament, God is also called the "God of Israel" and the "God of the Hebrews." Often, where God is identified as the "God of Jacob," the Hebrew people (rather than Jacob the patriarch) are intended.

BIBLE BACKGROUND:

IN SPITE OF EVERYTHING

The wonder of God's identification of Himself as the "God of Israel" is emphasized by even a cursory knowledge of Old Testament history. When the Israelites were freed from slavery in Egypt, and despite witnessing stunning miracles performed by the Lord to secure their release, they continued to doubt and reject His leading.

God built the nation of Israel from a group of slaves in Egypt.

This culminated in a refusal by the Exodus generation to enter Canaan when God commanded them to do so (Num. 14). As a result, that generation wandered in the wilderness for thirty-eight years, until all the rebels had died. Only then, as a new and obedient generation took their place, could the conquest of Canaan begin.

For some fifty years after the deaths of Joshua and the elders who had led the conquest, the Israelites remained faithful to God. But then an age of spiritual darkness began; it is called the era of the judges. For hundreds of years a pattern of rebellion and restoration marked the experience of God's people. Generation after generation fell into idolatry. Each succeeding apostasy led to divine judgment, as foreign peoples invaded the promised land and subjugated Israelite tribes. In desperation, the Israelites turned back to the Lord, who raised up leaders to liberate them. These judges first threw off the foreign yoke and then led God's people. Sadly, when these judges died, the people forgot the lessons of history and quickly returned to idolatrous pagan practices.

God eventually raised up David, who united the Hebrew tribes and established a strong kingdom that dominated the ancient Near East. For a time it seemed as if this golden age would break the sinful pattern noted above. But tragically, after the death of David's son Solomon, the united Hebrew kingdom was divided. In the north a series of kings followed the lead of the apostate Jeroboam I and maintained a national religion that counterfeited legitimate Old Testament institutions.

Within the first two decades of the division, those committed to the proper worship of the Lord migrated to the southern kingdom of Judah. During the nearly four hundred years that Judah survived as an independent kingdom, the nation experienced cycles of idolatry and return to God, much like those that marked the times of the judges. When godly kings ruled, the nation tended to be faithful to the Lord. But there were too many rulers in the south who led their people into idolatry, and ultimately centuries of sin brought the discipline of the Babylonian captivity.

Despite the faithlessness of God's Old Testament people, the Lord remained committed to them and to the covenant promises He had made to Abraham, Isaac, and Jacob. When the Israelites sinned, God disciplined them. But would God abandon His dearly loved people? Never!

It is striking that God wants Himself to be known as the God of the Hebrews. Certainly the Old Testament testifies that God's people all too often abandoned Him to worship idols. And all too often they ignored the righteous standards expressed in the Law of Moses. (For instance, injustice and oppression of the poor were commonplace during most of the years that Israel existed as a nation.)

Even more striking is the fact that God, who chose Israel, remained faithful to His people despite their apostasy. God's commitment of love remained fixed and firm. God expresses that love by speaking through the prophet Hosea. The Lord reveals that He was torn by pain as He faced the necessity of disciplining His sinning people.

I taught Ephraim to walk,
Taking them by their arms;
But they did not know that
 I healed them.
I drew them with gentle cords,
With bands of love,
And I was to them as those
 who take the yoke from their neck.
I stooped and fed them. . . .

How can I give you up, Ephraim?
How can I hand you over, Israel? . . .
My heart churns within Me;
My sympathy is stirred.
I will not execute the fierceness
of My anger;
I will not again destroy
Ephraim.
For I am God, and not a man,

The Holy One of Israel in your midst;
And I will not come with terror.
 Hosea 11:3, 4, 8, 9

In identifying Himself as the God of Israel and the God of the Hebrews, the Lord reveals Himself as One who loves His people unconditionally. God remains faithful, even when we are faithless. Truly, God is not a human being, for the kind of love God displayed in His relationship with Israel is a Calvary kind of love. It is a love that churns the heart. It will not let the loved one go, even though such love cost God the life of His only Son.

Yes, God is immanent. He is also intimately and actively involved in our lives. And through that involvement as the God of places, the God of persons, and the God of His Old Testament people, the Lord has made Himself known.

DESCRIPTIVE NAMES OF GOD

The exalted names of God tend to be compounds, such as Almighty God or God Most High. In these compounds, each element can be and often does stand alone. Thus we find "the Almighty" and "the Most High" standing alone in Scripture without "God."

The relational names of God are those in which the Lord is revealed as the "God of" a place, person, or people. When seeking the meaning of these names, we must go back to study each place or person and the way in which God acted at that place or related to the specific person or people.

The descriptive names of God are most often marked by the association of an adjective with "God" or "Lord," with the adjective making a specific declaration about God. In this arrangement, the descriptive names tend to be like the exalted names. In other words, they lift God up, and they declare some awesome reality about who He is. And who is He?

Moses affirmed the right of God to govern the affairs of His people.

❖

THE ETERNAL GOD/THE EVERLASTING GOD

'Olam is the Hebrew word translated as either "eternal" or "everlasting." The word occurs some 300 times in the Old Testament, and it is often translated as "forever," "ever," "everlasting," "perpetual," "old," or "ancient." God is called the eternal God or the everlasting God in only four Old Testament texts. Nevertheless, this descriptive name adds something important to our understanding of who God is. To be specific, the name 'el 'olam presents God as One who existed before the remotest time and who will exist in perpetuity. Simply put, this descriptive name of God reminds us that the Lord was, is, and ever more will be.

The name first occurs in Genesis 21:33. Abimelech (an early title of Caananite kings who lived in what later became the land of the Philistines) came to Abraham with Phichol, the commander of Abimelech's army. The two asked Abraham to make a treaty with them, for they said, "God is with you in all that you do" (v. 22). Abraham agreed, and made a covenant oath in which he swore friendship with them (vv. 23, 24). Verse 33 tells us that afterward Abraham planted a tree at the site of the treaty of friendship.

It was there that the patriarch "called on the name of the LORD, the Everlasting God." In doing so, Abraham affirmed his awareness that treaties between people are vulnerable to human failings. But once established, a relationship with God is secure, for the Lord is the everlasting God. He remains the same for all eternity.

This truth is echoed in Moses' final blessing on the tribes of Israel:

> The eternal God is your refuge,
> And underneath are the everlasting arms.
> Deuteronomy 33:27

THE GOD OF GLORY

Although found only one time in the Old Testament (namely, in Ps. 29:3), the title is significant. Psalm 29 is a poem written by David. He saw God's footprints in the creation, and he declared that the Lord is great and powerful. David's awe at the wonders of our world turned to awe of Yahweh, who not only made all things but who also governs them, and whose powerful voice is still heard in the storm. Thus David cried out,

> Give unto the LORD, O you mighty ones,
> Give unto the LORD glory and strength,
> Give unto the LORD the glory due to His name;
> Worship the LORD in the beauty of holiness.
>
> The voice of the LORD is over the waters;
> The God of glory thunders;
> The LORD is over many waters.
> The voice of the LORD is powerful;
> The voice of the LORD is full of majesty.
>   Psalm 29:1-4

The repetition of "LORD" and of "glory" in these verses is significant. In Hebrew the root meaning of the word translated "glory" is "heavy" or "weighty." The idea is that there is no more weighty or significant being in the universe than Yahweh, for He alone truly is majestic and high above all.

GOD IN HEAVEN

This descriptive phrase is found nine times in the Old Testament. In describing the Lord as "God in heaven," the writers of Scripture affirm several truths. Moses views God's position in heaven as giving Him the right to call on the Israelites to "keep . . . His commandments" (Deut. 4:39, 40). Rahab, a citizen of Jericho, saw Yahweh's position as God in heaven as one of power. He was well able to aid Israel and to crush Jericho's walls (Josh. 2:11). When the Lord is addressed as "God in heaven" in 1 Kings 8:23, 2 Chronicles 6:14, and 20:6, it is His uniqueness that is in view. All other so-called deities are idols whose realms are limited to the earth. They are the inventions of demons whose forms are fashioned by people.

Psalm 115:3-6 beautifully sums up what it means to know the Lord as God in heaven.

> But our God is in heaven;
> He does whatever He pleases.
> Their idols are silver and gold,
> The work of men's hands.
> They have mouths, but they do not speak;
> Eyes they have, but they do not see;
> They have ears, but they do not hear;
> Noses they have, but they do not smell.

What a contrast the above is with our God in heaven! It is a perfect reason for the psalmist to cry out,

> O Israel, trust in the LORD;
> He is their help and their shield.
> O house of Aaron, trust in the LORD;
> He is their help and their shield.
> You that fear the LORD, trust in the LORD;
> He is their help and their shield.
>   Psalm 115:9-11

Only God in heaven should be the object of our trust, for He alone is our help and our shield.

BIBLE BACKGROUND:

OF THEE WE SING

The various names of God have captured the imaginations of generations of believers.

God's names have also enriched worship, especially as many have been woven into the familiar hymns most of us know. Both words and music have functioned to lift our thoughts and hearts to God and encouraged us to praise Him for who He is. Here are phrases from hymns that we and our spiritual predecessors have sung:

"Be Thou My Vision"
High King of Heaven, Thou heaven's bright Sun,
O grant me its joys after victory is won;
Great Heart of my own heart, whatever befall,
Still be Thou my vision, O Ruler of all.

"His Name Is Wonderful"
His name is Wonderful, His name is Wonderful,
His name is Wonderful, Jesus my Lord.
He's the great Shepherd, the Rock of all ages,
Almighty God is He.

"Immortal, Invisible"
Immortal, invisible, God only wise,
In light inaccessible, hid from our eyes.
Most blessed, most glorious, the Ancient of Days,
Almighty, victorious, Thy great name we praise.

"O Worship the King"
O worship the King, all glorious above,
And gratefully sing His power and His love:
Our Shield and Defender, the Ancient of Days,
Pavilion'd in splendor and girded with praise.

The names of God truly enrich our praise, whether that praise is sung or pours out silently from a heart filled with love and adoration!

THE LIVING GOD

God is described as "the living God" ten times in the Old Testament and ten times in the New Testament. The key to understanding this descriptive name of the Lord is found in *The Theological Wordbook of the Old Testament*. The authors point out, "The OT speaks of life as the experience of life rather than as an abstract principle of vitality which may be distinguished from the body. . . . Life is the ability to exercise all one's vital power to the fullest" (p. 644).

In describing God as "the Living God," Scripture distinguishes between the Lord and all competing deities. Only the God of the Bible is the Living God, and He alone is able to exercise all His vital power to the fullest. It is significant that four of the ten occurrences of "Living God" are in the context of Assyria's insult to the Lord uttered in the time of Hezekiah. An Assyrian envoy had ridiculed the idea that the God of the Israelites could withstand Assyria's might any more than the deities of the many peoples Assyria had conquered. Hezekiah took the Assyrian ruler's insults to the Lord in prayer. Hezekiah said,

> O LORD God of Israel, the One who dwells between the cherubim, You are God, You alone, of all the kingdoms of the earth. You have made heaven and earth. Incline Your ear, O LORD, and hear; open Your eyes, O LORD, and see; and hear the words of Sennacherib, which he has sent to reproach the living God.
> 2 Kings 19:15, 16

Because God is the Living God and able to exercise fully all His vital power, He intervened on Hezekiah's behalf. In a single night, the Assyrian army was decimated, and not one Assyrian arrow flew over the walls of Jerusalem. Sennacherib returned home, and before another invasion of Judah could be mounted, he was assassinated by two of his sons (vv. 35-37).

Because God is the Living God, we can rely on Him completely. We can face our challenges courageously, and we can freely appeal to Him when we are in need.

THE LORD, THE KING

It is in the psalms that we find God described as King. For instance, Psalm 47 affirms that "the LORD Most High is awesome; He is a great King over all the earth" (v.2). How appropriate then it is to

Sing praises to our King, sing praises!
For God is the King of all the earth;
Sing praises with understanding.
God reigns over the nations;
God sits on His holy throne.
    Psalm 47:6-8

The Hebrew noun translated "king," *melek*, is an important term. In the ancient world, the king was responsible for all functions of government—the legislative, the executive, and the judicial. The *New International Encyclopedia of Bible Words* points out that the *melek* "provided whatever leadership and control were required to govern the people" (p. 376). And this authority rested, not so much in the office, as in the person who bore the title.

The encyclopedia briefly traces Scripture's vision of God as King.

On the day that Samuel presented Saul to Israel as their first king, he recalled sadly, "You said to me, 'No, we want a king to rule over us'—even though the LORD your God was your king" (1 Sa 12:12). Samuel affirmed that God had committed himself to personally provide the judicial, legislative, executive, and military leadership that his people needed. But God was invisible, and the enemies that surrounded Israel were all too visible. God was overtly rejected; Israel demanded a ruler they could see. They would rely on a human being rather than the Lord.

Samuel warned against reliance on mere human leadership (2 Sa 8:10-20). And biblical history records recurrent tragedies, with evil and inept kings leading Israel into apostasy.

The prophets, many of whom lived in the days of the monarchy, called Israel back to its original vision of God. God was Israel's Creator, King, and Redeemer (Isa 43:15; 44:6). He had to be recognized as the great King (Mal 1:14; cf. Zep 3:15). But it is Zechariah who sums up most clearly Israel's future hope. "The LORD will be king over the whole earth. On that day there will be one LORD, and his name the only name (Zec 14:9). After God personally intervenes to destroy Israel's wicked enemies, he will be personally present on earth. "Then the survivors from all the nations that have attacked Jerusalem will go up year after year to worship the King, the LORD Almighty, and to celebrate the Feast of Tabernacles" (Zec 14:16).

Thus, in speaking of God as King, the OT sees both his invisible but real rule over the course of human events and the coming day when he will appear on earth to bring everything under his personal control (pp. 376, 377).

There is, of course, another aspect of God's rule as King. David begins Psalm 145 with the words, "I will extol You, my God, O King" (v. 1). When we praise God as King "with understanding," we commit ourselves to be His subjects. We gladly acknowledge His right to legislate the kind of life we will live. And we trust Him completely to control the circumstances of our lives.

ANCIENT OF DAYS

This descriptive name of God is used only in Daniel 7:9. Even more significant, the Hebrew word translated "ancient," *'attiq*, is found only here in this unique name of God. While most take the phrase "Ancient of Days" to suggest enduring eminence, it is the context in which this name is used that is most significant.

In chapter 7, Daniel reveals a vision of the future. Beginning with verse 9, the focus shifts from earth to heaven. Daniel sees thrones being put in place, as in an ancient courtroom. There, seated on His throne and being ministered to by thousands, is the Ancient of Days. His first act as Judge is to see that an evil power (Antichrist) is condemned and slain. God's second act is to establish the dominion of the Son of man (a reference to Christ) on earth. The final act of the court is to end a last great rebellion, and make a judgment "in favor of the saints of the Most High, and the time came for the saints to possess the kingdom" (v. 22).

This is clearly an eschatological vision. The title "Ancient of Days" is a name that assures us of the final victory of God over evil. We are reminded that whatever evil and injustice may disturb us in our own day, from the beginning, from ancient times, God has been committed to establish a righteous kingdom for His saints.

THE TITLES OF OUR GOD

It's common in modern business. Workers are given titles instead of raises. Or, the title "Vice President" is given to salespeople to make potential clients feel they are receiving special treatment. Others bear titles of which they are not worthy. The character of a person can demean the office he or she holds and tarnish his or her title.

When we come to the many and varied titles of God, however, none of the caveats that make us suspicious of human titles apply. Each title the Lord bears is indeed meaningful, for it reveals more about who God is and who He is for us. And God's character infuses each title. He is worthy of all the praise and honor each title implies.

As with the many names of God, it's also possible to classify the many titles of God found in the Old Testament. There are exalted titles that emphasize His intrinsic power and authority. But most of all there are descriptive titles, which most often reveal what God has done or will do.

THE EXALTED TITLES OF GOD

CREATOR OF THE ENDS OF THE EARTH

In Isaiah 40:28, God is called "the everlasting God, the LORD" and given the title "the Creator of the ends of the earth." The context and the title emphasize "the greatness of His might and the strength of His power" (v. 26), for it is God who has brought all things into existence and who knows every star by name. For more on God as Creator, see page 8.

GOD OF HEAVEN AND EARTH
GOD OF HEAVEN
GOD ABOVE THE HEAVENS

While one of the descriptive names of the Lord is "God in heaven" (p. 43), He also bears the titles "God of heaven and earth," "God of heaven," and "God above the heavens." While the first title is found only in

Ezra 5:11, the other two occur some 23 times in the Old Testament.

In the Old Testament, the Hebrew word *samayim* is translated both as "heaven" and "heavens." The Bible understands the heavens as part of the created universe. Physically the heavens include everything in and above the sky, including the stars. But the heavens also are the realm of God. There is a certain parallelism between the physical and spiritual heavens. Both are "above," that is, beyond the capacity of human beings to experience directly. Both are vast and mysterious, comprehended fully only by God. Thus, Isaiah says,

"My thoughts are not your thoughts,
Nor are your ways My ways," says the LORD.
"For as the heavens are higher than the earth,
So are my ways higher than your ways,
And My thoughts than your thoughts."
Isaiah 55:8, 9

In giving the Lord the title "God of heaven," the Old Testament confronts us with the vast gap that exists between human beings and God, and reminds us that only God can cover the distance. We can never reach up to heaven to find Him. But God has stooped down to earth to touch our lives. No wonder the psalmist calls on us to

Give thanks to the God of heaven!
For His mercy endures forever.
Psalm 136:26

GOD OF TRUTH

The Lord is titled "God of truth" in several Old Testament passages. As Moses approached his own death, "God of truth" was one of the first titles he gave to the Lord in a teaching song (which Moses then had Israel memorize).

He is the Rock, His work is perfect;
For all His ways are justice,

A God of truth and without injustice;
Righteous and upright is He.
Deuteronomy 32:4

It's clear from this first occurrence of the title in Scripture that titling the Lord as "God of truth" is closely related to His moral character.

The New International Dictionary of New Testament Theology points out that "the Hebrews recognized the *logical* truth that others also recognized, that a true word can be relied upon because it accords with reality, and that both for a God of truth and for a man of truth, word and deed are one" (Vol. 3, p. 882). It may even be that the best way to translate most occurrences of "true" (Hebrew, *'emet*) in the Old Testament is with the word "reliable," for that which is true is reliable and can be counted on.

This is why Moses so clearly links the title "God of truth" with "justice" and "righteous." God's commitment to doing what is right is unshakable. He is the one reliable moral constant in the universe, regardless of what the modern world may hold about morality being relative and about actions being "right for me" without reference to an absolute standard. As God of truth, the Lord Himself is the standard, and His commitment to what is right makes Him a totally reliable person on whose word we can depend. It's no wonder the psalmist confidently says to the Lord,

You are my strength.
Into Your hand I commit my spirit.
Psalm 31:4, 5

And it is no wonder that Christ Himself uttered these very words on the cross, confident that His heavenly Father would not only receive the gift but also would raise the Son to everlasting life (Luke 23:46).

HIM WHO RIDES IN THE CLOUDS

HIM WHO RIDES IN THE HEAVEN OF HEAVENS

Both of these titles are found in Psalm 68. Verse 4 says, "Extol Him who rides on the clouds," and verse 33 calls on the reader to sing praises to the Lord, "to Him who rides on the heaven of heavens, which were of old." The image of "riding on" clouds or heavens indicates God's control, as the rider on a horse controls his or her steed. God is great, for only He controls not only the skies but also the heaven of heavens.

HOLY ONE OF ISRAEL

The title "Holy One of Israel" both describes the Lord and identifies His relationship with His covenant people. God is depicted as the "Holy One" 50 times in 48 Old Testament verses. In most of these verses the full title "Holy One of Israel" is given.

The Old Testament concept of "holy" is extremely important. The underlying thought is that whatever is holy is removed from the realm of the ordinary and transferred to the sphere of the sacred. Clearly God, being splendid in His essential power and glory, is infinitely set apart from His creation. As the Holy One, God Himself becomes the focus of the sacred realm.

There is also a clear emphasis in the Old Testament on the importance of God's people maintaining a distinction between secular and the sacred. Thus, the phrase "of Israel" is typically added to "Holy One." Why is this so? First, the title reminds us that Yahweh is the One who *defines* the sacred for His people. He Himself is quintessential holiness, the One who established Israel and who was Himself the standard by which Israel was to live.

Second, the phrase "Holy One of Israel" reminds us that Yahweh is the One who made Israel holy. In other words, God is the One who set the descendants of Abraham apart as His own special people.

Third, God is the One whom Israel must always reflect. In Leviticus 19:2 the Lord told Moses, "Speak to all the congregation of the children of Israel, and say to them: 'You shall be holy, for I the LORD your God am holy.'"

God's people were to be holy simply because they were *God's people*! Their lives were to reflect His character, and their ways were to bring glory to their God. It's no wonder that Proverbs 9:10 states, "the fear of the LORD is the beginning of wisdom, and the knowledge of the Holy One is understanding."

BIBLE BACKGROUND:

SET APART VERSUS ISOLATION

The underlying concept in the Hebrew word rendered "holy" is "set apart to God." In Old Testament times this involved separation. For instance, implements used in temple worship were not to be employed for any other purpose. Many of the more peculiar dictates of Old Testament ritual law were intended to underscore the fact that Israel itself was set apart from all the other peoples of the ancient world. While the Old Testament contains several examples of pagan peoples who came to know the Lord, the wall of separation erected by the Law was maintained. There was to be no confusion about who and what was holy to the Lord.

The gospel introduced a radical change in the concept of holiness. God's Old Testament people were both a nation and a faith community. God's New Testament people, formed of individuals who trusted in Jesus as their Savior, were a faith community, not a nation. Instead, Christians were called to live among pagan peoples—living in the same apartment buildings, working side by side with unbelievers, and sharing meals and customs with them. Holiness could no longer be expressed in isolation from pagan influences.

The Law dealt with every aspect of an Israelite's life, constantly reminding God's people that they were set apart to Him.

Nowhere is this stated as clearly as by Paul in 1 Corinthians 5:9-13 (NIV).

I have written you in my letter not to associate with sexually immoral people—not at all meaning the people of this world who are immoral, or the greedy and swindlers, or idolaters. In that case you would have to leave this world. But now I am writing you that you must not associate with anyone who calls himself a brother but is sexually immoral or greedy, an idolater or a slanderer, a drunkard or a swindler. With such a man do not even eat. What business is it of mine to judge those outside the church? Are you not to judge those inside? God will judge those outside. "Expel the wicked man from among you."

From this passage we derive several principles. First, individual Christians are not to "leave this world" but rather to live in it as witnesses. In fact, one of the clearest of Christian witnesses is a holy life. Such is not measured by "dos" and "don'ts" but rather by one's dynamic inner commitment to love, to do only good deeds, and to remain uncontaminated by the sins of others.

Second, Christians should maintain membership in a Christian community that is a holy fellowship, that is committed to following Jesus, and that rejects the contrary values of society at large. In the early church, it was in bonds formed between members of such a holy community that individual believers drew strength to live godly and holy lives in the world.

At times throughout church history the Old Testament expression of holiness—which truly involved an element of isolation from pagan peoples surrounding Israel—has crept in to distort the understanding of Christians concerning what holy living involves. For believers holiness is a quality of life and a commitment to God's ways and values. Such a mindset enables us to live among people whose beliefs and behaviors are godless. It's only when we understand holiness as a commitment to God and His ways—even though we live in a hostile world—that we will be able to experience the moral purity and spiritual growth to which God has called us in Jesus Christ.

What holiness involved. In the Old Testament, holiness had both strong cultic and moral elements. The cultic element involved a ritual holiness that was summed up in the requirement that Israel avoid all things that God had identified as "unclean," and perform those ritual duties that were prescribed. For instance, a Hebrew was not to mix fabrics in a garment or plow with two different animals yoked together (Deut. 22:10). Such proscriptions were not moral in nature; rather, they were cultic.

Keeping these rather strange commandments, or even the more familiar commands not to eat unclean animals (Lev. 11:24-47), was never a matter of morality. Instead, all such cultic rules were intended to remind the Israelites that they truly were a people set apart to God; thus, they were different from all the peoples around them.

It was the responsibility of the priests to "distinguish between holy and unholy, and between clean and unclean, and . . . teach the children of Israel all the statutes which the LORD has spoken to them by the hand of Moses" (Lev. 10:10, 11). Israel was to be holy in the "set apart" sense. Also, the rules that patterned daily life, the year, and an individual's life-cycle, were all intended to remind the nation of its special relationship with the Holy One of Israel.

Moral holiness. While ritual holiness was a significant element in the lifestyle of Israel, moral holiness was also emphasized. The first commandments given Israel by God at Sinai were moral in character, not ritual. A person set aside to God was not to be involved in idolatry, theft, lying, immorality, murder, and so on. Later commandments of a moral nature were frequently punctuated with the reminder, "I am the LORD."

One of the major themes of the prophets was to remind the Israelites that God called them to a moral way of life and to a commitment to doing good. For those who were set apart to God by His own actions, both ritual and moral holiness were required.

While the Old Testament emphasizes the "set apartness" of the way of life called for by the Holy One of Israel, a distinct change of emphasis is found in the New Testament. There the emphasis is placed on a dynamic holiness. It is an active moral commitment that reflects the work of the Holy Spirit of God within a human personality. While Old Testament saints separated themselves from sinners, New Testament believers are to live holy lives in the context of sinful human societies, and so to "overcome evil with good" (Rom. 12:21).

Ultimately for saints in either era, the title Holy One of Israel reminds us that we are to pattern our lives on the perfections of our God. We are to distinguish between good and evil (as we are taught in God's Word), and so set ourselves apart to Him.

THE RELATIONAL TITLES OF GOD

It is possible to treat some of the titles of God as relational. For instance, "God our healer" clearly emphasizes the relationship between the believer and the Lord. Yet it is preferable to treat most of the titles of God found in the Old Testament as descriptive titles. This is because most of the Old Testament's titles describe something that God does or will do. For this reason the rest of the titles of God examined in this chapter will be identified as descriptive titles.

DESCRIPTIVE TITLES OF GOD

How is God to be described? In Scripture the two most common functions of God's descriptive titles are to affirm a role of God, such as King, or to portray actions of God, such as "He who forgives." The 38 descriptive titles of God explored here further enrich our understanding of who God is and our awe at His love and grace.

GOD OF JUSTICE

One of the roles that Scripture ascribes to the Lord is that of doing justice. This role is intimately linked to God's role as Ruler of the universe He created and maintains.

Two Hebrew verbal roots are important in helping us understand the implications of this title. The first root, *sapat*, incorporates all functions of government, including the judicial. Justice deals with a person's rights and duties under law, and to give God the title "God of justice" means in part that He establishes those rights and duties as Lawgiver (Is. 33:22). God also functions as Judge (Ps. 7:11) and metes out justice.

The other Hebrew root is *sadaq*, and words constructed on this root are translated by "right" and "righteous" as well as by "just" and "justice." The underlying idea is that moral and ethical standards exist and that our actions can be and are measured against them. Actions that are in harmony with the standards are "just," while those that violate the standards are "unjust." As God of justice, the Lord not only establishes the standards, but also His own actions are always in full harmony with them.

The New International Encyclopedia of Bible Words makes several important points about God and justice.

Ultimately our understanding of justice has its source in the person of the one who gave mankind his law. "He is the Rock, his words are perfect, and all his ways are just. A faithful God who does no wrong, upright and just is he" (Dt 32:4). God's historic punishments of Israel for deviation from the revealed norms are also an aspect of justice. Again and again Israel was forced to admit, "In all that has happened to us, you have been just" (Ne 9:33; cf. 2 Ch 12:5-6).

Justice, then, is rooted in the very nature of God, and his character is the true norm or standard. All his acts are just and right, even those we may not be able to understand. But in Scripture, God has given us norms that we can grasp. These standards, expressed in the OT in the Mosaic Law and in the Prophets, take justice from the realm of the abstract and make it a practical issue indeed (p. 369).

The great mystery in Scripture's portrait of the Lord as God of justice is that there is also room for mercy. Isaiah 30:18 combines the themes of mercy and justice.

Therefore the LORD will wait,
 that He may be gracious to you;
And therefore He will be exalted,
 that He may have mercy on you.
For the LORD is a God of justice;
 Blessed are all those who wait for Him.

The mystery is that while strict justice calls for punishment, the Lord, as God of justice, encourages His people to rely on His grace and mercy. Isaiah 30:18 clearly links God's gifts of grace and mercy to His role as God of justice.

The Old Testament does not explain how the conflict between justice and mercy can be resolved. But the New Testament Book of Romans reveals how God dealt with this apparently irresolvable moral dilemma.

Now the righteousness of God apart from the law is revealed, being witnessed by the Law and the Prophets, even the righteousness of God, through faith in Jesus Christ, to all and on all who believe. For there is no difference; for all have sinned and fall short of the glory of God, being justified freely by His grace through the redemption that is in Christ Jesus, whom God set forth as a propitiation by His blood, through faith, to demonstrate His righteousness, because in His forbearance God had passed over the sins that were previously committed, to demonstrate at the present time His righteousness, that He might be just and the justifier of the one who has faith in Jesus (Rom. 3:21-26).

Since all have sinned, divine justice demands that all be condemned. But Jesus paid the penalty justice required, freeing God to be just while offering sinners a salvation received by faith. In the death of Christ on the cross, God at last revealed how He could be gracious to Old Testament saints whose sins He seemed to have ignored. Before the beginning of time, God knew that to create the human race and to give people moral freedom would ultimately cost Him the life of His Son.

Truly the God of justice has been exalted! In His commitment to do what is right, He not only maintained His integrity through Calvary, but also through that same act poured out grace upon an undeserving humankind.

GOD OF KNOWLEDGE

After the birth of Samuel, his mother Hannah, who had prayed desperately for a son, praised God in a prayer recorded in 1 Samuel 2. Filled with joy, Hanna exulted,

There is none holy like the LORD,
For there is none beside You,
Nor is there any rock like our God.
Talk no more so very proudly;
Let no arrogance come from your mouth,
For the LORD is the God of knowledge;
And by Him actions are weighed.
　1 Samuel 2:2, 3

Only Jesus' cross was able to reconcile the inherent conflict between the justice and the mercy of God.

The Hebrew word translated "knowledge" (v. 3) is a general term for knowledge typically gained by personal involvement. The same word is also used for technical knowledge, which we would call "know-how." As a God of knowledge, the Lord is aware of all things, even though the wicked foolishly question His ability to know (Ps. 73:11). The Lord also has the "know-how" to accomplish all His purposes. In the 1 Samuel context, it's clear that the title "God of knowledge" emphasizes this first aspect of knowledge. God is aware of all that human beings say and do, and God uses this knowledge when He weighs the actions of people.

GOD OF MY SALVATION

This special title of God appears in Psalm 88:1. There the psalmist begins,

O Lord, God of my salvation,
I have cried out day and night before You.
Let my prayer come before You;
Incline Your ear to my cry.
Psalm 88:1, 2

This entire psalm is a plea to God to act and to deliver the believer.

Salvation in the Old Testament. In the Old Testament the concept of salvation, or deliverance, focuses on concrete situations. While eternal salvation is not ignored in the Old Testament, that doctrine is not fully developed. When Old Testament saints called on God to save them, they typically meant being rescued from dangers in their immediate circumstances. Thus the psalmist explains,

For my soul is full of troubles,
And my life draws near to the grave.
I am counted with those who go down to the pit:
  Psalm 88:3, 4

Also intimately involved in the concept of salvation is the awful awareness that unless someone acts, all is lost. There is no way that people on their own can extricate themselves from their desperate situation. The psalmist admits,

I am like a man who has no strength,
Adrift among the dead,
Like the slain who lie in the grave,
Whom You remember no more,
And who are cut off from Your hand.
Psalm 88:4, 5

In addressing the Lord as "God of my salvation" (v. 1), the psalmist acknowledged God as the only one who could relieve the pressures under which he lived. Even though the rest of Psalm 88 inquires as to why God had not yet acted, the underlying conviction that the Lord is a God of salvation shines through.

New Testament parallels. In the New Testament, the emphasis shifts from situational salvation to eternal salvation. God is still seen as being able to deliver us from dangerous circumstances (Phil. 1:12-19). But what is celebrated is the work of Jesus, who has saved those who believe from the penalty of sin, who is saving those who believe from the power of sin, and who will save those who believe from the presence of sin.

While the emphases differ in the two testaments, there are close parallels between them. Individuals portrayed in the Old Testament found themselves in danger of physical death. The New Testament portrays all humanity as in danger of spiritual death. Individuals portrayed in the Old Testament were powerless to deliver themselves from their enemy. The New Testament portrays all humankind as powerless to deliver themselves from the grip of sin or to escape punishment. Individuals portrayed in the Old Testament called on God for help, and He rescued them by defeating their enemies. The New Testament portrays God as acting in Christ to defeat death, and to provide eternal life to all who trust in Jesus.

Thus, even though the emphases differ between the testaments, Scripture is totally consistent in developing the doctrine of salvation. In salvation, people are seen as helpless before a threat to their very lives, and only divine intervention can avail.

Today, as in ancient times, we celebrate the Lord as "God of my salvation." He is our best and only hope. And God is Savior enough.

GOD OUR HEALER

Shortly after the Israelites crossed the Red Sea on their journey out of Egypt, God announced to them, "I am the Lord who heals you" (Ex. 15:26).

This title, *Yahweh Rophe*, which is often taken as a name, was announced shortly after the Lord purified a spring of bitter waters so that the Israelites might have something to drink. At that time, the Lord (through Moses) told the Israelites, "If you diligently heed the voice of the LORD your God and do what is right in His sight, give ear to His commandments and keep all His statutes, I will put none of the diseases on you which I have brought on the Egyptians. For I am the LORD who heals you" (v. 26).

The title "the God who heals you" has captured the imagination of Christians over the centuries, especially as people have yearned for the healing touch of God. Many take this title as a promise that God is committed to heal people of faith. Those who hold this view link this Old Testament title to Isaiah 53:5, which says, "and by His stripes we are healed." They argue that physical healing is ours in the atonement, and that the believer need only claim the power of the blood of Christ for healing to be assured.

It is certain that God has the power to heal and that He often exercises that power on our behalf. But it is not at all sure that God *must* heal believers on demand.

The Exodus text. Exodus 15:26, in which God titles Himself "the LORD who heals you," links freedom from those diseases that troubled Egypt with Israel's faithfulness in keeping God's Law. In context, the point God made is clear. God sent plagues upon Egypt because the Egyptians had refused to heed His command. Only by listening and responding to God's commandments could the Israelites avoid similar plagues. In calling Himself "the LORD who heals you," God reminded Israel that He controlled the health of His people as well as all things. God likewise is able to gift us with health, just as He is able to gift us with wealth or any other blessing (Deut. 8:18).

Isaiah 53. This great prophecy depicting Christ's death and resurrection expresses several of the benefits Jesus won for us on

Jesus remains free to heal or not to heal today, just as during His years on earth.

the cross. However, the phrase "by His stripes we are healed" (v. 5) need not refer to physical healing. Isaiah uses the image of sickness and debility as a depiction of sin, and healing may well refer to the restoration of spiritual well-being (see 1:5, 6). Even if physical health were the primary issue in 53:5, that healing referred to may well take place in the Resurrection. Until then, both believers and unbelievers are subject to illness and other tragedies, for all people (whether saved or unsaved) live as sinners in a fallen world.

The New Testament's testimony. While Jesus did heal during His time on earth, and while miracles of healing are described in the Book of Acts, there is no guarantee of physical healing stated in the New Testament. James 5:13-15 is the only exception. There healing is described as an answer to the prayer of church elders combined with medical treatment (namely, anointing with oil). We need to remember that even after Paul's prayer for his own physical healing, God did not take away the apostle's ailment. Paul learned that God's strength shines more clearly through human weaknesses (2 Cor. 12:7-10).

Retaining focus. In general, the context in which the Scriptures first introduce a new concept or reveal a new name or title is critical to our interpretation. In Exodus 15:26, where God is revealed as "the LORD who heals you," the context clearly argues for a simple explanation. Human beings remain spiritually healthy and often are more healthy physically when they live in a right relationship with God. God wants us to stay close to Him so that we might be as whole and healthy as possible in every way. When we turn away from God, we make ourselves vulnerable to illness, certainly as a judgment, but also because we are weakened when cut off from God.

Yes, God is our healer. He is the source of spiritual health, and the person who is at peace with God spiritually will tend to live a healthier and happier life than would be possible if he or she were alienated from the Lord.

GOD WHO AVENGES ME

This unusual title of God is found near the close of Psalm 18. In the psalm, David recalls his deliverance from many dangers and his victories over enemies, and he credits God. In view of all God has done for him, David cries out,

> The LORD lives!
> Blessed be my Rock!
> Let the God of my salvation be exalted.
> It is God who avenges me.
>   Psalm 18:46, 47

This title, "God who avenges me," reminds us of two great truths taught in Scripture. The first is clearly expressed in 2 Thessalonians 1. There Paul describes Christ returning from heaven "with His mighty angels, in flaming fire taking vengeance on those who do not know God" (vv. 7, 8). Paul also reminds us that "it is a righteous thing with God to repay with tribulation those who trouble you" (v. 6).

The Lord does not hesitate to reveal Himself as a God of judgment as well as grace. While God will joyfully receive sinners who put their trust in Christ, God will also punish those who scorn His grace. When God proclaimed His name (that is, revealed more of His essential nature) to Moses, God announced Himself as

> The LORD, the LORD God, merciful and gracious, longsuffering, and abounding in goodness and truth, keeping mercy for thousands, forgiving iniquity and transgression and sin, by no means clearing the guilty.
>   Exodus 34:6, 7

It is no wonder the Scriptures announce, "'Vengeance is mine, I will repay,' says the Lord" (Rom. 12:19; see Deut. 32:35).

The second great truth revealed in this title is that, since God will take vengeance, we do not have to! This is a wonderful gift given by God to His people. While we as a society are to be committed to doing justice, as individuals we simply are not responsible to deal with every miscarriage of justice. When the guilty escape the penalty of law, when the corrupt prosper, and when the immoral are lionized by press and people, it is a great comfort for us to remember that the Lord says, "Vengeance is Mine, I will repay" (Rom. 12:19).

When King Saul's army was pursuing David, David slipped into Saul's camp one night and found his enemy asleep. One of David's men pointed out that the Lord had delivered Saul into David's hand. Now was the moment to murder Saul! But David refused and explained, "As the LORD lives, the LORD shall strike him, or his day shall

God alone does great wonders, and He is able to supply all our needs.

come to die, or he shall go out to battle and perish. The LORD forbid that I should stretch out my hand against the LORD's anointed" (1 Sam. 26:10, 11). To kill Saul there would have been murder, making it a personal rather than judicial killing. Thus, David would not take vengeance into his own hands, even though he was in constant danger from the jealous and hostile Saul.

David remembered that vengeance belongs to God, and it may well be that David thought about this incident when, under the Spirit's guidance, he gave the Lord the title, "God who avenges me" (Ps. 18:47).

GOD WHO SEES

This title was given to the Lord by a desperate Egyptian slave woman who was fleeing the harsh treatment of her mistress. The slave woman's name was Hagar, and at the time she was pregnant with a son by Abraham (Gen. 16:1-9).

Although God had promised Abraham a son, none had been born to Sarah. After ten years of seemingly futile waiting in Canaan, Sarah was convinced that it was too late for

her to bear her husband a child. Thus, Sarah followed established custom and, like other childless wives, supplied her husband with a surrogate. According to the law of those times, the child the surrogate bore would be Sarah's, and she would thus have fulfilled her duty to give Abraham a son.

But Sarah had not consulted God, and when Hagar became pregnant, everything began to go wrong. The two women became increasingly hostile and finally Hagar, although pregnant, could stand it no longer. She fled into the wilderness to hide. But there the Angel of the Lord spoke to Hagar. The angel, who many believe was God in visible form, told her what to name the unborn child within her womb and promised her a bright future: "I will multiply your descendants exceedingly, so that they shall not be counted for multitude" (v. 10). It was there that Hagar called the Lord "the-God-Who-Sees" (v. 13).

God had seen Hagar's plight and stooped to speak with her. And as God looked ahead, He saw the future that Hagar had been almost ready to throw away. Hagar trusted God's vision of the future, and she returned to Sarah's tent.

What an encouragement this title of God is to us! God sees our plight, too. And God also sees the future that He has in store for us. Because God truly does love us, that future indeed is bright.

HE WHO ALONE DOES GREAT WONDERS

HE WHO BY WISDOM MADE THE HEAVENS

HE WHO LAID OUT THE EARTH ABOVE THE WATERS

HE WHO MADE GREAT LIGHTS

HE WHO STRUCK EGYPT IN THEIR FIRSTBORN

HE WHO DIVIDED THE RED SEA

HE WHO LED HIS PEOPLE THROUGH THE WILDERNESS

HE WHO STRUCK DOWN GREAT KINGS

HE WHO GIVES FOOD TO ALL FLESH

These titles are all ascribed to God in one of Scripture's greatest praise psalms. The psalmist focused his attention on the Lord and described His wonderful works for His people. Each alternating line of Psalm 136 proclaims, "For His mercy *endures* forever."

This passage of Scripture is known as a "history psalm," for it focuses on God's works in history and praises Him for each act. The first title is a general one that sums up the rest. God is "Him who alone does great wonders" (v. 4). The Hebrew term rendered "wonders" emphasizes the response of people to God's miraculous acts. Immediately the believer is struck by the fact that God's acts are marvelous and wonderful. Each of the subsequent titles in this psalm points to something marvelous God has done that should fill us with awe.

The next three titles in the psalm honor God as the Creator. By wisdom He made the heavens (v. 5). He laid out the earth above the waters (v. 6). He made great lights, namely, the sun, moon, and stars (vv. 7-9).

These designations are followed by four titles that recall God's deliverance of His people from slavery in Egypt and His gift to them of the land of Canaan. God struck down Egypt's firstborn (v. 10). God divided the Red Sea and led the Israelites through it (v. 13). God also led His people safely through the wilderness (v. 16). And because of God, the Israelites conquered the promised land, for the Lord struck down great kings (v. 17).

It is significant that the two wonders emphasized in this psalm are God's creation of all things and His deliverance of Israel from Egypt. Throughout the Old Testament, believers looked back on these two historic events as miracles that defined God's power and demonstrated His commitment to His covenant people.

As the psalm ends, the writer adds another title, one that brings God's wonders into contemporary focus. God is He "who gives food to all flesh" (v. 25). The God of history—who acted in the past—is present with us as well. His grace is revealed in the provision He has made not just for humankind but also for every creature.

HE WHO FORGIVES

The title "God-Who-Forgives" is found in Psalm 99:8. There the psalmist reminds God's people of the following:

> The King's strength also loves justice;
> You have established equity;
> You have executed justice and
>   righteousness
> in Jacob.
> Exalt the Lord our God,
> And worship at His footstool—
> He is holy.
> vv. 4, 5

It is in this context of celebrating justice and righteousness that the psalmist shares the wonderful title, "God-Who-Forgives" (v. 8). Despite Israel's failings,

> You answered them, O Lord our God;
> You were to them God-Who-Forgives,
> Though You took vengeance on their deeds.

The juxtaposition of forgiveness and vengeance may seem strange. But we need to understand that forgiveness of sin does not imply immunity to its consequences. The man who gets drunk and drives his car into a tree, killing his wife and child, may cry out to God and be forgiven. But forgiveness does not mean that his family will be restored to him in this life. The young man who robs a store at gunpoint may turn to the Lord and be forgiven, but this does not mean he won't have to serve time in prison.

The fact that God forgives does not mean that He relieves us of the temporal consequences of our actions. As moral Ruler, God has structured a universe in which there are consequences for wrong actions. And in this sense God does "take vengeance" on deeds for which we can be and have been forgiven.

Nevertheless it is clear that, to God's people, it is His forgiveness that counts. People without faith express regret, not so much because they seek forgiveness but because they fear the penalty. People of faith accept the consequences of their actions as their due, and rejoice in the forgiving grace of God.

David, who wrote many of the Old Testament psalms, understood full well that it is forgiveness that counts. Sadly, he learned this lesson by personal experience. After David sinned by committing adultery with Bathsheba and murdering her husband, Uriah the Hittite (2 Sam. 11), David wrote about the inner turmoil he experienced while outwardly pretending all was well. In Psalm 32:3-4 he admitted,

> When I kept silent, my bones grew old

> Through my groaning all the day long.
> For day and night Your hand was heavy upon me.
> My vitality was turned into the drought of summer.

For the person who is sensitive to God, the Spirit so disturbs the conscience that he or she has no peace. It is no wonder then that in verses 1 and 2, David exclaims,

> Blessed is he whose transgression is forgiven,
> Whose sin is covered.
> Blessed is the man to whom the Lord does not impute iniquity,
> And in whose spirit there is no guile.

People who lie to themselves and to God about their sin will never know the blessedness of having their iniquities forgiven. Like David, we are to say, "I will confess my transgressions to the Lord" in full confidence that when confession has been made, "You forgave the iniquity of my sin" (v. 5).

BIBLE BACKGROUND:

WHEN WE FORGIVE

Paul wrote in Colossians 3:13, "bearing with one another, and forgiving one another, if anyone has a complaint against another; even as Christ forgave you, so you also must do." From this verse we see that God's readiness in Christ to forgive sinners stands as both an example and a challenge. As God has shown Himself ready and willing to forgive, ever maintaining a forgiving attitude toward those who have offended Him, so also we are to nurture an attitude of forgiveness. Thus, holding on to hostility and anger simply is not the path we are to travel.

At the same time, while God displays an attitude of forgiveness toward all, this does not mean all are automatically reconciled to Him.

It was God who enabled Israel to win military victories.

The gospel comes with a message that must be received and with an offer that must be accepted. However great God's willingness is to forgive, reconciliation cannot take place until sinners acknowledge their transgressions and receive God's pardon through faith in Christ.

A similar dynamic exists in our relationships with others. We freely forgive those who harm us. Nevertheless, no reconciliation can take place until our forgiveness is accepted. Those who refuse to acknowledge that any harm has been done will reject our willingness to forgive and perhaps even see it as an insult.

It's important to make a distinction between a forgiving attitude and reconciliation. We should be willing to forgive, for God is willing to forgive. But until forgiveness has been offered and accepted, interpersonal harmony cannot be restored. Yes, we are responsible to maintain a forgiving attitude, which cleanses our hearts of anger and hostility. But we are not responsible for the other person's response to our offer of forgiveness.

We are to forgive as unconditionally as the Lord forgives. And in Christ a door is opened to sinners to find peace with God. But neither God nor we are responsible for harmony with those who refuse to walk by faith through that open door.

With our sins forgiven, a right relationship with God is restored. In the context of that restored relationship, God promises,

> I will instruct you and teach you
>   In the way you should go;
> I will guide you with My eye.
>   v. 8

Then the forgiven believer experiences the reality described in verses 10 and 11:

> He who trusts in the LORD,
>   mercy shall surround him.
> Be glad in the LORD and rejoice,
>   you righteous;
> And shout for joy, all you upright in
>   heart!

"God-Who-Forgives" (Ps. 99:8)—what a marvelous title for our wonderful and loving God!

HE WHO TRAINS MY HANDS FOR WAR

God is given this title only in Psalm 144:1. Yet in 2 Samuel 22:35 and Psalm 18:34, David also gives God credit for teaching his hands to make war.

On the one hand, this truth about God may seem strange to peace-loving people. David is clearly convinced that God has given him the gifts he needs to be a warrior. While this notion may trouble pacifists, there remains a role for warriors in our sinful world.

More significantly, however, the title challenges some of our assumptions. Perhaps we're used to thinking about giftedness as something "spiritual." For instance, God gifts us to be teachers of His Word, to counsel and show compassion, and so on.

Nevertheless, the Old Testament reminds us that practical abilities are also divine gifts. When it came time to construct the Old Testament tabernacle, Moses told the Israelites, "See, the LORD has called by name Bezalel the son of Uri, the son of Hur, of the tribe of Judah; and He has filled him with the Spirit of God in wisdom and understanding, in knowledge and all manner of workmanship, to design artistic works, to work in gold and silver and bronze" (Ex. 35:30-32).

In the same way, Moses reminded the Israelites while they were still in the wilderness, "You shall remember the LORD your God, for it is He who gives you power to get wealth" (Deut. 8:18).

The title "[He] who trains my hands for war" (Ps. 144:1) reminds us that it is God who gives us *any* of our abilities, whether those needed to be a warrior, an artist, or a successful business person. God equips us

Today, as in ages past, those who turn away from God bring disaster on themselves and their loved ones.

❖

for our calling in the world as well as for our calling within the community of faith. The "secular" abilities we possess are just as much gifts from God as are the spiritual gifts provided by the Holy Spirit (1 Cor. 12:4-6).

THE HOPE OF ISRAEL

This title is found in Jeremiah 14:8. There the prophet cries out for divine aid in a time of drought. He says,

O LORD, though our iniquities testify
    against us,
Do it for Your name's sake;
For our backslidings are many,
We have sinned against You.
O the Hope of Israel,
his Savior in time of trouble.
                              Jeremiah 14:7-8

As "Lawgiver" God points the way to a happy and healthy life and away from a lifestyle that brings disaster.

The context tells us much about God as the "Hope of Israel," and as our own hope.

Two of the Hebrew words translated "hope," *miqweh* and *tiqweh*, imply looking ahead eagerly and confidently. To hope in God is to yearn for His involvement and also to expect it. Each word, however, also implies patience, for what we hope for lies in the future.

A third Hebrew word, *yahal*, is dominant in the psalms and prophets. This word reminds us that while we wait for God to act, we are to concentrate on living godly lives now. God will act, for He is our deliverer. Our part is to wait and to courageously face each new day.

"Hope," then, is essentially a relational term that emphasizes trust. We have confi-dence in God, trusting Him completely, and thus we live each day without surrendering to despair. David in Psalm 119 affirms, "You have given me hope. My comfort in all my suffering is this: Your promise preserves my life" (vv. 49, 50 NIV).

The words of Jeremiah are particularly significant in view of this biblical concept of hope. Jeremiah was well aware of the failures of God's people. The prophet knew their iniquities and backslidings. Yet, despite all the flaws of God's people, He remained the "Hope of Israel" (Jer. 14:8). God continues in the covenant relationship He has established with His people; God's love is unshaken. And because God continues to care for His own, even sinners and backsliders have hope.

Our life may be dreary and we may feel spiritually dry. But we should not lose hope, for our God is the "Hope of Israel," and our hope, too.

JEALOUS GOD

It is the Lord who presents Himself as a "jealous God." This title is found six times in the Old Testament (Ex. 20:5; 34:14; Deut. 4:24; 5:9; 6:15; Josh. 24:19).

The first occurrence is in Exodus 20:5, which is part of the Ten Commandments. The Lord directed His people to worship Him alone, and warned them against turning aside to false gods and bowing down to carved idols. The passage says,

> You shall not bow down to them nor serve them. For I, the LORD your God, am a jealous God, visiting the iniquity of the fathers upon the children to the third and fourth generations of those who hate Me.

This passage appears puzzling, for some take God's warning of the long-term impact of turning away from Him as a rather vindictive threat. However, when rightly understood, the title "jealous God" is not a threat at all, but rather an encouragement.

The Hebrew word *qana'* can be translated either as "jealousy" or "zeal." The Hebrew portrays a very powerful emotion, a passionate desire, which can have either a positive or negative connotation. When the passionate desire is to seize another's rightful honor or possessions, the yearning is sinful. In this case "jealousy" is an appropriate translation. But when the passionate desire is for another's *benefit*, the yearning is godly. In this case "zeal" is a more appropriate rendering. Thus, when the Lord presents Himself as a jealous God, we recognize Him as being truly passionate, that is, zealous about doing good to us.

How then do we explain the reference in Exodus 20:5 to visiting the consequences of iniquity down to the fourth generation? We do so by remembering that this statement is a warning, not a threat. God has called on His people to worship Him rather than turn to pagan deities and idolatry. The commandment is given for Israel's good. Only if Israel maintains a right relationship with the Lord will He then bless them.

But what will happen if God's people turn aside and become idolaters? Then, the choice of evil will have a tragic impact on that family for generations!

This is really no surprise to us. We see the phenomenon today in families of alcoholics. Much research shows that even if the children do not become alcoholics themselves, living in the home of alcoholics affects their lives significantly and adversely. It is the same thing in abusive households. Children of abusive parents tend to abuse their own children, establishing a pattern that can persist through several generations. And even if they do not abuse, their self-image has been so affected that it is difficult for them to establish healthy relationships with a spouse and children.

Simply put, sinful choices echo down through the generations. In this sense God visits the iniquity of parents on their children. God has so created human beings that the choices of parents, both godly and evil, have an impact on the children whom they nurture.

As a jealous God, the Lord has a passionate desire that we make choices that will bring blessings on ourselves and our children. This helps make known a basic underlying motive of God in giving us commandments. We need to know what is right so that we might choose and do it! And it is especially important that we remain committed to the Lord, for should we abandon Him, this choice is sure to have a disastrous impact on us and our offspring.

It's no wonder the Lord tells us that we are to worship Him alone and stay away from idols. It's also no wonder that a God who cares so intensely for us would, in this context, present Himself as jealous.

JUDGE OF ALL THE EARTH

This title is found only in Genesis 18:25, although it is not unusual for God to be spoken of as Judge. In the following two paragraphs, the *New International Encyclopedia of Bible Words* sums up the implications of the Old Testament's portrait of God as Judge:

> The OT makes it clear that the ultimate ruler of the universe is God. All human governing authority is derived from him. Often where the OT speaks of God as judge, it is his ultimate sovereignty as governor of the universe, and not simply his role as moral arbiter, that is in view. We see the interplay clearly in Psalm 96:10-13, where God is pictured as "judge" in all the rich meaning of that word. "Say among the nations, 'The LORD reigns.' The world is firmly established, it cannot be moved; he will judge the peoples with equity. Let the heavens rejoice, let the earth be glad; let the sea resound, and all that is in it; let the fields be jubilant, and everything in them. Then all the trees of the forest will sing for joy; they will sing before the LORD, for he comes, he comes to judge the earth. He will judge the world in righteousness and the peoples in his truth.
>
> God's judicial acts are but one aspect of his rule. To affirm God as judge is to assert that he is governor of all, not only with every right to command but also with responsibility to vindicate and to condemn (p. 363).

Abraham gave to the Lord the title "Judge of all the earth" (Gen. 18:25). God had told Abraham that He had come to destroy Sodom and Gomorrah "because their sin is very grave" (v. 20). But this troubled Abraham. He wondered whether there might be some good people in the wicked cities. He thus asked the Lord whether He would destroy the city if there were fifty righteous

people in it. Abraham evidently thought it would unfair for the Lord to "destroy the righteous with the wicked" (v. 23). And Abraham was sure that God would be fair, for he asked, "Shall not the Judge of all the earth do right?" (v. 25).

Abraham continued to press the Lord and finally the patriarch was satisfied when God promised that He would not destroy the city if there were even ten righteous people in it. Apparently to Abraham this number of people was a satisfactory price to pay to rid the land of Sodom and Gomorrah. But strikingly, God was not satisfied!

The angels whom the Lord sent to Sodom found only one righteous man there, namely, Lot. And before the city was destroyed, God made sure that His angels had removed Lot and his family. God was not willing that *any* righteous person should perish with the wicked!

Sometimes we think of divine judgment as dark and frightening, and we conjure up images of God as vindictive and (or so it seems to some) unfair. Yet God's title as "Judge of all the earth" (especially in its biblical context) focuses our attention not on judgment but on God's grace and His commitment to do what is right. In punishing sin, God will never let the necessity for justice overcome His own commitment to love and to care for humankind. We can rest assured that the Judge of all the earth *will* do what is right; and in so doing, He will be far more fair and loving than we could ever be.

KING
KING OF GLORY

See the discussion of "The Lord, the King" on page 45, and also the discussion of "God of Glory" on page 43.

LAWGIVER

Isaiah 33 looks ahead to a time when God's people will "see the King in His beauty" (v. 17). Jerusalem will be restored, and "there the majestic LORD will be for us a place of broad rivers and streams" (v. 21). It is in the context of this idyllic setting that the prophet explains, "for the LORD is our Judge, the LORD is our Lawgiver, the LORD is our King; He will save us" (v. 22). It is fascinating to see the title "Lawgiver" nestled between the titles "Judge" and "King" in a passage affirming that it is this God—Judge, Lawgiver, and King—"[who] will save us."

We have seen earlier that both "Judge" and "King" are positive titles assigned to the Lord. But to many people, the idea of "Lawgiver" is troubling. Aren't "laws" all too often restrictive and unbending? Don't "laws" often force us into patterns of life that we would not choose for ourselves, and often resent?

While there are negatives to the notion of "law" when applied to human legislation, this simply isn't the case with the laws that God has given His people. Yes, those laws are not a way of salvation, and they were never intended to be. But God's laws have always functioned as a revelation of His goodness and as a window into His moral character.

The laws of God have also been a guide to those who wish to please Him. Believers obey His commands, not simply because they *must* obey, but more so because they delight in pleasing the Lord.

BIBLE BACKGROUND:

LAW IN OLD TESTAMENT USE AND LIFE

The Hebrew noun rendered "law" in the Old Testament is *torah*, which means "teaching" or "instruction." In the Hebrew sacred writings, these instructions were focused on how one should live rather than on mere academic facts. It should come as no surprise, then, that the Old Testament view of law is rich and positive. One is left with the impression that a fatherly God stooped lovingly to share with His people how they were to live in His love and dwell lovingly with one another.

Moses told Israel, "Therefore be careful to observe [these commands]; for this is your wisdom and your understanding in the sight of the peoples who will hear all these statutes, and say, 'Surely this great nation is a wise and understanding people.' . . . And what great nation is there that has such statutes and righteous judgements as are in all this law which I set before you this day?" (Deut. 4:6, 8). In this quote we see a developed meaning of *torah*. God's instructions were binding instructions, and they regulated the social, ceremonial, and religious life of His people.

In time, the Hebrew noun rendered "law" came to indicate everything that God had revealed to Israel through Moses. In fact, the term was used to refer the entire Pentateuch. Thus, in the Old Testament "law" may refer to divine revelation in general, to a specific set of instructions, to written divine revelation in general, or to the writings of Moses. Whichever of these meanings is in view, *torah* ("law") is at heart divine instruction that God provided as a gift to His people.

The Law was a historically necessary gift. God had established a covenant relationship with Abraham and his descendants. This is seen in God's deliverance of the Israelites from slavery in Egypt. Their continued unresponsiveness to Him demonstrated their need for specific guidance and discipline (Ex. 15:22—17:7). God provided that guidance in the Law given at Sinai.

This legal code explained the consequences of disobedience and obedience. The person or generation who wandered from the Law would meet disaster, while the person or generation who lived by it would be blessed. Thus, the Law was a great gift to ancient Israel. It was like a well-marked road sign that pointed the way to an experience of God's very best and greatest blessings.

The Old Testament Law was not simply the great moral code expressed in the Ten

Commandments. The Law also provided an overall structure for Israel's life. It guided individual acts and worship. It structured social life and laid down criminal law. It provided the constitution for Israel as a nation, and it designated Israel's worship system. In short, everything in the life of the Old Testament believer and in later Jewish society was governed and regulated by the Law.

The godly Israelite did not see this law as a set of rigid, burdensome regulations. Rather, to the individual who enjoyed a personal relationship with the Lord, His Law signified His loving voice of instruction. Two of David's psalms reflect the correct attitude that Old Testament believers had about the Law.

> The ordinances of the LORD are sure
>   and altogether righteous.
> They are more precious than gold,
>   than much pure gold;
> they are sweeter than honey,
>   than honey in the comb.
> By them is your servant warned;
>   in keeping them there is great reward.
> Psalm 19:9-11 NIV

> I rejoice in following your statutes
>   as one rejoices in great riches.
> I meditate on your precepts
>   and consider your ways.
> I delight in your decrees;
>   I will not neglect your word.
> Psalm 119:14-16 NIV

While the true believer responded in obedience to God (whose voice was recognized in the Law), the Law as a system failed to make Israel righteous. The nation and individuals within it fell short of practicing justice and righteousness. Despite the fact that Israel knew what was good, generation after generation failed to live this way. The prophets recognized this limitation in the Law and looked ahead to a day when God would take another approach to righteousness. Jeremiah foresaw a day when

the Mosaic covenant would no longer be in force and when God would supplant the Law with a new covenant. Then, He would "put My law in their minds, and write it on their hearts" (Jer. 31:33).

We who study the Old Testament today as God's revelation for us as well as for Israel must be careful in our thinking about the Law. On the one hand, we must not jump to the conclusion that the Law was less than just and good, for God gave it to His people to bless them. On the other hand, we must not jump to the conclusion that the Law is essential if God is to produce truly good people. After all, the Old Testament promises that God will one day introduce a better way to produce righteousness.

God's better way has been introduced in Christ. And God's ultimate approach in making human beings truly good is for them to trust in Jesus as their Savior from present as well as past sins. They also are to rely on the Spirit to produce His fruit in their lives.

But there is another quality of God's laws that makes "Lawgiver" a wonderful title for the Lord. God's laws point us toward a way of life that brings blessings and warn of choices that will surely bring disaster. For instance, when the Lord says don't commit adultery, His intent is not to spoil our fun, but rather to protect us and our loved ones from a choice that, while offering momentary pleasure, will ultimately lead to pain and misery. The laws that God has given us are rooted deeply in His love for us, for God truly wants us to have a happy and blessed life.

It's no wonder then that Isaiah adds "Lawgiver" to the list of titles given to a God who "will save us" (v. 22). Assuredly, when we trust in Christ, God will save us by forgiving the sins we commit. But God the Lawgiver will also save us from hurt and harm by the signposts of His commandments posted along the path of our life journey.

THE MERCIFUL
MY MERCIFUL GOD

Moses stated it beautifully in his sermon to a new generation of Israelites who were poised to enter the promised land. He declared, "(the LORD your God is a merciful God), He will not forsake you nor destroy you, nor forget the covenant of your fathers which He swore to them" (Deut. 4:31).

It is fascinating that Moses emphasized God's mercy here, when we might be tempted to see the commitments expressed as more closely related to God's faithfulness. In reality, the explanation is seen in the meaning of the Hebrew verbs most frequently translated by "mercy."

One of the Hebrew roots, *raham*, is used primarily of the love of a superior for an inferior. God loves us, not because we are His equals, but rather despite the fact that we fall so far short of all that He is.

The other Hebrew root, *hanan*, focuses on the response of one person who is able to help another person who is helpless. The verb implies a strong feeling of compassion, which moves a person to offer aid even though the other is undeserving. Frequently this word, *hanan*, is rightly translated "grace." *The New International Encyclopedia of Bible Words* notes that "mercy is condescending love, reaching out to meet a need without considering the merit of the person who receives the aid" (p. 440).

It is this truth that makes Moses' use of the title "merciful God" so appropriate in Deuteronomy 4:31. Why will God "not forsake you nor destroy you"? Why will He not "forget the covenant of your fathers which He swore to them"? We are secure in our relationship with God, not because we deserve His love, but rather because He has chosen to love us despite ourselves. Looking back over the history of a rebellious Israel,

Nehemiah celebrates God's faithfulness and recalls that despite the fall of Jerusalem and the Babylonian captivity, "in Your great mercy You did not utterly consume them nor forsake them" (Neh. 9:31).

How can we be sure that God will continue to love us despite our failures? The same verse states the reason clearly: "For You are God, gracious and merciful."

REDEEMER
REDEEMER FROM DEATH

In the Old Testament a redeemer was someone who acted to free another person who was in bondage or danger. The Hebrew words expressing this concept were all ordinary words people used in daily life. One word, *padah*, referred to a purchase, in which ownership was transferred from one person to another.

Another word, *ga'al*, meant to "play the part of a kinsman." This referred to the fact that a close kin had both the right and the obligation to help a relative out. While the emphasis in *ga'al* is on the relationship, the idea of rushing to the aid of a person unable to help himself or herself is also implicit.

A third word, *koper*, is usually translated "ransom." Its basic meaning is "to atone by substituting a payment." For instance, each year Israelite males were to place a shekel in the temple treasury as a symbolic payment for their life. This served as a remembrance of how God spared the firstborn sons of Israelite families when He struck down the firstborn of the Egyptians (Ex. 30:11-16).

Thus, redemption was a well-known and in many ways ordinary concept in ancient Israel. One redeemed an item by buying it. One redeemed a relation by making a payment that released him or her from an obligation. And one acknowledged God's right to every Israelite by paying an annual ransom at the temple.

The Old Testament applies the language of redemption to explain God's actions on behalf of His people. And the New Testament carries this language over to explain the significance of Jesus' death on Calvary.

BIBLE BACKGROUND:

THE KINSMAN-REDEEMER

The Hebrew noun, *go'el*, has an important specialized meaning in the Old Testament. Under the Law a near relative had certain privileges and obligations. One responsibility was to avenge murder. If a member of the *go'el's* family was murdered (in distinction from an accidental homicide), it was the duty of the *go'el* to do justice by putting the murderer to death.

One of privileges was that of redeeming a poor relative from slavery by paying his or her debt. The kinsman could even redeem a relative's sold property by paying what the relative had been given for the sale of the land. This explains why some English versions translate *go'el* not simply as "kinsman" but rather as "kinsman-redeemer."

The classic example of the kinsman-redeemer in Scripture is Boaz, who appears in the Book of Ruth. Boaz was a close relative of Naomi, the mother-in-law of Ruth. Naomi and her husband had left Israel some years before the main account took place. When Naomi and Ruth returned to Israel, Boaz "purchased" the family lands by marrying Ruth. This allowed their firstborn son to be counted in the line of Ruth's deceased husband, who was the rightful heir to the property.

The concept of a kinsman who was qualified to redeem a destitute relative and his or her property has theological implications, for it anticipates the person and work of Christ. In ancient Israel, only a near relation was qualified to redeem. Thus, Christ took on humanity so that He might be our near kinsman. Also, in Old Testament times, only someone who possessed the necessary resources could aid a destitute

relative. Christ alone had the resources of an endless divine life to pay the price of our sin. Thus, after being crucified on the cross, He rose from the dead to grant us not only forgiveness but also eternal life.

God as Redeemer in the Old Testament. In Psalm 78 we see a clear application of the concept of redemption to God's acts in history. This is an historic psalm; in other words, it is a poem reviewing the history of the Israelites and their relationship with God. In this passage of Scripture, the psalmist (Asaph) recounts miracles God performed on behalf of His people.

> Marvelous things He did
>   in the sight of their fathers,
> In the land of Egypt, in the field
>   of Zoan.
> He divided the sea and caused them
>   to pass through;
> And He made the waters
>   stand up like a heap.
>   vv. 12, 13

Asaph goes on to recount more of God's actions, and then he records Israel's response.

> But they sinned even more
>   against Him
> By rebelling against the Most
>   High in the wilderness.
>   v. 17

Against the backdrop of God's intervention and Israel's unresponsiveness, Asaph reports,

> Then they remembered that
>   God was their rock,
> And the Most High God
>   their Redeemer.
>   v. 35

All God's actions on behalf of His people were to be viewed through the lens of redemption. God rushed to the Israelites' aid because He had established a relationship with them and paid the price necessary to make them His own. The language of redemption is particularly strong in the Book of Isaiah, where that prophet again and again refers to the Lord as "your Redeemer" (41:14; 43:14; 44:6, 24; 47:4; 48:17; 49:7, 26; 54:5, 8; 59:20; 60:16; 63:16).

Christ as Redeemer in the New Testament. Romans 3:23 and 24 clearly state the New Testament doctrine of redemption. "For all have sinned and fall short of the glory of God, being justified freely by His grace through the redemption that is in Christ Jesus." Jesus paid the price to release us from sin by substituting His own shed blood for ours. By that sacrificial act, He transferred us from the kingdom of Satan to the kingdom of God. Ephesians 1:7 likewise declares, "In [Christ] we have redemption through His blood, the forgiveness of sins, according to the riches of His grace."

The doctrine of redemption also helps to explain the necessity of the Incarnation. In Bible times, only a near relative had the right to redeem. Hebrews 2:14 and 15 says, "Inasmuch then as the children have partaken of flesh and blood, He Himself likewise shared in the same, that through death He might destroy him who had the power of death, that is, the devil, and release those who through fear of death were all their lifetime subject to bondage."

Jesus was born a baby so that God might become our kinsman. Also, Christ died on the cross to pay the price for our sins. And because of the redemption that He purchased, we who believe belong to God forever. Surely, God in Christ is our Redeemer!

SAVIOR
DELIVERER

See the discussion on "God of my salvation" on p.53.

God initiated mankind's redemption when God the Son enter our world as an infant.

THE LORD MIGHTY IN BATTLE
THE LORD STRONG AND MIGHTY

These two titles occur in Psalm 24:8. The psalm is messianic and fits together with Psalms 22 and 23.

Psalm 22 looks forward to the Messiah's crucifixion. It contains prophetic images of Calvary, including Christ's cry from the cross, "My God, My God, why have You forsaken Me?" (v. 1). The psalm also contains this description of events at Calvary:

They pierced My hands and My feet;
I can count all My bones.
They look and stare at Me.
They divide My garments among them,
And for My clothing they cast lots.
vv. 16-18

"God our Peace" provides an inner and outward harmony that is independent of external circumstances.

Psalm 23 celebrates Christ as Shepherd. The resurrected Christ watches over His sheep by leading, guiding, and caring for them (John 10).

Psalm 24 looks beyond the cross and the present age to Jesus' return as the "King of glory" (v. 8).

> Lift up your heads, O you gates!
> And be lifted up, you everlasting doors!
> And the King of glory shall come in.
> Who is this King of glory?
> The LORD strong and mighty,
> The LORD mighty in battle.
> Lift up your heads, O you gates!
> Lift up, you everlasting doors!
> And the King of glory shall come in.
> vv. 7-9

The unresisting Christ of Calvary, the exalted and hidden Christ who now shep-herds His own people, will one day be revealed as the King of glory. When He comes in power, the whole world will acknowledge Him, for then He will be seen not as the quiet carpenter of Nazareth but rather as the "LORD strong and mighty" and the "LORD mighty in battle."

THE LORD OUR MAKER

See the discussion of God as Creator and Maker, page 8.

THE LORD IS PEACE

The Hebrew phrase *Yahweh Shalom*, which means either "the Lord is peace" or "the Lord our peace," is not properly a title of God but rather the name of an altar that Gideon constructed in the time of the judges. The Angel of the LORD (most likely God

Himself in a cloaked form) had appeared to young Gideon and commissioned him to lead Israel against the Midianites, who were overrunning the promised land. Gideon, however, had his doubts.

Then, when the Angel of the Lord performed a miracle and disappeared from sight, Gideon became terrified. He exclaimed, "Alas, O LORD God! For I have seen the Angel of the LORD face to face" (Judg. 6:22). In response, the Lord said to Gideon, "Peace be with you; do not fear, you shall not die" (v. 23).

It was on that spot that Gideon quickly built an altar to the Lord, and Gideon called the altar, "The LORD-Shalom," which means "the Lord is peace" (v. 24). The name of that altar has so captured the imagination of many Christians that "the Lord is peace" or "the Lord our peace" has become a favorite title for God—and with good reason.

The nature of peace. In the earlier portions of the Old Testament, "peace" refers primarily to international or interpersonal harmony. It may also refer to an individual's health or general well-being. We read in 2 Kings 4:26 that Elisha sends his servant to ask a friend about an emergency. The questions the servant asks are "Is it well with you? Is it well with your husband? Is it well with your child?" The key Hebrew word in each of these questions is *shalom*. In conventional language, the servant would be asking, "Are you alright?" A person who is at peace, who is in a state of *shalom*, is healthy and thus "alright."

The Hebrew word takes on deeper meaning in the later portions of the Old Testament. *Shalom* refers to an experience of inner harmony and fulfillment that grows out of our relationship with God and that reflects His blessing on our life (Ps. 29:11). Those without faith can never understand or experience this peace, which exists independent of external circumstances. God is the source of peace and healing for the righteous. However, "the wicked are like the troubled sea, when it

cannot rest, whose waters cast up mire and dirt. 'There is no peace,' says my God, 'for the wicked'" (Is. 57:20, 21).

The *New International Encyclopedia of Bible Words* sums up the Old Testament meaning of "peace":

> Peace in the OT, then, speaks of the blessings of inner and outer harmony that come to a person or people who live in a close relationship with God. Believers can, like David, experience peace despite dangerous circumstances by being conscious of God's presence, or at least of his sure promises. Ultimately the world will know international and interpersonal peace as well, as the very presence of God in the person of Jesus halts strife and war (p. 480).

The New Testament promise of peace. The meaning of peace established in the Old Testament is carried over into the New Testament. This meaning infuses the Greek word *eirene* when it is used. Various New Testament letters remind us that our Lord is the "God of peace," and as such the source of our well-being (Rom. 15:33; Phil. 4:9; 1 Thess. 5:23).

We first begin to experience peace when we establish a personal relationship with God through faith in Jesus. Romans 5:1 reminds us that since we have been justified by faith, we have peace *with* God "through our Lord Jesus Christ." The New Testament also reminds us that we have peace *from* God. Jesus said, "Peace I leave with you, My peace I give to you; not as the world gives do I give to you. Let not your hearts be troubled, neither be afraid" (John 14:27). The only peace the world can offer is the temporary cessation of overt hostility. But the peace Jesus provides is a deep awareness of inner well-being regardless of whatever situation we may find ourselves in.

On the one hand *Yahweh shalom*, "the Lord our peace," is not a title of God but rather the name Gideon gave to a pile of stones commemorating his first contact with

Lord. On the other hand, "the Lord our peace" does rightly stand as a title of our God, for He truly is our peace. Making peace with Him and experiencing the peace He gives lie at the heart of our personal relationship with the Lord.

THE LORD WHO BROUGHT YOU OUT OF EGYPT

Two great events lay at the root of Israel's understanding of God. One of those events was the creation of the universe. This established God as greater than anything that might be seen or imagined in the visible or invisible realm.

BIBLE BACKGROUND:

GRAVEN VERSUS MENTAL IMAGES

Early in the list of the Ten Commandments given in Exodus 20, we find the following injunction: "You shall not make for yourself a carved image—any likeness of anything that is in heaven above, or that is in the earth beneath, or that is in the water under the earth" (v. 4). Despite this, Scripture is filled with mental images intended to enrich our understanding of God. Why did the Lord issue the prohibition against graven images if verbal imagery was not only acceptable but also frequently emphasized in the Old Testament?

First, a "carved image" referred to something material in nature. To attempt to represent God by any material object is to limit and in some sense distort His essential nature. John 4:23 and 24 says, "true worshipers will worship the Father in spirit and in truth; for the Father is seeking such to worship Him. God is Spirit, and those who worship him must worship in spirit and truth."

Second, a "carved image" referred to something that people had made. This remains true of any kind of image fashioned by people, whether it was made from cast metal or drawn or painted. Graven images represent an implicit denial of God's divine nature, for He is the Creator of all. Thus, people who attempted to represent God by any humanly fashioned object distorted His essential nature.

Third, the prohibition is rooted in humankind's response to material representations of God. Exodus 20:5 says, "you shall not bow down to them nor serve [or worship] them." Fallen human beings tend to rely on what can be seen and touched. And all too quickly humankind moves from worshiping the God an object is supposed to represent to worshiping the object itself *as God*. Anyone who doubts this truth need only review Old Testament history and consider the testimony of humankind's ancient and modern religions.

The mental images we find in Scripture are very different from graven images for the following three reasons. First, mental images are not material in nature. Also, rather than representing God Himself, they are simply used to enable the worshiper to contemplate some aspect of His nature. Second, the mental images are not created by people. Rather, they are inspired concepts revealed by God in Scripture. Third, we contemplate mental images in the realm of the spirit. Also, they prompt us to focus on the Lord's glorious, divine nature.

Clearly, there is a great difference between material images fashioned by human beings to represent God and those mental images revealed in Scripture to help us appreciate some facet of the divine nature and character. Graven images quickly become abhorrent objects of worship, while mental images serve as an aid to acceptable forms of worship. There is no way in which the mental images of God revealed in Scripture violate the commandment recorded in verse 4.

The other event was God's rescue of His people from slavery in Egypt. God's intervention in history on behalf of His people once and for all established the Lord as a covenant-keeping, trustworthy God, who was able to rescue and protect His people. Because God proved Himself able to act in our world of space and time, there was no way the Lord could be confused with the idols that pagan worshipers claimed to be divine. Gladly then Asaph records God's proclamation: "I am the LORD your God, who brought you out of the land of Egypt" (Ps. 81:10).

THE LORD WHO PROVIDES

This title is one that also rightly captures our imagination. *Yahweh Yireh*, which means "the Lord will provide," is a title that Abraham gave to the Lord.

God had told Abraham to take his only son Isaac, whom he loved, to Mount Moriah. There Abraham was to sacrifice his son. The command went against everything Abraham knew about God and against all the promises that God had made to Abraham. Central to those promises was their fulfillment through Abraham's offspring. Isaac was the patriarch's only legitimate son, the one through whom God was to keep His covenant promises.

Nevertheless, the morning after God had told Abraham what to do, the patriarch rose early and, taking Isaac and two servants, set out for the mount, which was some three days' journey distant. On the way, young Isaac was puzzled. The donkeys that they brought along carried wood for the sacrificial fire. But where was the lamb for the offering? It was in answer to Isaac's question that Abraham confidently replied, "My son, God will provide for Himself the lamb for a burnt offering" (Gen. 22:8).

And God did provide. As Isaac lay bound on the altar constructed by his father, God spoke to Abraham. The patriarch was not to slay his son, but rather to look in the nearby thicket for a ram whose horns had become entangled. As Abraham had confidently believed, so the Lord did provide. Thus, the patriarch "called the name of that place, The-LORD-Will-Provide" (*Yahweh Yireh*; v. 14).

The Lord would not—and could not—ask Abraham to surrender the life of his only and dearly loved son. Yet nearly two thousand years later God would Himself do what He would not ask Abraham to do. On that same Mount Moriah, where David built an altar and Solomon constructed his temple, God would surrender His only and beloved Son, Jesus. God would offer up Jesus as a sacrifice, and accept that sacrifice as payment for our sins, so that we might be forgiven and have eternal life.

Will God provide? The answer is *yes*! God has provided salvation for us. And the title *Yahweh Yireh* must be one of those titles that arouses our awe and awakens our love for God.

THE LORD WHO SANCTIFIES YOU

Here we have a title that God Himself announced when He emphasized the significance of keeping the Sabbath. The announcement is found in Exodus 31:13: "Speak also to the children of Israel, saying: 'Surely My Sabbaths you shall keep, for it is a sign between Me and you throughout your generations, that you may know that I am the LORD who sanctifies you.'" The Hebrew word translated "sanctify" means to "set apart" or to "make holy." For a discussion of its meaning, see the article on the "Holy One of Israel," on page 49.

YOU WHO HEAR PRAYER

This title is found in Psalm 65:2, where David tells God that praise awaits Him in Zion. David addresses God as "You who hear prayer."

While the title is not repeated in the Old Testament, it is clear that God's people viewed Him as a person who heard and answered their prayers. The psalms are filled

The name "You Who Hear Prayers" is intended to give us confidence to bring every concern to the Lord.

with praises and emotional cries for help addressed to God. The significance that God's people placed on prayer is reflected not only in the many petitions and praises recorded in the Old Testament, but also in the extensive vocabulary used in prayer. All of the following Hebrew words may be translated "prayer," and each one provides additional shades of meaning.

Hebrew words for prayer. The uses of the Hebrew words in Scripture demonstrate the Bible's emphasis upon our dependence on the Lord and on His love for us.

Palal, "to pray." This is one of the most common Hebrew words for prayer. It expresses dependence on God and also an appeal for God to view the situation and act to meet the individual's need.

Tepillah, "prayer." This Hebrew word occurs 75 times in the Old Testament, usu-

ally in narrative passages that indicate individual and corporate prayer. Several kinds of prayer are described by this word, from entreaty to thanksgiving to confession.

Na'. This Hebrew particle is found some 400 times in the Old Testament. It expresses entreaty, although it is translated in a variety of ways. At times it is rendered "we pray," but in the psalms it is frequently viewed as an interjection and translated "O."

'Atar, "to entreat." This Hebrew word is often simply translated "pray." However, in the Hebrew it conveys a sense of urgency or intensity that is often lost in the English translation.

Sa'al, "to ask" or "to inquire." This Hebrew word, which is used some 170 times in the Old Testament, indicates asking for some object, favor, or information. It is not just a religious term, and the seeker may ask of other individuals as well as of the Lord.

'Anath, "to answer." This Hebrew word is used in the imperative to express a request, such as "Hear me!" Otherwise, the word refers to God's answer or response to His people's prayers.

Paga', "to intercede." The idea here is to use one's influence to help another. This Hebrew word is used in Isaiah's description of the work of the coming Savior: "He bore the sin of many, and made intercession for the transgressors" (Is. 53:12).

Hanan, "to be gracious." In one form this Hebrew word becomes a plea for God to meet the need of the one who prays. It is closely related to showing pity or kindness.

The very breadth of the Old Testament prayer vocabulary helps us sense how important it was to God's people that He truly is "You who hear prayer" (Ps. 65:2).

Key Old Testament prayers. The psalms have been called the "prayer book of Scripture." Anyone who wishes to deepen his or her prayer life can hardly do better than to saturate himself or herself in the psalms, and so learn to pray as God's Old Testament saints prayed. There are several prayers recorded in the Old Testament that are particularly helpful in enriching our appreciation for God as One who hears prayer.

Abraham intercedes for Sodom
    Genesis 18:16-33
Moses intercedes for Israel
    Exodus 32:11-14
Hannah gives thanks
    Samuel 2:1-10
David prays for his ailing son
    2 Samuel 12:13-23

Solomon dedicates the temple
    Kings 8:22-53
Jehoshaphat seeks relief
    2 Chronicles 20:5-12
Ezra confesses Judah's sins
    Ezra 9:5-15
Hezekiah prays for help
    Isaiah 37:14-20

For an enriching exploration of prayer in Scripture, see the companion volume in this series, *Every Prayer in the Bible*.

GOD IN SIMILE AND METAPHOR

One of the most delightful things about the Hebrew language is its use of vivid images. Instead of saying "I feel depressed" or "I'm really down," an ancient Hebrew was likely to say the following:

My eye wastes away with grief,
Yes, my soul and my body!
For my life is spent with grief,
And my years with sighing; . . .
And my bones waste away.
Psalm 31:9, 10

While someone might argue that this is poetry, the fact remains that the ancient Hebrews tended to think in images rather than abstract concepts. For instance, Amos calls wealthy women who lived in luxury at the expense of the poor "cows of Bashan" (4:1), vividly bringing to mind fattened cattle. Furthermore, Amos describes the coming "day of the Lord" as "darkness, and not light," and he says, "It will be as though a man fled from a lion, and a bear met him!" (5:18, 19).

The use of vivid images, of simile and metaphor, not only enrich the Scriptures, but also make translation of the Old Testament into other languages both a challenge and a joy. How it enriches our sense of who God is when He is called a rock or a fortress. What warmth is communicated when God presents Himself as our shepherd.

As the names and titles of God found in Scripture help us see Him more clearly, so do images of God provided in simile and metaphor—images we will look at in this chapter.

EXALTED IMAGES OF GOD

Just as there are names and titles of God that exalt Him by emphasizing His majesty and power, so there are exalted images of God.

CONSUMING FIRE
WALL OF FIRE

When Moses warned Israel against turning from God to the worship of idols, he used the following metaphor: "the LORD your God is a consuming fire, a jealous God" (Deut. 4:24).

The phrase "consuming fire" (or "devouring fire") is found seven times in the Old Testament. Exodus 24:17 tells us that the "glory of the LORD was like a consuming fire on the top of" Mount Sinai. The metaphor of God as a consuming fire emphasizes both divine anger and the sinner's innate terror of God. Three verses from Isaiah illustrate this point.

"Behold, the name of the LORD comes from afar, burning with His anger, and His burden is heavy; His lips are full of indignation, and His tongue like a devouring fire" (Is. 30:27).

"The LORD will cause men to hear his majestic voice and will make them see his arm coming down with raging anger and consuming fire" (Is. 30:30 NIV).

"The sinners in Zion are afraid; fearfulness [terror] has seized the hypocrites: 'Who among us shall dwell with the devouring fire? Who among us shall dwell with everlasting burnings?'" (Is. 33:14).

While the metaphor of God as a consuming fire strikes terror into the hearts of sinners, not all people are terrified. Isaiah answers the question "Who among us shall dwell with the devouring fire?" by saying the following:

He who walks righteously and speaks uprightly,
He who despises the gain of oppressions,
Who gestures with his hands, refusing bribes,
Who stops his ears from hearing of bloodshed,
And shuts his eyes from seeing evil:
He will dwell on high.
Isaiah 33:15, 16

God terrifies sinners, but there is no fear in the hearts of God's own, who walk with Him. Believers who are faithful to God's covenant "dwell on high."

Perhaps the account of Shadrach, Meshach, and Abednego illustrates what I'm saying. These three Hebrew officials in Nebuchadnezzar's empire refused to bow down to an idol the ruler had erected. As a punishment they were hurled into a furnace of fire.

Daniel describes the king's astonishment when the three men were seen walking, unhurt, in the middle of the raging fires, accompanied by a fourth figure. When the three stepped out from the fires in response to the king's call, all "saw these men on whose bodies the fire had no power; the hair of their head was not singed nor were their garments affected, and the smell of the fire was not on them" (Dan. 3:27).

What an image of deliverance! God the consuming fire terrifies sinners, but those who have known His grace and who follow Him walk in the midst of the flames, not only unhurt, but also rejoicing in their fellowship with the Lord.

What then of God as a "wall of fire"? This image is found in Zechariah 2:5. While God as a "consuming fire" strikes terror in the hearts of sinners, God as a "wall of fire" comforts believers. God shows Zechariah an angel measuring Jerusalem for the future blessing promised the city and her people. The angel tells the prophet to run with the good news. The day is coming, the Lord says, when "[I] will be a wall of fire all around her, and I will be the glory in her midst."

The God who will judge sinners with consuming fire guards His own with a wall of fire. And we are comfortable in the flames, for we walk with God.

FORTRESS
STRONG TOWER

In Old Testament times even smaller cities were often walled. Fields around the

God our Fortress remains today a powerful symbol of security.

city were cultivated during the day, and the farmers came inside the walls when night fell. Cities also had "daughters," a name given to clusters of four or five outlying homes near the city. In times of danger the people who lived in these tiny settlements also hurried to the walled city for protection. The walled city was the fortress of ancient times (2 Sam. 5:7), within which a person felt secure.

Larger cities not only were protected by walls but also contained one or more "strong towers." These towers were strongholds within the fortress cities, where resistance could continue even if the outer defenses fell.

While the fortress cities of the ancient world provided security against raiding enemies, a determined and powerful foe could take the strongest fortress. Siege engines battered the walls. Fires were set to weaken the limestone out of which the walls were built. Often ramps of dirt and stone were constructed that reached the top of a city's walls and over which an invading army might advance. While earthly fortresses offered some security, however great a city's walls

might be, the only true security a believer could find was in God.

And so David, looking beyond earthly walls made of stone, celebrates the Lord as the fortress in whom he places ultimate trust. "You, O God, are my fortress" (NIV), David cries out in Psalm 59:9. He wrote this psalm as he lay huddled in his home and while Saul's troops watched his house, waiting to kill him (1 Sam. 19:11). In the midst of this turmoil, David imagined God as being a fortress. David confidently affirmed, "My God of mercy shall come to meet me" (Ps. 59:10).

The metaphor of God as a fortress, stronghold, or place of refuge is found many times in the Old Testament, primarily in the Psalms, but also in Isaiah 17:10 and Jeremiah 16:19. Yet perhaps the clearest expression of what it means to know the Lord as a fortress is seen in Psalm 61:3 and 4, where God is portrayed as a strong tower.

For You have been a shelter for me,
A strong tower from the enemy.

I will abide in Your tabernacle forever;
I will trust in the shelter of Your wings.

HORN OF MY SALVATION

This image occurs only in 2 Samuel 22:3 and Psalm 18:2. The Hebrew noun, *qeren*, is used literally of the horns of various animals. Symbolically the horn stands for the animal's strength or power. For instance, in Daniel 8:5, 8, 9, and 21, the "horn" is used to indicate powerful rulers or nations. However, no human power can stand against the Lord, who promises the following:

> All the horns of the wicked
>   I will also cut off,
> But the horns of the righteous
>   shall be exalted.
>   Psalm 75:10

The *Theological Wordbook of the Old Testament* explains the reference to God as "horn of salvation" by saying that since "God is the source of all true salvation, he is termed the horn of salvation" (2:816). The fact that God is greater than any worldly power guarantees the salvation He provides for His own.

ROCK

The first usage of Rock as a metaphor for God is found in Genesis 49:24. In this verse Jacob calls the Lord the "Mighty One of Jacob" (NIV) and says that He is the "Rock of Israel." Here we find Jacob relying on the Lord, his Rock, to both help and bless his offspring.

The Hebrew noun *sur* (often translated as "rock" or "stone"), which is most frequently used in this metaphor, refers to boulders or massive stone formations, the material from which mountains are made. While "rock" has a number of metaphorical uses, it is most frequently a metaphor for God Himself.

BIBLE BACKGROUND:

THE ROCK OF MATTHEW 16

In Matthew 16:16, Peter confessed that Jesus is "the Christ, the Son of the Living God." In response Jesus said, "Blessed are you, Simon Bar-Jonah, for flesh and blood have not revealed this to you, but my Father who is in heaven. And I also say to you that you are Peter, and on this rock I will build My church" (vv. 17, 18).

Various early church leaders argued that the "rock" is Peter (supposedly the first pope), or his confession of Christ, or Christ Himself. The first theory seems strange. The Greek noun rendered "Peter" means "pebble." However, the Greek noun translated "rock," while built on the same verbal root, refers to a giant bolder or rock formation. It's thus hard to see how a pebble can serve as the foundation for a mighty church, especially when Jesus Himself spoke of the church as resting on a foundation of solid rock.

The second theory seems more likely than the first. Peter had confessed his belief in Jesus as the promised Messiah (Christ) of the Old Testament and as the Son of the living God. Certainly no one is a true Christian who does not share this faith of Peter's. The church is made up of those who acknowledge Jesus, not only as the Son of God, but also as our only Savior and Lord. Those who believe are the church, not its foundation.

The third theory seems most likely. Christ Himself is the Rock on which the church rests. This fits with the imagery of God as a rock (a metaphor that is used in the Old Testament). It also fits with the statement of Paul in 1 Corinthians 3:11: "No other foundation can anyone lay than that which is laid, which is Jesus Christ."

Yes, Jesus Christ is the church's foundation. He is the Rock on which our faith and life rests. Thus the image of God as a rock in the Old Testament clearly points to the Messiah.

As the Rock, God is faithful (Deut. 32:15), holy (1 Sam. 6:14), a stronghold, and a refuge (2 Sam. 22:3). The *Theological Wordbook of the Old Testament* suggests that the underlying impression is one of total reliability. "He is a sure source of strength, and he endures throughout every generation" (2:762).

Anyone who has driven through the mighty Rockies or stood below the peaks of the Tetons will understand the awe and the comfort that the image of God as a Rock provides. Surely the mountains can never be moved, and the same is true of those who take their stand in God. As David wrote in Psalm 62:1, 2,

> From Him comes my salvation.
> He only is my rock and my salvation;
> He is my defense;
> I shall not be greatly moved.

SHIELD

The shield in ancient warfare was used for defense. Most shields were made of layers of hardened cowhide, and some were strengthened with metal studs. Shields were used in close combat to turn the thrusts of enemy swords and to deflect rocks thrown from city walls. While shields were not offensive weapons, they were essential in battle.

It is striking that the sword is never used as a metaphor for God. How fascinating then that God is depicted as a shield some twelve times in the Psalms and twice in Proverbs. Perhaps the people of Israel, surrounded by hostile nations, were more concerned with defense than with conquest. What was important to Israel was preservation in the land God had given them so that they might wait for the promised Messiah to appear and bring in the golden age. With no driving

The ancient shield represents the fact that God protects and defends us.

urge to conquer foreign lands or to build a great empire, what was important to the men and women of the Holy Land was that they could count on the Lord to shield them.

In our day, too, we are not to attack others, but we do need defense from those who are hostile to us because of our allegiance to Christ. How good, then, to have a relationship with a God who "is a shield to those who put their trust in Him" (Prov. 30:5).

SUN

The meaning of the metaphor seems uncertain, simply because it can be interpreted in so many ways. The sun is the source of light. As a sun, does God reveal the steps we are to take or enable us to distinguish good from evil? The sun is also the source of warmth. As a sun, does God comfort our hearts as He pours out love on His own? The sun is a source of life, and plants especially depend on the light given off by the sun. Does the metaphor of a sun have an agricultural emphasis?

One of the problems with metaphors is that they can be pressed too far. We need to let Scripture itself interpret its metaphors, especially metaphors of God Himself. Thus we need to look at the context in which a metaphor is used, and limit our interpretation to its meaning in that context.

The metaphor of God as a sun is found only in Psalm 84:11. It occurs near the end of the psalm, as the sons of Korah express their wonder at God's graciousness toward people and their delight at being in His presence. They write the following:

> For a day in Your courts is better than a
>   thousand.
> I would rather be a doorkeeper in the
>   house of my God
> Than dwell in the tents of wickedness.
> For the LORD God is a sun and shield;
> The LORD will give grace and glory;
> No good thing will He withhold
> From those who walk uprightly.
>   Psalm 84:10, 11

God as a sun is the source of grace and glory. He pours out blessings on all who live in His warmth. Those who live close to God share His light, while those who "dwell in the tents of wickedness" stumble about in the cold and the darkness.

RELATIONAL IMAGES OF GOD

The most powerful metaphors for God in the Old Testament are relational. While we appreciate those passages in which God is seen as a rock or a shield, we rightly are struck with wonder when God presents Himself in human guise as the believers' father, husband, shepherd, and helper.

FATHER

The Hebrew noun rendered "father" (*'ab*) occurs 1,191 times in the Old

Testament. In only a few of these passages is "father" a metaphor for God. In most cases "father" indicates biological descent, usually from a parent or grandparent. In fact, in Hebrew genealogies "father" often indicates a more distant ancestor.

Nevertheless, "father" is also used in other senses. At times "father" is simply an expression of respect, and is used when a common citizen addresses a governor or priest, or when a servant addresses a master. "Father" is also used in the sense of a founder of a guild, or tribal or family line. For example, when Genesis 4:21 speaks of Jubal as the "father of all those who play the harp and flute," it is simply saying that he invented both stringed and wind instruments.

God is identified as "Father" only a few times in the Old Testament. We should look at several of these references to discern just what is and is not implied by this metaphor.

God as the Father of Israel (Deut. 32:6). In the prophetic song that Moses taught Israel near the end of his life, he called on the nation to show respect for God and to honor Him.

> Is He not your Father, who bought you?
> Has He not made you and established you?
>   Deut. 32:6

It's clear in this passage that the metaphor of God as Father is rooted in the fact that God established and redeemed Israel. Israel owes its existence to the Lord, and thus Israel owes Him a "father's" respect.

Most references to God as Father in the Old Testament portray Him as the originator of Israel as a corporate entity. It is because God called Israel into existence that the nation owes God the respect due to a human father. Thus, through Jeremiah, God says the following to rebellious Israel:

> How gladly would I treat you like sons
> and give you a desirable land, the most
> beautiful inheritance of any nation. I

thought you would call me "Father" and not turn away from following me. But like a woman unfaithful to her husband, so you have been unfaithful to me, O house of Israel.

Jeremiah 3:19, 20 NIV

In this and other key Old Testament passages (Is. 63:16; Jer. 31:9; Mal. 1:6), God's fatherhood is corporate rather than individual and is based on His creation of the nation.

God as the Father of David (Ps. 89:26). In this prophetic psalm, God says of David, "He shall cry to Me, 'You are my Father.'" Other passages in the Old Testament identify David or his son Solomon as having a relationship with God as Father (2 Sam. 7:14; 1 Chr. 17:13; 22:10; 28:6). Yet, when we examine such passages, it is clear that God is a "Father" to David or Solomon in the same sense that He is a "Father" to Israel. God called David's royal line into being. God is the founder and originator, and in this sense He is a "Father."

God acts as a father in nurturing and caring for His own.

❖

God as "father of the fatherless" (Ps. 68:5). One of the virtues about the Lord for which David praises Him is that He is "a father to the fatherless, a defender of widows."

The role of a father in the Old Testament's patriarchal society was clear. He was the head of the family, and as such was to be respected. But as head of the family, the father was also responsible for its well-being. The father was responsible for the physical well-being of his wife and children, and so was to provide food and shelter. The father was also responsible for the spiritual well-being of the family, and so was to teach and to discipline his children. To describe God as "a father to the fatherless" meant that God Himself took on the responsibility for caring for those who had no biological father.

Many provisions of Old Testament Law were designed to make sure that widows and orphans were cared for. The Law gave widows and the poor the right to glean (harvest leftovers) in the fields of others. The Law provided for a tithe to be collected every third year for the care of the poor. The Law provided for interest-free loans and even for the forgiveness of debts. In this way God functioned as a father to the fatherless, providing for them and taking care of their needs.

God also acted as a father might in caring for Israel. This is illustrated in a number of passages. God brought Israel safely through years of wandering in the wilderness, carrying them "as a man carries his son" (Deut. 1:31). In the same way God also disciplined His people. "As a man chastens his son, so the LORD your God chastens you" (Deut. 8:5). Drawing on the same analogy David says, "As a father pities his children, so the Lord pities those who fear Him" (Ps. 103:13).

While the Old Testament thus uses parent-child relationships to help Israel understand the motives behind God's actions, none of these analogies indicates that an actual father-child relationship existed between the Lord and individual Israelites, or between God and Israel.

When Jesus spoke of a father-child relationship with God that individual believers could experience, He uttered a truly new revelation, as we will see in chapter 7. This is because the Old Testament carefully limits its use of the Father metaphor. God is moved by a father-like love to care for Israel. But where God reveals Himself as a Father, that metaphor is limited to His role as the originator of the covenant people and founder of the Davidic line. It is only in the New Testament that God is revealed to be our Father in the deepest, most personal sense.

HUSBAND

Marriage is the basic institution of any society. From the beginning it was intended to be the union of one man and one woman who commit themselves to live their life on earth together. Commitment is utterly basic to the biblical concept of marriage. Each spouse is to be faithful to the other. Each is to be deeply aware that they form an indissoluble unit and are to function as one.

It is not surprising, then, that the prophets saw parallels between marriage and the relationship of Israel with God. Israel was the wife and God was the husband. Tragically, while God remained the faithful husband, Israel acted as an unfaithful wife.

God as a husband (various passages in Isaiah and Jeremiah). Isaiah is the first to make explicit reference to the analogy. In 54:4 and 5, the Lord comforts an unfaithful Israel:

Do not fear, for you will not be ashamed;
Neither be disgraced, for you will not be
    put to shame.
For you will forget the shame of your
    youth,
And will not remember the reproach of
    your
widowhood anymore.
For your Maker is your husband,
The Lord of Hosts is His name;
And your Redeemer is the Holy One of
    Israel.
                    Isaiah 54:4, 5

While Israel had been unfaithful to the Lord, God remained committed to His people.

Jeremiah uses the analogy to reveal the significance of Judah's idolatry and also as a basis for God's call to His people to return to Him in repentance and faith.

"Return, O backsliding children," says
the LORD; "for I am married to you"
                    (Jer. 3:14).

And

"Surely, as a wife treacherously departs
from her husband, so have you dealt
treacherously with Me, O House of
Israel," says the LORD (Jer. 3:20).

Israel's hope for the future rests on God's willingness to make a new covenant with His people, a covenant unlike the Mosaic covenant "which they broke, though I was a husband to them, says the LORD" (Jer. 31:32).

The case of Hosea. The most poignant revelation of the implications of God's Old Testament role as a husband is found in the Book of Hosea. Hosea was a prophet who ministered in the northern kingdom of Israel from 750-715 B.C. (In 722 B.C. the Assyrians conquered the land and deported its people.)

God called on Hosea not only to preach to Israel, but also to model in his own relationship with his wife the relationship that existed between God and Israel. The prophet tells us that God told him to "go, take yourself a wife of harlotry" (1:2). In other words, Hosea was to marry a woman who was (or who would become) a prostitute.

This woman's name was Gomer. In time she abandoned her husband and their children to live with various paramours. During those difficult years, Hosea continued to love Gomer. Even when one lover after another abandoned her, Hosea saw to it that Gomer had adequate food and shelter (2:8). Finally, Gomer was forced to sell herself into slavery because of her debts. When that happened, Hosea bought her back and then brought her home (3:2, 3).

Chapters 1 through 3 of Hosea tell the account of the prophet and his wife, and in doing so reveals the heart and intentions of God toward Israel. How hurt and angry were Hosea and God, and how those emotions at first seemed to harden their hearts against Gomer and Israel. Yet the unfaithful wife was still loved. In fact, despite such infidelity, Hosea and God would make every effort to bring back their respective wives.

"And it shall be in that day," says the LORD,
"That you will call Me 'My husband,'
and no longer call Me 'My Master.'
For I will take from her mouth
the names of the Baals," . . .

I will betroth you to Me forever;
Yes, I will betroth you to Me
In righteousness and justice,
In lovingkindness and mercy;
I will betroth you to Me in faithfulness,
And you shall know the LORD."
   Hosea 2:16, 19, 20

As a husband, God presents Himself in the Old Testament as an utterly faithful person. He remains committed to Israel, His wife, despite her unfaithfulness. In the end, God will act to change the heart of the unfaithful wife. In that day, God and Israel will be united forever.

SHEPHERD

The Old Testament shepherds' role was to care for, protect, and provide pasture for their sheep. Shepherds lived in the fields with their flocks much of the year. As the seasons changed, they found grass for the sheep to eat and water for them to drink.

The first reference to God as a shepherd is early. Around 1859 B.C., Jacob spoke of the "God who has been my Shepherd all my life to this day" (Gen. 48:15 NIV). Jacob is the first person in Scripture to use this metaphor, identifying God as "the Shepherd, the Rock of Israel" (Gen. 49:24 NIV).

Rulers were also called shepherds. Israel's kings were called by God to "shepherd My people [Israel]" (1 Chr. 17:6). Psalm 78:72 tells us that David "shepherded them according to the integrity of his heart, and guided them by the skillfulness of his hands." The human rulers whom God gave to Israel were charged with caring for His people and with keeping their hearts in tune with the Lord. Even the Persian ruler Cyrus is called "My shepherd" (Is. 44:28) by the Lord, for Cyrus would encourage the return of the exiles to Judah from Babylon.

Jeremiah describes the religious leaders of his day as shepherds, but ones who "have become dull-hearted, and have not sought the LORD" (Jer. 10:21). These were shepherds who abandoned the Lord and who "destroyed My vineyard. They have trodden My portion underfoot; they have made My pleasant portion a desolate wilderness" (12:10).

The unfaithfulness of the shepherds who were commissioned to care for God's sheep, the children of Israel, led to the spiritual and literal ruin of the nation. It's no wonder the Lord had Ezekiel prophesy judg-

The image of God as the Shepherd of His people has roots in the earliest book of the Old Testament.

ment on the shepherds of Israel, who only "feed themselves! Should not the shepherds feed the flocks?" (Ezek. 34:2).

Ezekiel introduced a special promise. Since the secular and religious leaders of Israel had failed, God said, "As a shepherd seeks out his flock on the day he is among his scattered sheep, so will I seek out My sheep and deliver them" (v. 12). Ezekiel conveys God's promise, "I will feed My flock" (v. 15).

The prophet then reveals that David's descendant, the Messiah, "will feed them" (v. 23) and "be their shepherd." This identification of the coming Shepherd with both God Himself and the Messiah is strong evidence for the deity of Christ. Micah 5:4 says of the Messiah, "He shall stand and feed His flock in the strength of the LORD, in the majestic name of the LORD His God; and they shall abide, for now He shall be great to the ends of the earth."

The Old Testament does the following:

- Portrays God as a shepherd
- Identifies kings as under-shepherds
- Identifies religious leaders as under-shepherds
- Condemns the failure of both to truly care for God's flock
- Promises that one day God Himself will shepherd Israel in the person of the Messiah, the greatest descendant of David.

God's shepherding ministry. God presents Himself as the Shepherd of Israel. Interestingly, David viewed God as his own personal Shepherd. Psalm 23 makes it clear that in the Old Testament the metaphor of God as a Shepherd conveyed a sense of being in a close personal relationship with the Lord much more powerfully than did the metaphor of God as a Father. Note in this psalm how God fulfills the role of a shepherd.

The LORD is my shepherd;
    I shall not want.   (God provides)
He makes me to lie down in
    green pastures;
He leads me beside the
    still waters.   (God leads)
He restores my soul;
He leads me in the
    paths of   (God gives moral
righteousness   guidance)
For His name's sake.
Yea, though I walk though
    the valley of the shadow
    of death   (God gives peace)
I will fear no evil;
For You are with me;   (God protects)
Your rod and Your staff, they
    comfort me.
You prepare a table before me
    in the presence of my
    enemies;   (God saves)

You anoint my head with oil;
    My cup runs over.   (God blesses)
Surely goodness and mercy
    shall follow me
All the days of my life;   (God gives
And I will dwell in the   eternal life)
    house of the LORD
    forever.

God's sheep. In casting God as a Shepherd, the Bible also casts believers as His sheep. This is hardly a flattering metaphor. Sheep are far from intelligent animals. The reason they need to be constantly accompanied by a shepherd is simply that sheep lack the sense required to care for themselves. Without constant supervision they will wander off to places where they might be lost, hurt, or captured by wild animals. Isaiah 53:6, which describes the substitutionary sacrifice of the coming Messiah, reminds us that "all we like sheep have gone astray; we have turned, every one, to his own way."

It is only in the New Testament that the full import of God's identification of Himself as our Shepherd is understood. Jesus speaks of Himself as the Good Shepherd. He cares so much for His sheep that He gave His own life for them. Yet even in the Old Testament the metaphor of God as a Shepherd powerfully conveyed to His people that He loved them both individually and corporately. With David, each Old Testament believer could gladly say the following:

The LORD is my Shepherd!
The LORD is my Shepherd!
The LORD is my Shepherd!
            Psalm 23:1

HELPER

David, who celebrated God as his Shepherd in Psalm 23, says in 54:4 that "God is my helper." The Hebrew noun translated "helper," 'ezer, refers to a person who comes alongside someone else to offer assistance.

The *Theological Dictionary of the Old Testament* describes the uses of the Hebrew verb from which the noun is derived. While frequently military assistance is in view, the verb also indicates personal assistance, particularly in the Psalms.

> The Lord is seen as the helper of the underprivileged; the poor (Ps 72:12) and the fatherless (Ps 10:14; cf. Job 29:12). The psalmist confesses that he has no help but God (Pss 22:11; 107:12). He is conscious of divine assistance at a time of illness (Ps 28:7), at a time of oppression by enemies (Ps 54:4), and at a time of great personal distress (Ps 86:17). God's hand (Ps 119:173) and his laws (Ps 119:175) were sources of assistance to the psalmist (2:661).

As a Helper, God is willing and able to stand beside the believer in any and every need. Thus the psalmist exults, "The LORD is with me; he is my helper. I will look in triumph on my enemies" (Ps. 118:7 NIV).

It is interesting that this same Hebrew noun, 'ezer, is used by God to describe Eve. After God's creation of Adam, the Lord provided a suitable helper for Adam. Nothing appropriate could be found in the animal creation, so the Lord fashioned Eve from Adam's rib. When God brought Eve to Adam, he recognized immediately that she shared his identity as a human being. Because they had so much in common, Eve could establish a truly personal relationship with Adam. It was in the context of that relationship that she functioned as a helper to him.

When God created humankind, He gifted us with His own image-likeness (Gen. 1:26, 27). In some mysterious way, He made us enough like Himself so that we might have an intimate relationship with Him. As our Helper, God comes alongside us, feeling what we feel and knowing what we know. He also comes alongside to give us aid in our time of need.

God is our hiding place. We turn to Him in every time of trouble.

❖

DESCRIPTIVE IMAGES OF GOD

Metaphors and similes are used to help us better understand God and what He intends to be for us. To accomplish this purpose, God is often spoken of in unlikely ways. For instance, in the Old Testament the Lord is presented to us as a lamp, a potter, and a refiner. Each of these images (and more) conveys fresh insights into who the Lord intends to be for us.

HIDING PLACE

David says of God, "You are my hiding place; You shall preserve me from trouble; You shall surround me with songs of deliverance" (Ps. 32:7). Isaiah also refers to a hiding place. But the prophet has scorn for those who make lies their hiding place, and he warns that the waters of God's judgment will sweep away the hiding place of the wicked (Is. 28:15, 17).

The Hebrew noun rendered "hiding place" (KJV, NIV) or "secret place" (NASB) comes from a verb that means "to conceal." To others the believer may seem vulnerable and exposed. But all the while we have a secret place to which we can retreat. There, in God's presence, we know that we are secure. While the sinner tries to hide behind lies, the believer turns to God and finds peace in prayer.

There is one other reference to God as a hiding place. This time it is a reference to the Messiah. But here we find a very different Hebrew word. When Christ reigns, our place of safety will no longer be a secret. Isaiah 32:1 and 2 tells us,

> Behold, a king will reign in righteousness,
> And princes will rule with justice.
> A man will be as a hiding place from the wind,
> And a cover from the tempest,
> As rivers of water in a dry place,
> As the shadow of a great rock in a weary land.

KEEPER

When the psalmist wrote, "The LORD is your keeper" (Ps. 121:5), he chose a common Hebrew noun whose verbal root occurs hundreds of times in the Old Testament. The underlying meaning is "to be responsible for someone or something," whether the reference is to keeping God's commandments or to watching over another's possessions.

Long ago Cain asked God, "Am I my brother's keeper?" (Gen. 4:9). Cain's question was a denial of responsibility. Yet the fact remains that he was responsible to love his brother. Tragically, however, Cain murdered Abel. In calling Himself our Keeper, the Lord reassures us of His protection. He has accepted responsibility for our well-being, and He will never let us down.

LAMP

The "lamp" referred to in Scripture was a shallow bowl filled with olive oil, in which a bit of flax was dropped to serve as a wick. Each night in Hebrew homes such a lamp was left burning, indicating that the home was occupied. Thus, the absence of a lamp symbolized an unoccupied home.

When Proverbs 20:20 warns that "whoever curses his father or his mother, his lamp will be put out in deep darkness," the saying reflects the Law's promise of long life to those who honor their mother or father (Ex. 20:12). Those who ignore the commandment and curse parents can expect to die young, leaving their house dark and unoccupied. The same message is conveyed in Proverbs 24:20: "There will be no prospect [future] for the evil man; the lamp of the wicked will be put out."

People in ancient Israel also used lamps to light their way when walking outside. This use is reflected in Psalm 119:105, where David writes, "Your word is a lamp to my feet and a light to my path." The imagery here was also well understood by the original readers of the Hebrew text. A modern flashlight casts a beam of light well ahead of the person holding it. But the lamp of Bible times only cast its circle of light around the feet of the person holding it, showing only the next step along the path.

Today we tend to want to look far ahead, as though we could know what the future holds. Yet regardless of whatever plans we might make, the future remains hidden from us. All we can really do is be careful that the next step we take in life is guided by God's Word and Spirit. It is this truth that David had in mind when he says, "You are my lamp, O LORD; the LORD shall enlighten my darkness" (2 Sam. 22:29). We do not know our future, but God does. In His time, He will show us the next step we

An unlit lamp symbolizes a home empty of God.

❖

are to take, and in this way guide us along His path.

LIGHT
LIGHT TO THE GENTILES

Both light and darkness are powerful metaphors applied in a variety of ways in the Old and New Testaments. But what does David mean when he writes, "The LORD is my light and my salvation; whom shall I fear?" (Ps. 27:1).

The *New International Encyclopedia of Bible Words* sums up the ways in which "light" is used in the Old Testament.

> God set the sun in the sky to "give light to the earth" (Ge 1:15). He accompanied Israel through the wilderness in a fiery pillar "to give them light" (Ex 13:21). These historic acts provide images that are picked up and expanded by the psalmists. God is called "my

The image of God as a potter emphasizes His sovereign ability to mold history and human lives.

❖

light and my salvation" (Ps 27:1). It is only in relationship with the Lord that one's life is illumined, for "in [his] light we see light" (Ps 36:9). Light is linked with divine revelation (Ps 43:3; 119:130), with life (Ps 49:19; 56:13), with salvation (Ps 27:1), and with God's presence (Ps 89:15; 90:8). God's people are called to "walk in the light of the Lord" (Isa 2:5), and the prophets promise that one day God himself will live among men, to replace the sun as their "everlasting light" (Isa 60:19-20).

As we will see, the New Testament presents Jesus as *the* light of the world (John 8:12). The fact that David's experience of God as light and salvation is one day to be made available to all who have trusted in Christ is clearly predicted in the Old Testament.

In what are called Isaiah's "servant songs"—passages that refer to the coming Messiah as God's Servant—Isaiah 42:6 and 7 portrays Him as "a light to the Gentiles, to open blind eyes, to bring the prisoners from the prison, those who sit in darkness from the prison house."

In another servant song, God says the following:

> Indeed He says,
> "It is too small a thing that
>   You should be My Servant
> To raise up the tribes of Jacob,
> And to restore the preserved
>   ones of Israel;
> I will also give You as a
>   light to the Gentiles,
> That You should be My
>   salvation to the ends of the earth."
>   Isaiah 49:6

Thus, salvation seems to be the primary emphasis in passages that portray God or His Messiah as light. It is the recognition of God as our Savior that opens our eyes and frees us from the darkness in which all those who do not know God live.

POTTER

There are few images that evoke a stronger reaction than that of God as the potter and human beings as the clay. Isaiah 64:8 states this truth clearly.

> But now, O Lord,
> You are our Father;
> We are the clay, and You our potter;
> And all we are the work of Your hand.

For some the image is troubling because it seems to portray human beings as passive entities who have no real responsibility or influence over the course of their lives. On the surface, this notion seems to be strengthened by the prophet's use of the metaphor.

> Surely you have things turned around!
> Shall the potter be esteemed as the clay;
> For shall the thing made say of him who
>   made it,

"He did not make me"?
Or shall the thing formed say of him who
    formed it,
"He has no understanding"?
                    Isaiah 29:16

Again,

Woe to him who strives with his Maker!
Let the potsherd strive with the
    potsherds of the earth!
Shall the clay say to him who forms it,
    "What are you making?"
Or shall your handiwork say,
    "He has no hands"?
                    Isaiah 45:9

In 29:15, we find Isaiah speaking to those who "seek deep to hide their counsel far from the LORD."

"O house of Israel, can I not do with you as this potter," says the LORD. "Look, as the clay is in the potter's hand, so are you in My hand, O house of Israel."
                    Jeremiah 18:6

When we look at the context of these verses, however, we quickly see that the image of God as a potter in no way denies human responsibility.

In Isaiah 29:15 the prophet ridicules those who "seek deep to hide their counsel far from the LORD." Assuredly they "have things turned around" (v. 16). They are acting as if they, rather than God, were the Creator, or as if they, rather than God, were sovereign over all things.

In Isaiah 45:9, the prophet addresses those who strive against their Maker. This, too, is turning things upside down. Compared to God, people are like potsherds, namely, broken pieces of a clay pot. They may struggle against other people—potsherd against potsherd—but how foolish it is to imagine that people might succeed in striving against God, the Potter.

In Jeremiah 18:6, the prophet warns a rebellious house of Israel, "Can I not do with

you as this potter?" Judah has forgotten that the Lord is God, in sovereign control of history. He is capable of establishing and tearing down kingdoms. Thus God says to His people, "Return now every one from his evil way, and make your ways and your doings good" (v. 11).

In each context, the Lord is speaking to those who are acting as if He is irrelevant, and as if they are capable of determining their own future without Him. The image of God as a potter is a reminder that, compared to the Lord, we are mere clay. In contrast, the reference in Isaiah 64:8 is a statement of trust expressed by a believer who knows that God is sovereign and rejoices in that reality.

It has been suggested that there are only two rules to remember in order to get along with God.

Rule 1: Remember that the Lord is God.
Rule 2: Remember that we are not.

Israel and Judah forgot these two basic rules. In the analogy of God as the potter and human beings as the clay, God is simply reminding His people of these rules and calling them back to Him in repentance and faith.

REFINER

Malachi 3:2 compares God to a "refiner's fire." Verse 3 says, "He will sit as a refiner and purifier of silver; He will purify the sons of Levi, and purge them as gold and silver, that they may offer to the LORD an offering of righteousness."

The refiner in ancient times (as in our own) subjected the metal to be purified to intense heat. As metal melts and bubbles, impurities rise to the top and are removed by the refiner. Gradually the metal is purified, becoming more and more pure. In the same way God permits us to experience difficult and painful times. But His goal is always that of the refiner, not to harm, but to purify. God's goal is that we, too, might be to Him an offering of righteousness.

The New Testament picks up this same image in 1 Peter 1:7. There the apostle reminds those who are distressed by various trials that "the genuineness of your faith, being much more precious than gold that perishes, though it is tested by fire, may be found to praise, honor, and glory at the revelation of Jesus Christ."

In any era, God intends the sufferings that challenge our faith only for our good.

REFUGE

David says, "The LORD also will be a refuge for the oppressed, a refuge in times of trouble" (Ps. 9:9). The Hebrew word translated "refuge" can also mean "stronghold" or "secure height."

Before the Israelites conquered the promised land, God instructed Moses to establish "cities of refuge" (Num. 35:11). In the earliest days of Israel's history, there were no national or local police to enforce the laws and capture criminals. It's true that local elders adjudicated disputes, but when a person killed another, the responsibility for bringing the murderer to justice belonged to the "avenger of blood" (Deut. 19:12). This person was the nearest relative of the murdered person. The avenger was responsible for finding and executing the killer, as required by Genesis 9:6 and Numbers 35:21.

There was always the possibility that someone might kill another accidentally. In this case the death would not be murder. The problem, however, was that in the heat of anger over the death of a relative, the avenger of blood might find and kill the one responsible for the death before it was determined whether the crime was murder or accidental homicide.

This is where the cities of refuge came in. A person who killed another was to immediately flee to the nearest city of refuge. He was to remain there until the elders of his own city could hear his case.

If it was determined that the killing was intentional, the offender was turned over to the avenger. But if it was determined that the death was accidental, the offender was to stay in the city of refuge until the death of the current high priest. Then the offender would be free to return home, and the avenger of blood could not harm him.

The sites of these cities of refuge were selected carefully. They were placed so that anyone in Israel was within a day's journey of a city of refuge, for only in the city of refuge could a person be safe.

What a picture of our relationship with God! Despite the fact that we are guilty of many sins, God has provided a refuge that is immediately accessible to us. We can hurry to Him in our times of trouble, and only in Him will we be eternally secure.

ST IN THE
TESTAMENT

A number of the names and titles in the Old Testament are given to the Messiah. The term "messiah" means the "anointed." The title "Christ" in the New Testament has this same meaning, and is the Greek translation of the Hebrew word.

In Old Testament times special persons selected to serve God and the nation were set apart for their mission by being anointed with olive oil. Thus Aaron and his sons were anointed when they were consecrated as Israel's priests (Ex. 28:41; 29:7), and Israel's kings were anointed when they were commissioned to the royal office (cf. Judg. 9:8; 1 Sam. 16:12).

In predicting the appearance of a person to be called the "Messiah," the Old Testament practice of anointing foreshadowed His role. The Messiah would be both Priest and King. As Priest, He would represent the people before God and offer a sacrifice that restored harmony between people and God. As King, the Messiah would conquer evil, punish sinners, and establish God's rule on earth.

Both of these ministries, the priestly and the kingly, are reflected in the names and titles given to the Messiah in the Old Testament. These names and titles also establish another important truth. The coming Messiah, while a human being, was to be God Himself.

Some have excused the failure of the religious leaders of the first century to recognize Jesus as the Messiah because He did not come as the conqueror predicted in the Old Testament Scriptures. Others have excused their fanatic opposition to His claims to be the Son of God and thus one with the Father (in other words, equal to Him in nature and essence; John 10:30). However, as we examine the names and titles of the Messiah found in the Old Testament, we discover that the reason for the religious leaders' rejection of Jesus cannot be explained simply as a lack of awareness of who the Messiah was to be.

The Scriptures make it plain that the Messiah was to be God enfleshed, and that He would serve God both as Priest and King. Some passages featuring the names or titles

The title Messiah, Anointed One, emphasizes Christ's commissioning to carry out a mission for God.

❖

of the Messiah emphasize His deity, His priestly ministry, or His royal commission. Yet in many passages featuring the Messiah's names and titles, two or all three of these themes are interwoven.

PRIMARY NAMES OF CHRIST IN THE OLD TESTAMENT

Among the many names and titles of Christ revealed in the Old Testament, several can be called primary. They are "primary" because they unmistakably identify Him. At the same time the context of the Scripture passage often clearly identifies His ministries.

ANOINTED ONE (MESSIAH)

As noted above, individuals were anointed with oil to commission them for some special service to God and His people.

In a stunning prophecy speci[...] weeks" from a command to rest[...] Jerusalem, the prophet Daniel [...] the coming of Messiah the Prince [...] "make an end of sins," make "reco[...] for iniquity," and "bring in everlast[...] teousness" (Dan. 9:24). Daniel also p[...] the death (cutting off) of the Messiah [...] not for Himself" (v. 26), a subseq[...] destruction of Jerusalem, and the app[...] ance of an enemy who will desecrate t[...] holy place until he is put down (v. 27).

In this prophecy, which blends the [...] priestly and kingly aspects of the Messiah's ministry, He is also give the divine title, "the Most Holy" (v. 24)

BIBLE BACKGROUND:

DANIEL'S 70 WEEKS

Daniel discovers Jeremiah's promise that the captivity will last 70 years (Jer. 25:11-14). Now, in 538 B.C., the appointed years are almost complete. So Daniel pleads with God to act.

The angel Gabriel appears as Daniel is praying, to give God's answer. Daniel is told that a set period of time is determined "for your people and your holy city to finish transgression, to put an end to sin, to atone for wickedness, to bring in everlasting righteousness, to seal up [i.e., to fulfill] vision and prophecy, and to anoint the most holy" (24). This is a unique prophecy in that rather than being indefinite about time, the whole prophecy focuses on time and announces in advance a prophetic time framework.

Some have taken these figures in the literal sense that Daniel clearly intended. The best interpretation, viewing each "time" as a year, and each "week" or "seven" as seven years, takes the "decree to restore Jerusalem" as that given by Artaxerxes to Ezra in 458 B.C. The first seven (49 years) takes us to 409 B.C., when Nehemiah and Ezra complete the task of walling in and populating the city. The next group of 62 sevens (434 years) brings us to A.D. 26 and the baptism of Jesus (e.g., the "anointing of the most holy")(cf. Matt. 4; Luke 4).

What about the last group of seven years? Daniel says that "after the sixty-two sevens the anointed one will be cut off and have nothing" (26). "Cut off" is used in the OT to indicate execution (cf. Lev. 7:20; Ps. 37:9; Prov. 2:22). This is "after" the anointing. Thus the text implies an indeterminate time gap between the sixty-ninth and seventieth week. The final seven-year span begins when an evil ruler comes and makes a seven-year treaty with God's people, which he will break at midpoint.

To those who take prophecy in a literal way, the picture of Jesus crucified stands out in bold relief. So does a fact not known to OT prophecy—that the Messiah will suffer and die, and that a great gap of time exists between the first coming of Jesus and his second coming. When this gap finally closes, the last week of Daniel, like the first sixty-nine, will see prophecy fulfilled as literally and strikingly as Daniel identified the empires of Greece and Rome.

The Illustrated Bible Handbook,
pp. 371-372

Daniel's prediction concerning the Messiah is not the only place where His deity is affirmed. Psalm 2, recognized by ancient Jewish commentators as well as by Christians as a messianic psalm, speaks of the "nations" (v. 1) raging against "the Lord and . . . His Anointed" (v. 3). Then in verses 7 through 9, the Messiah speaks.

I will declare the decree:
    The LORD has said to Me,
    "You are My Son,
        Today I have begotten You.
Ask of Me, and I will give You
    The nations for Your inheritance,

And the ends of the earth for
    Your possession.
You shall break them with a
    rod of iron;
    You shall dash them to pieces
    like a potter's vessel."

Here the Messiah, seen in His royal role as Conqueror, is identified as the Son of God.

The Scriptures presenting the Messiah (the Christ) as the Anointed One clearly establish the fact that the Person who will come to deal with sin and establish His righteous rule is indeed God Himself.

BRANCH

The term "branch" is a common metaphor for family relationships. As a branch grows from a tree, so metaphorically the Messiah is said in Scripture to be David's "Branch of Righteousness" (in other words, a descendant of that king; Jer. 23:5). Similarly, Isaiah 11:1 predicts that "a shoot will come up from the stump of Jesse [David's father], and from his roots a Branch will bear fruit" (NIV). Jeremiah 33:15 quotes the Lord as saying, "I will cause to grow up to David a Branch of righteousness." But the Messiah is more than a descendant of David. He is also called the "Branch of the LORD" (Is. 4:2). Jeremiah is even more clear in giving the Messiah a divine title, *Yahweh sidkenu.* Jeremiah 23:6 says,

In His days Judah will be saved,
    And Israel will dwell safely;
Now this is His name by
    which He will be called:
THE LORD OUR RIGHTEOUSNESS.

In passages where the Messiah is identified as the Branch, both His human nature and His deity are affirmed. There was no basis for the religious leaders of Jesus' time to be shocked that in presenting Himself as the Messiah, Jesus also affirmed His deity. For

The messianic title, Branch, emphasizes Jesus' descent from David and thus His right to rule Israel.

the fact that the Promised One was to be God Himself is clearly taught in the Old Testament!

But what aspect of the Messiah's ministry is in view where He is spoken of as the Branch? In Isaiah and Jeremiah, the Messiah's role as Conqueror and Ruler is emphasized. Jeremiah 23:5 says of Him, "a King shall reign and prosper, and execute judgment and righteousness in the earth." And Isaiah 11:2-4 says,

> The Spirit of the LORD shall rest upon Him,
> The Spirit of wisdom and understanding,
> The Spirit of counsel and might,
> The Spirit of knowledge and of the fear of the LORD.
> His delight shall be in the fear of the LORD,
> And He shall not judge by the sight of His eyes,
> Nor decide by the hearing of His ears;
> But with righteousness He shall judge the poor,
> And decide with equity for the meek of the earth;
> He shall strike the earth with the rod of His mouth,
> And with the breath of His lips He shall slay the wicked.

Zechariah, however, emphasizes the priestly ministry of the Branch. In 3:9 we learn that the Lord, through His Servant the Branch, "will remove the iniquity of that land in one day." In 6:12 and 13 we read that "the Man whose name is the BRANCH" is to "sit and rule on His throne; so He shall be a priest on His throne."

In the Messiah, in Christ, the ministries of priest and king are united. In His death,

Jesus our High Priest offered His own blood as a purifying sacrifice. And when Jesus returns, He will come to rule.

IMMANUEL

This name is associated with perhaps the most famous prophecy in the Bible. The prophet Isaiah, some seven hundred years before Christ, is sent to King Ahaz of Judah. The king is terrified because Rezin of Syria and Pekah of Israel are negotiating a treaty with a view to invade Judah. Isaiah bears good news: the conspiracy will fail.

However, when Isaiah tells Ahaz to ask for a sign (that is, a miracle, authenticating the message as being truly from God), the apostate king refuses. In response Isaiah declares, "the Lord Himself will give you a sign: Behold, the virgin shall conceive and bear a Son, and shall call His name Immanuel" (Is. 7:14). Isaiah continues and, referring to his own infant son Sher-Jashub, whom he is carrying, tells Ahaz that before the child is old enough to be weaned, the two kings Ahaz fears will no longer be a threat to Judah (vv. 15, 16).

The second prophecy was fulfilled, as both of the hostile nations Ahaz feared were overrun by Assyria. This was a "near term" prophecy, fulfilled within a short span of time and thus authenticating the prophet's message as being from God. That fulfilled prophecy not only demonstrated that Isaiah was God's spokesman, but also guaranteed the "long term" prophecy of a virgin birth, and more!

The promised child was not simply to be miraculously conceived, but also was given a name that in Hebrew means "God with us." In fact, the way the name is constructed gives it a slightly different emphasis: "WITH US is God!" God is not just to be "with us" in the traditional sense, but is to be WITH US in a unique sense. The One who is to be born of a virgin is God, come to earth as a true human being! He is to be with us in our humanity, born into the world as an infant as we are, and yet at the same time fully God.

GOD'S SERVANT

A number of chapters in Isaiah are dedicated to the description of a person called the Lord's Servant. It is clear from these passages, called "servant songs," that God had chosen Israel to be His servant, charged with glorifying Him among the nations. But Israel failed in this mission. So Isaiah introduces God's coming individual who will serve Him as a Servant and who will accomplish the mission God gives to Him.

We can best understand this title of Christ in the Old Testament by summarizing the chapters in which the Servant appears.

Isaiah 42:1-13. The gentleness of the Servant is emphasized in verses 1-3, while verses 4-9 describe His mission. God's Servant is to redeem the lost and release the captives. Verses 10-13 reveal that the work of the Servant will give the peoples of the earth a new song to sing—a song of praise to the Lord.

Isaiah 42:14-25; 43:1-28. This second "servant song" presents Israel as God's failed servant (42:14-25). Israel not only failed to do God's will, but also was completely unresponsive to His discipline. Yet Israel is not to fear, for God will redeem His people (43:1-13). And God will blot out His people's sins (vv. 14-28).

Isaiah 49. Isaiah now introduces an individual, called from the womb to be God's Servant, who will light the way to God for the Gentiles (vv. 1-7). He himself will also be

a covenant to the people [Israel],
To restore the earth,
To cause them to inherit the
    desolate heritages;
That You may say to the
    prisoners, "Go forth."
  v. 8

The phrase "a covenant to the people," found here and also in 42:6, is a reference to the new covenant of Jeremiah 31:31-34, which Christ inaugurated in His death on Calvary.

When God's Servant has accomplished His mission of redemption, redeeming Israel and humbling hostile world powers, the whole world will know that the Lord is Israel's Redeemer.

Isaiah 50. In contrast to disobedient Israel, God's Servant will be responsive to God even though His obedience brings suffering. In the end the Servant will be vindicated by the Lord Himself (vv. 1-9). Those who rely on God will obey "the voice of His Servant" and "trust in the name of the LORD" (v. 10).

Isaiah 52:13—53:12. This song begins with God's affirmation, "My Servant shall deal prudently; He shall be exalted and extolled and be very high" (52:13). But Isaiah goes on to note that at first the Servant will be unrecognized. Moreover, He will be "despised and rejected by men, a Man of sorrows and acquainted with grief" (53:3).

Isaiah 53 describes the death of the Servant, in which He is "wounded for our transgressions" and "bruised for our iniquities" (v. 5). This stunning prophetic passage not only describes the death of Christ on Calvary, but also makes its redemptive purpose utterly clear. The chapter also pictures His resurrection and exaltation, all because "He bore the sin of many, and made intercession for the transgressors" (v. 12).

Robert T. France has summarized the servanthood of Jesus, as revealed in Isaiah.

The Servant was chosen by the Lord (42:1; 49:1) and endowed with the Spirit (42:1). He was taught by the Lord (50:4), and found his strength in him (49:2, 5). It was the Lord's will that he should suffer (53:10); He was weak, unimpressive, and scorned by men (52:14; 53:1-3, 7-9); meek (42:2), gentle (42:3), and

uncomplaining (50:6; 53:7). Despite his innocence (53:9), he was subjected to constant suffering (50:6; 53:3, 8-10), so as to be reduced to near despair (49:4). But his trust was in the Lord (49:4; 50:7-9); he obeyed him (50:4-5), and persevered (50:7) until he was victorious (42:4; 50:8, 9).

The many chapters in Isaiah devoted to Jesus as God's Servant make the title "Servant" one of the most significant of the names and titles of Jesus in the Old Testament.

A CHILD BORN
A SON GIVEN
WONDERFUL
COUNSELOR
MIGHTY GOD
EVERLASTING FATHER
PRINCE OF PEACE

Isaiah has been called the evangelist of the Old Testament. This is due in part to the second half of Isaiah's prophecy, which emphasizes salvation rather than judgment. But the primary reason Isaiah is called the evangelist of the Old Testament is that his book is filled with images and prophecies concerning the coming Savior.

One of the clearest and most powerful of these prophecies is found in Isaiah 9:6 and 7. There Isaiah writes,

> For unto us a Child is born,
>   Unto us a Son is given;
> And the government shall be
>   upon His shoulder,
> And His name will be called
>   Wonderful, Counselor, Mighty God,
> Everlasting Father, Prince of Peace.
>   Of the increase of His
>   government and peace
>   There will be no end,
> Upon the throne of David and
>   over His kingdom,

Frequent references to the throne of David emphasize the fact that Jesus was born a king, and at history's end He will rule over all.

To order it and establish it with
  judgment and justice
From that time forward, even forever.
The zeal of the Lord of hosts
  will perform this.

The references to David and his throne make it unmistakably clear that this passage is about the Messiah. It not only predicts an everlasting and peaceful rule for the Messiah, but it also contains several names and titles.

A Child is born. This title is a clear reference to the Messiah's humanity. He will enter the world as a child through the normal process of birth. As Isaiah later wrote, "He shall grow up before Him as a tender plant, and as a root out of dry ground. He has no form or comeliness, and when we see Him, there is no beauty that we should desire Him" (Is. 53:2). As Jesus

lived His life on earth, there seemed nothing special about Him. In one sense, He was simply a faithful first-century Jewish man who worked as a carpenter. After Joseph's death, Jesus assumed the responsibility for taking care of His mother and younger half-brothers and half-sisters.

The surprising ordinariness of Jesus is emphasized in the Gospels. When Jesus came to John the Baptist to be baptized, John, who was most likely Jesus' cousin, refused at first (Matt. 3:13-15). The reason for John's reluctance was not because he understood Jesus' messianic identity. Rather, John realized that Jesus was a truly good person, someone who did not need a baptism that signified a commitment to change one's way of life.

John's baptism implied confession of sins for which one needed to repent. But John was sure that this was inappropriate for Jesus. Only when Jesus pointed out that in being baptized He would identify Himself with righteousness and with John's message did the latter permit Christ to be baptized.

The next day John identified Jesus to some of his disciples as the Lamb of God, and observed, "I did not know Him, but He who sent me to baptize with water said to me, 'Upon whom you see the Spirit descending, and remaining on Him, this is He who baptizes with the Holy Spirit'" (John 1:33).

Even those who knew Jesus best, while viewing Him as a truly good person, saw nothing supernatural. As a humanly born child, Jesus had no special form or comeliness that would prompt people who saw Him to immediately acclaim Him as their Messiah and King.

A Son is given. The Savior, while born into this world as a child, was more than that. Isaiah 9:6 titles Him a "Son . . . given." This title clearly calls to mind John 3:16:

> For God so loved the world that He gave His only begotten Son, that whoever believes in Him should not perish but have everlasting life.

While the Old Testament does not expressly imply the doctrine of the Trinity (though the New Testament does), that later revelation makes it clear that God has from eternity existed in three Persons, namely, the Father, the Son, and the Holy Spirit. Looking back from the perspective of the New Testament, we understand perfectly Isaiah's prophecy of a "Son . . . given." And we understand that the promised Messiah was at the same time to be both fully human and fully divine.

BIBLE BACKGROUND:

THE TRINITY

Christians have never been able to explain the Trinity or even understand how one God exists as three Persons. . . . While we soon become confused when we try to conceptualize the Trinity and while our analogies break down, we really aren't troubled by so-called logical contradictions. After all, human beings don't understand many things in the material universe. Why should we expect to be able to comprehend God? But the real reason we aren't troubled by our failure to understand the Trinity is that God's threeness and oneness are taught in Scripture.

God is three. Plural language is found even in the Old Testament. The name of God used in Genesis 1, *Elohim*, is plural, and in making human beings, God uses plural language: "Let *us* make man in *our* image" (Gen. 1:26, italics added). Even the Hebrew word in Israel's great affirmation, "the LORD our God is *one* LORD" (Deut. 6:4, italics added), uses a Hebrew term that emphasizes plurality in unity. Beyond this, we look back and see an Old Testament filled with references to God's Spirit, and we suspect that in many instances the "angel of the Lord" was a pre-incarnate Jesus.

We see these hints of plurality in the Old Testament because we look back with the perspective given by the New Testament revelation where we find bold statements. We see Jesus presented as one who was with God and was God from eternity (John 1:1-3). We hear Jesus speak of the Father as "the only true God" and yet affirm that "I and the Father are one" (John 10:30; 17:5). In towering statements, the Bible speaks of Jesus as God incarnate, one with and yet distinct from the Father (Phil. 2:5-11; Col. 1:15-20). In the same way Jesus identifies the Holy Spirit as one like himself (John 14:15-17). He is given divine attributes (1 Cor. 2:1-11; Heb. 9:14) and is identified with God in his acts (2 Cor. 12:4-6). In Ephesians 1, we see the role of Father, Son, and Spirit spelled out for us, with each acknowledged as God. We may not understand how it can be, but we are comfortable in the knowledge that the Bible presents one God who exists eternally as three: Father, Son, and Holy Spirit.

Zondervan Dictionary of Christian Literacy, pp. 358, 359

———————————— ❖ ————————————

Wonderful, Counselor. The Hebrew word in Isaiah 9:6, *pehleh*, means "wonderful" in the sense of a wonder or miracle. Asaph describes the Lord as "the God who does wonders" (Ps. 77:14). The verb form of this Hebrew word is found in Exodus 3:20, where God promises Moses to "strike Egypt with all My wonders."

The name "Wonderful, Counselor" (Is. 9:6) clearly indicates that the child born, who is also a Son given, is a miracle. His nature and existence can only be explained as a supernatural intervention by God, and not by the normal process of cause and effect at work in the material universe.

"Wonderful, Counselor" is a compound name in Hebrew, with the second component being "counselor." The root, *ya'as*, means "to advise," "to counsel," "to purpose," or "to plan." While most take the name "Wonderful, Counselor" to suggest that the Messiah's plans and purposes for humankind are wonderful, it seems more appropriate to see in this title a reference to the fact that the miracle of the Messiah will fulfill the eternal plan and purpose of God.

Mighty God. Psalm 89:8 describes God as being mighty. Truly, God is strong and powerful. But in Psalm 50:1, "Mighty One" is a title of "God the LORD." The assignment of the same title in Isaiah 9:6 to the Messiah is truly significant.

The Psalm 50:1 reference makes it clear that "Mighty One" is a title belonging to *Yahweh*. And the titles of *Yahweh* are His exclusively. This is emphasized in Isaiah 42:8, in which God says, "I am the LORD [*Yahweh*], that is My name; and My glory I will not give to another, nor My praise to carved images." Thus to call the Messiah the "Mighty God" (9:6) is tantamount to identi-

fying the miracle child, who is also a Son, as *Yahweh* Himself.

Jesus' claim to be one with the God of the Old Testament is thus clearly in harmony with Scripture's teaching concerning the Messiah, the Christ. Any first-century rabbi familiar with the Old Testament Scriptures should have understood Isaiah's prophecy and its import.

Everlasting Father. This is a third compound title that Isaiah 9:6 gives to the coming Messiah. E.W. Hengstenberg, in *Christology of the Old Testament*, explains.

> This allows for a twofold explanation. Either, we may suppose, that Father of eternity is the same as Eternal Father, when the meaning would be, that the Messiah will not, as must be the case with an earthly king, however excellent, leave his people destitute after a short reign, but rule over them and bless them for ever. Or we may explain it by the usage of the Arabic, in which he who *possesses* a thing is call *the father of* it, e.g., the father of mercy, the merciful. We have the more reason to suppose this usage is adopted here, since in respect to proper names especially it very often occurs in Hebrew. Thus e.g. *Father of strength*, strong; *Father of knowledge*, intelligent; *Father of glory*, glorious; *Father of goodness*, good; *Father of compassion*, compassionate; *Father of peace*, peaceful. According to all these analogies, *Father of eternity* is the same as *eternal*. According to both explanations, the latter of which is much to be preferred, a Divine attribute is here ascribed to the Messiah (p. 196).

Before all time, before the world was created, the coming Messiah eternally existed, and He Himself is source of all that now is.

Here again we have a title that uncompromisingly affirms the full deity of the Child-Son who was to be born. The deity of the Messiah, the Christ sent by God, is so

The title "Banner" reflects the fact that Gentiles as well as Jews would one day rally to Jesus, God's Messiah.

clearly taught that only those who were willfully ignorant could deny it.

Prince of Peace. This is the fourth and final compound title of the Messiah in Isaiah 9:6. The name, implying the "Ruler who brings peace," serves as a natural transition to verse 7: "Of the increase of His government and of peace there will be no end." The One who is coming will sit on the throne of David and rule over his kingdom, "to order it and to establish it with judgment and justice from that time forward, even forever." (See also the discussion of "The Lord is Peace" on page 70.)

OTHER OLD TESTAMENT NAMES AND TITLES

This title is found in Isaiah 11:10, which states that in the time of the Messiah "there shall be a Root of Jesse, who shall stand as a banner to the people; for the Gentiles shall seek Him." The two titles here stand in contrast. The root is the underground source of the trunk and branch. The

root is present but hardly prominent. Thus, Jesse is the source of David's line, from which the Messiah will spring. Conversely, a banner (namely, an ensign or standard) is a highly visible rallying point for all. The Messiah coming from Jesse's line will indeed be prominent.

The image of the Messiah as Banner reflects an incident that took place during Israel's wilderness wanderings. A plague of poisonous snakes caused terror in the Israelite camp. God told Moses to make a replica of a snake and attach it to the top of a pole. God promised "and it shall be that everyone who is bitten, when he looks at it, shall live" (Num. 21:8). Later, Jesus compared His death to that event. He said, "And as Moses lifted up the serpent in the wilderness, even so must the Son of Man be lifted up, that whoever believes in Him should not perish but have eternal life" (John 3:14, 15).

Jesus, from the root of Jesse, has been lifted up on the cross, and as such stands out, that all people everywhere may rally in faith to Him and be saved.

COMPANION, FELLOW

In Zechariah 13:7, God through the prophet speaks about the death of His Shepherd (see p. 172). The prophet records God's words as follows:

"Awake, O sword, against
My Shepherd,
Against the Man who is My
Companion,"
Says the LORD of hosts.
"Strike the Shepherd,
And the sheep will be
Scattered."

This too is a messianic prophecy that is referred to in the Gospels. In fact, Jesus quoted it to His disciples the last night of His life on earth. He warned, "All of you will be made to stumble because of Me this night, for it is written: 'I will strike the Shepherd, and the sheep of the flock will be scattered'" (Matt. 26:31; Mark 14:27).

What is significant here is that the title "My Companion" (Zech. 13:7), or "My fellow," again presents the Shepherd-Messiah as God's equal.

COVENANT OF THE PEOPLE

The concept of covenant is central to the Old Testament's portrait of a relationship between God and people. When a covenant that God has made with human beings is in view, "covenant" has the force of a promise or oath. For a more thorough analysis of biblical covenants, see the companion volume in this series, *Every Promise in the Bible*.

In Isaiah 42:6 and 49:8, the Lord speaks about His Servant as a "covenant." God says to His Servant, the Messiah, "I, the LORD, have called You in righteousness, and will hold Your hand; I will keep You and give You as a covenant to the people, as a light to the Gentiles" (42:6). Later God again speaks through the prophet. "In the day of salvation I have helped You; I will preserve You and give You as a covenant to the people" (49:8).

As is common in the Old Testament, "the people" is a reference to Israel, namely, God's chosen people. Jeremiah 31:31 and 32 makes it clear that God intends one day to "make a new covenant with the house of Israel and with the house of Judah—not according to the covenant that I made with their fathers in the day that I took them by the hand to lead them out of the land of Egypt." According to verse 34, this new covenant will bring forgiveness and transformation to God's people, "for I will forgive their iniquity, and their sin will I remember no more."

According to Isaiah 42:6, Israel's Messiah will be a "light to the Gentiles." Moreover, the Messiah will Himself *be* the covenant. The covenant promise of forgiveness is not made *by* the Messiah, but *in* the Messiah. Thus, it was at the Last Supper that Jesus told His disciples about "the new covenant in My blood, which is shed for you" (Luke 22:20). Clearly, in the names and titles of Christ in the Old Testament, the redemptive mission of Jesus can be foreseen.

DESIRE OF ALL NATIONS

On the seventeenth of October in 520 B.C., the prophet Haggai delivered a second message from God to the people of Judea. After the destruction of Jerusalem in 586 B.C. the Jews had been deported from their homeland and taken to Babylon. In 538 B.C., 42,360 Jews returned to Judah under a permit issued by Cyrus the Persian, who had conquered the Babylonian Empire. On arriving in Judea, the returning Jews immediately erected an altar for worship. They also laid the foundation of a second temple on the site where Solomon's temple had once stood.

Life, however, was difficult for the returnees, and the temple was not completed. For some eighteen years the people struggled to make a living from the land. And then God spoke through Haggai and his contemporary Zechariah, urging the people to again put God first and complete work on the temple.

The people responded to Haggai's first message, which he delivered on August 29, and enthusiastically set out to complete the temple. The theme of Haggai's second sermon was that God was with them, and that the temple they were then working on would one day be filled with glory. "I will shake the nations," the Lord promised, "and they shall come to the Desire of All Nations, and I will fill this temple with glory" (Hag. 2:7). The prediction that God would fill the second temple with glory was fulfilled when Jesus, God Himself, entered it half a millenium later.

BIBLE BACKGROUND:

THE SECOND TEMPLE

The temple that Solomon finished building in 959 B.C. (1 Kings 6:38) was destroyed by the Babylonians in 586 B.C. (2 Kings 25:9). At that time the Hebrew population was resettled in Babylon.

The foundations of what is known as the second temple were laid in 536 B.C. after a group of 42,360 Jewish pilgrims returned to their homeland in 538 B.C. (Ezra 2:64; 3:8). The return was made possible by Cyrus the Persian's overthrow of the Babylonian Empire. He reversed Babylonian policies and permitted exiled populations to return to their homelands. The Jewish returnees were committed to rebuild the temple. In fact, they carried with them gold and silver vessels that had been used in the Solomonic temple and that had been taken away by the Babylonians.

While the foundation was quickly laid, opposition to the building project caused the work to cease for sixteen years (from about 536 to 520 B.C.; 4:24). It took the combined ministry of the prophets Haggai and Zechariah to rekindle religious zeal

(5:1). As a result of their influence, work on the second temple began again in 520 B.C. (v. 2), and it was completed in 515 B.C. (6:15).

Rebuilding the temple was an important affirmation of faith. But the motivation had even deeper roots. The earlier prophets had outlined God's plan for Israel's future. They had envisioned a great war and a worldwide divine judgment. They had also foreseen the advent of the Messiah, a Deliverer to emerge from David's royal line.

In their prophecies, the Jerusalem temple played a significant role. Ezekiel saw the glory of the Lord returning to Jerusalem and settling down in a new temple that had been built to receive His presence (Ezek. 43:1-5). Also, Micah envisioned the Gentiles humbly coming to God's temple (Mic. 4:1-4). Isaiah likewise shared this same vision (Is. 2:2-4). Thus, only if the temple were rebuilt could the promised Savior appear!

Over the centuries the second temple was added to and its grounds extended. The greatest expansion and beautification of the temple began around 19 B.C. under King Herod the Great. Workers completed the main part of the project in ten years, but other parts of the work continued on for several more decades (John 2:20). The structure was not finally completed until around A.D. 64, under Herod Agrippa.

By the time of Christ, the Herodian temple was one of the most impressive structures of the ancient world (Matt. 24:1). It was made of massive blocks of stone bedecked with gold ornamentation, and its buildings consisted of gleaming white marble. It was there in the temple grounds that Jesus taught. And it was there that He drove out the money changers, insisting that God's sanctuary should be used as a house of prayer, not as a den of thieves (21:12, 13).

For over five hundred years, the second temple stood in Jerusalem, giving its mute witness to the expectation of God's people that a Deliverer would one day appear. Yet, when Christ came, He was rejected by His own people (John 1:11) and ultimately was crucified (19:17, 18). Within four decades of Jesus' crucifixion, the Romans under Titus destroyed the temple, along with the rest of Jerusalem (A.D. 70). The plowed ground where the city and its temple had stood was strewn with salt, and the Jews were forbidden to enter its environs.

Despite this catastrophic end, the second temple had served its purpose. It had stood for half a millennium, waiting for the Savior to appear. And appear He did, performing the work of salvation for us. Then, with its purpose fulfilled, the second temple faded into history. Despite its grandeur, its splendor was lost in the brightness of the One who came as the "light of the world" (8:12).

But what about the title, "Desire of All Nations" (Hag. 2:7)? One of the covenant promises that God made to Abraham around 2100 B.C. was that "all the nations of the earth shall be blessed" (Gen. 18:18) in Abraham's offspring. Solomon picks up this thought when he says concerning the Messiah, "men shall be blessed in Him; all nations shall call Him blessed" (Ps. 72:17). Isaiah 66:18 also looks forward to a time when "all nations . . . shall come and see My glory."

While the nations (that is, the Gentile world) stumbled about in darkness, ignorant of God and unwilling to seek Him, the Messiah remained their only hope. All that every person desires and needs is made available to us in Christ. In this sense Christ is— and one day will be recognized by all—as the "Desire of All Nations" (Hag. 2:7).

HORN OF THE HOUSE OF ISRAEL

Ezekiel 29:21 speaks about "that day," a phrase that most often refers to the time of history's end when the visions of all the prophets will be fulfilled. God announced, "In that day I will cause the horn of the house of Israel to spring forth." As we have

seen, "horn" in Scripture is a symbol of strength or power (p. 80). In other words, the Messiah is the strength of Israel, for He alone will enable God's people to fulfill their destiny.

HOLY ONE

"Holy One" is one of the exalted titles of God Himself (p. 49). Yet the same title is given to the Messiah in Psalm 22:3 (NIV) and in 89:18. Perhaps the most striking application of this title to Christ is seen in 16:10.

> For You will not leave my soul in Sheol,
> Nor will You allow Your Holy One to
>   see corruption.

In the first recorded sermon in the Book of Acts, the apostle Peter quoted Psalm 16:10 as evidence that Christ's resurrection was in full harmony with the Old Testament. On the day of Pentecost, while speaking to thousands in Jerusalem, Peter argued that Jesus of Nazareth, "a Man attested by God to you by miracles, wonders, and signs" (Acts 2:22), was the promised Savior. Peter noted the following:

> Him, being delivered by the determined purpose and foreknowledge of God, you have taken by lawless hands, have crucified, and put to death; whom God raised up, having loosed the pains of death, because it was not possible that He should be held by it. For David says concerning Him:

> "I foresaw the LORD always
>   before my face,
> For He is at my right hand, that
>   I may not be shaken.
> Therefore my heart rejoiced,
>   and my tongue was glad;
> Moreover my flesh also will
>   rest in hope,
> For You will not leave my soul
>   in Hades,

An image of a capstone or cornerstone reminds us that Jesus has always been the central element in God's plan of salvation.

❖

Nor will you allow Your Holy
One to see corruption.
You have made known to me
the ways of life;
You will make me full of joy
in Your presence."

Men and brethren, let me speak freely to you of the patriarch David, that he is both dead and buried, and his tomb is with us to this day. Therefore, being a prophet, and knowing that God had sworn with an oath to him that of the fruit of his body, according to the flesh, He would raise up the Christ to sit on his throne, he, foreseeing this, spoke concerning the resurrection of the Christ.

Acts 2:23-31

Here again we see a divine title, "Holy One" (v. 27), ascribed to the Messiah. Without question the promised Christ is identified as God in the Old Testament.

KING OF GLORY

The title "King of glory" occurs only in Psalm 24, a psalm that is clearly messianic. For a detailed discussion of this title and its use in Psalm 24, see page 64.

MAN OF SORROWS

This familiar title is found in Isaiah 53:3, the prophet's powerful preview containing many details of the death and resurrection of God's Servant, Jesus. The title reflects the fact that all during Jesus' earthly ministry as God's Servant, His life was filled with grief. The Hebrew word rendered "sorrows" is often translated "sicknesses," and this translation is appropriate as long as we understand that Christ's sufferings were both physical and spiritual in nature. Yes, He was crucified. But Jesus was also rejected by the same people He came to save. In this the Messiah was truly a "Man of sorrows."

PRECIOUS CORNERSTONE
THE STONE THE BUILDER'S REJECTED
SURE FOUNDATION

These distinctive titles of the Messiah are found in Isaiah and the Psalms. The title "sure foundation" is found in Isaiah 28:16.

> Behold, I lay in Zion a stone
>   for a foundation,
> A tried stone, a precious
>   cornerstone, a sure
>   foundation;
> Whoever believes will not act
>   hastily.

A parallel title, "the stone which the builders rejected," comes from Psalm 118:22. The *Revell Bible Dictionary* describes the cornerstone as follows (p. 254):

The keystone in a structure, either the corner of the foundation (Job 38:6; Jer. 51:26) or the final stone (capstone) of an arch (Ps. 118:22). In both testaments, the cornerstone (the first or last stone placed) serves as an image of the Messiah, God's alpha and omega, his first and last. New Testament writers seem fond of Ps. 118:22, "The stone the builders rejected has become the capstone," quoting it five times (Mt. 21:42; Mk. 12:10; Lk. 20:17; Acts 4:11; 1 Pet. 2:7). Despite rejection by his own people, Jesus is precious to those who acknowledge him as the cornerstone of their salvation.

In Ephesians, Paul pictures the Church as a building, a "holy temple," built on the ministry of the apostles and prophets, "with Christ Jesus himself as the chief cornerstone" (2:20).

Similar imagery is found in 1 Corinthians 3:11, where the apostle states, "For no other foundation can anyone lay than that which is laid, which is Jesus Christ." There is no way that a person can construct a life unless the Messiah, Jesus Christ, is the central and foundational figure.

BIBLE BACKGROUND:
LAYING THE CORNERSTONE

During the reign of godly King Josiah (640-609 B.C.), an amazing discovery was made. A lost book of God's Law was found in the temple. Josiah had come to the throne at the age of eight, experienced a personal conversion at the age of sixteen, and by the age of twenty had set about to restore the temple and worship of the Lord.

The restoration was long overdue. Josiah's grandfather, Manasseh, who had ruled for fifty-five years (697-642 B.C.), proved to be the most evil of Judah's kings. A dedicated enemy of the worship of Yahweh for most his life, Manasseh had closed the temple, erected pagan idols in Jerusalem, assassinated priests and prophets, and burned all copies of the Scriptures he could find.

It was not surprising, then, that Josiah and his reformers where thrilled to discover a lost copy of God's Law in the temple. Immediately Josiah had the scroll read to him. Through its words the king realized how far the people of Judah had strayed from God's pathway. Josiah committed to reestablishing Yahweh worship and the rule of His Law in Judah.

But where was the scroll of the Law found? We would probably be mistaken to assume that it lay forgotten on some dusty shelf, for Manasseh had been too eager to destroy all copies of the Scriptures. One likely possibility reflects a practice followed in the ancient world and indeed in the United States prior to the twentieth century. That practice was to place documents in foundation stones—and particularly the cornerstones—of important buildings.

In the United States, the practice was intended to provide a "time capsule" that would contain for posterity images of the period in which a building was constructed. The motivation of the practice in ancient times is less certain and may have been symbolic. But whatever the reason, the practice is well attested. It's possible that Josiah's workmen, while making extensive repairs on the temple (which had been abandoned for about half a century), found God's Law preserved in the foundation of the sanctuary, which had been laid over three centuries earlier!

PRINCE OF PRINCES

The Hebrew phrase rendered "Prince of princes" (Dan. 8:25) means "Leader of leaders" or "supreme Leader." The broader context of the passage describes a person we call the Antichrist. He will be a king "having fierce features, who understands sinister schemes" (v. 23). Ultimately, he rises up against the "Prince of princes" (v. 25), the supreme ruler of the universe, God Himself. After this uprising, "[Antichrist] shall be broken without human means."

When we compare this with other prophecies concerning that future rebellion (2 Thess. 1:7, 8; 2:8), it is clear that the rebellion will be put down by Christ. At His Second Coming, Jesus will be revealed as the supreme Ruler, the Prince of princes, who will firmly establish His rule over all the earth.

REPROACH OF MEN

Psalm 22:6 is the source of this title of the Messiah. It echoes the theme of Isaiah 53, namely, that people will reject the Messiah before He accomplishes His mission and opens the door for all to a saving relationship with God. Psalm 22 not only describes the Messiah in these painful terms, but also predicts the same words spoken to Jesus on the cross by enemies who ridiculed Him in His time of suffering (Matt. 27:39-44; Luke 23:35, 36).

> But I am a worm, and no man;
> A reproach of men, and
>   despised by the people.
> All those who see Me ridicule Me;
> They shoot out the lip, they
>   shake the head, saying,
> He trusted in the LORD, let
>   Him rescue Him;
> Let Him deliver Him, since He
>   delights in Him!
>   Psalm 22:6-8

ROOT OF JESSE

See the article on "Banner of the People" on page 102.

RULER

Micah 5:2 predicts, "But you, Bethlehem Ephrathah, though you are little among the thousands of Judah, yet out of you shall come forth to Me the One to be Ruler in Israel, whose goings forth are from old, from everlasting."

This familiar verse pinpointing the little town of Bethlehem as the birthplace of the Messiah is read in countless churches each Christmas. The verse emphasizes both the birth and the destiny of the Messiah. While born an infant, the child in Bethlehem was destined to be King.

The Hebrew word translated "Ruler" is *masal*, which simply means "to rule" or "to have dominion." The *Theological Wordbook of the Old Testament* notes that this word, as with other "words for oversight, rule, government must be defined in relation to the situation out of which the function arises" (Vol. 1, p. 534). It is clear from many of the Old Testament prophets that at history's end Christ will rule supreme, having put down all God's enemies and established peace in His universe.

SEED

The Hebrew word rendered "seed" means "offspring" or "descendant." This name or title is found in Genesis 3:15, which is the Bible's first prophecy concerning the Messiah.

In Eden, God had warned Adam not to eat the fruit of one particular tree. After Adam and his wife Eve disobeyed the divine command, the Lord found the now fallen couple hiding in the garden. There God explained the consequences of their tragic choice. But first God spoke to Satan, who had acted through a serpent to deceive Eve and lead the first couple into sin.

> And I will put enmity
> Between you and the woman,
> And between your seed and
>   her Seed;
> He shall bruise your head,
> And you shall bruise His heel.
>   Genesis 3:15

Eve understood this as a promise of restoration to the first couple's state of innocence. Thus, when she bore her firstborn, she said, "I have acquired a man [literally, "the man"] from the LORD" (4:1). Eve could hardly have been more wrong. For that son, Cain, grew up to murder his brother, Able.

Nevertheless, the divine promise remained of a descendant who would crush the head of Satan (Rom. 16:20). The Savior would destroy the devil's power, despite the fact that He Himself would be bruised (that is, crucified) in the cosmic battle (Col. 2:14, 15; Heb. 2:14, 15).

The messianic promise recorded in Genesis 3:15 was repeated to Abraham after he had entered the land of Canaan. God told Abraham, "To your descendants I will give this land" (12:7). While the Hebrew word here is appropriately translated "descendants," it is in fact a singular word that literally means "seed."

It is not unusual for a word to function both as a singular or a plural, depending on the context. For instance, we might say either "I saw a deer" or "I saw a herd of deer." Whether "deer" is to be understood as referring to one animal or many animals depends on the context in which the word is used. It is the same way with the Hebrew word rendered "seed." Paul, taking note of this dual meaning, argued that there is a deep theological significance in God's choice of the Hebrew word, which could stand for many offspring or for one descendant. Galatians 3:16 says the following about Genesis 12:7,

> Now to Abraham and his Seed were the promises made. He does not say, "And to seeds," as of many, but as of one. "And to your Seed," who is Christ.

This interpretation of the Old Testament text by the Holy Spirit affirms that in Christ, the promised Messiah of Israel, all God's promises find their fulfillment. Also through Christ—the Seed of the woman and the Seed of Abraham—humankind can find redemption.

STAR OUT OF JACOB

The messianic title "a Star shall come out of Jacob" (Num. 24:17) was uttered by a pagan prophet. A man named Balaam, who lived around 1450 B.C., had gained a reputation as a seer with supernatural powers. When the great crowd of Israelites whom Moses had freed from Egypt approached the lands of Moab and Midian, Balaam was hired to curse Israel. The people of that time believed that such a curse would sap the power of an enemy and thus make them easier to defeat.

Balaam sacrificed cattle and tried several times to curse God's people. However, all Balaam could utter were blessings rather than curses! It is in the context of these blessings, which are reported in Numbers 23 and 24, that Balaam cried out the following in 24:17:

> I see Him, but not now;
> I behold Him, but not near;
> A Star shall come out of Jacob;
> A Scepter shall rise out of Israel,
> And batter the brow of Moab,
> And destroy all the sons of tumult.

While the Hebrew term rendered "Star" was not typically used of royal figures in Israel, it is used in this sense in Isaiah 14:12. The usage was also common in other cultures of the ancient Near East. The parallel reference to "a Scepter" (Num. 24:17) makes it clear that the "Star" in this verse is a royal figure. The royal figure about whom the pagan seer foretold would emerge as the Conqueror of Israel's enemies. However, it would not be in Balaam's day.

BIBLE BACKGROUND:

STARGAZERS

The prophecy of Balaam recorded in Numbers 23—24 is often seen as the source of the interpretation of wise men who, Matthew 2:1-12 reports, sought out the Christ child a millennium and a half later. Who were these wise men? What discipline led them to their interpretation of a phenomenon observed in the sky? What was the star of Christmas?

The wise men were magi—members of a learned class that emerged in ancient Persia as advisors to powerful kings. The original magi were trained in agriculture, mathematics, history, the occult, and especially in astronomy and astrology. In the ancient world, the last two disciplines were joined together. It was not just about studying and charting the motions of stars and planets. More importantly, the stars were believed to influence the course of nations and especially the destiny of royal families. It was undoubtedly the magi's careful and constant observation of the heavens that caused them to discover the unusual star that shone in their western sky. But how would they be able to discern the significance of the star?

The Old Testament was among the works studied in the days of the Persian Empire. Remarkably, Babylon was a center of Jewish learning and especially the source of what is known as the Babylonian Talmud (which has equal standing in much of Judaism with the Jerusalem Talmud). The magi, whose thirst for knowledge undoubtedly was insatiable, might have been familiar with the Hebrew sacred writings and puzzled over its prophecies.

But what was the nature of the "star" the magi saw and recognized? A number of theories have been suggested.

1. The star was a supernova, bursting in the nighttime sky with unparalleled brilliance.
2. The star was a rare conjunction of Jupiter and Saturn, which are the two brightest planets in the sky.
3. The star was a comet flashing through the sky.
4. The star was a supernatural appearance of God's glory.
5. The star was an angel sent by God, for angels are sometimes referred to as stars in ancient writings.

Astronomers have reconstructed the condition of the heavens around the time of Jesus' birth. They think that several of the above phenomenon probably occurred in the ancient Near East. For instance, a supernova was observed in March/April of 5 B.C. A conjunction of Jupiter and Saturn occurred in May, October, and December of 7 B.C. And a conjunction of Jupiter and Venus could have been seen on June 17, 2 B.C.

Most likely we will never know for sure the exact nature of the Christmas star. Yet assuredly it was seen, and its significance was understood. Also, wise men from the East did journey to Judah to worship the King of Jews. Moreover, as bumper stickers remind us, wise people still seek the Messiah.

Most Bible scholars believe that Balaam's reference to a star that would rise out of Judah is the reference that alerted the wise men to the birth of Jesus.

The question of "when" was answered nearly a millennium and a half later, when Jesus was born. Matthew 2:2 tells us of wise men from the East who traveled to Judea in search of the child who had been born King of the Jews. These men, magi from the old Persian Empire, were scholars versed not only in religious writings but also in astronomy and other sciences. When they arrived in Jerusalem, they explained their coming by saying, "We have seen His star in the East and have come to worship Him."

The star representing Israel's Ruler-to-be had appeared in the heavens. The time for the promised Ruler of Israel to appear had come at last!

THE NAMES AND TITLES
OF GOD
IN THE NEW TESTAMENT

The Old Testament revelation of God unfolded slowly and gradually over millennia. Traditions about the Creation, the Fall, and the Flood had been woven into the human consciousness from the beginning. Yet the stories were gradually confused and corrupted, especially as human beings sought to distance themselves from a God whom they feared and did not understand.

Then, around 2100 B.C. in Mesopotamia, God spoke to a man named Abram and gave him a series of wonderful promises. These promises, stated in what we know as the Abrahamic covenant, set out the course of history and expressed what God intended to do to provide redemption for humankind. In those earliest of times, God was known to the Hebrews simply as *Elohim*, the Most High God, and His distinguishing characteristics were that He was the Creator of all and that He was the God of Abraham.

The next great revelatory moment occurred over half a millennium later, around 1450 B.C., when the Lord appeared to Moses and commissioned him to free Abraham's descendants, the Israelites, from slavery in Egypt. At that time God revealed to Moses His personal name, *Yahweh*, the LORD. As Moses confronted Pharaoh and called down miraculous judgments on Egypt, another defining characteristic of God was unveiled. The Lord was made known not only as Creator but also as Redeemer. God was One who could and would use His power to intervene in time and space on behalf of His covenant people.

Throughout the Old Testament, God's creation name, *Elohim*, and His redemptive and revelatory name, *Yahweh*, are primary. But as the centuries passed, the seers and prophets God sent to Israel, and those who recorded the history of God's people, added to our understanding of God by sharing fresh names, titles, and images of God. This rich heritage of the Old Testament's revelation of God is foundational to our reading of the New Testament. No Old Testament name, title, or image of God is discarded. They remain the same, and what they reveal about God's nature, character, and purpose is as valid today as it was in the Old Testament era.

Nevertheless, there is something striking about the New Testament's vision. First, while the Old Testament revelation took place over millennia, the New Testament revelation was completed within some six *decades*, that is, from the A.D. 40s until the end of the first century. In the Old Testament, as in lighting candles one at a time over a period of days and weeks, the light gradually becomes brighter and brighter. In contrast, the New Testament is like the appearance of the sun after an eclipse. What had been hidden in shadow was suddenly illuminated in a light almost unbearably bright.

Second, while Old Testament names, titles, and images of God do reveal Him *accurately*, the New Testament reveals God *fully*. While the Old Testament revelation of God is in harmony with the fact that He exists as one God in three Persons, only the New Testament defines these Persons as Father, Son, and Holy Spirit. While Old Testament names and titles foreshadow the work of each Person of the Godhead, only the New Testament defines those works.

In the Old Testament, God is revealed as the Shepherd, yet only in Christ do we see what it means for God to come to us as the Good Shepherd who gives His life for the sheep. While the Old Testament reveals God as a Father in a limited sense, the New Testament reveals the first Person of the Trinity as *our* Father, who calls us to an intimate personal relationship with Him as spiritual children in His heavenly family.

As we come to the New Testament, then, we build on everything taught about God in the Old Testament. And we also add names, titles, and images of the Father, Son, and Holy Spirit that reveal each Person of the Trinity with a clarity and sharpness simply not possible in the older revelation. In the New Testament, the sun breaks out from behind clouds, and in what seems like a moment in time, God presents Himself to

our eyes as being wonderful, exalted, and awesome in His glory and grace!

NAMES AND TITLES OF GOD THE FATHER

God the Father is usually identified as the first Person of the Trinity. In the New Testament, "Father" is frequently used in tandem with "Son" to distinguish the first and second Persons of the Trinity. While there is some sense in which Jesus could say, "My Father is greater than I" (John 14:28), Christ also affirmed that the Father and Son were at the same time one in nature and essence (10:30). While the Trinity remains a mystery that we are unable to fathom, it is also a reality clearly taught in the New Testament. It is this truth that leads us to consider separately the names and titles of each Person of the Godhead.

THE NAMES AND TITLES OF GOD THE FATHER IN THE GOSPELS

When we read the Gospels, one of the first things we note is the absence of Old Testament names and titles of God. Zechariah refers to Him as "the Lord God of Israel" (Luke 1:68), and a wondering crowd responded to Jesus' miracles by praising "the God of Israel" (Matt. 15:31). But these are the only Gospel references to the "God of Israel."

Similarly there are only two references to "the God of Abraham, the God of Isaac, and the God of Jacob" (Mark 12:26; Luke 20:37), and both of these are in quotes of Exodus 3:15. There are seven references to "the Lord your God" in the Gospels, and each of these too is found in an Old Testament passage quoted by Jesus (Matt. 4:7,10; 22:37; Mark 12:30; Luke 4:8, 12; 10:27). The only other familiar Old Testament title of God in the Gospels is a reference to Him as "the Highest." This is found in words the angel Gabriel spoke to Mary when announcing God's choice of her as the mother of the Messiah (Luke 1:35).

Other than these few references, God the Father is referred to in the Gospels simply as "God" or as "Father."

GOD

There are some 293 references to God in 260 verses in the Gospels. The Greek word used in these references is *theos*. This was the common Greek term for deity. But the Greeks believed in many gods and goddesses, who were like human beings in that they had both base and honorable motives. The *New International Encyclopedia of Bible Words* says the following about these deities:

> They were limited in their powers. Typically, the Greek gods were not concerned with mortals, though they might be influenced to help them at times.
>
> In later Greek philosophy, the gods and goddesses of mythology were discounted, and the deity was thought of more as an abstract principle or force. The biblical concept of God, as defined by the OT, was foreign to Greek thought.
>
> Thus when *theos* was used in the Septuagint and NT, it was purified and transformed. The vague notions of the Greeks were cleansed, and the clear images of the OT were imported. The God of the NT is the God of the OT (p. 314).

The age of the Gospels remained essentially a part of the Old Testament era. It was not until the death of Christ instituted the new covenant that the New Testament age began. Thus, as the author above points out, the "God" of the Gospels is not the *theos* of the Greeks but rather the *Elohim-Yahweh* of the Old Testament. Whenever speakers in the Gospel use the term "God," the God they refer to is the Creator and Redeemer whose nature and character are unveiled in the Old Testament Scriptures.

Gabriel identified God as "the Highest" when informing Mary that she had been chosen to become the mother of the Messiah.

FATHER

While the term "God" is stabilized in the Gospels by the Old Testament revelation, a stunning transformation of another Old Testament title of God takes place. In the Gospels, God is referred to as "Father" almost exclusively by Jesus, some 137 times in John, 64 times in Matthew, 56 times in Luke, and 18 times in Mark. In speaking about God as "Father," Jesus transformed the title into a name—a name that becomes the primary and defining one for God, the first Person of the Trinity.

God as the Father of Jesus. Leon Morris, in his *New Testament Theology*, has an extensive discussion of the relationship between the Father and Jesus. His summary is well worth noting.

Jesus emphasized an "in secret" relationship between believers and God as "your heavenly Father."

John's association of the Father and the Son begins in the prologue. There we find that the *Logos* was in the beginning, was with God, and was God (1:1, cf. V.18). At the end of the Gospel, Thomas says to Jesus, "My Lord and my God" (20:28). Jesus was accused of making himself equal with God (5:18) and of making himself God (10:33). He is uniquely from the Father (1:14; cf. 16:27-28), he is "in the bosom of the Father," and he had revealed the Father (1:18). The word "bosom" denotes intimacy and affection, and here it indicates that he comes to us from the very heart of God. It is because of this close relationship that he can reveal God to us in the way he does. He gives us genuine and intimate knowledge of the Father because of his relationship with the Father. He "came out from God" (8:42).

Jesus has a special relationship to God, for it is only he who has seen the Father (6:46). The Jews recognized that he regarded God as his Father in a special sense; they saw this as blasphemy and tried to kill him for it (15:18), and they asked Jesus where his Father was (8:19). When Jesus said, I am ascending to "my Father and your Father and to my God and your God," he indicated that there is a difference between his relationship to the Father and ours.

It is a persistent strand of Johannine teaching that the Father and the Son are in some sense one (10:30). This must be understood carefully, for there is also a sense in which Jesus could say, "The Father is greater than I" (14:28). This is probably to be understood in terms of the Incarnation, which means a voluntary acceptance of certain limitations. But that the two are very close is clear throughout this Gospel. Jesus came "in the name" of his Father (5:43). He repeatedly ascribed his teaching to the Father (8:38, 40; 12:49-50; 14:24) and spoke of receiving commands from him (10:18; 14:31; 15:10). The deeds he did were "the works the Father" had given him to do (5:36; cf. 10:32, 37); they were done "in the name" of the Father (10:25); indeed it was the Father dwelling in Christ who did the works (14:10). "Of God" characterizes his relationships: he is "the Son of God" (1:34 and many other references), "the Lamb of God" (1:29, 36), "the bread of God" (6:33), "the holy one of God" (6:33).

To know the Son is to know the Father (8:19; 14:7; 16:3); neither the Father nor the Son it seems can be known apart from the other. God is with Jesus, who is "a teacher come from God" (3:2). To see the Son is to see the Father (14:9). There were people who had seen and hated both the Son and the Father (15:23-24). So it is that Christ knows the Father, and the Father knows the Son (10:15), the Father is in him and he is in the Father (10:38). All that the Father has is the Son's (16:15), and vice versa (17:10). Each is "in" the other (17:21), and the two are a unity (17:11, 22). Small wonder that Christ says, "No one comes to the Father except through me" (14:6) (pp. 248-49).

As Morris so thoroughly summarizes, many references to God as Father in the Gospels, and especially in John, depict the special relationship between God the Father and Jesus. God is the Father of Jesus and Jesus is the Son of God in a unique sense. While our relationship with God as our Father may be likened to a relationship between a father and son, the relationship between God the Father and Jesus is significantly different.

Nevertheless, as we read the Gospels, we note that in naming God as "Father," something special is also said about the relationship of believers with God.

God as our Father. When the disciples asked Jesus to teach them to pray (Luke 11:1), the first words He taught them to utter were "Our Father" (v. 2). These two words indicate a stunning transformation from the "Father as originator" of the Old Testament to the "our Father" of intimate personal relationship of the Gospels and New Testament Epistles. Perhaps the best way to grasp the significance of the fact that God is by nature "Father" and that He has chosen in Christ to become "our Father," is to look at especially relevant passages in the Gospels.

Your Father in heaven (Matt. 6:1-8). In the Sermon on the Mount, Jesus spoke of God as "your Father" in heaven. While religious hypocrites did charitable deeds, prayed, and fasted publicly to establish a reputation for piety, God's true children were to nurture an "in secret" relationship with Him. Yes, they were to do charitable deeds, pray, and fast. But they were to avoid ostentatious public displays, confident that their heavenly Father knew all that they did to honor Him and that He would reward them eternally.

Our Father (Matt. 6:9-13). On that occasion Jesus told His followers to address their prayers to God as "our Father." In the first century, as in later Judaism, those who addressed prayers to God were careful to display respect. Typical rabbinic prayers (quoted by Jacob Neusner in *The Classics of Judaism*) begin as follows:

> Blessed are you, our God, King of the world (p. 438).

> Praised are you, Lord our God and God of our fathers, God of Abraham, God of Isaac, God of Jacob, great, mighty, revered God, exalted, who bestows loving kindness and is Master of all things (p. 424).

While these prayers are truly pious and reflect a view of God deeply rooted in the Old Testament, their tone is very different from the intimacy and simplicity expressed in the words Jesus taught us to utter when we pray. Although what we know as the Lord's Prayer goes on to acknowledge God's mastery of all things and His sovereignty in our lives, those first words, "Our Father" (Matt. 6:9) place this prayer in a relational context that is radically new.

BIBLE BACKGROUND:

THE LORD'S PRAYER
MATTHEW 6:9-13

The Prayer	The Kingdom Attitude
Our Father . . .	Affirms a personal relationship with God
In heaven . . .	Recognizes God as Lord over all
Hallowed be Your name	Honors God as living, powerful, and real
Your kingdom come . . .	Accepts God's right to rule in our lives
Your will be done on earth as it is in heaven . . .	Submits completely to God's will now as a guide to life on earth
Give us this day our daily bread . . .	Recognizes God's involvement in our daily experiences and His supply of our needs

Forgive us our debts as we also have forgiven*	Expresses readiness to live as a forgiven and forgiving people
Lead us not into temptation, but deliver us from evil*	Asks protection from the trials always associated with establishing God's kingdom on earth.

Illustrated Bible Handbook, p. 474

Your heavenly Father knows (Matt. 6:25-34; Luke 12:22-34). Jesus told His disciples, "Do not worry about your life, what you will eat or what you will drink." The fact that God is a Father to Jesus' own followers should free them from anxiety about getting their basic needs met. Instead, they can "seek first the kingdom of God and His righteousness." Certainly the God who feeds the birds and clothes the lilies will care for those who are His spiritual children.

Your Father gives good things (Matt. 7:7-11). Jesus encouraged His disciples to pray by pointing out that even evil people tend to give good gifts to their children. "How much more," Jesus said, "will your Father who is in heaven give good things to those who ask Him!"

If God were your Father (John 8:37-47). When the religious leaders angrily confronted Jesus over His claim that God was His Father, they asserted that their own relationship with God was based on the fact that they were physical descendants of Abraham. Thus, God was their Father in the Old Testament sense of Originator or Founder of a line. Jesus, however, dismissed this claim as invalid. If the religious leaders truly were the *spiritual* descendants of Abraham, they would have loved Jesus, for He came from the Father whom Abraham had known and trusted. The religious leaders' hostility toward Jesus proved that their spiritual heritage was traced back to Satan, "for he is a liar and the father of it."

Jesus taught that only human beings who trust in Him have a relationship with God as their heavenly Father. And only they can count on the eternal benefits of that relationship, as explained by Jesus in the Sermon on the Mount.

Jesus' presentation of God as "our Father" (Matt. 6:9) establishes two stunning truths. First, in His essential nature, God is a Father, with all of a father's love for his family. As a good Father, God watches over His own, responding to their prayers, meeting their needs, and always giving them good gifts.

Second, not all human beings have a Father-child relationship with God. Only those who trust in Jesus, the Son of God and God the Son, have the intimate personal relationship with the Creator that is implicit in His name, "Father."

Reflections of the Gospels' teaching in the Epistles. Just as the Old Testament names, titles, and images filled the term "God" with meaning, so the teaching of Jesus about God as Father carry over into the New Testament Epistles. What Jesus taught about God as His Father, as the Father, and as our Father, are all reflected in the Epistles.

Five times in the Epistles the phrase "the God and Father of our Lord Jesus Christ" is found (Rom. 15:6; 2 Cor. 1:3; 11:31; Eph. 1:3; 1 Pet. 1:3). This continues the identification of God as Jesus' Father. Three times "God the Father and the Lord Jesus Christ" are linked, twice as the source of grace and peace (Eph. 6:23; 1 Thess. 1:1; 2 Thess. 1:2), thus emphasizing the unity of Jesus with the Father. Ten times God is spoken of as "God our Father," emphasizing the relationship that exists between God as Father and believers in Jesus (Rom. 1:7; 1 Cor. 1:3; 2 Cor. 1:2; Gal. 1:3; Eph. 1:2; Phil. 1:2; Col. 1:2; 2 Thess. 1:1; 2:16; Philem. 1:3).

We will examine several of these verses when we look at the Epistles' revelation of the roles of God the Father. It is clear for now, however, that Jesus' focus on God as Father—not only His Father but also as the

Father and as our Father—provided a fresh way to look at God, and that that fresh revelation has shaped the Christian faith.

THE NAMES AND TITLES OF GOD THE FATHER IN THE ACTS OF THE APOSTLES

A few of the Old Testament's names and titles of God are found in the Book of Acts. As in the Gospels, the Old Testament names and titles are most frequently found in quotations or when an evangelist is addressing a Jewish audience. God is the "Lord of heaven and earth" (17:24) and the "Lord of all" (10:36). He is the "God of Abraham, Isaac, and Jacob" (3:13; 7:32), and the "God of our fathers" (3:13; 5:30; 22:14; 24:14). He is also the "God of glory" (7:2).

However, Luke (who wrote Acts) most often prefers to simply use the term "God." This occurs 163 times in 154 verses. And, as the term *theos* is infused in the Gospels with meaning drawn from the Old Testament, so in Acts *theos* is infused with that same meaning plus all that has been revealed about God by Jesus when He was here on earth. Strikingly, the term "Father" is used of God only four times in Acts, with two of the uses by Jesus Himself (Acts 1:4, 7).

By far the most common name given God the Father in Acts is "Lord." Of the 103 uses of the term, at least 37 are specific references to the Lord Jesus, and two are references to the Holy Spirit as "the Spirit of the Lord" (5:9; 8:39). The rest of the references seem to be to God the Father. As Lord, the Father adds to the church those who are being saved (2:47), and He raised up Jesus as a Prophet (3:22). As sovereign Lord, the Father "made heaven and earth and the sea, and all that is in them" (4:24). As Lord, the Father forgives (8:22), sends angels to rescue the saints (12:7) and to punish the wicked (v. 23), and opens hearts to receive the gospel (16:14). In fact the gospel is itself the "word of the Lord Jesus" (19:10).

In Acts references to "God" are infused with the rich meaning of all the names and titles of God found in the Old Testament.

God the Father then is seen in Acts to be actively involved, with the Holy Spirit, in creating and shaping Jesus' church. The Father also answers the prayers of Jesus' people, and guides and protects those charged with proclaiming the gospel to the world.

THE WORKS OF GOD THE FATHER IN THE EPISTLES

The number of names and titles ascribed to God the Father in the New Testament rivals those found in the Old Testament. Before we look at them, however, it is helpful to review works specifically ascribed in the Epistles to God as Father.

AN OVERVIEW

God the Father is, with Jesus, the source of grace and peace for believers (Rom. 1:7; 1 Cor. 1:3). Christ was raised from the dead through the Father (Rom. 6:4). He is the source not only of all things but also of our life in Christ (1 Cor. 8:6). When the end comes, Christ will hand over the kingdom to the Father (1 Cor. 15:24).

The Father is compassionate and "the God of all comfort" (2 Cor. 1:3). The Father, with Jesus, chose Paul to be an apostle (Gal. 1:1). Christ died for our sins to rescue us "according to the will of our God and Father" (Gal. 1:4). The Father has provided us with every spiritual blessing in Christ (Eph. 1:3). As a glorious Father, God answers intercessory prayers (v. 17). The Father is over and through all (4:6).

The Father has "qualified us to be partakers of the inheritance of the saints" and has "delivered us from the power of darkness, and conveyed us into the kingdom of the Son of His love" (Col. 1:12, 13). The Father has loved us and given us "everlasting consolation and good hope" (2 Thess. 2:16). The Father has given us new birth into a living hope through Christ's resurrection (1 Pet. 1:3). The Father also judges each person's work impartially (v. 17).

Today believers who walk in the light have fellowship with the Father and with Jesus (1 John 1:3). And the Father has lavished His love on us, calling us "children of God" (3:1).

EPHESIANS 1

In Ephesians 1, the apostle Paul distinguishes the role of each Person of the Godhead in providing salvation. Briefly, it was the role of the Son to redeem lost humankind by dying for them (vv. 7-12), and it was the role of the Holy Spirit to take up residence in believers as the guarantee of their ultimate salvation (vv. 13, 14). Verses 3-6 summarize the role of God the Father:

> Blessed be the God and Father of our
> Lord Jesus Christ, who has blessed us
> with every spiritual blessing in the heav-

enly places in Christ, just as He chose us in Him before the foundation of the world, that we should be holy and without blame before Him in love, having predestined us to adoption as sons by Jesus Christ to Himself, according to the good pleasure of His will.

Regardless of whatever position one may take on the nature of predestination, it is clear that the Father is the One who planned, determined, chose, and willed the salvation of all believers. He is the One who designed the plan of salvation, while the Son and the Spirit executed the Father's plan.

It is clear from the brief survey in Ephesians 1 that God the Father is presented in the New Testament as a Person distinct from the Son and the Holy Spirit, with His own specific role to play in our salvation. It is also clear that in all things God truly is a Father to us, for He loves and cares for us as members of His own family.

PREDESTINATION AND ELECTION

The issue of predestination and election is raised in Ephesians 1. Because the doctrine is so easily twisted and because it is central to our understanding of the role of God the Father, I want to focus on it indepth here.

Probably no other doctrine has caused more dispute between Christians or more concern in individual hearts. Does God sovereignly choose individual Christians for salvation? Is the rest of humankind utterly without hope? If individuals are so chosen, how can we know if we are among the select company?

On the one hand, those who believe in absolute predestination insist that only this doctrine guards the freedom and sovereignty of God and makes salvation something that is truly of grace. On the other hand, those who deny absolute predestination insist that the doctrine robs human beings of freedom, casts God in the role of an unjust monster, and makes the gospel offer of salvation for "whosoever will" a mockery.

The doctrine of predestination is closely linked with other beliefs that characterize differing theological systems. Because the links are so complex, it is impossible in a brief overview to offer a harmonizing position. So in this article, I want to sketch the linked beliefs of two representative Christian understandings of what the Bible teaches, and then I will explore the Bible's use of the words "predestine" and "election."

Predestination and election in Calvinism. Calvinism is a major Protestant theological tradition, represented by Reformed and Presbyterian churches. Calvinism emphasizes both the sovereignty of God and human ruin by sin. A Christian understanding of God must begin with the recognition that He truly is God, in total control of all events in the universe. God has planned the whole from before Creation itself, and His power guarantees that His every purpose will be realized. In it all, God made His choices freely, moved only by His love and His grace and not at all affected by the choices that He foresaw human beings would make.

The fact that salvation rests completely on God's action in carrying out His purpose is demonstrated by the Bible's teaching on sin. Adam's fall ruined the race, making it impossible for any human being to choose to obey or respond to God. Human choices are made freely, but sin has so warped human beings that the free choices of unsaved persons will never be in true harmony with God's will.

Thus, both the sovereignty of God and the depravity of humanity make it clear that an active work of God, changing people within so that they will choose to believe and thus be saved, is utterly necessary. Predestination is the simple confession that personal salvation is a result of God's purpose and His actions in us.

It is important to note that while God chooses those destined for salvation and acts to move them by irresistible grace, He does not predestine the unsaved in the same sense. That is, God does not actively choose those who will be lost for damnation, nor does God act to move them to unbelief. His activity is focused on salvation. It is only human sinfulness and unwillingness to respond to God that result in condemnation.

Predestination and election in Wesleyanism. Wesleyanism, represented by Methodist and Wesleyan Methodist churches, reflects an Arminian position. God is sovereign, and His purposes will be worked out in our universe. While God knew from eternity the people who would be saved, He did not predestine them in the active, irresistible, Calvinistic sense. Instead, God provided humanity with sufficient grace that, despite the impact of sin, any person may choose to respond to the gospel.

It follows that sin has not had as drastic an impact on human beings as is supposed by Calvinists. Although the person's free will must be exercised in cooperation with God's grace, the choice of the individual neither initiates nor merits salvation. Salvation is still completely of grace. God has been able to structure all things in the universe according to His plan, not because He acts to make some believe, but because He knew from the beginning who would choose to believe.

Predestination in Scripture. The Greek word for "predestine" occurs only six times in the New Testament (Acts 4:28; Rom. 8:28-30; 1 Cor. 2:7; Eph. 1:5, 11). It means to "mark out ahead of time" or "to predetermine." In each biblical reference just what God has predetermined is carefully identified. In Acts 4:28, it is the events culminating in Jesus' Crucifixion, which unfolded as God's "power and will had decided beforehand that should happen." In Romans 8:29, those who love God are "predestined to be conformed to the likeness of His Son."

The 2 Corinthians 2 passage looks at God's plan of redemption, calling it "destined for our glory before time began." And Ephesians 1:5 focuses again on believers, affirming that in love God "predestined us to be adopted as His sons through Jesus Christ, in accordance with His pleasure and will." Verse 11 of the same chapter adds that "in Him we were chosen, having been predestined according to the plan of Him who works out everything in conformity to His will."

Calvinists see these verses as proof of their position. Wesleyans, however, note that none of the passages says anything about the role of the human will in believing. Instead, it is those who do believe who are predestined, not to salvation, but to adoption as heirs and to conformity to Jesus' likeness. While "predestine" appears only a half dozen times, other words that are translated "appointed," "determined," or "destined" affirm God's final control over all things.

Election in Scripture. Both the Old and New Testaments frequently portray God making choices. Terms from the Greek word group meaning "to choose" are used to express the idea of election. The word "election" is used in the Bible and theology to affirm God's sovereign choice of places and especially of persons.

The Old Testament shows God making a number of significant choices. For instance, God chose Jerusalem, where His temple would be erected. More importantly, God chose Israel from all the peoples of the world (see, for example, Deut. 7:6; Ps. 33:12; Is. 14:1; 45:4). God also chose individuals. He chose Abraham (Gen. 18:19; Neh. 9:7), Moses (Ps. 106:23), and David (1 Kin. 8:16; 1 Chr. 28:4).

In each case, these choices were free, motivated only by God's own love and purpose. We see it clearly in Deuteronomy 7:7 and 8: "The Lord did not set His affection on you and choose you because you were more numerous than other peoples, for you were the fewest of all peoples. But it was because

the Lord loved you and kept the oath He swore to your forefathers."

The apostle Paul picks up this theme in Romans 9 and argues against those who try to find a reason for God's choice in some supposed human merit or inherited right. God chose Isaac but rejected Ishmael. Jacob and Esau were twins, yet before their birth, before either "had done anything good or bad—in order that God's purpose in election might stand; not by works but by Him who calls," their mother was informed that God had chosen the younger to receive the covenant promises (vv. 6-13).

Paul's point is that "it does not depend on man's desire or effort, but on God's mercy" (v. 16). All rests on grace, and grace, flowing solely from the character and the love of God, is expressed in God's free and sovereign choice.

When the references that deal with God's choices are traced through the Old Testament, it is clear that in eternity past the Lord determined to provide the salvation that His church now enjoys. But Christians still disagree as to whether these passages indicate that He has chosen some for salvation and neglected to choose others. It is clear, however, that in most New Testament contexts, God's choices are linked with the believing community rather than individual Christians.

How do we explain these different points of view about election and predestination? It seems that each camp has chosen to emphasize different strands of biblical teaching. The Calvinist emphasizes the sovereignty of God and the sinfulness of human beings. The Wesleyan emphasizes the gospel offer of salvation to all who believe, and the love of God for lost human beings. Wesleyans do not believe that sin has had the totally destructive impact on the human will that the Calvinists do. Neither group denies God's sovereignty. Neither denies that human beings are sinful and lost. Neither denies the transforming power of the gospel. But the differences in emphasis have led to the disagreement about predestination and election sketched above.

So which position is right? In the New Testament two logically contradictory truths are both taught. First, everything related to salvation is ascribed to God's free and sovereign choice. Salvation isn't a joint enterprise, part from God and part from human beings. Second, human beings are responsible persons, invited and called to make a real decision about the gospel.

While these two truths may seem logically contradictory, there is no biblical contradiction. God chooses and human beings are invited to choose. Many are convinced that God's choice overrides every other consideration, that only predestination can adequately express that reality. Others are convinced that a person's choice is free, yet made without violating the ultimate freedom of God to accomplish every purpose and plan of His own.

The personal impact of predestination.
Predestination is a doctrine that has troubled many people since its first clear articulation. Some are upset because they feel that predestination implies unfairness on God's part. Others have been deeply troubled, fearing that they are not among the elect. Every momentary uncertainty convinces them that they do not really believe or that their belief is something less than saving faith. Probably as long as a person's focus is on the doctrine of predestination rather than on Christ, he or she is bound to be troubled.

Martin Luther points a way out: "When a man begins to discuss predestination, the temptation is like an inextinguishable fire; the more he disputes, the more he despairs. Our Lord God is opposed to this disputation and accordingly has provided against it baptism, the Word, the sacraments, and various signs. In these we should trust and say: 'I am baptized; I believe in Jesus Christ; what does it concern me, whether or not I am predestined?' He has given us ground to stand on, that is, Jesus Christ, and through Him we

may climb to heaven. He is the one way and the gate to the Father."

How wise Luther was. Salvation does not hinge on belief in or rejection of predestination. It is Jesus that God sets before us, promising all who believe in Him forgiveness of sins. We may discover when we meet the Lord in glory that our salvation was predestined in the fullest sense of that word. Or we may discover that our response to the gospel was simply foreknown. But what will count then—and what counts now—is that our faith is placed in Jesus and in Jesus alone. Whether or not our faith was predestined, our faith has saved us.

Without dismissing the doctrine or the important issue with which it deals, Christians may still say with Luther, "I believe in Jesus Christ; what does it concern me, whether or not I am predestined?" I believe. Jesus is mine, and I am His—forever.

THE NAMES AND TITLES OF GOD THE FATHER IN THE EPISTLES

ABBA

Of all the names of God, *Abba* most powerfully expresses the intimacy of the believer's new relationship with the Father. In Romans 8:15 the apostle Paul wrote, "You did not receive the spirit of bondage again to fear, but you received the Spirit of adoption by which we cry out, 'Abba, Father.'" And in Galatians 4:5, Paul similarly writes about adoption as sons, teaching that "because you are sons, God has sent forth the Spirit of His Son into your hearts, crying out, 'Abba, Father!'"

In each context the name "Abba" is associated with our adoption by God. It is important to understand just what "adoption" involved in the first-century Roman world. The roots of Paul's references to adoption lie in the Roman rather than Greek or Jewish

Believers are invited to come to God, the Creator and Ruler of the Universe, and to address Him as "Daddy."

❖

world. In the Roman legal system, a father's authority over his family was a fundamental reality. As a legal act, "adoption" transferred an individual from the authority of his old *pater familias* to the authority of the one adopting him. *The New International Encyclopedia of Bible Words* explains:

> In adoption an individual's old relationships were severed. Old debts and obligations were canceled. The person was placed under the authority of the father of his new family. The father was considered owner of all the adoptee's possessions and was believed to have the right to control the adoptee's behavior. The father also had the right of discipline and became liable for the new son or daughter's actions. Each was committed by the act of adoption to support and to help maintain the other.

What does this mean for us who have been adopted by God? It means that we owe no allegiance to our old masters (cf. Gal. 3:26—4:7). We now owe total allegiance to God the Father, and all that we have is his. On his part, God commits himself to guide us and to discipline us, that we might bring credit to his household.

For his part God has given us the Holy Spirit to guarantee our release from all that once enslaved us (Gal. 4:6-7). The Spirit's presence assures us that at the resurrection we will experience fully every benefit belonging to God's heirs (Rom. 8:23) (p. 21).

With the legal relationship described above comes the most intimate of personal relationships, expressed in the name "Abba." "Abba," which was one of the first words uttered by a Jewish or Arab child, simply means "Daddy."

CREATOR

A foundational concept from the Old Testament is that God is the Creator of all that exists. Three New Testament references specifically refer to God the Father as Creator.

In Romans 1, Paul writes about humankind's response to God. In this context "God" is used as in the Old Testament, without distinguishing the Persons of the Godhead. In general, when "God" is used in this way in the New Testament it's best to assume reference to the Father as representative of all three Persons of the Godhead.

In Romans 1, Paul argues that what may be known about God through the witness of the creation is evident to all, not only because it is logical to assume that a system so complex and balanced had to be created, but also because God implanted in human beings intuitive knowledge about Him that is triggered by the creation (vv. 19, 21). The proof that human beings truly are sinners and separated from God is that despite knowing God, people have "exchanged the truth of God for the lie, and worshiped and served the creature rather than the Creator, who is blessed forever" (v. 25).

In Colossians 3:10, Paul writes that the believer has been raised in Christ to a new life, and is in fact a new person "who is renewed in knowledge according to the image of Him who created him." Here God the Father is distinguished from Christ, and the Father is described as the Author of that new creation, which is the transformation of the believer by a special work of God in conversion.

The last reference to God as Creator, where again the Father is clearly intended, is in 1 Peter 4:19. Peter has written about the suffering that Christians may experience as they follow the Lord. The apostle concludes his words of encouragement by writing "therefore let those who suffer according to the will of God commit their souls to Him in doing good, as to a faithful Creator."

In recognizing God as Creator, then, the appropriate response for the unconverted would be to acknowledge and worship Him. For believers the appropriate response is to acknowledge Him as the source of our new life and to reflect His character in our words and deeds. Also, when we as believers undergo trials, we are to simply trust ourselves to God as a faithful Creator, relying completely on His wisdom, knowledge, love, and power.

FATHER OF GLORY
FATHER OF MERCIES
FATHER OF LIGHTS
FATHER OF SPIRITS

In discussing the Old Testament name of Christ as "Father of eternity" (p. 101), we noted that in Hebrew and Arabic to call someone the "father of" something is the same as to attribute that quality to him. Thus, the phrase "Everlasting Father" (Is. 9:6) would identify Christ as eternal. Likewise, to call God the "Father of mercies"

(2 Cor. 1:3) would be to identify God as merciful.

The Father of glory. In following this Old Testament convention, to call God the "Father of glory" would be the same as calling Him the glorious One. This is certainly the sense of Ephesians 1:17, which speaks of "the God of our Lord Jesus Christ" as "the Father of glory." He is the glorious Father, for His gift of knowledge to His saints (namely, that we might know the hope of His calling and the riches of His inheritance in the saints) surely brings glory to Him.

The Father of mercies. The NKJV plural rendering "Father of mercies" in 2 Corinthians 1:3 (see the NASB) could also be translated "Father of compassion" (as in the NIV) to emphasize the compassionate nature of God. In His compassion for His own, God comforts believers in trouble so that we in turn might share His comfort with others who are in similar straits. In fact God in His compassion may allow us to experience troubles and difficulties in order to equip us to comfort others.

The Father of lights. In the New Testament where God is identified as the "Father of X" and "X" is in the plural rather than the singular form, different linguistic conventions control.

Consider the phrase "Father of lights" in James 1:17. James is writing about temptations, and also about our tendency to blame God when we find ourselves in a situation where we are tempted. James points out that what we experience as temptations (namely, that pull toward wrong or sinful choices or the weakness that makes us give in) has its roots in our sinful nature and not in God or in the situation. James writes that God "cannot be tempted by evil, nor does He Himself tempt anyone" (v. 13).

Nevertheless, God is in control of the situations in which we find ourselves. How then do we explain God's involvement in

In calling God the "Father of lights" James emphasizes the fact that His actions are as consistent as the behavior of the stars in the heavens.

what we experience as temptations? James' answer is that "every good and perfect gift is from above, and comes down from the Father of lights, with whom there is no variation or shadow of turning" (v. 17). What does James mean?

Most likely the "lights" referred to here are the stars, known for their regularity and consistent movement. Ancient astronomers used the term "moving shadows" to describe what they saw as the irregular movement of some of the planets. What James is saying in calling God the "Father of lights" is that He is totally consistent in all that He does. When it comes to His relationship with us, He is consistent in shaping every situation and every experience as a good and a perfect gift.

Temptations, then, are not divine tricks intended to trip us up. Any "temptation" associated with situations is rooted within us, not the situation. In putting us in a difficult or painful situation, God intends our good. While we may see situations as a source of temptation, in reality our every situation is an opportunity to respond in faith with a commitment to do what is right. In this way every situation, however difficult, is an opportunity for growth and the maturing of our Christian life. Indeed, this is a divine gift!

Father of spirits. This title of God occurs in Hebrews 12:9. The author is writing about discipline. He points out that children who are disciplined by their human fathers show respect and learn from the discipline. The author writes, "Shall we not much more readily be in subjection to the Father of spirits and live?" (Other versions—such as the NIV and the NASB margin—render the passage "the Father of our spirits.")

The writer's point is well taken. Our human fathers were concerned with our life on earth, and they disciplined us as they saw fit to enable us to be productive and successful in the here and now. But God is the Father of our spirits. His concern is that we might be productive and successful in our relationship with Him both now and for eternity. Not only is God deeply concerned for us as a Father, but also He has a perspective that differs radically from that of our human fathers.

In saying that we had respect for our human fathers, the writer of Hebrews is alluding to the fact that children don't always understand the purpose that parents have for disciplining them. A child's perspective is limited to his or her present, while a parent is concerned with the child's future. Children simply have to accept the fact that "father (or mother) knows best," and they show respect by accepting the discipline, even though they do not fully understand its purpose.

Similarly, we often find ourselves in painful circumstances whose purpose we may not grasp. As God's children, we are to show respect for Him by believing that He has a good purpose in what is happening. Also, we should show respect by continuing to trust and obey Him daily. As the Father of our spirits, God knows what is best for us. Every situation in which He places us truly is a good gift, regardless of whether we see the good in it.

GOD OF ALL GRACE

The title "God of all grace" occurs only in 1 Peter 5:10. "Grace" is one of those terms given unique meaning in Scripture. In the first century, the Greek word used in the New Testament, *charis*, simply meant to show kindness or favor. It was also used in expressions conveying gratitude for a favor. In the New Testament Epistles, the word's rather mild approval of a pleasing human quality became a technical theological term to communicate the deep realities that lay at

the heart of what God has done for us in Christ.

Ephesians 2:1-10 most clearly summarizes the basic realities expressed in the biblical concept of grace:

> And you He made alive, who were dead in trespasses and sins, in which you once walked according to the course of this world, according to the prince of the power of the air, the spirit who now works in the sons of disobedience, among whom also we all once conducted ourselves in the lusts of our flesh, fulfilling the desires of the flesh and of the mind, and were by nature children of wrath, just as the others.
>
> But God, who is rich in mercy, because of His great love with which He loved us, even when we were dead in trespasses, made us alive together with Christ (by grace you have been saved), and raised us up together, and made us sit together in the heavenly places in Christ Jesus, that in the ages to come He might show the exceeding riches of His grace in His kindness toward us in Christ Jesus. For by grace you have been saved through faith, and that not of yourselves; it is the gift of God, not of works, lest anyone should boast. For we are His workmanship, created in Christ Jesus for good works, which God prepared beforehand that we should walk in them.

In this passage Paul portrays human beings as utterly lost, spiritually dead, and under divine wrath. In this deplorable condition, human thoughts and actions express the sin that has corrupted our very nature so that we are utterly without hope. But God loves us despite our sinfulness, and God acted in Christ to make us spiritually alive. God not only gave us new spiritual life, but also He lifted us up in Christ, raising us from the depths of condemnation to heaven itself. Throughout eternity what God has done for us in Jesus will display the riches of His grace so that the entire universe might stand in awe.

As the God of all grace our Lord reaches out to us in our helplessness.

In view of this and other defining passages (such as Romans 4, 5:15-21, and 11:1-6), we can say that "grace" is God's free action. It is based on Jesus' death and resurrection and motivated by love. God's grace is intended to redeem believing sinners and to impute His righteousness to them.

BIBLE BACKGROUND:

GRACE

Grace is a vital biblical term, one that makes a basic statement about how God relates to human beings. To appreciate the message of the Bible, we must understand grace more accurately.

The concept of grace is given full expression in the New Testament. There is no exact parallel for it in the Old Testament. Nevertheless, one Hebrew term, *hesed*, comes close. It speaks of favor and of being merciful and gracious. Psalm 51:1 clearly pictures the force of this beautiful Old Testament idea.

David cried out, "Have mercy upon me, O God, according to Your lovingkindness; according to the multitude of Your tender mercies, blot out my transgressions." David's petition reveals his sense of helplessness. He turned away from self-reliance and depended only on the loving compassion of the Lord. Yahweh's nature as a loving, caring God was the basis for David's appeal.

Charis is the Greek term commonly rendered as "grace" in the New Testament. In ancient Greek culture, the word indicated a favor or benefit given. *Charis* was also used to refer to a response of gratitude. Paul used *charis* as a technical theological term to sum up what Christ has done and to denote all that the gospel affirms about being in a personal relationship with God.

Human religions approach being in relationship with God from a common point of view. They assume that people are able to please God by their actions and that being in a relationship with God depends to some extent on what a person does. This makes salvation a reward, namely, something a person merits or deserves.

Christianity approaches being in a relationship with God in a totally different way. People are viewed as spiritually lost, that is, as being dead in trespasses and sins (Eph. 2:1). They are unable to please God because sin is woven into the fabric of their being. It is only by God's free and spontaneous action in Jesus that salvation comes. Even the righteousness that increasingly marks the Christian's experience is a result of God's action in us, not mere human effort.

Religion focuses on self, relies on works of the Law, and results in condemnation. In contrast, Christianity focuses on the Messiah, relies on His saving work for us, and results in new life and personal righteousness. All of this is summed up in the New Testament concept of grace.

Ephesians 2:1-10 is a key New Testament passage concerning grace. Verses 1 and 2 (NIV) reveal that at one time all humanity lay dead in "transgressions and sins" and followed "the ways of this world and the ruler of the kingdom of the air." (The latter is a reference to Satan.) Here we learn that in their fallen state, people are spiritually helpless (Rom. 5:6).

Ephesians 2:4 and 5 (NIV) declare, "But because of his great love for us, God, who is rich in mercy, made us alive with Christ even when we were dead in transgressions—it is by grace you have been saved." Verses 8 and 9 (NIV) reveal that God's grace is mediated to us "through faith—and this not of yourselves, it is the gift of God—not by works, so that no one can boast."

Grace views human beings as helpless. Also, grace affirms God as a loving, compassionate Creator who, moved solely by His great goodness, has acted in Christ to free all who believe from their bondage to sin. The Lord freely and unconditionally gives them eternal life, and this becomes the foundation for a practical righteousness.

While it is important to see the role of God's grace in salvation, it is just as important to realize that grace is the key to a vital Christian experience. Perhaps the impact is most clearly seen in Paul's vision of a holy life, which he summed up in Romans 6—8. In chapter 6, Paul showed that believers are united by faith to Jesus in His death and resurrection. That union frees them from a legalistic approach to the Christian life in which their own efforts are the key to pleasing God. Instead, that union places them in the realm of grace. Now they can rely on God to enable them to do good and righteous acts. As they yield themselves to God and trust in Him daily, the Lord overcomes their innate helplessness and enables them to do His will.

Grace is not simply an orientation to relationship with God. It is also a practical approach to living the Christian life. If we try to follow our Lord in our own strength, we will fail (Gal. 5:4). But if we rely on Christ and the Holy Spirit, we will succeed in living a holy, loving life.

Romans 7 illustrates these truths by describing Paul's own failure to achieve righteousness through obedience to the Law. In chapter 8, Paul described the great release that came as he learned to rely on grace and to count solely on the Holy Spirit within to move him to do good. Grace, then, is not only the way of salvation but also a way of life. Grace is a continuing reliance on God to make us holy even as we first relied on Him to forgive our sins.

What does it mean for us to recognize and rely on the grace of God? It means that we accept the impossibility of pleasing God by our own efforts. It also means that we acknowledge God's great love expressed in Jesus, and that we trust God to welcome us into His family for Jesus' sake. Moreover, it means that we continue to rely on Jesus as we live daily. We count on His strength to enable us to make those choices that are pleasing to our Lord. When we know God's great heart of love and the compassion that moved Him to reach out to save us, we will "approach the throne of grace with confidence" (Heb. 4:16 NIV).

While the title "God of all grace" occurs only in 1 Peter 5:10, "grace" in the developed sense discussed above is found no less than 106 times in 98 verses. It is indeed a defining term of the Christian faith, for the Father, as the "God of all grace," has chosen to call "us to His eternal glory by Christ Jesus."

GOD OF ALL COMFORT

This title is found only in 2 Corinthians 1:3. In that context Paul explains that God comforts us in all our troubles. In so doing He equips us to comfort others who are afflicted "with the comfort with which we ourselves are comforted by God" (v. 4).

The Greek words translated "comfort" occur over 100 times in the New Testament in verb and noun forms. But those words have several different meanings in Greek, ranging from "to invite" to "to exhort." In the 17 times where the translation "comfort" is found (1 Cor. 14:3; nine times in 2 Cor. 1; 2:7; 7:6, 7; 13:11; Phil. 2:1; Col. 4:11), the meaning is roughly "to come alongside to comfort and encourage." In our distress God comforts us, providing the encouragement we need to live through our most difficult times. Ultimately, it is only God who can bring us through. He is indeed the "God of all comfort."

GOD OF LOVE AND PEACE

Though this title of the Father occurs in only 2 Corinthians 13:11, it is buttressed by numerous references in the Epistles to the love of God and the peace He brings. The above verse is Paul's farewell to the Corinthian believers. The apostle wrote, "Become complete. Be of good comfort, be of one mind, live in peace; and the God of love and peace will be with you."

God of love. "Love" is another Greek word that the writers of the New Testament chose to fill with fresh meaning. At least three words for love were available to the writers of the New Testament. One, *eros*, was associated with sexual desire and passion. Another, *philia*, was associated with friendship and mutual enjoyment of a relationship. A third word, *agape*, conveyed fondness. The New Testament adopted this third word and transformed it by using it as the defining term for God's attitude toward human beings as expressed in Jesus Christ.

We can sense the depth of meaning given *agape* by glancing at just one passage in which it is central, namely, Romans 5:6-10.

> For when we were still without strength, in due time Christ died for the ungodly. For scarcely for a righteous man will one die; yet perhaps for a good man someone would even dare to die. But God demonstrates His own love toward us, in that while we were still sinners, Christ died for us. Much more then, having now been justified by His blood, we shall be saved from wrath through Him. For if when we were enemies we were reconciled to God through the death of His Son, much more, having been reconciled, we shall be saved by His life.

While *eros* expressed desire for one we find beautiful and *philia* expressed enjoyment of a mutually pleasurable or beneficial relationship, *agape* came to express the determined choice of God to act for the benefit of an enemy, even at the cost of the life of His own Son.

God's commitment to sinners in Christ forever transformed the concept of love. Love passed from the realm of emotion to the realm of choice. Love passed from the realm of personal benefit to the realm of self-sacrifice. And love passed from the realm of focus on one's own concerns to a focus on what will benefit the other.

The New Testament speaks of three love relationships. There is the love of God for human beings. There is the love of the believer for God. And there is the love believers are to have for each other. In each case the meaning of "love" is defined by God's expression of His love in Jesus Christ. In each case "love" is a conscious commitment to benefit another, whatever the cost to us. Surely God the Father is rightly titled the "God of love!"

God of peace. While the title "God of love and peace" occurs only in 2 Corinthians 13:11, God the Father is titled the "God of peace" five times (Rom. 15:33; 16:20; Phil. 4:9; 1 Thess. 5:23; Heb. 13:20). The *New International Encyclopedia of Bible Words* notes that "in the Epistles, 'peace' is most often that restored wholeness that Jesus brings to our relationship with God and others, although this cannot be separated from the inner sense of well-being that accompanies them" (p. 481). New Testament verses that use this title suggest several aspects of the peace that God provides.

Release from fear. "And the God of peace will crush Satan under your feet shortly" (Rom. 16:20).

Fellowship with God. "The things which you learned and received and heard and saw in me, these do, and the God of peace will be with you" (Phil. 4:9).

Inner transformation and wholeness. "Now may the God of peace Himself sanctify

Christ showed Himself to have power over life and death in calling Lazarus from his tomb.

you completely; and may your whole spirit, soul, and body be preserved blameless at the coming of our Lord Jesus Christ" (1 Thess. 5:23). Also, "Now may the God of peace who brought up our Lord Jesus from the dead, that great Shepherd of the sheep, through the blood of the everlasting covenant, make you complete in every good work to do His will, working in you what is well pleasing in His sight, through Jesus Christ, to whom be glory for ever and ever" (Heb. 13:20, 21).

GOD OUR SAVIOR

This title occurs six times in the New Testament Epistles (1 Tim. 1:1; 2:3; Titus 1:3; 2:10; 3:4; Jude 1:25) The title "Savior" is given both to the Father and to Jesus, as in Titus 1:3 and 4. For more information, see the discussion of "Savior" in Chapter 8, page 183.

GOD WHO GIVES LIFE TO THE DEAD

GOD WHO CALLS THOSE THINGS WHICH DO NOT EXIST AS THOUGH THEY DID

These titles are found in Romans 4:17. Together they indicate God's miracle-working power. In context, the apostle Paul reviews history and notes that the birth of Isaac, Abraham and Sarah's son, was a miracle. Sarah's womb was dead as far as its capacity to carry a child was concerned, for at ninety she was long past menopause. Nevertheless, God promised that she and Abraham would have a son, even though it meant giving life to her dead womb and calling into existence a child who was not yet born.

The apostle Paul sees in this Old Testament account a foreshadowing not only of the resurrection of Jesus, but also of the gift of life to those who believe in Him. Later, in 8:11, the apostle reminds us that "if the Spirit of Him who raised Jesus from the dead dwells in you, He who raised Christ from the dead will also give life to your mortal bodies through His Spirit who dwells in you." God, as One who gives life to the dead, is able to infuse even our sinful personalities with new life, so that we are able to live godly lives pleasing to the Lord.

HOLY ONE

This title of God is found only in 1 John 2:20 in the Epistles. God is frequently identified as the "Holy One" in the Old Testament (see the discussion beginning on p. 105). Here John writes, "But you have an anointing from the Holy One, and you know all things."

"Anointing" here refers to divine enabling, specifically enabling to discern the truth. The Holy Spirit is our Enabler and Anointer. Also, the Spirit is God the Father's gift to us who believe. Thus, the "Holy One"

here refers to the Father rather than the Holy Spirit.

BIBLE BACKGROUND:

QUESTIONING THE CULTS

It doesn't take long for those studying theology to discover that Christian denominations tend to have their own distinctions. One group will emphasize the sovereignty of God and argue for predestination. Another group will emphasize the love of God and argue for free will. Some will insist that speaking in tongues is evidence of true spirituality, while others will insist that this spiritual gift was phased out when the last New Testament book (Revelation) was written and distributed.

It's important to remember that this kind of debating is essentially a family matter. In other words, the denominations and groups that hold one view or another are truly "Christian." They rely on Christ for salvation, and they take their stand on the Incarnation (namely, the physical death and literal resurrection of our Lord).

There are other religious groups, however, whose members might use the same words that Christians use but who are not true followers of the Savior. These groups are cults, for their teachings deny the essential truths of Christianity and their "faith" is not in the Jesus of the Bible.

When a person representing a "church" or group that you're not familiar with begins a conversation with you, what questions can you ask that will help you differentiate between a fellow believer whose views may differ from your own and a member of a cult whose theological foundations are not at all Christian? Here are some questions you might ask and answers you might receive. Any one of the answers on the right should warn you that you are speaking with a member of a cult rather than a genuine Christian.

The Questions	The Christian's Response	The Cultist's Response
Do you believe that Jesus is God?	Yes	Jesus is a god. Jesus became a god.
Do you believe that one God exists as three Persons?	Yes	The Father, Son, and Spirit are aspects of the one God
Do you believe that Jesus is the Creator?	Yes	Jesus is a created being. Jesus made the material universe but is still a created being.
Do you believe in the incarnation of Jesus?	Yes	Jesus was just a human being whom God used.
Do you believe in the physical resurrection of Jesus?	Yes	Jesus' resurrection was spiritual, not physical, in nature.

Through the Spirit, God enables Christians to distinguish the false from the true. We are enabled to distinguish antichrists from genuine teachers sent by God. While the Spirit within gives us discernment, there is also an objective test we can use to identify false teachers (namely, antichrists). John points out that "whoever denies the Son does not have the Father" (2:23) and that "every spirit that does not confess that Jesus Christ has come in the flesh is not of God. And this is the spirit of the Antichrist" (4:3). No teaching of anyone who denies that Jesus Christ is both fully human and fully divine can be trusted. Such a person is not a Christian at all.

THE KING ETERNAL, IMMORTAL, INVISIBLE

GOD WHO ALONE IS WISE

These titles of God are found in 1 Timothy 1:17. They are part of an expres-

sion of praise that bursts forth from Paul in view of the grace given him in Christ. To this God, the one and only King who alone is eternal, immortal, invisible, and wise, Paul says, "be honor and glory forever and ever. Amen."

King. To affirm God as King is to assert His sovereignty over all. For a detailed look at the Old Testament roots of this title, see the discussion beginning on page 151.

Eternal. The *New International Encyclopedia of Bible Words* offers the following explanation: "Essentially, the eternal is that which is not limited by time. The eternal has no beginning and no end but stands outside of and beyond time. God is like this. His nature (Rom 1:20) and his purposes (Eph 3:11) are timeless, for he created the material universe and set in motion the processes by which time is measured" (p. 150).

As the Eternal, God is truly unique and beyond comparison. While the Creator, He is more than this. He is the self-existent One who is, was, and evermore will be.

Immortal. Two Greek words, *aphtharisa* and *aphthaartos* (found a total of 15 times in the New Testament), can be translated either "immortal" or "imperishable." However rendered, these Greek words convey the concept of immunity to decay. Since the Fall, our universe has been dying, being subject to deterioration and decay. All nature, Paul says in Romans 8, is subject to "futility" (v. 20) and "corruption" (v. 21).

In contrast, God is untouched by this kind of change. He Himself is imperishable (Rom. 1:23; 1 Tim. 1:17). Even more, God has by planting His own incorruptible seed within us (1 Pet. 1:23) released *us* from bondage to the forces of death and decay. Ultimately, we will be raised from the dead to share with Christ a resurrection life that is like God's own. And because God's life truly is eternal, we who have that life through faith in Christ will live forever with the Lord.

Invisible. The fact that God is invisible (that is, unable to be seen) is expressed four times in the New Testament (Rom. 1:20; Col. 1:15; 1 Tim. 1:17; Heb. 11:27). The "visible" is whatever can be apprehended by mortal powers of sight. To say that God is invisible, or to speak of an invisible realm (Col. 1:16), casts no doubt on their reality. It simply means that we must apprehend the invisible by some means other than sight.

First Peter 1:8 puts the invisible in perspective. God the Father and Jesus Christ are those "whom having not seen you love. Though now you do not see Him, yet believing, you rejoice with joy inexpressible and full of glory." Through the eyes of faith, we pierce the veil between material and spiritual realities, and although we cannot see God with our eyes, we can and do experience His presence.

God who alone is wise. This title is found in Jude 1:25. (A number of early Greek manu-

scripts delete "wise," *sopho*, so that the original text may have read "the only God." But let's assume that the Greek manuscripts underlying the NKJV are correct.) The word group from which *sopho* comes was typically used to indicate philosophical or speculative knowledge. But this is not the sense in which that word group is used in the New Testament.

In the New Testament, "wisdom" is the capacity to evaluate real life situations and make a correct choice. Our "God who alone is wise" is the One to whom we look to make prudent choices in our lives. As far as God's choices are concerned, they are always wise, for He understands every issue involved in each choice. Also, He always acts in harmony with His own character, which is perfect and good.

LAWGIVER

While God is clearly portrayed in the Old Testament as the giver of Israel's law, the title "Lawgiver" is found only once in the New Testament, in James 4:12, which reads, "There is one Lawgiver, who is able to save and to destroy. Who are you to judge another?" However, a number of other versions (working from different Greek manuscripts) read, "there is only one Lawgiver and Judge" (NIV, NASB).

While God is unquestionably viewed throughout Scripture as the giver of the Ten Commandments, this title in James implies more. God is our Lawgiver in the sense of being the source of all standards of right and wrong, for these flow from His character. Indeed, God has planted in the heart of every human being knowledge of what constitutes a moral issue (Rom. 2:14, 15).

The fact that all ethical standards have their source in God's character makes Him the only authentic Judge of others. God, who knows us perfectly, is alone able to evaluate not only behavior but also motive and intent. James is speaking out against those who "slander" (4:11 NIV) others. Only the

As Lawgiver and Judge, God measures human beings by the standard of His own perfect character.

"Lawgiver" (v. 12) is able to judge whether a person's actions are in harmony with His perfect moral standard. And as Lawgiver, God alone has the right and obligation to judge others by the Law, which reflects His own perfect character.

BIBLE BACKGROUND:

"JUDGING" IN THE NEW TESTAMENT

Luke, James, and Paul all deal with "judging." Each says clearly that believers are not to take it on themselves to evaluate one another. "There is only one Lawgiver and Judge," James says, "the one who is able to save and destroy. But you—who are you to judge your neighbor?" (James 4:12). Paul develops this theme in Romans 14. He teaches that Jesus died and rose again "that he might be Lord of both the dead and the living. . . . why [then] do you judge your brother? Or why do you look down on your brother?" (14:9, 10). . . .

These sharp prohibitions of judging sometimes cause confusion when compared with two NT passages which speak of church discipline and the settlement of disputes (1 Cor. 5). In the case of discipline, the church is not called on to judge others but to take a stand with God against actions which he has clearly specified in his Word to be sin. In disputes between believers, the facts of the particular situation are to be evaluated. In these two cases we are to judge, in the sense of discerning.

In contrast, "judging" in James and Romans involves a critical attitude toward the beliefs, motives, or convictions of another person. Such judging is strictly prohibited by God.

Illustrated Bible Handbook, p. 521.

LIGHT

"Light" is a significant term in the New Testament. Jesus stated that He is the "light of the world" (John 8:12). This title has implications that are explored in both the Gospels and the Epistles.

However, in one very significant New Testament passage God the Father is spoken of as Light. In fact, John asserts there that "God is light" (1 John 1:5). Because this passage is so significant, we definitely need to understand what John is saying when he asserts, "God is light and in Him is no darkness at all." Verses 5-10 read as follows:

This is the message which we have heard from Him and declare to you, that God is light and in Him is no darkness at all. If we say that we have fellowship with Him, and walk in darkness, we lie and do not practice the truth. But if we walk in the light as He is in the light, we have fellowship with one another, and the blood of Jesus Christ His Son cleanses [literally, "keeps on cleansing"] us from all sins. If we say that we have no sin, we deceive ourselves, and the truth is not in us. If we confess our sins, He is faithful and just to forgive us our sins and to cleanse us from all unrighteousness. If we say that we have not sinned, we make Him a liar, and His word is not in us.

John begins his first epistle by focusing our attention on living in fellowship with God. This is something the apostle has experienced, and he wants us to experience it, too (vv. 3, 4).

However, if we are to experience true fellowship with God, we must realize that He is light, and that "in Him is no darkness at all" (v. 5). Our understanding of this title of God (and our grasp of John's teaching) depends on understanding a particular characteristic of light. Where there is light, nothing is hidden or misrepresented. In the light, everything is exposed for what it actually is. John thus is saying that to have fellowship with God we must "walk in the light" (v. 7). We must live our life with God with uncompromising honesty.

With this principle laid down, John introduces the topic of sin, for it is *pretence about sin* that disrupts our fellowship with

God. We cannot say that we have fellowship with God if we pretend we do not sin. When we are honest about our sins and confess them to God, He "is faithful and just to forgive us our sins " (v. 9) and to continue the cleansing process initiated by the Holy Spirit. If, on the other hand, we lie to ourselves and to God by asserting "we have no sin" (v. 8), we are walking in darkness and are out of fellowship with God.

Some insist that "walking in the light" (v. 7) means living a sinless life. This interpretation, however, is utterly wrong, for John says that if we are walking in the light, Christ's blood "cleanses us from all sin." But if we were truly sinless, we would hardly need His spiritual cleansing. John also says that those who claim to have no sin deceive themselves, and the truth is not in them (v. 8). It is only by being honest about the true nature of our sinful thoughts and deeds that we open ourselves up to God's transforming power.

Too many Christians excuse anger as "righteous indignation," put a pious label on gossip, and explain away meanness as "truth telling." It is only by being truly sensitive to God's Spirit and being willing to acknowledge to ourselves and to God the true nature of our thoughts and actions that we will experience fellowship with the Lord, who is Light.

LORD ALMIGHTY

God the Father is referred to as the "LORD Almighty" in 2 Corinthians 6:18. For a fuller discussion of the title "Lord Almighty," see page 33.

LORD GOD

The name "Lord God" appears in 1 Peter 3:15 in the NKJV. However, other versions, being based on different Greek manuscripts, read "Christ as Lord" (NIV, NASB). For a discussion of this passage and the title "Lord" as applied to Jesus in the New Testament epistles, see page 156.

LORD OF PEACE

This title occurs only in 2 Thessalonians 3:16, "Now may the Lord of peace Himself give you peace always in every way." For a discussion of titles incorporating "peace," see pages 70 and 71.

MAJESTY IN THE HEAVENS
MAJESTY ON HIGH

Hebrews 8:1 describes Jesus as the believers' High Priest seated at the right hand of "the Majesty in the heavens." Hebrews 1:3 uses a similar image to portray Jesus. He is said to have finished the work of redemption and is now sitting down at the right hand of "the Majesty on high." In each verse the Greek word rendered "Majesty" is *megalosunes*. The term is used in the New Testament in place of the divine name, and means "loftiness" or "majesty." *Megalosunes* is also found in Jude 25, where Jude closes by ascribing "glory and majesty, dominion and power" to God "both now and forever."

MOST HIGH GOD

This distinctive Old Testament title of God is found in the New Testament only in Hebrews 7:1, where the writer refers to Melchizedek as a priest of the Most High God (Gen. 14:18-20). For a discussion of this title, see page 34.

SAVIOR

This title is given both to God the Father and to Jesus. Both are intimately and actively involved, with the Holy Spirit, in the process of bringing salvation to humankind. For a discussion of the significance of the term "Savior" and of "salvation," see page 69.

As our High Priest Jesus represents us before God's throne, guaranteeing our salvation by the sacrifice of Himself.

THE NAMES AND TITLES OF GOD THE FATHER IN REVELATION

The Book of Revelation is a unique New Testament document. Classified as apocalyptic literature, it contains stunning visions of divine judgments associated with the final triumph of God over evil. In this context, God is consistently seen as the ultimate power in the universe, exercising that power to put down evil and once and for all establish the victory of good. When looking at the names and titles of God in this final book of the New Testament, it is important to remember that each is enhanced by and gives expression to the theme of the book.

The names are discussed here in the order in which they appear in Revelation, most likely written by the apostle John in the A.D. 90s.

HIM WHO IS AND WHO WAS AND WHO IS TO COME

This title is first found in Revelation 1:4, where each person of the Trinity is mentioned. John writes, "Grace to you and peace from Him who is and who was and who is to come, and from the seven Spirits who are before His throne, and from Jesus Christ" (vv. 4, 5). The title is also used in 11:17, where the Father is also referred to as the "Lord God Almighty." Here the Father is praised because "You have taken Your great power and reigned." A very similarly worded title is found in 16:5, where an angel praises God "because You have judged these things."

The title stresses the eternity of God. He alone exists outside of time and before the Creation of the world. As such, God is the ultimate power in the universe. In the scenes depicted in Revelation, God the Son steps from eternity into time, not to suffer for us but to triumph.

LORD GOD ALMIGHTY

Like other titles, this one also emphasizes the power of God. It is found in Revelation 4:8, 15:3, 16:7, and 21:22. In 4:8, we see a special class of angelic beings whose role is to continually praise God as both holy and eternal. In 15:3, God is praised for His victory over the beast, an enemy who appears at history's end.

In 16:7, God is again addressed as "Lord God Almighty," and again the theme of angelic praise emphasizes the fact that God has now acted in judgment. In 21:22, John describes the establishment of a new heaven and a new earth after sin and evil have been judged and banished. The Lord God Almighty, who created all things, will for eternity be known for His victory over sin and evil. This is a victory more significant than any won during the previous course of history.

LIVING GOD

God is described as "the living God" in Revelation 7:2. This title too has Old Testament roots, which are discussed on page 44.

GOD OF THE EARTH
GOD OF HEAVEN

Each of these titles is found in Revelation 11, the first in verse 4 and the second in verse 13. Chapter 11 describes judgment being poured out on the people of the earth during a span of 1,260 days. During this time, two witnesses with supernatural protection announce God's judgment. The ministry of these two witnesses, despite every effort by people to kill them, demonstrates the Lord's position as the "God of the earth" (v. 4). He is in control of all that happens. Later in the chapter, John describes the heavenly source of the judgments that strike the earth. This reinforces the truth that the Lord is the "God of heaven" (v. 13).

KING OF THE SAINTS

Most of the names or titles of God appearing in Revelation are found in joyful expressions of praise offered by angels and believers. This is true of 15:3, which says, "Just and true are Your ways, O King of the saints!" Some Greek manuscripts, however, read "King of the nations" (NASB) or "King of the ages" (NIV). Regardless of which reading is preferred, the main truth remains clear. God is praised because His judgments were not only purifying but also gracious. Because God has acted, the nations as well as God's own people will worship Him.

Great and marvelous are Your works,
Lord God Almighty!
Just and true are Your ways,
O King of the saints!
Who shall not fear You,

O Lord, and glorify Your name?
For You alone are holy.
For all nations shall come and
  worship before You,
For Your judgements have been mani-
    fested.

Revelation 15:3, 4

LORD GOD OMNIPOTENT
THE GREAT GOD

In a chapter that describes the triumphant return of Christ and the destruction of God's enemies, the Father is rightly called "the Lord God Omnipotent" (Rev. 19:6) and "the great God" (v. 17). From this we see that in the end, God the Father will indeed reign. Also, all will acknowledge Him to be the "Lord God Omnipotent" (v. 6), that is, the truly "great God" (v. 17).

NAMES AND TITLES OF JESUS CHRIST

The New Testament contains a number of names and titles of God the Father and the Holy Spirit. But a quick review of the names and titles of Jesus Christ makes it very clear that He is without question the focus of the New Testament revelation. The four Gospel portraits of His life on earth take up approximately half the New Testament. And the New Testament gives Jesus Christ over ninety names and titles! Through these we are given a clearer awareness of Jesus' deity, His humanity, and His mission as the ultimate Savior of humankind.

NAMES AND TITLES EMPHASIZING JESUS' DEITY

No honest reader of the Gospels can claim that Jesus failed to identify Himself as God or that from the beginning Christians have firmly believed in the full deity of Jesus as God incarnate. This doctrine is so central to biblical Christianity that the apostle John makes the confession "that Jesus Christ has come in the flesh" (1 John 4:2) the central objective test to distinguish true Christians from false prophets and teachers (v. 3, 15). Also, many of the names and titles of Jesus used in the New Testament emphasize His deity.

ALMIGHTY

"Almighty" is a descriptive name of God found in the Old Testament (see page 33). It is also a primary name of God the Father in the Book of Revelation, where it emphasizes the Lord's overarching power exercised in His final triumph over sin and evil. In 1:8, Jesus identifies Himself as the Almighty, as well as by a title borne only by Christ, "the Alpha and the Omega."

ALPHA AND OMEGA

This distinctive title occurs with "the Almighty" in Revelation 1:8. It is also found in two passages near the end of Revelation. In Revelation 21:6 God the Father, while seated on His throne, says, "I am the Alpha and the Omega, the Beginning and the End." Then in 22:13 and 14, Christ states,

> And behold, I am coming quickly, and My reward is with Me, to give to every one according to his work. I am the Alpha and the Omega, the Beginning and the End, the First and the Last.

It is significant that the title is used of the Father and the Son interchangeably. And it follows that in Revelation 1:8 the other titles given the Father would also apply to the Son. Concerning this verse, the *Zondervan NIV Bible Commentary* (Vol. 2) notes the following:

> Of the many names of God that reveal his character and memorialize his deeds, there are four strong ones in this verse. (1) "Alpha and Omega" are the first and last letters of the Greek alphabet. Their mention here is similar to the "First" and "Last" in v. 17 and is further heightened by the "Beginning" and the "End" in 21:6 and 22:13. Only this book refers to God as the "Alpha and Omega." (2) He is the absolute source of all creation and history, and nothing lies outside him. Thus he is the "Lord God" of all. (3) He is the one who "is, and who was, and who is to come." (4) He is continually present to his people as the "Almighty" (lit., "the one who has his hand on everything").

The application of the title "Alpha and Omega" to both God the Father and the Son is incontrovertible evidence of Christ's full deity.

AMEN

While the word "Amen" occurs frequently in the New Testament, only in Revelation 3:14 is a person of the Godhead identified as "the Amen." "Amen" is the transliteration of a Hebrew word that refers to something being firm, reliable, or true. The Gospels report that Jesus frequently

introduced a significant teaching by saying "Amen, Amen,"—a phrase that modern versions frequently render as "truly, truly."

As the "Amen" (Rev. 3:14), Jesus is the reliable foundation on whom the promises of God rest. Second Corinthians 1:20 says concerning Jesus, "all the promises of God in Him and Yes, and in Him Amen, to the glory of God." Jesus not only confirms the promises of God, but also ensures the fulfillment of the Father's plans.

BLESSED AND ONLY POTENTATE

In 1 Timothy 6:15, Paul calls Jesus "the blessed and only Potentate." Other versions translate the phrase as the "blessed and only Sovereign" (NASB, NRSV) or the "blessed and only Ruler" (NIV).

The significance of the title "Potentate" in this verse is reflected in the accompanying phrases "King of kings and Lord of lords." These defining phrases are also found in Revelation 17:14 and 19:16, and are associated with the ultimate triumph of Christ at His Second Coming. Thus, to call Jesus the "blessed and only Potentate" (1 Tim. 6:15) is to ascribe to Him ultimate authority and power, something which can belong only to God.

BRIGHT AND MORNING STAR

Jesus claims this unusual descriptive title. In Revelation 22:16 we read, "I, Jesus, have sent My angel to testify to you these things in the churches. I am the Root and the Offspring of David, the Bright and Morning Star."

Two other passages also refer to the morning star. Second Peter 1:19 speaks about the day dawning and the morning star rising in the hearts of believers. And Revelation 2:28 records Jesus' promise to give to those who overcome "the morning star."

Commentators differ concerning the significance of this title. Most agree that in ancient times the morning star, Venus, was known as the herald of the dawn. Its appearance supposedly announced the coming of the day. If this is the idea behind Jesus' declaration of being the "Bright and Morning Star" (22:16), then perhaps He was saying that He will announce in His Second Coming the dawning of God's new day.

Others see in the title an allusion to Numbers 24:17, which predicts the appearance of a King who is destined to rule and crush Israel's enemies. Still others look to the Greek concept of the stars as rulers of humankind's destiny. In this regard, they see Christ's gift of the morning star to those who overcome as symbolic of their destiny to share in Jesus' rule over creation.

Whatever the basis for the analogy, the title "Bright and Morning Star" (Rev. 22:16) presents Jesus as the fulfillment of God's purposes and the Ruler of eternity.

BRIGHTNESS OF [GOD'S] GLORY

In calling Jesus the "brightness of [God's] glory" (Heb. 1:3), the writer of Hebrews asserts that Jesus is the One through whom God's glory radiates. The *Illustrated Bible Handbook* notes that "there is a strong affirmation here of the full deity of Jesus. He is the radiant source of that Glory which, in the OT, marks the very presence of God" (p. 742).

"Glory" is a significant term in the Old Testament. When used in reference to human beings, it indicates impressiveness or worthiness. And when used of God, the concept of glory is closely linked to His self-revelation. The *New International Encyclopedia of Bible Words* says the following:

"Glory" implies much more than a disclosure by God of who he is. It implies an invasion of the material universe, an expression of God's active presence among his people. Thus, the OT consistently links the term "glory" with the presence of God among Israel (e.g., Ex 29:43;

Eze 43:4-5; Hag 2:3). God's objective glory is revealed by his coming to be present with us, his people, and to show himself by his actions in our world.

Jesus, then, as the radiance of God's glory, is both God present with us and God revealed to us. Christ is, without question, God.

DAYSPRING

The title "Dayspring" occurs only in Luke 1:78. This verse is part of a hymn of praise uttered by Zacharias, the father of John the Baptist. In it Zacharias praises God that John will serve Him as a prophet and give knowledge of salvation "through the tender mercy of our God, with which the Dayspring from on high shall visit us." In the NIV, "Dayspring" is rendered as "the rising sun" who will come to us. And the NASB has "the Sunrise from on high."

Many see in this prophetic utterance a reference to Malachi's description of a coming day when God will actively intervene in history. Malachi 4:2 speaks of "the Sun of Righteousness" who "shall arise with healing in His wings." The image of a rising sun is also found in Psalm 84:11, which says "the LORD God is a sun and a shield." As the "Dayspring" (Luke 1:78), Jesus not only fulfills prophecy, but also is and must be the Lord God of the Old Testament.

EMMANUEL
IMMANUEL

The spelling of this word differs in English versions, but they each mean the same thing: *With us is God!* Matthew 1:23 quotes the Isaiah 7:14 prediction that a child would be born to a virgin and that this child would be God's own Son. In His coming to earth, the Son is in a unique sense "God with us." See the discussion of this name on page 97.

BIBLE BACKGROUND:

INCARNATION

The concept of Incarnation is captured in the name "Immanuel." "Incarnation" means "enfleshed." It reflects the teaching that in Jesus, God took on a true human nature and became a man. I've summarized this important doctrine in another work.

It was hard even for some early Christians to grasp. And the idea has been ridiculed by ancient and modern skeptics. Yet it is clearly taught in the Bible and is basic to our faith. In the person of Jesus Christ, God has come to us in the flesh. This is the Christian doctrine of incarnation. We believe that God has pierced the barrier between the seen and the unseen, and in history's greatest miracle, God became a true human being.

The Bible does not attempt to explain this reality, but it clearly and forcefully teaches the Incarnation. John's Gospel begins by identifying Jesus as the Word who "was with God, and the Word was God" (John 1:1). This Word "became flesh and lived for a while among us . . . the one and only Son, who came from the Father, full of grace and truth" (John 1:1-14). The eternally existing Word took on flesh, becoming a true human being, who for a few brief years lived among other human beings on planet earth.

Galatians 4:4-5 picks up the theme of preexistence—the fact that the one who came was the Son with the Father from eternity. "When the time had fully come," the Bible says, "God sent his Son, born of a woman, born under the law, to redeem those under law, that we might receive the full rights of sons."

Philippians 2 is one of the clearest and most powerful biblical expressions of the incarnation. It presents Jesus Christ "who, being in very nature God" yet "made himself nothing, taking on the very nature of a servant, being made in human likeness." As a human being the Son of God "humbled himself and became obedient unto death—even death on a cross." Exalted now, Jesus has been given "the name that is above every name" and will hear "every tongue confess that Jesus Christ is Lord" (Phil. 2:5-11).

A fourth passage is found in Colossians. There Jesus is described as the "[express] image [the exact representation] of the invisible God." It was "by him all things were created: things in heaven and on earth, visible and invisible. . . . He is before all things and in him all things hold together," for "God was pleased to have all his fullness dwell in him [Jesus]" (Col. 1:15-19). It was Jesus Christ whom God invested with humanity and who is the agent of salvation. Through Jesus, God chose to "reconcile to himself all things . . . by making peace through his blood, shed on the cross" (Col. 1:20). And the same passage emphasizes the fact that the Incarnation was no mere illusion: God has reconciled us "by Christ's physical body through death" (Col. 1:22).

Given the fact that the Bible teaches the Incarnation, why make an issue of it? Why view the incarnation of Christ as central to Christian faith? Simply because so much hinges on it.

Before the first century A.D., philosophers despaired of ever really knowing God. He was so wholly "other." Whoever or whatever "God" might be, whether Aristotle's "unmoved mover" or Neoplatonism's "pure spirit," God was so removed from humankind's universe that he was unknowable. And then, in an obscure little country on the fringe of the mighty Roman Empire, this unknowable God arrived. He came not in majesty but as an infant. He lived as a real human being, not among the political movers but among the common people. And he died, not a victim but a Victor. Because God the Creator entered his own universe, the hidden God that humanity despaired of knowing was fully unveiled. And because God acted to free humanity from bondage to sin, the distant God that humanity feared was discovered to be lovingly near, inviting each of us to truly know him in an intimate, personal relationship.

This is, of course, the real reason for and necessity of the Incarnation. Sin's ruin had devastated our whole race, alienating us from God, and so warping our outlook that we were actually "enemies in [our] minds because of [our] evil behavior" (Col. 1:21). Only God's personal intervention could deal finally with sin, reveal the full extent of his love for us, and transform us from enemies into children. No one could do for us what Jesus did, and so Jesus had to come, impelled by the necessity imposed by God's deep love.

Yes, Christians believe in the Incarnation. We believe that God loved us enough to enter the universe and take on human nature. We believe that God loved us enough to live among us and die for us. And because we do believe, we acknowledge Jesus of Nazareth as fully God, and we worship him.

The Zondervan Dictionary of Christian Literacy, pp. 207-09.

EXPRESS IMAGE OF [GOD'S] PERSON

This descriptive title of Jesus is found in Hebrews 1:3 and is particularly significant. In our day, "image" suggests a copy of the real thing. But this notion doesn't apply to the Greek phrase rendered "express image." (The NIV and NASB render it "exact representation.") The *Bible Reader's Companion* explains, "The phrase 'The exact representation of his [God's] being' is the *charackter*. In the first century this indicated the imprint of a die, such as the impression on coins. Jesus 'bears the stamp' of the divine nature itself" (p. 855). This phrase, then, indicates an identity with God so complete that Christ perfectly represents who God the Father is.

FAITHFUL AND TRUE

The phrase occurs as a name or title only in Revelation 19:11. It is found in a vivid description of Jesus' return as Conqueror and Judge. Verses 11-16 are so powerful and so overwhelmingly present Jesus as God that they are worth quoting here:

Now I saw heaven opened, and behold, a white horse. And He who sat on him was called Faithful and True, and in righteousness He judges and makes war. His eyes were like a flame of fire, and on His head were many crowns. He had a name written that no one knew except Himself. He was clothed with a robe dipped in blood, and His name is called The Word of God. And the armies in heaven, clothed in fine linen, white and clean, followed Him on white horses. Now out of His mouth goes a sharp sword, that with it He should strike the nations. And He Himself will rule them with a rod of iron. He Himself treads the winepress of the fierceness and wrath of Almighty God. And He has on His robe and His thigh a name written: KING OF KINGS AND LORD OF LORDS.

After reading this passage of Scripture, there can be no doubt that the Jesus presented here is God.

FIRSTBORN

In the New Testament the title "firstborn" (Greek, *prototokos)* occurs nine times. Twice it refers to Jesus in a literal way. Luke 2:7 says that Jesus was Mary's "firstborn Son." Mary and Joseph offered the temple sacrifice required for every Jewish couple's firstborn male (v. 23). Once there is a historical reference to God's deliverance of the firstborn of the Israelites during the Exodus period (Heb. 1:6).

In most cases, however, the title "firstborn" is used of Jesus in a technical theological sense that has its roots in the Old Testament. Some cults, ignoring the biblical roots, have taught that to call Jesus "firstborn" implies that rather than being fully God, the Son was a creation of the Father. This misconception of the term as it is used in the New Testament is clearly refuted by the many passages, names, and titles of Jesus that clearly teach that the Son is and always was God.

In the Old Testament, "firstborn" renders the Hebrew term *bakar*, a word that literally means "to be born first." It is important to understand the role of the firstborn son in a Hebrew family. The firstborn received a double portion of the family estate (Deut. 21:17), and had a right to the special blessing of his father (Gen. 27). The blessing firstborn received included leadership of the family and a right to the intangible assets of the family. In the case of Isaac and Jacob, the intangible assets were the covenant promises of God that passed to them from Abraham and through them to their descendants. The firstborn, then, was the head of the family through whom material and spiritual blessings were channeled.

With this background in mind we can see the theological significance of the title "firstborn" being given to Jesus. As the "firstborn among many brethren" (Rom. 8:29), Jesus is the One through whom we are to be blessed with an inner transformation that will ultimately make us spiritually like Him. As the "firstborn over all creation" (Col. 1:15), He is in control of the universe. And as the "firstborn from the dead" (Col. 1:18; Rev. 1:5), Jesus is the One through whom the blessing of being resurrected is transmitted to His spiritual body, the church.

The title "firstborn," far from subordinating Jesus, exalts Him "that in all things He may have the preeminence" (Col. 1:18) and be "ruler over the kings of the earth" (Rev. 1:5).

LORD OF GLORY

This title, found in 1 Corinthians 2:8, reflects a Hebrew idiom and can be paraphrased "glorious Lord" (NLT). The concept of God's glory is discussed on page 143 under the title "the brightness of God's glory."

GOD

In the Gospels, Acts, and Epistles, references to "God" (*theos*) are typically references to God the Father (see page 145). In this way the writers of the New Testament consistently maintained a distinction between the three Persons of the Trinity—the Father, the Son, and the Holy Spirit. Jesus is typically referred to as "Jesus," "Christ," "Jesus Christ," "the Lord Jesus Christ," and "the Son of God."

This statement, however, in no way suggests that Jesus is viewed in the New Testament as anything less than God. During His life on earth, Jesus' enemies undoubtedly understood Him to claim equality with the Father as God (John 5:18; 8:57-59), and they tried to murder Him for blasphemy. One of the strongest affirmations of Jesus' deity is found in the prologue to John's Gospel, where the apostle identifies Jesus as the Word and the Word as God (1:1, 2, 18; see also the article on the title of Jesus as "Word," page 160).

Other New Testament passages also emphasize both Jesus' preexistence and His deity. In Colossians 1:19, Paul writes that "in [Jesus] all the fullness [of deity] should dwell." Perhaps the clearest expression of the fact that Jesus is God is found in Philippians 2:6-10. There the apostle traces Christ's entrance into the human race, which involved the voluntary temporary surrender of the prerogatives (though not the reality) of deity so that He might suffer and die for us.

> [Jesus] being in the form of God, did not consider it robbery to be equal with God, but made Himself of no reputation, taking the form of a bondservant, and coming in the likeness of men. And being found in appearance as a man, He humbled Himself and became obedient to the point of death, even the death of the cross. Therefore God also has highly exalted Him and given Him the name which is above every name, that at the name of Jesus every knee should bow.

There are many other passages that emphasize the deity of Jesus. For instance, the writer of Hebrews devotes his first chapter to demonstrating that, as God, Jesus is higher than angels even though He was "made a little lower than the angels, for the suffering of death" (2:9).

Indeed, after proving from the Old Testament that the Christ must indeed be God, the writer argues that it is entirely appropriate, "as the children have partaken of flesh and blood" (2:14) that "He Himself likewise shared in the same, that through death He might destroy him who had the power of death."

Thus, while most references to "God" in the New Testament are to the Father, it remains clear that Jesus too always has been God.

Although as God the Son Jesus is high above the angels, in the Incarnation He was "made a little lower than the angels" that He might lift us up to God.

things" is made by God Himself. The Hebrew word to which this title can be traced is *yaras*, which means "to take possession" or "to inherit." The emphasis in the Old Testament is on the right of the heir to possess what belongs to the Father. Through faith in Jesus, we become God's spiritual children and heirs to all His eternal promises (Gal. 4:7; see also Rom. 4:13). But Jesus alone has been designated by God the Father as "heir of all things" (Heb. 1:2), for through Jesus, God also made the "worlds" (or "ages").

HEIR OF ALL THINGS

This title is introduced in Hebrews 1:2. The appointment of God's Son as "heir of all

HOLY ONE OF GOD

The Old Testament speaks of God as the "Holy One of Israel" (see p. 149). "Holy One" is also a name of God the Father in the New Testament (see p. 132). But the title "Holy One" is also used of the Messiah in the Old Testament (see p. 105). It should be no surprise then to find this title applied to Jesus in the Gospels.

What may be surprising is to discover that in Mark 1:24 and Luke 4:34 this title was uttered by demons, who recognized and were repelled by Jesus. They sensed His divine nature, masked though it was by His flesh to the eyes of His contemporaries. Mark 1:23-25 illustrates:

> Now there was a man in their synagogue with an unclean spirit. And he cried out, saying, "Let us alone! What have we to do with You, Jesus of Nazareth? Did You come to destroy us? I know who You are—the Holy One of God." But Jesus rebuked him, saying, "Be quiet, and come out of him!" And when the unclean spirit had convulsed him and cried out with a loud voice, he came out of him.

Not only did the demons recognize Jesus as the Holy One of God, but also Christ demonstrated His power over these minions of Satan by casting them out of those whom they possessed.

John 6:69 is another passage where the title "Holy One of God" occurs in a few Greek manuscripts. (This translation is reflected in the NIV and NASB; the NKJV renders the same verse "Son of the living God.") Here we find a record of the confession of faith made by Jesus' disciples. They too pierced the veil of Christ's humanity, and using the title "Holy One of God" in its Old Testament sense of designating the promised Messiah, the disciples acknowledged Jesus as the fulfillment of God's promise to come and live among humanity, first to save us and ultimately to rule over us.

I AM

"I AM" is the traditional translation of the four consonants that make up the Old Testament's personal name of God, *Yahweh*. That most significant of Old Testament names is discussed at length in chapter 2 of this book.

Jesus called Himself the "I AM" (John 8:58). At the time Jesus was under attack by a group of angry scribes and Pharisees, religious leaders whose authority Jesus' teachings had undermined. These leaders angrily debated Christ's claim to represent God the Father on earth, and they ridiculed His offer of freedom to those who believed in Him. The scribes and Pharisees insisted that as descendants of Abraham they were free and had never been in bondage. They made this claim despite Rome's domination of Judah.

Jesus, however, was speaking about spiritual freedom and bondage to sin. Nevertheless, the religious leaders kept on insisting that they were in the line of Abraham and therefore of the family of God. Jesus rejected their claim. If they had been of Abraham's family line, they would have acted as Abraham did when God spoke to him. In rejecting Jesus as the Messiah, the leaders of Israel showed that they were related spiritually to Satan. Jesus went on to say that Abraham had looked forward to the Messiah's day with rejoicing. The religious leaders scoffed at this claim: "You are not yet fifty years old, and You have seen Abraham?"

In response Jesus made a statement that His listeners clearly understood to be a claim of deity:

> Jesus said to them, "Most assuredly, I say to you, before Abraham was, I AM." Then they took up stones to throw at Him; but Jesus hid Himself and went out of the temple, going through the midst of them, and so passed by.
> vv. 57, 58

In making this statement, Jesus identified Himself as Yahweh, the God of the Old Testament who had spoken to Moses (Ex. 3:14), and who throughout the history of the Israelites had been the focus of revelation itself.

Public announcements were made at the "judgment seat" (bema) in Corinth.

JUDGE

Second Timothy 4:8 is one passage in which Jesus is given the title "Judge." In fact, Paul calls Christ "the righteous Judge" and looks forward to that time when Christ, as Judge, will reward the apostle for having "fought the good fight" and for keeping the faith (v. 7).

Despite this single usage, there is no question that the title "Judge" rightly belongs to Christ. Jesus stated that God has given the Son "authority to execute judgment also, because He is the Son of Man" (John 5:27). All that is said about God as Judge is also true of Christ, into whose hands the work of judging as well as that of salvation has been placed. See also the comments on "Judge of all the Earth" (p. 134) and "Lawgiver" (p. 64).

BIBLE BACKGROUND:

JUDGMENT DAY

The New Testament Greek words translated "judge" or "judgment" mean either "evalu-

ate" or "distinguish." At times these words are used in a legal sense, with God cast as a judge on the bench and humankind cast as the criminals before the bar.

Christians believe that God is the only One truly qualified to judge us, for He alone is able to evaluate all things accurately. And we have complete trust that His judgment is fair. But we also believe God has already reached His verdict. The Bible unveils not only the standards by which God evaluates but also the conclusions He has drawn. Bluntly stated, God's evaluation is that "there is none righteous, no, not one" (Rom. 3:10), for "all have sinned and fall short of the glory of God" (v. 23).

All that is left is for these conclusions to be expressed in an act of judgment, which Christians are convinced lies ahead. Paul spoke about the future judgment to mocking skeptics in Athens: God "has appointed a day on which He will judge the world in righteousness by the Man whom He has ordained" (Acts 17:31). Jesus, who lived history's only perfect life, has been granted authority to judge (John 5:22, 27), and Jesus' verdict has already been announced. The world is "condemned already" (3:18). When Judgment Day comes, all who find themselves standing before the divine bar, to be evaluated on the basis of what they have done, will be cast into what the Bible calls "the lake of fire" (Rev. 20:15).

Christians take this revelation of human failures and peril as one of God's greatest gifts. Why? Because God has announced His judgment and our sentence long before that sentence is to be executed. According to 2 Peter 3:9, execution is delayed; it is withheld by God's kindness and tolerance in order to give human beings an opportunity to repent and believe. Until the Day of Judgment comes, human beings are invited to acknowledge their sin and turn to Christ in faith for forgiveness. For those who believe in Jesus, there is no condemnation, for He has already taken our punishment and offers us eternal life in Him (John 5:21-30).

A Judgment Day is coming. But for Christians Judgment Day is past. Judgment Day occurred nearly two thousand years ago when the Son of God died for our sins at Calvary. What awaits us now is life—an eternity to be spent with our Redeemer and Lord!

JUST ONE

In Revelation 15:3 and 4, John hears heaven reverberate in praise to God and the Lamb. In the "song of Moses . . . and the song of the Lamb," God is not only praised for His great and marvelous works but also for being "just and true" in His ways. When we realize that justice is a foundational characteristic of God, we should not be surprised to discover that Jesus is also called the "Just One" or "Righteous One."

In possibly the first evangelistic sermon preached after Jesus' resurrection, Peter accused his listeners of denying "the Holy One and the Just" (Acts 3:14). Stephen also used this title in his powerful condemnation of the Jewish religious leaders, for which he was stoned to death. Stephen shouted out,

"Which of the prophets did your fathers not persecute? And they killed those who foretold the coming of the Just One, of whom you now have become the betrayers and murderers" (7:52).

It is almost as if Peter and Stephen chose the title "Just One" to heighten the contrast between the life Jesus lived and the injustice perpetrated against Him by His own people.

In John's first epistle, he assures the believers to whom he writes that when they sin they have an Advocate with the Father, "Jesus Christ the Righteous [or Just] One" (1 John 2:1 NIV). The words "righteous" and "just" are used interchangeably in many versions for the simple reason that a single Greek word is translated both "just" and "righteous." Also, the same verbal root stands both for "justice" and "righteousness." The concept of justice or righteousness applies equally to God's saving work in forgiving the sins of believers and to His punishment of sinners. The *New International Encyclopedia of Bible Words* examines both aspects of the divine justice.

Romans 3 develops the first theme. Because all have sinned, human beings must be redeemed. Salvation is given freely, as a gift of grace, through "the redemption that is in Christ Jesus." Paul explains that "God presented him as a sacrifice of atonement, through faith in his blood. He did this to demonstrate his justice, because in his forbearance he had left the sins committed beforehand unpunished—he did it to demonstrate his justice at the present time, so as to be just and the one who justifies those who have faith in Jesus" (Rom 3:24-25).

Paul's point is that God, as governor of the universe, is morally bound to condemn the guilty. Since all have sinned, God might be criticized for failure to condemn OT saints. The death of Christ has at last demonstrated that there is a basis on which God as judge could validly leave sins unpunished. And Jesus' self-sacrifice provides a basis on which God can be just and offer salvation to people today. Because of the Cross, God can remain true to his own moral commitment to what is right, and still freely acquit sinners (cf. 1 Jn 1:9).

The second theme is found in a number of NT passages. God is not unfair in punishing sinners. In 2 Thessalonians, Paul graphically portrays the destiny of those "who do not know God and do not obey the gospel of our Lord Jesus Christ" (1:8). When Christ returns, they will be punished everlastingly. Paul affirms, "God is just; he will pay back those who trouble you and give relief to you who are troubled" (1:6-7). The emphasis on just punishment is also seen elsewhere in the NT (e.g., Rom 3:5-6; 9:14; Heb 2:2; Rev 15—16).

It is important to note that in these passages the Bible is neither defending God nor trying to explain his actions. After all, God is the standard of morality in the universe. Human beings may resist and challenge the "humanity" of God's decisions. But God is himself the measure of righteousness. Thus the Bible simply affirms that God is just. In both salvation and condemnation, God's actions are in full harmony with his righteous character (pp. 371-372).

What does it mean then to give Jesus the title of "Just One"? The best answer is that in Him both aspects of divine justice find their fullest expression. In Jesus the forgiving love of God has been shed abroad so that God might be gracious to sinners. And in Jesus' return to earth from heaven, He will be the One who executes God's judgment on those who have failed to respond in obedience to His revelation of Himself.

KING

As a descendant of David, Jesus was qualified to take the throne of Israel. Meeting this requirement was a primary qualification of the promised Old Testament Messiah (Matt. 1:1—2:6). In the Gospels, the title of "King" is most often applied to Jesus at the

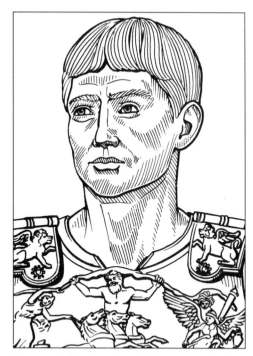

Augustus's "kingdom" was the Roman world wherever his authority was acknowledged.

end of His earthly life. It was Pilate, a Roman and an unbeliever, who insisted that a sign be posted above Jesus as He hung on the cross to proclaim Him "KING OF THE JEWS" (Matt. 27:37; Mark 15:26; Luke 23:38; John 19:19).

When Jesus returns, He is to be acknowledged by all as the ultimate Ruler, the "Lord of lords and King of kings" (Rev. 17:14). Yet to grasp what it means today to acknowledge Jesus as our king, we need to understand more of what the term meant in the first century A.D.

The meaning of kingdom. Today we think of a kingdom as a geographical district with national borders. A "king" is a person who rules a kingdom. But in biblical times, a kingdom was not so much a land as it was the sphere of authority enjoyed by a ruler. And this authority need not have geographical boundaries.

While the kingdom of the Roman emperor Augustus extended throughout the empire, the authority of, say, a King of Phrygia, was recognized even by Phrygians who lived in the Roman Empire. Similarly today we acknowledge the authority of the government of the country where we live. But as citizens of Jesus' kingdom, we acknowledge Christ's authority as being supreme.

In the New Testament, too, a kingdom is a realm in which a king exerts control and authority. Thus, the "kingdom of God" is not necessarily a place, and it need not have geographical borders. The kingdom of God is any realm over which God exercises control.

Kingdom in the Old Testament. In the Old Testament, two concepts of kingdom are developed. The first one is that God is King over the entire universe, for ultimately He is in control of everything. Regardless of whether that control is acknowledged by human beings, God's controlling influence over the course of events and in human lives nevertheless exists (Dan. 4:34, 35).

Of course, the Old Testament prophets look forward to a future expression of God's rule that will be visible and unmistakable. In that future kingdom, a descendant of David is to rule the earth, and all nations everywhere will submit to God's Anointed One (Ps. 2). In fact the Old Testament uniformly and consistently envisions a day when earth will be ruled by the Messiah, and "the kingdom shall be the Lord's" (Obad. 21). It is over this kingdom that Jesus will rule as King of kings and Lord of lords at history's end (Rev. 19:16).

Kingdom in the New Testament. The New Testament assumes both aspects of God's kingdom expressed in the Old Testament. Indeed, after His resurrection, Jesus' disciples asked Him whether this was the time when He would "restore the kingdom to Israel" (Acts 1:6). Jesus responded, "It is not for you to know the times or the seasons which the Father has put in His own authority" (v. 7). The kingdom the prophets foresaw will be established when Christ returns. But until then God will exercise His rule in a totally unexpected way. In other words, a form of His kingdom not revealed in the Old Testament will emerge!

That form of God's kingdom is a hidden one in which believers acknowledge Christ as King and submit to His will. Meanwhile unbelievers all around us are blind to the reality of this kingdom. The framework of Christ's hidden kingdom is revealed in the Gospels, and how we are to live as citizens of Jesus' kingdom is developed in the Epistles.

Jesus' present kingdom in the Gospels. The Sermon on the Mount (Matthew 5—7) is best understood as Jesus' statement of how people of any age live when they acknowledge God's sovereignty and abandon themselves to His will. The *New International Encyclopedia of Bible Words* offers the following summary:

> The Beatitudes describe the values of a person living a kingdom lifestyle (Mt 5:3-12). Jesus then gives a series of illustrations, showing how inner values find expression in lifestyle (5:17-42). As king, Jesus acts to transform the character of his subjects. Jesus in the present kingdom is working in our inner selves to change our outward behavior. Jesus goes on to show how we can experience this transforming power. We focus on our "in secret" relationship with the Lord, not on visible piety (6:1-18). We give priority to seeking God's kingdom and righteousness, and we trust our Father to supply our material needs (6:19-33). We relate to other kingdom citizens as brothers and sisters and reject every claim of a right to judge or control them (Mt 7:1-14). Instead of relying on human leaders, we rely on the simple words of Jesus and commit ourselves to obey them (p. 380).

The kingdom as described in the Gospels is a hidden one, whose existence is not visible

BIBLE BACKGROUND:

Kingdom parables in Matthew 13.	Expected form as prophesied	Unexpected form for New Testament era
1. Sower vv. 3-9, 18-23	Messiah turns Israel and all nations to Himself	Individuals respond differently to the gospel
2. Wheat/tares vv 24-30, 36-43	The kingdom's citizens rule with the King	Citizens live among people of the world until harvest time
3. Mustard seed vv. 31, 32	The kingdom initiated with power and glory	The kingdom seems insignificant at first. Its greatness is a surprise
4. Leaven v. 33	Only the righteous enter the kingdom	The kingdom is implanted in sinners and grows to fill the personality with righteousness
5. Hidden treasure v. 44	The kingdom is public, for all	The kingdom is hidden, for individual purchase
6. Priceless pearl vv. 45, 46	The kingdom brings all valued things to its citizens	The kingdom calls us to surrender all other values
7. Dragnet vv. 47-50	Kingdom launched with separation of the righteous and unrighteous	Kingdom ends with the separation of the righteous and unrighteous

to those who refuse to believe. But to those who commit themselves to Jesus as King and gladly obey Him, God's present kingdom is indeed real.

Matthew 13 develops a series of parables about the kingdom. These parables contrast the present form of Jesus' rule with the form of His rule described in the Old Testament and expected by first-century Jews.

Jesus' present kingdom in the Epistles. Paul tells us that through Christ believers have been delivered from "the power of darkness and conveyed . . . into the kingdom of the Son of His love" (Col. 1:13). As citizens of Jesus' present kingdom (1 Cor. 15:50; Gal. 5:21; Eph. 5:5; James 2:5), we acknowledge Jesus as our Ruler. In doing His will here on earth, we not only are becoming living expressions of the present kingdom of

God, but also we are placing ourselves under the sovereign rule of King Jesus, who controls every circumstance of our lives. And because King Jesus is present within His own, the unmatched power of God can find supernatural expression through our lives.

LIGHT

Earlier we explored the significance of the title "light" as applied in 1 John to God the Father (see p. 135). It is even more significant that Christ is titled the "light of the world" (John 8:12) and that many more references to Him as "light" occur in Scripture.

Light and darkness are natural metaphors found in all languages and cultures. In the Old Testament, light is linked with salvation (Ps. 27:1), with divine revelation (43:3; 119:130), and with God's presence (89:15). God's people are to walk in the "light of the LORD" (Is. 2:5), remaining faithful in their commitment to Him.

In the New Testament, references to Jesus as "light" primarily stand for illumination. He claimed, "I am the light of the world" (John 8:12). He also declared, "He who follows Me shall not walk in darkness, but have the light of life." Those who fail to trust in Jesus stumble about in darkness, for He alone can provide not only perspective on reality but also life itself (3:16-21). Those who respond in faith to the good news about Jesus are freed from the realm of darkness to become children of light (Eph. 5:8; Col. 1:12). They even become lights to people of the world (Matt. 5:1-16).

Several key passages in John's Gospel develop the significance of Christ's title as "light of the world" (8:12).

John 1:4-9. Jesus is the true light. When He entered the world, He revealed reality to all human beings, enabling them to see what had not been clear before His coming. In the gospel message, Jesus' light continues to shine in our sin-darkened world, revealing an eternal life that exists beyond our few paltry years on earth.

John 3:19-21. The coming of Jesus shed a brilliant light that revealed the depths of God's love for human beings. Humanity's reaction to that love demonstrates the reality of our alienation from God because of sin. Rather than welcome the light that Jesus sheds, most people scurry deeper and deeper into spiritual darkness. Verse 19 says, "This is the condemnation, that the light has come into the world, and men loved darkness rather than light, because their deeds were evil."

John 8:12. Only by following Jesus, the Light of the world, can people be released from the grip of sin's darkness and receive eternal life. As the Light of the World, Jesus illumines the reality of humankind's sin and reveals the depth of God's love. Only in Jesus' light can we find salvation.

LIFE

Jesus told His disciples, "I am the way, the truth, and the life. No one comes to the Father except through Me" (John 14:6). Throughout Scripture, "life" consistently stands in contrast to death. Both are used as powerful metaphors for spiritual realities. While the Bible portrays human sin as the source of biological and spiritual death, God is the source and giver of our life here on earth, of spiritual life, and of eternal life. Both the Father and the Son "have life in" (5:26) themselves. Thus, they are the source of every aspect of life.

Several key New Testament passages develop the theme of life as it is related to Jesus.

- John 3:15-26. The person who trusts in Jesus receives eternal life. In contrast, those who reject Him receive eternal condemnation.

- John 5:21-26. Jesus has "life in Himself" (v. 26). He is the possessor and source of every aspect of life, from biological to eternal.
- John 6:27-69. Jesus came down from heaven to bring the gift of eternal life to humankind.
- John 10:10-28. As the Good Shepherd, Jesus gave up His own life in order to make eternal life available to His followers.
- John 11:1-44. Jesus is the "resurrection and the life" (v. 25). His power over death is demonstrated by His restoring Lazarus to life. He is Himself the promise of resurrection and endless life for those who believe in Him.

As the Life, Jesus is the only antidote to sin. He also is the only hope for release from the sentence of eternal death passed on to us because of our sin. Because Jesus truly is life and the giver of life, our hope indeed is real.

BIBLE BACKGROUND:

THE NEW TESTAMENT VIEW OF LIFE

In the New Testament, the focus shifts away from our biological life to our spiritual life. Now, too, death is viewed in its aspect as alienation from God, as being cut off from the source of all life and being.

There are several words in the Greek language for life. *Bios* focuses on the externals: on a person's lifestyle, his or her wealth and possessions. This word is seldom used in the New Testament, and when it is, it is used negatively (Luke 8:14; 1 John 2:16). *Psuche* stands for the conscious life and often means the inner person or the personality. Jesus gave his life (his very self) as a ransom for us (Matt. 20:28). And Jesus warns that to save one's life (*psuche*, the inner, true self), a person must lose himself or herself for the Lord. Only by surrendering ourselves to Jesus can our full potential be realized, can we become the person we can be.

The third Greek word is *zoe*, which in the New Testament is a theological term. It shifts our vision from this earth to the life that spans time and eternity. This is the distinctive word with which Christians are most concerned as we explore what the Bible teaches about spiritual life and death.

In the New Testament this life is everywhere contrasted with death. Adam and Eve sinned and brought our race death—alienation from God and a corruption of human capacities and powers. With that curse came biological death as well. But Jesus brings us life in every sense of the term. He restores us to relationship with God, he frees us to find fulfillment, and ultimately he will release us from corruptibility through a glorious resurrection. As Jesus said, "I tell you the truth, whoever hears my words and believes on him who sent me has eternal life and will not be condemned; he has crossed over from death to life. I tell you the truth, the time is coming and now is when the dead will hear the voice of the Son of God and those who hear will live. For as the Father has life in himself, so he has granted the Son to have life in himself" (John 5:24-26). Relationship with Jesus releases the vitality of a fresh, spiritual life which the Bible calls eternal.

The Bible's vision of eternal life contains a promise of endless personal existence of fellowship with God. Dying Christians can face death in the assurance that their biological end is nothing less than a new beginning. Ahead, too, is resurrection, when the promise comes true that "death has been swallowed up in victory" (1 Cor. 15:53-55).

But eternal life means even more to us than this. God's gift of life in Christ means that "the old has gone, the new has come." We can experience fulfillment through being what humanity was originally created to be: creatures who glorify God and who enjoy him now and forever.

The Zondervan Dictionary of Christian Literacy, pp. 242, 243

Thomas was convinced that Jesus is Lord when Christ showed him the prints of the nails in His hands.

LORD

"LORD" (printed with the first letter capitalized and the rest of the words in small capital letters) is used wherever the name "Yahweh" appears in the Hebrew text of the Old Testament. A quite different convention underlies the New Testament use of the word "Lord." In the New Testament, the Greek noun *kyrios* is most often translated and printed either as "lord" or "Lord."

In ordinary speech, *kyrios* often served as a term of respect when used to address a superior. In such cases, "master" or "sir" are appropriate translations. Often when Jesus is addressed as "Lord" in the Gospels, the speaker is simply showing customary respect for a teacher or rabbi, rather than acknowledging Jesus as God. However, when Jesus spoke about Himself as "Lord even of the Sabbath" (Matt. 12:8), or when

Thomas confessed Jesus as "My Lord and my God" (John 20:28), the Greek term rendered "Lord" clearly reflects the Old Testament name of deity.

It is significant that after Jesus' resurrection, the church immediately and consistently affirmed Him as Lord. This affirmation constituted a confession of faith in His full deity. Philippians 2:9-11 indicates that the title "Lord" is "the name which is above every name, that at the name of Jesus every knee should bow, of those in heaven, and of those on earth, and of those under the earth, and that every tongue should confess that Jesus Christ is Lord, to the glory of God the Father."

What then does it mean for Christ to be Lord and for us to acknowledge Him as such? First, it means He holds all authority. Everything is subject to Him, for He is God (Eph. 1:21; 1 Pet. 3:22). Second, it means that Jesus exercises personal authority over believers. In Romans 14 Paul points out that the lordship of Jesus over every person means that each of us is responsible directly to Him for our actions and convictions. We are not to judge each other but rather to acknowledge that Christ alone exercises authority over our fellow believers.

Third, the fact that Jesus is Lord means He exercises pervasive authority over His church. We live "in" and "under" and "through" our Lord. These phrases occur repeatedly in the New Testament, reminding us that the presence and power of Jesus are central in our spiritual experience. Fourth, at history's end Christ's lordship will be obvious to all, for it will be demonstrated in His return and final victory over sin.

God calls on us to acknowledge Jesus as Lord, and we are to honor Him as God. But more than that, we are to willingly submit ourselves to Him and His will. The key to vital Christian experience is not found simply in agreeing that Jesus is Lord but also in fully submitting ourselves to His will, so that He might work out all that His lordship implies in our lives.

LORD OF THE SABBATH

Jesus identified Himself as Lord of the Sabbath on an occasion reported in both Matthew 12:8 and Luke 6:5. First-century rabbis were especially concerned about obeying the commandment to remember the Sabbath day and keep it holy (Ex. 20:8). The Hebrew Scriptures specified that no work was to be done on the Sabbath.

Tragically, the experts in the Mosaic Law assigned to themselves the task of defining "work" down to the minutest detail. According to their rulings, plucking heads of grain to eat while walking along a pathway was defined as "work." Thus, when Jesus' disciples were seen doing this one Sabbath, the religious leaders censured Jesus for it (Matt. 12:1, 2). Later that day the religious leaders took issue with Jesus for healing a man with a withered hand on the Sabbath (vv. 9-13).

It was during the controversy over Sabbath labor that Jesus called Himself Lord of the Sabbath (v. 8). As God, Jesus had given the Israelites the Sabbath commandment. Surely then Jesus, the Lord of the Sabbath, was the only One who could give a definitive interpretation of what the commandment did and did not imply. In their legalistic approach to the Sabbath, the religious leaders had missed the meaning of the holy day and had made their own humanly devised traditions—which distorted God's original intent—of equal weight to the Word of God.

ONLY BEGOTTEN
ONE AND ONLY

Each of these phrases (which appear in different English translations) renders the same Greek phrase. In Scripture, the phrase is understood to mean the object of a father's special love. Isaac is said to be the "only begotten" (Heb. 11:17) of Abraham, even though Isaac had a half-brother named Ishmael.

Jesus is identified as God's one and only Son in John 1:14, 18; 3:16, 18; and 1 John 4:9. Far from suggesting that Jesus was a creation of God the Father, "only begotten" emphasizes the deep love that God the Father has always had for Jesus, His Son.

PRINCE

In his second recorded evangelistic sermon, Peter announced that Jesus has been "exalted to [God's] right hand to be Prince and Savior" (Acts 5:31). This is the only reference in the New Testament to Jesus as Prince, although the Messiah is spoken of in the Old Testament in these terms. There He is indeed called the "Prince of princes" (see page 108), a title that emphasizes the authority Jesus has been given over all.

RIGHTEOUS ONE

See the discussion of "Just" and "Just One" beginning on page 52.

ROCK

In the Old Testament God is often called a Rock, a metaphor suggesting the building blocks of mountains. This image conveys the idea of strength, reliability, and security (see p. 81). In the New Testament, Christ is called "Rock" only in 1 Corinthians 10:4. Paul is reviewing Israel's experience of God during the Exodus. The apostle notes that they "all drank the same spiritual drink. For they drank of that spiritual Rock that followed them, and that Rock was Christ."

This passage is a warning. Although Israel enjoyed many spiritual privileges, this did not make God's people immune to the temptation of idolatry. Similarly, the Corinthians' spiritual privileges, including

Christ's miracles authenticated His claim to be the Son of God.

❖

participation in Christ, did not mean they could expect immunity, especially if they exposed themselves to the same sort of temptation.

Some commentators think that Paul's reference to the Rock following the Israelites is an example of midrash (or rabbinic interpretation). It is claimed that the rock from which Israel twice was given water moved to be with them (Ex. 17:5-7; Num. 20:10). But Paul's thought is better understood as a reference to that fact that God's grace followed Israel throughout the wilderness wanderings and that Christ, the spiritual Rock, never abandoned them.

RULER

See the section entitled "Blessed and only Potentate" on page 142.

SON OF GOD

This is one of the principal divine names of Jesus. It occurs forty times in the New Testament, with sixteen of these in the Epistles and one in Revelation. Only in Matthew 27:54 is the phrase possibly something less than an affirmation of deity. The NKJV renders the centurion's statement as follows: "Truly this was the Son of God!" However, the NASB margin indicates that this statement could also be rendered as either "a son of God" or "a son of a god."

During Satan's attempts to entice Jesus to sin, the devil said, "If You are the Son of God" (4:3, 6). In referring to Jesus in this way, Satan tacitly admitted Jesus' deity, for the "if" used by Satan has in the Greek the sense of "since." In other words, since Jesus is the Son of God, He should call upon His powers as God to change stones into bread. In response Jesus said, "Man shall not live by bread alone" (v. 4), which indicated that He chose to trust the Father to meet His physical needs.

As the Son of God, Christ cast out demons. These evil spirits clearly knew Jesus' identity as the Son of God and referred to Him as such (Matt. 8:29; Mark 3:11; Luke 4:41).

Paul begins the Book of Romans by pointing out that God the Father confirmed Christ's claim to deity. Jesus was "declared to be the Son of God with power according to the Spirit of holiness, by the resurrection from the dead" (1:4). The resurrection of Jesus—an unmistakable work of God—serves as the Father's documentation of Jesus' identity as God the Son.

A careful study of the Scriptures leaves no doubt concerning the full deity of Jesus. John Jefferson Davis, in his *Handbook of Basic Bible Texts*, lists the following key passages that tell us who Jesus is:

BIBLE BACKGROUND:

JESUS, THE SON OF GOD

Co-equal with God, the second person of theTrinity	Is. 9:6; Mic. 5:2; John 1:1-3; 6:38; 8:56-58; 17:4-5; Gal. 4:4-5; Phil. 2:5-7; Rev. 22:12, 13, 16
Virgin born, conceived by the Holy Spirit	Is. 7:14; Matt. 1:18-25; Luke 1:26-38
Without a sinful nature, clear of acts of sin	Luke 1:35; John 8:29, 46; 14:30-32; Acts 3:14; 2 Cor. 5:21; Heb. 4:15, 26, 28; 9:14; 1 Peter 1:18, 19; 2:22, 23; 1 John 3:4, 5
Truly and fully God, with divine titles	Is. 9:6; Matt. 26:63-66; Mark 1:2, 3; Luke 1:17; 3:1; Acts 2:21
Possessor of divine attributes	Matt. 28:20; John 1:1; 17:5; Eph. 1:22, 23; Phil. 21:5-7; Rev. 22:13
Possessor of divine power	John 1:3, 14; 5:21, 26; 11:25; Col. 1:16, 17; Heb. 1:2
Possessor of divine prerogatives	Matt. 25:31, 32; Mark 2:5-7; John 5:22, 27; Acts 8:59
Equal in every way with the Father	John 1:1; 20:28; Titus 2:13; Heb. 1:8; 1 Peter 1:1
Resurrected in the body and taken into heaven to guide and empower His church	Matt. 28:9; Luke 24:36-39, 50, 51; John 20:19; Acts 1:1, 2, 9-11; Rom. 1:2-4; 15:3-6, 17, 20; 1 Cor. 2:32, 33; Eph. 1:19-21; Phil. 2:9-11; Heb. 4:14; 7:26; Rev. 1:5

STAR

See "Bright and Morning Star" on pages 142 and 143.

STONE

"Stone" is one of the images of Christ in the Old Testament. The promised Messiah is to be a precious cornerstone, a sure founda-tion, and yet the stone that the builders reject. In each image, the Messiah is either the keystone on whom God's building is founded or the One who completes the structure.

The image of the stone being rejected by the builders is referred to most frequently in the New Testament. Jesus is presented as the rejected keystone in Matthew 21:42, Mark

12:10, Luke 20:17, and Acts 4:11. In each passage, the "builders" are the spiritual leaders of Israel who refuse to acknowledge Christ as the one critical element in their faith. In Romans 9:32 and 22, Paul refers to Isaiah 8:14, where the prophet presents God's keystone as a "stone of stumbling and rock of offense."

Peter also quotes this same passage when referring to those who reject Jesus as the Messiah (1 Peter 2:7, 8). Verses 4-8 put the whole matter in perspective:

Coming to Him as to a living stone, rejected indeed by men, but chosen by God and precious, you also, as living stones, are being built up a spiritual house, a holy priesthood, to offer up spiritual sacrifices acceptable to God through Jesus Christ. Therefore it is also contained in the Scripture,

> "Behold, I lay in Zion
> A chief cornerstone, elect, precious,
> And he who believes on Him
> will by no means be put to shame."

Therefore, to you who believe, He is precious; but to those who are disobedient,

> "The stone which the builders rejected
> Has become the chief cornerstone,"

and

> "A stone of stumbling
> And a rock of offense."

Jesus is the focus of our faith. We who make Him the cornerstone become living stones in God's new creation. To all who fail to trust Him, Christ is the stumbling stone whose rejection seals their eternal condemnation.

TRUTH

Jesus' claim to be "the way, the truth, and the life" is recorded in John 14:6. This means He is the way to God, the truth about God, and the source of life from God.

It is important to understand the biblical concept of truth. In both the Old and New Testaments, the underlying idea is one of reliability, rooted in the fact that what is true is of necessity in complete harmony with reality. When Jesus affirms that God's Word is truth (John 17:17), He is stating that every word of God is in total harmony with reality. Because of this, we can completely trust God's Word and, as we live by it, we will come to "know [by experience] the truth, and the truth shall make you free" (John 8:32).

As the Truth, Jesus is the One in whom all reality finds its focus. Only in Him will all the illusions of humankind be stripped away. In Him alone will we be able to know and live the life that God intends for us.

WORD

John begins his Gospel, not with an account of the birth of Jesus, but rather with statements about Jesus' preexistence as God in eternity past, before the creation of the universe. The apostle introduces us to the preincarnate Christ, giving Him the title "the Word" (John 1:1). Verses 1-3 read as follows:

> In the beginning was the Word, and the Word was with God, and the Word was God. He was in the beginning with God. All things were made through Him, and without Him nothing was made that was made.

Verse 14 declares, "the Word became flesh and dwelt among us, and we beheld His glory, the glory as of the only begotten of the Father, full of grace and truth." It is clear that John identifies Jesus as the eternal Word. But what is the significance of the name or title "the Word"?

Ancient Greek had two primary terms for "word." *Rhema* generally indicated a specific word or utterance. *Logos*, the word chosen by John, had broader application. The phrase "word of God" focuses on communication. God has spoken, revealing both truth and Himself to us.

In calling Jesus "the Word" (v. 1), John reminds us that the incarnation of Jesus so fully expresses who God is that Christ could say, "No one has seen God at any time. The only begotten Son, who is in the bosom of the Father, He has declared Him" (v. 18).

Thus, the Word expresses God's vital self-expression through the totality of His involvement in His universe and in our lives. When we acknowledge the Word of God, we affirm that Scripture is God's revelation to us. But we also confess our belief that God has fully and perfectly expressed Himself in Jesus. Christ shows us who the Father is and who He wants to be for us.

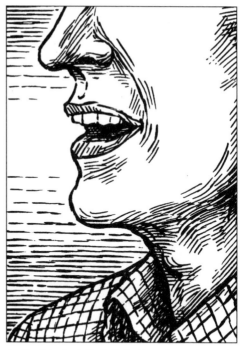

As the Word of God Christ has always been the Person of the Godhead who communicated with human beings.

NAMES AND TITLES OF JESUS EMPHASIZING HIS HUMANITY

The Jesus of Scripture is a true human being. He lived among us as a man. He experienced hunger and thirst, knew exhaustion, and felt deeply the rejection of His own people. A host of passages in Scripture make it unmistakably clear that while He is eternally God, Jesus Christ was also fully human.

One incident is particularly significant. Before Christ began His public ministry, the Holy Spirit led Him into the wilderness. There Jesus fasted for forty days and forty nights. Then, when Jesus was physically weak and exhausted, Satan came to tempt Him. Many years earlier the devil had succeeded in tempting Eve and Adam. Now Satan was intent on enticing Jesus (the Second Adam) to sin. The devil wanted to trick Jesus into abandoning God's will (Matt. 4:1, 2).

The first temptation focused on the fact that, because Jesus was a true human being, He was famished. Hunger, which deserts a

person during a long fast until all stored up bodily resources are expended, had returned. Satan's first temptation was focused on this fact. Thus, he said to Jesus, "If [since] You are the Son of God, command that these stones become bread" (v. 3).

Jesus, who would perform far more significant miracles, refused to do what the devil suggested. Instead, Jesus responded by quoting Deuteronomy 8:3, "It is written, 'Man shall not live by bread alone, but by every word that proceeds from the mouth of God'" (Matt. 4:4).

Jesus was living proof of the reality of this truth. He had set aside the prerogatives of deity to live on earth as a true human being (Phil. 2:5-7). Thus, the Son of God would meet Satan's temptations by relying only on the resources available to us! Jesus refused to perform a miracle to satisfy His hunger, for the suggestion to turn stones into

greatest wonder in the universe is the fact that God the Son chose to become a human being.

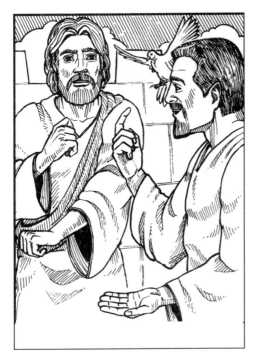

Jesus overcame Satan's temptations by depending only on resources within His human nature, setting an example for us.

❖

bread had come from Satan, not from God. As a human being, Jesus was committed to do the will of God, regardless of how great some might think the benefit of acting on His own would seem.

In asserting, "Man shall not live by bread alone" (Matt. 4:4), Jesus took His stand alongside us. He would not "cheat" by drawing on resources that are not available to us, His fellow human beings (Heb. 2:17, 18). Jesus was determined to live His life on earth subject to the same limitations under which we labor. Even Jesus' miracles would not be performed in His own power, but rather in the power of the Spirit, so that the Father's will might be accomplished (Matt. 12:28).

It is not surprising, then, to find that many of the names and titles of Jesus found in the New Testament emphasize His humanity rather than His deity. Perhaps the

❖

BIBLE BACKGROUND:

PASSAGES EMPHASIZING JESUS' HUMANITY

"Then Jesus was led up by the Spirit into the wilderness to be tempted by the devil. And when He had fasted forty days and forty nights, *afterward He was hungry*" (Matt. 4:1, 2).

"Now when He got into a boat, His disciples followed Him. And suddenly a great tempest arose on the sea, so that the boat was covered with waves. But *He was asleep*" (Matt. 8:23, 24)

"And *Jesus increased in wisdom and stature*, and in favor with God and men" (Luke 2:52).

"Behold My hands and My feet, that it is I Myself. Handle Me and see, for a spirit does not *have flesh and bones as you see I have*" (Luke 24:39).

"And the *Word became flesh and dwelt among us*" (John 1:14).

"Now Jacob's well was there. Jesus therefore, *being wearied from His journey*, sat thus by the well" (John 4:6).

"After this, Jesus, knowing that all things were now accomplished, that the Scripture might be fulfilled, said, *'I thirst!'*" (John 19:28).

"But when they came to Jesus and *saw that He was already dead*, they did not break His legs. But one of the soldiers *pierced His side with a spear, and immediately blood and water came out*" (John 19:33, 34).

"Inasmuch then as the children have partaken of *flesh and blood, He Himself likewise shared in the same*. . . . Therefore, *in all things He had to be made like His brethren,* that He might be a merciful and faithful High Priest in things pertaining to God, to make propitiation for the sins of the people. For in that *He Himself has suffered, being tempted,* He is able to aid those who are tempted" (Heb. 2:14, 17, 18).

THE LAST ADAM

Luke's genealogy traces Jesus' line back to Adam, establishing that Jesus is a true human being. Paul sees an even more significant relationship between Jesus and Adam. In 1 Corinthians 15:45, the apostle's great chapter on resurrection, he says, "The first Adam became a living being" (a quote from Genesis 2:7). Paul then says, "The last Adam became a life-giving spirit" (1 Cor. 15:45).

The first Adam launched our race, but in his fall into sin carried humanity away from God. The last Adam, Jesus, launched a renewal of humanity and led believing humankind's return to God.

Paul develops this theme in Romans 5:12-21. He compares and contrasts the first and last Adams. It was "through one man [that] sin entered the world, and death through sin, and thus death spread to all men" (v. 12). This was Adam's dark contribution to the millennia of tragedy and sorrow that followed. But it was also through one man's "righteous act [that] the free gift came to all men, resulting in justification of life. For as by one man's disobedience many were made sinners, so also by one Man's obedience many will be made righteous" (vv. 18, 19).

Our heritage from Adam is one of sin, death, and alienation. But now through faith we belong to Christ, the Founder of a new spiritual race, and our heritage in Him is righteousness and life.

BRIDEGROOM

Scripture views marriage as a delightful state. The bride and the groom are portrayed as finding joy in one another (Ps. 45:9; Song 1:1—8:14; Jer. 7:34; 16:9). The wedding was especially the focal point of joy. The celebration often lasted a week, and during this time the bride and groom were treated as king and queen.

Each of the synoptic Gospels reports that Jesus adopted this imagery when He answered a question about fasting (Matt. 9:15; Mark 2:19, 20; Luke 5:34, 35). In ancient times, fasting was a sign of grief and sorrow. In contrast, the wedding was a symbol of joy and celebration. The disciples of the Pharisees and even of John the Baptist might fast. However, during Jesus' earthly ministry, His followers would eat and drink, for Jesus was the Bridegroom, and His followers were the guests who were to accompany Him to the wedding. They couldn't fast while He, the Bridegroom, was with them.

Jesus' choice of this metaphor clearly underscored the reality of His humanity. People were comfortable in His presence and sought Him out for help, advice, and teaching. Being around Jesus was a source of joy for many, whether disciple or "sinner." Jesus was filled with a love that made many around Him (except the religious leaders, who were His enemies) feel like celebrating!

There are, of course, deeper implications to the image of Christ as a Bridegroom. When it came time for a Jewish couple to marry, the groom and his friends left his home and traveled to the home of the bride. This trip usually took place in the evening, and the guests of the bridegroom carried torches. The festive group laughed and sang as they approached the home of the bride. There the bride and her friends would be waiting with their own torches (Matt. 25:10). They were eager for the arrival of the bridegroom, and ready to

As the eldest son Jesus would have worked as a carpenter with Joseph.

❖

accompany the bride back to the groom's home, where the wedding would take place.

The Old Testament prophets used the image of the bride and groom to depict the relationship between God and Israel. We learn that in the future, a great restoration of Israel will come. It will be like a wedding not only because of the joy it will bring but also because it marks the union of God with His people.

Jesus adopted this prophetic language. Thus, in Matthew 25:1-13, He applied it to His own return for the church. After His death and resurrection, Jesus would return to heaven. As the Bridegroom of the church, His return might not be for a long time. Nevertheless, Jesus assuredly would return as the Bridegroom, eager to gather us, His waiting bride.

THE CARPENTER

Mark 6:3 indicates that Jesus worked as a carpenter. The second synoptic Gospel tells of a time when Jesus, after He had gained some fame as an itinerant teacher and healer, returned to Nazareth. That Sabbath He was invited to teach in His hometown synagogue (vv. 1, 2).

Being invited to teach was not unusual. The synagogue service began with a recitation of blessings, followed by a reading from the Pentateuch. By the first century A.D., the first five books in the Old Testament had been organized into several hundred readings, which took a congregation through the writings of Moses every three years. The reading of the Torah was followed by a reading from the Haptorah, the Prophets. After this, a member of the congregation or a visitor was invited to make spontaneous comments on the Scriptures read. Thus, when Jesus returned to Nazareth after ministering elsewhere, it was natural that His curious townspeople would want to hear what He had to say.

According to Mark 6:2 and 3, those in the synagogue were "astonished, saying, 'Where did this Man get these things? And what wisdom is this which is given to Him, that such mighty works are performed by His hands? Is this not the carpenter, the Son of Mary, and brother of James, Joses, Judas, and Simon? And are not His sisters here with us?' So they were offended at Him." This brief passage tells us much about Christ's humanity.

Jesus worked in Nazareth as a carpenter. In biblical times, the oldest son typically learned his father's trade. This suggests that Joseph had been a carpenter and that as a youth Jesus had been Joseph's apprentice. The fact that Jesus was called "the carpenter" (Mark 6:3) by the people of Nazareth suggests that Joseph had died and that Jesus was no longer viewed as just "the son of the carpenter" but rather as "the carpenter."

The *Revell Bible Dictionary* describes the work of a first-century carpenter and explains the reaction of the people of Nazareth.

> What did these woodworkers make in biblical times? Wood was generally scarce in Palestine, and most homes were constructed of stone, but roof beams and often doors were made of wood. The many fishing boats that crossed the Sea of Galilee were wooden, and fashioning them called for special skills. Probably Joseph and Jesus, working in Nazareth some miles from the water, made farm tools like plows and sickles, and furnishings for the homes of their neighbors: chairs, tables, and bedframes.
>
> Jesus' neighbors found it difficult to grasp the fact that the carpenter who had made yokes for their animals was in fact the Messiah. It is easy to lose sight of God in the commonplace. We too may fail to realize that our Lord most often reveals himself in the simple things of daily life (p. 195).

Jesus took on the role of head of the family. After Joseph died (the most likely possibility, given all the biblical evidence), Jesus, as the eldest son, became the head of the family. He thus was responsible for the care of his mother, for in ancient times the bulk of the family estate passed to the eldest son, not to the widow.

The fourth Gospel reports that as Jesus hung on the cross, He saw His mother, Mary, and a disciple named John standing nearby. There, as the last act before Jesus' death, the Savior directed Mary's attention to John and said, "Woman, behold your son!" (John 19:26). Then Jesus directed John's attention to Mary, and said, "Behold your mother!" (v. 27). The text says, "From that hour that disciple took her to his own home."

It's striking to see that on the cross Jesus was moved by the very human concern of a son for His mother's welfare. Indeed, Jesus was human in the very best sense of the word.

Jesus grew up in a family with brothers and sisters. Some try to explain away the clear teaching of John 7:5 by claiming that the Greek noun *adelphos*, which is usually rendered "brother," can also be translated "cousin." This argument, however, is rooted in the desire of some to see Mary as a perpetual virgin rather than as a Jewish mother who loved her husband and rejoiced in the privilege of giving him many children (Matt. 13:55, 56).

For Jesus, the birth of brothers and sisters meant that He grew up in a large family. As the eldest son, Jesus undoubtedly helped to care for His younger siblings. We can hardly imagine a more typical childhood for a first-century Jewish youth. It is striking that, even after Christ had become well known in Galilee, "even His brothers did not believe in Him" (John 7:5). They could not imagine that their brother was also the Son of God.

Christ was so truly and fully human—so much a son, neighbor, and brother—that the reality of His messiahship was at first denied by His own siblings. (Later some of Jesus' brothers did come to faith. For instance, James became the leader of the Jerusalem church as well as the author of the epistle that bears his name.) We need only look at the reaction of the people of Nazareth and of Jesus' family, who knew Him best, to be convinced that God the Son had become a real human being in His Incarnation.

CHILD

Isaiah prophesied, "For unto us a Child is born, unto us a Son is given" (Is. 9:6). This prophecy clearly indicates that the promised Messiah was to be both a human being, entering the world through the natural process of childbirth, and God the Son, given supernaturally.

The Gospels frequently refer to Jesus as a child, carefully establishing the fact of His full human nature. Matthew 1:18 says that

Firstfruits—the first ripened of the crop—were offered to God in thanksgiving for the coming harvest.

❖

Mary—who was pledged to be married to Joseph but had not yet had sexual relations with him—was "found to be with child through the Holy Spirit" (NIV). While settled in Mary's womb, Jesus developed as did any human fetus. Luke 2:7 describes Jesus' entry into the world through natural childbirth: "[Mary] brought forth her firstborn Son, and wrapped Him in swaddling cloths, and laid Him in a manger."

As an infant and a toddler, Jesus was as dependent on His parents as any child would be. When Herod sought to kill the One born King of the Jews, Joseph, having been warned in a dream, took the child and His mother to Egypt (Matt. 2:14). Jesus, at this time a helpless young child, was guarded and nurtured by Joseph and Mary.

Luke 2:51 says that even after Jesus' twelfth birthday, He was "subject" (or "obedient") to His parents. We also learn

that Jesus "increased in wisdom and stature" (v. 52).

In all this we see clear evidence of the full humanity of Jesus. He was conceived, born, and grew up as a child. First Timothy 3:16 affirms this truth: "And without controversy, great is the mystery of godliness: God was manifested in the flesh, justified in the Spirit, seen by angels, preached among the Gentiles, believed on in the world, received up in glory." Truly, the Christ child born in Bethlehem was at the same time God the Son!

FIRSTFRUITS

In 1 Corinthians 15:20-24, Paul refers to Jesus as the "firstfruits":

> But now Christ is risen from the dead, and has become the firstfruits of those who have fallen asleep. For since by man came death, by Man also came the resurrection of the dead. For as in Adam all die, even so in Christ all shall be made alive. But each one in his own order: Christ the firstfruits, afterward those who are Christ's at His coming.

The historic roots. The title "firstfruits" (1 Cor. 15:20) goes back to a principle established in the Mosaic Law. The *Nelson Encyclopedia of the Bible* defines the firstfruits as follows:

> [The] firstborn child or animal or first parts of any crop which, in Hebrew thought, were considered as holy and belonging to the Lord. The first fruits, as a foretaste of more to come, were offered to God in thanksgiving for his goodness in providing them (p. 791).

In verse 20, the resurrected Jesus is portrayed as the "firstfruits," that is, the first installment of a harvest to eternal life. As Jesus was resurrected, so will all human beings be who believe in Him.

In verse 21, Paul argues that "since by man came death, by Man also came the resurrection of the dead." This is a recurring theme in the Epistles—it was only because Christ came and shared our human nature that He was qualified to bear our sins. And it is through our spiritual union with Christ—the man who died and who was made alive—that we have been freed from the grip of sin and given new life through faith in Him. Moreover, it was Christ's resurrection as a man that made Him the firstfruits. In other words, He is the sure and certain foretaste of what is yet to come for us who believe.

HIGH PRIEST

The Book of Hebrews emphasizes the fact that Christ is a "merciful and faithful High Priest in things pertaining to God" (2:17). The high priesthood of Jesus is referred to in no less than eight of Hebrews thirteen chapters! These chapters, which contain some fifteen references to Jesus' high priesthood, make it clear that Jesus *must have been* human.

The Old Testament background. The role of the high priest in Israel's religion was clearly established in the Old Testament. The *Revell Bible Dictionary* offers the following summary:

> The functions of the OT priesthood are outlined in Deut. 33:8-10. Priests, drawn from the tribe of Levi and the family of Aaron, (1) guard God's covenant by (2) teaching God's precepts and Law, and (3) offer incense and sacrifice on God's altar. In teaching God's Law, the priests spoke to men on God's behalf. In presenting sacrifices and offerings, the priests spoke to God for men. Thus their role was mediatorial, intended to bond God's covenant people to him.
>
> Any of the priests could teach God's written Law and offer sacrifices on behalf of those who committed unintentional sins. But the high priest was unique. The high priest alone bore on his chest, in a sacred pouch,

the Urim and Thummim. Through the Urim and Thummim, God gave specific guidance concerning his will in situations not covered in the written Word. Furthermore, the high priest alone could enter the Holy of Holies on the Day of Atonement. There he offered the blood of a sacrifice, making atonement for all the sins of God's people, both unintentional and intentional (Lev. 16). In these two ministries, the high priest was the sole mediator of the covenant that God made with Israel. Thus, in these functions, the high priest was a type, or living portrait, of Jesus Christ.

The Book of Hebrews describes the ministries of Jesus in view of His appointment as high priest. Jesus made atonement for sins (2:17); He interceded with God for sinners (4:15); and in offering Himself on Calvary, Jesus made the sacrifice necessary to win our forgiveness (8:3).

Christ's priesthood and Jesus' humanity. The Book of Hebrews makes it clear that Jesus simply must have been fully human to serve, as He does, as our high priest (2:14-18).

Jesus had to be human to understand experientially human nature and needs. Hebrews 2:17 points out that Jesus "had to be made like His brethren, that He might be a merciful and faithful High Priest." If Jesus were to represent humanity before God, it was necessary that He personally suffer, "being tempted" (or "tested," v. 18), so that He might be "able to aid those who are tempted."

A similar point is made in 4:15 and 16. We learn that "we do not have a High Priest who cannot sympathize with our weaknesses, but was in all points tempted as we are, yet without sin. Let us therefore come boldly to the throne of grace, that we may obtain mercy and find grace to help in time of need."

Being tempted does not imply sin, but rather natural human weaknesses. Just as we are subject to the pressures of hunger, hurts, frustrations, and rejection, Jesus too, in living a human life, subjected Himself to all these pressures. He lived with our weaknesses—weaknesses that are intrinsic to the human condition. Nevertheless, He did so without ever once *surrendering to* any temptation and thus falling into sin.

Jesus does understand what it means to be human and what it means to be weak. Thus He can and does sympathize with us. We can come to Him boldly, whether for mercy after we have given in to temptations or for grace to help us withstand temptations, for He knows by experience what it is like to be one of us.

Jesus had to be human to qualify as our High Priest. Hebrews 5:1 says, "Every high priest is selected from among men and is appointed to represent them in matters related to God, to offer gifts and sacrifices for sins" (NIV). No angel could serve as our High Priest. Even God the Son could not perform that function until He had taken on humanity. It thus was utterly necessary that Jesus be appointed by the Father as humankind's representative. Christ needed to become human in order to offer Himself as an atoning sacrifice for sins and thereby bring believing sinners to God.

Though Jesus was qualified by His humanity to be our high priest, He also had to be appointed to this office by the Father. One might initially conclude that this would be a problem, for all Old Testament priests had to be from the family of Aaron of the tribe of Levi. Jesus' family line was traced back to the tribe of Judah not Levi (v. 14). The issue is resolved when we realize that God was replacing the Levitical system with a new Priest, who would offer a new sacrifice under a new covenant. God appointed Jesus as a high priest according to the order of Melchizekek, not Aaron (7:11).

The Aaronic priests eventually died and were replaced by others. But, as the writer of Hebrews notes, there is no record in Scripture of the death of Melchizedek (v. 3). This per-

son, being both a king and a priest, is mentioned briefly in Scripture as blessing the patriarch Abraham (Gen. 14:18-20). But aside from this brief passage, we know nothing about the birth or death of Melchizekek.

Verse 17 quotes God's promise in Psalm 110:4 that the Messiah would be a priest "forever according to the order of Melchizedek." As our resurrected Lord, Jesus will never die again. He is always available to represent us before the throne of God.

The writer of Hebrews rightly concludes that in Jesus, the God-man, we have a high priest who meets our spiritual needs. He alone is "holy, innocent, undefiled, separated from sinners and exalted above the heavens" (Heb. 7:26 NASB). Once again we see clearly that the Scriptures present Jesus not only as the Son of God but also as a real human being.

JESUS OF NAZARETH
NAZARENE

Fifteen times in the Gospels and in Acts Christ is called "Jesus of Nazareth." Four times in these documents Jesus is referred to as "the Nazarene."

Some think that by calling Jesus "the Nazarene," people were simply identifying Him with His hometown of Nazareth. However, it is more likely that at first the title was used to distinguish Jesus the Messiah (namely, the Anointed One from Nazareth) from many other Jews of the day who bore the name "Jesus."

It's helpful for us to realize that there was no great pool of names from which a Jewish couple could draw upon when naming their sons or daughters. Typically, the names given children were family names, borne by generation upon generation of ancestors. It was typical in the Roman Empire for a woman named Julia (for instance) to also name each of her three daughters "Julia." They would then by known as Julia Major, Julia Secunda, and

Julia Tertia—that is, Julia the first, Julia the second, and Julia the third!

Most likely "Jesus" ("Joshua" in Hebrew or Aramaic) was one of those common Jewish names favored by God's people. Understandably, then, people identified the Jesus of the Gospels as "Jesus of Nazareth." In other words, He was *that* Jesus (as opposed to some other person named "Jesus").

This having been said, there is an even greater significance in identifying the Messiah as "Jesus of Nazareth." Just as the first century is a specific period in time, so Nazareth in Galilee was a specific location in space.

Thus, calling the Savior "Jesus of Nazareth" reminds us that the account of Jesus is neither a myth nor one of those far-fetched stories found in pagan religions about false gods and goddesses. Rather, God the Son—named "Jesus of Nazareth"—entered our world of space and time. He is a historic figure, a person who actually lived, died, and rose again in the "real world.' Testifying to the historicity of all those events recorded in the New Testament, we have the witness of people who knew and who spoke about the Messiah as Jesus "of Nazareth."

MAN
SON OF MAN

Every now and then people would refer to Jesus simply as that "man." For example, after witnessing one of Jesus' miracles, even His disciples wondered aloud, "What kind of man is this?" (Matt. 8:27 NIV).

Those few passages in which Jesus was spoken of simply as a man pale in significance to one of Jesus' favorite titles for Himself. No less than 82 times in the Gospels Jesus refers to Himself as the "Son of Man." We can tell from this repeated use that the title "Son of Man" was particularly significant to Jesus. This title was not only important to Him, but it also has great theological significance. *The New International*

Encyclopedia of Bible Words summarizes them succinctly.

First, [the title Son of Man] emphasizes Jesus' humanity. In the OT, "son of man" is often used in addressing Ezekiel. In the context of that book, it is clear that the title simply means "man," and carries there a special emphasis on the distinction between humanity and God. The NT makes it clear that Jesus took on true human nature, and the implication of the title is to affirm [and emphasize] his humanity.

Second, it is used in place of "I." There are a number of passages in which it seems best to take the phrase in this way (e.g., Mt 12:8; 17:22; 19:28; 20:18, 28).

Third, it identifies Jesus as the focus of OT eschatological prophecy. Daniel reported his vision of history's end, saying, "In my vision at night I looked, and there before me was one like a son of man, coming with the clouds of heaven. He approached the Ancient of Days and was led into his presence. He was given authority, glory and sovereign power; all peoples, nations and men of every language worshipped him. His dominion is an everlasting dominion" (Dan 7:13-14). The phrase "like a son of man" undoubtedly means that Daniel saw a being who, in contrast to the exotic figures he had just described (7:1-12), simply looked human. But the phrase is given more meaning in the eschatological passages in the Gospels. Jesus is *the* human being Daniel saw, who will fulfill Daniel's prophecy in times to come (Mt 13; 24; Mk 13).

Fourth, it identifies Jesus with humanity in his suffering for us. Often this phrase was chosen by Jesus when he spoke of his coming suffering and death (e.g., Mt 12:40). Jesus the Son of Man did come from heaven (Jn 3:13), but he had to be lifted up in crucifixion, suffering for all so that all who believe in him may have eternal life (Jn 3:14).

It would be difficult to exhaust the significance of the title "Son of Man." But surely it is intended to draw our attention to Jesus as fully human, to make us aware of Jesus' sufferings

Peter, who knew Jesus as a friend before he became a disciple, was stunned when he recognized Jesus' deity.

for us, and to awaken wonder that the eternal Son of God truly entered the world to bring us, victorious, to His eternal glory.

MASTER

In the Gospel of Luke, Jesus is addressed as "Master" some six times, five of them by His disciples and once by lepers seeking His aid (17:13). The term is capitalized in both the NKJV and the NIV as if it were a title of deity. However, the Greek noun that Luke uses, which is found only in his Gospel, is *epistates*, which might be translated "chief" or "commander." While this word implies authority to give orders, it does not indicate unlimited authority.

It is interesting that the disciples used this term during the early stages of their relationship with Jesus (Luke 5:5; 8:24, 45; 9:33, 49). While they were quickly awed by

Jesus and by His authority over nature, sickness, and even demons, they had not yet fully realized His messianic identity. It is only later in Luke's Gospel that the disciples begin to address Jesus as "Lord."

SON OF DAVID

The Gospels refer to Jesus as the "Son of David" sixteen times. The phrase establishes Jesus as a descendant of David and thus a member in the royal line. Joseph, too, is referred to as a son of David (Matt. 1:20), but not in the same sense as is Jesus. While Joseph was *a* descendant of David, Jesus was *the* Son of David, that is, the promised Messiah who was to come from the line of Israel's greatest king.

Both the Gospels of Matthew and Luke provide genealogies of Jesus. Each genealogy is intended to establish Jesus' lineage and thus His right to the messianic throne as a legitimate offspring of King David. Nevertheless, Luke's genealogy goes further by tracing Christ's ancestry back to Adam. Jesus was indeed a true human being, a member of our race whose roots can be traced back to the first man, Adam. Thus, the title "Son of David" looks both to Jesus' identity as a human being with a known and specific family line and to His role as the long-promised Messiah.

BIBLE BACKGROUND:

THE TWO GENEALOGIES OF JESUS

The Bible contains orderly lists tracing the human ancestry of Jesus the Messiah. These are found in Matthew 1:1-17 and Luke 3:23-38. Some have seen a conflict in the two genealogies, for at one point the ancestors listed diverge. The explanation for this and something of the significance of these two genealogies is contained in the *Revell Bible Dictionary* (pp. 423, 425).

Biblical genealogies characteristically include only selected ancestors. This is illustrated by Luke's list of some 20 ancestors between David and the Exile, while Matthew has only 14. A significant difference between the two is that Matthew traces Jesus' line through Solomon and Judah's kings, while Luke traces the line through Nathan, another son of David by Bathsheba (1 Chr. 3:5). The two primary explanations assume (1) that Matthew traces the legal line and Luke the biological line of Joseph, or (2) that Luke gives the genealogy of Mary, while Matthew lists the genealogy of Joseph. This second view is supported by Jeremiah's curse on Jehoiachin, a king in Solomon's line, whose descendants were never to occupy Israel's throne, even though the legal right was theirs (compare Jer. 22:30; Mt. 1:11). If this second explanation is correct, Jesus' legal right to the throne

is established through Joseph, while his biological descent from David is established through Mary. This view may be reflected in Romans 1:3, which affirms that Jesus "as to his human nature was a descendant of David."

Two other features of these genealogies are of note: (1) Each genealogy guards the doctrine of the virgin birth. Christ was the son "so it was thought, of Joseph" (Lk. 3:23; *see also* Mt. 1:16); (2) Matthew includes four women in Jesus' genealogy, which is contrary to Hebrew practice, and even more unusual are the women selected: Tamar (Mt. 1:3), who became pregnant by her father-in-law, Gen. 38; Rahab (Mt. 1:5), who was the believing prostitute who survived the destruction of Jericho, Josh. 2; 6:25; Ruth (Mt. 1:5), who was a Moabitess; and Bathsheba (Mt. 1:6), who was the adulterous wife of Uriah, a victim of David's passion, 2 Sam. 11; 12. God's grace not only reached out to save these women but also placed them in the line of the Redeemer.

Thus, the genealogies show both that Jesus fulfills Israel's messianic expectations and that, through the incarnation, the redemption Christ won is for all of humanity.

RABBI

The Gospels report fourteen incidents in which Jesus was addressed as "Rabbi." Only Luke chose not to report such an incident.

In ancient times "rabbi" was a title of respect. It was used when addressing a person who was recognized as an expert in the Law of Moses. John 1:38 notes, "They said to Him, 'Rabbi!' (which is to say, when translated, Teacher), 'where are you staying?'"

By the first century A.D., the usual route through which a person might obtain the knowledge of the Law necessary to gain recognition as a rabbi was by apprenticeship to a recognized expert in the Law. The eager student

Nicodemus, a member of the Sanhedrin, admitted that the religious leaders were well aware that Jesus was a teacher sent to them by God.

would become the disciple of a well-known rabbi, and for a number of years actually live with him. The student would listen to the rabbi's teaching, observe his way of life, ask him questions, and seek to imitate not only his master's teachings but also his lifestyle.

During the years that a disciple spent with a rabbi, he was expected to serve the rabbi, and the rabbi was expected to support his disciple, often through gifts given by those who sought the rabbi's advice or who simply wished to be associated with him. The benefit to the student was that he would one day be personally recognized as a rabbi. The benefit to the rabbi was that his particular insights and interpretations would be passed down to others and hopefully become an integral part of Judaism.

One reason the religious establishment resented Jesus was because He had suddenly laid down His carpenter's tools and begun teaching and preaching as a rabbi. Rather than first becoming the disciple of a rabbi, Jesus instead had begun to teach with an authority that seemed even greater than that of Judaism's' recognized sages (Matt. 7:29).

Nevertheless, it was clear even to the religious establishment that Jesus truly was an expert in Old Testament lore and law. Even Nicodemas—a member of the Sanhedrin, who came to visit Jesus one night early in the Savior's public ministry—addressed Jesus as "Rabbi" and confessed that "we [the religious leaders] know that You are a teacher come from God; for no one can do these signs that You do unless God is with him" (John 3:2).

"Rabbi," then, was a title that carried no implication of deity, but instead was granted to a human being who, like other persons, struggled to grasp the deeper meaning of God's Law. While "Rabbi" was a title of utmost respect within the first-century Jewish community, it was also a very human title. Though it conveyed profound respect, it was a respect that fell far short of worship.

All these names and titles of Jesus—"the Last Adam," "the Bridegroom," "the Carpenter," "Child," "Firstfruits," "High Priest," "Jesus of Nazareth," "Son of Man," "Master," "Son of David," and "Rabbi"— emphasize the fact that Jesus lived as, and indeed was, a human being. The Messiah was like us in every way—except for lost humankind's natural bent toward sin (Heb. 4:14).

NAMES AND TITLES OF JESUS EMPHASIZING HIS MISSION

Scripture assigns to Jesus names and titles that emphasize His deity and His humanity. But Jesus also bears names and titles that give us insight into His mission both here on earth and subsequently in heaven. As we consider these names and titles, we are impressed not simply with who Jesus is, but also with who Jesus is *for us*.

ADVOCATE

John tells us that "if anyone sins, we have an Advocate with the Father, Jesus Christ the righteous" (1 John 2:1). The Greek noun rendered "Advocate" is *parakletos*. It is used only by John in the New Testament, typically in references to the Holy Spirit. However, in this verse John uses *parakletos* in a legal sense, one that was well-established in the first century A.D.

In Bible times, the *parakletos* was a "helper in court," namely, someone who defended another person by offering evidence to support his or her innocence. In the above mentioned verse, John pictures Jesus as our "helper in court." When we sin, Jesus steps forward and pleads the efficacy of His own blood, which He offered as a sacrifice in payment for our sins. As verse 2 says, "He himself is the propitiation for our sins, and not for ours only but also for the whole world."

Jesus' role as our Advocate is a present ministry. But it is also an essential element of His mission to make salvation available to all humankind. While not all people will respond to Him with faith and be saved, His sacrifice is sufficient to pay for the sins of all humankind.

APOSTLE

In Hebrews 3:1 Jesus is called the "Apostle and High Priest" whom Christians confess. This is the only place in Scripture where Jesus is called an apostle. Nevertheless, it is clear from the rest of the New Testament that Jesus was in fact the premier apostle.

The Greek noun rendered "apostle" is *apostolos*. By the first century A.D., it carried the idea of a personal representative of a dignitary or ruler. In philosophy, the word came to be used with a religious connotation. Thus, an apostle was someone who spoke as authorized by a deity.

In both senses Jesus is indeed the premier apostle. He is God the Father's personal representative. Also, Jesus is God the Son! Thus, everything He has taught bears the stamp of divine approval, for He as well as His statements are the Word of God.

The Father's commissioning of the Son to represent Him was indeed a central aspect of Jesus' mission to earth. As the Father's personal representative, Jesus came to reveal who God truly is. Also, Jesus came to reveal more fully God's saving plans and purposes.

As the Apostle and High Priest whom Christians confess, Jesus is the One whose revelation of the Father's love and whose promise of forgiveness we believe implicitly.

BIBLE BACKGROUND:

"APOSTLE" IN THE NEW TESTAMENT

The Gospels focus our attention on twelve men whom Jesus chose to be His apostles (Matt. 10:2-4; Luke 6:13-16). The Savior chose these men to be His representatives and authorized them to speak for Him when the church was established.

The title "apostle" was also given to other church leaders, such as the apostle Paul (1 Tim. 2:7). In a significant way, Paul ranks with the Twelve as a spokesperson of the risen Christ.

There is, however, another use of "apostle" in the New Testament. Individuals like Barnabas (Acts 14:14) and possibly Andronicus (Rom. 16:7) are referred to as "apostles," and this role was clearly filled by several in the first-century church (1 Cor. 12:28). It is likely that these lesser apostles—lesser in comparison to the Twelve and Paul—were what we today would call missionaries. They traveled throughout the Roman Empire as Christ's representatives and proclaimed the gospel to all who would listen.

AUTHOR

The Greek noun translated "author" appears three times in the New Testament in reference to Jesus, although the word is rendered "author" only once in the NKJV. Jesus is called the author of our faith (Heb. 12:2 NKJV), the author of our salvation (2:10 NASB), and the author of eternal life (Acts 3:15 NIV).

The Greek noun is *archegos*, and it was frequently used when referring to a city's founder or to the founder of a philosophic school. As used in reference to Jesus, the term marks Him as the Pioneer who has opened the way for us to salvation and eternal life. In fulfilling His redemptive mission by His sacrificial death and resurrection, Christ bridged the gap between humankind and God. Jesus also became the source of eternal life and salvation for us.

BREAD

It was Jesus who called Himself the "bread of life" (John 6:35), using what was a powerful metaphor in biblical times. Long ago in Palestine, bread was the primary food. It was made from a variety of grains, often with ground beans or lentils mixed in the flour. Bread was typically baked flat. A loaf of dough was about a half-inch thick. It was slapped against the outside of a beehive-shaped clay oven to bake.

Bread has great significance in the Bible, for it literally and symbolically represented the maintenance of life. Thus, it should come as no surprise that Jesus taught His disciples to pray, "Give us this day our daily bread" (Matt. 6:11). This request reminds us of our constant dependence on God for all the necessities of life. But the most significant metaphorical reference to bread is found in John 6:35, where Jesus announced that He is the "bread of life."

The setting (John 6:1-27). A large crowd had followed Jesus out into an isolated place. As the day wore on, Jesus asked Philip (and undoubtedly the rest of the disciples) where bread could be purchased to feed all the hungry people. The query was a test, one that Philip and the other disciples failed. Perhaps shocked, Philip objected that a great sum of money would be necessary to buy enough bread to feed the vast crowd.

Jesus then took the five barley loaves and two small fish a boy had brought and multiplied them. The crowd of thousands was fed,

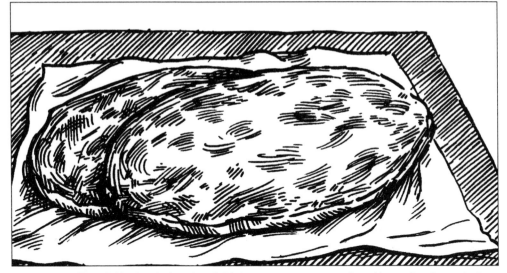

Flat loaves of bread, like the pita bread available in grocery stores, were viewed in Israel as the staple that sustained life.

and there were twelve baskets of fragments left over. The miracle excited the crowd. They reasoned that not only must Jesus be the Messiah, but if He were to rule them, they would never go hungry again! Jesus sensed their intent to take Him by force and acclaim Him their king, so He quickly left the area.

The next day the crowds found Jesus again. It was then that He rebuked them for focusing on food for the body, rather than on "the food which endures to everlasting life" (John 6:27).

The sermon on the bread of life (John 6:28-66). What Jesus said on that occasion both puzzled and alienated many of His listeners. *The Teacher's Commentary* (1988, pp. 723, 724) traces the flow of Jesus' message to the people of His time, and explores the meaning of His identification of Himself as the Bread of Life.

"I am the Bread of Life" (John 6:35-40). Each statement Jesus made stressed the continuing benefits of the life He brings. *You will never be hungry*. God will, in Jesus, keep on supplying that which sustains our new life. *You will never*

be thirsty. A human being can go without food for weeks without dying, but he cannot go without water. Jesus promises to satisfy even that most intense of needs; He will see that we lack nothing we need. *I will never drive [him] away . . . I shall lose none of all that He has given me*. We can be sure Jesus will extend God's grace to us in a daily experience of eternal life as well as in a permanent relationship with God.

"I am the Bread that came down from heaven" (John 6:41-51). The manna God provided for the Israelites during the Exodus is a picture of Jesus as "living bread." When God's people traveled through the wilderness, they had to depend on God to provide their food supernaturally. God provided the food in a way that would also teach the people something about their relationship with Him. Every day God gave enough food for that day. No one could gather more than a day's supply. There had to be a continual, constant dependence on God; He was the only source of sustenance.

The Jews murmured against Christ's claim to be "Bread that came down from heaven." They knew this Man and His family;

how could He claim a heavenly origin? Jesus answered that it would be God who would draw men to Christ. And Jesus then went on to promise that anyone who believed in Him would have eternal life, and anyone who fed on the living Bread "will live forever."

"Eat the flesh of the Son of man" (John 6:52-59). Many see in these words a reference to the Communion service. "This is My body, given for you," Jesus would say as He instituted the memorial service. This is "My blood which is poured out for you." But to "eat" and "drink" the body and blood of Jesus means far more than to participate in a shared memorial, as the rest of our passage suggests. "Whoever eats My flesh and drinks My blood remains in Me" (v. 56). "He who feeds on this bread will live forever" (v. 58). "The words I have spoken to you are spirit," Jesus said (v. 63).

Jesus was using *body* and *blood* to represent everything needed to sustain and support life. Our lives will be supported so completely that we will never hunger or thirst. Our spiritual lives will be sustained so completely that they will endure until Jesus raises us up on the last day.

When Jesus called Himself the Bread of Life, then, He was referring to His mission to give and sustain spiritual life. Christ fulfilled His mission to be our Bread of Life by dying on the cross and being resurrected. We complete the transaction when, by faith, we figuratively "eat" and "drink" (that is, spiritually appropriate) His body and blood.

CHIEF CORNERSTONE

The Old Testament refers to Jesus as a precious cornerstone, as the stone the builders rejected, and as our sure foundation (see p. 159). In Ephesians 2:20, Paul carries this theme further. The apostle views the church, the household of God, as being "built on the foundation of the apostles and prophets, Jesus Christ Himself being the chief cornerstone."

Similar imagery is adopted by Peter, who calls Jesus a "living stone, rejected

indeed by men, but chosen by God and precious" (1 Peter 2:4). The apostle goes on to quote several Old Testament passages in which the Messiah is identified as the chief cornerstone (vv. 6-8).

The point in each of these passages is that Christ came to be the key not only to our spiritual life but also our spiritual growth. As Paul says in 1 Corinthians 3:11, "No other foundation can anyone lay than that which is laid, which is Jesus Christ."

CHRIST

Jesus is identified as the "Christ" no less than 530 times in the New Testament in some 499 verses. This title, the equivalent in Greek of the Hebrew "Messiah," or "Anointed One," is one of the most significant names of Jesus to be found in Scripture. (For more information on the title "Messiah," see page 94.)

In Old Testament times, anointing someone set that person apart. He or she was commissioned for a special mission. Thus, the name "Messiah," or "the Anointed One," emphasizes the fact that God set Jesus apart to accomplish a redemptive mission.

The Jews considered the primary mission of the Messiah to be the reconciliation of God's people to Himself, their purification from sin, and the elimination of sin and evil worldwide. There are Old Testament passages that emphasize other aspects of the Messiah's mission, such as providing physical healing (Is. 35:1-3) and salvation from sin (chap. 53). Nevertheless, the mission of the Messiah that most captured the imagination of Israel was that of establishing the rule and justice of God on earth.

In the New Testament Epistles, "Christ" becomes as much a name as a title. Nevertheless, it remains clear that Jesus' identification as the "Christ" implies that He too was anointed, or set apart, for a special mission. In one sense, the entire New Testament revelation is an unveiling of the redemptive mission for which God sent Jesus to earth. (In contrast, the Old Testament gives partial

The fish was chosen as an early Christian symbol because the letters of its Greek name, *ichthus,* were the initial letters of the Christian confession, "Jesus Christ, Son of God, Savior."

glimpses of what God commissioned Jesus to do.) Understandably, then, it is valuable to examine the New Testament Epistles where Jesus is called "the Christ" and discern what aspects of His redemptive mission are associated with this special name.

BIBLE BACKGROUND:

CHRIST'S MISSION

PASSAGE	MISSION
ROM. 1:1	TO REPRESENT GOD AS AN APOSTLE
ROM. 1:6	TO GATHER A PEOPLE BELONGING TO HIM
ROM. 2:16	TO BE THE STANDARD BY WHICH PEOPLE'S SECRETS ARE JUDGED
ROM. 3:22	TO BE THE SOURCE OF RIGHTEOUSNESS TO ALL WHO BELIEVE
ROM. 3:24	TO REDEEM LOST HUMAN BEINGS
ROM. 5:1	TO BRING BELIEVERS INTO A STATE OF PEACE WITH GOD
ROM. 5:6	TO DIE FOR THE UNGODLY
ROM. 5:8	TO DIE FOR US, SHOWING GOD'S UNCONDITIONAL LOVE FOR HUMANKIND
ROM. 5:11	TO RECONCILE US TO GOD
ROM. 5:15	TO BRING US THE GIFT OF GOD'S GRACE
ROM. 5:17	TO PROVIDE THE GIFT OF RIGHTEOUSNESS
ROM. 5:21	TO BRING US ETERNAL LIFE
ROM. 6:3	TO UNITE US SPIRITUALLY TO HIMSELF IN HIS DEATH
ROM. 6:4	TO UNITE US SPIRITUALLY TO HIMSELF IN HIS RESURRECTION
ROM. 6:23	TO BRING US THE GIFT OF ETERNAL LIFE
ROM. 7:4	TO ENABLE US TO DIE TO THE LAW SO THAT WE MIGHT BEAR FRUIT TO GOD
ROM. 8:1	TO RELEASE US FROM CONDEMNATION
ROM. 8:2	TO SET US FREE FROM THE POWER OF SIN AND DEATH
ROM. 8:10	TO MAKE US SPIRITUALLY ALIVE
ROM. 8:17	TO MAKE US CO-HEIRS WITH HIM OF GOD THE FATHER

ROM. 8:35, 39	TO SECURE US AS HIS OWN FOREVER
ROM. 10:4	TO MAKE THE LAW NO LONGER NECESSARY FOR THOSE WHO BECOME ACCEPTABLE TO GOD BY FAITH
ROM. 10:17	TO STIMULATE FAITH THROUGH HIS WORD
ROM. 12:5	TO UNITE BELIEVERS INTO A SINGLE SPIRITUAL BODY
ROM. 14:9	TO BECOME LORD OF BOTH THE DEAD AND THE LIVING
ROM. 15:6	TO ENABLE US TO GLORIFY GOD
ROM. 15:7	TO WELCOME LOST HUMAN BEINGS
ROM. 15:8	TO CONFIRM THE PROMISES MADE TO THE PATRIARCHS
ROM. 15:16	TO SANCTIFY THE GENTILES, MAKING THEM AN OFFERING ACCEPTABLE TO GOD
ROM. 16:27	TO BRING GLORY TO GOD
1 COR. 1:2	TO SANCTIFY AND MAKE HOLY THOSE WHO CALL ON HIS NAME
1 COR. 1:3	TO BE THE SOURCE OF GRACE AND PEACE FOR BELIEVERS
1 COR. 1:4	TO BE THE AGENT THROUGH WHOM GOD GIVES BELIEVERS HIS GRACE
1 COR. 1:10	TO LEND HIS NAME TO OUR PRAYERS
1 COR. 1:23	TO BE CRUCIFIED
1 COR. 1:24	TO DISPLAY THE POWER AND WISDOM OF GOD
1 COR. 2:16	TO REVEAL GOD'S MIND; FOR EXAMPLE, TO GUIDE US IN OUR LIVES
1 COR. 3:11	TO BECOME THE FOUNDATION OF OUR FAITH
1 COR. 5:7	TO BE SACRIFICED FOR US, AS A PASSOVER LAMB
1 COR. 8:6	TO BE THE SOURCE OF OUR NEW LIFE WITH GOD
1 COR. 8:11	TO DIE FOR THE STRONG AND THE WEAK CHRISTIAN
1 COR. 15:3	TO DIE FOR OUR SINS
1 COR. 15:22	TO MAKE ALIVE THOSE WHO DIED IN ADAM
1 COR. 15:23	TO RISE FROM THE DEAD AS THE FIRSTFRUITS OF OUR SALVATION
1 COR. 15:57	TO GIVE US VICTORY OVER DEATH
2 COR. 1:20	TO AFFIRM AND CONFIRM THE PROMISES OF GOD
2 COR. 4:6	TO GIVE US KNOWLEDGE OF THE GLORY OF GOD
2 COR. 5:17	TO MAKE US NEW CREATIONS
2 COR. 5:19	TO RECONCILE THE WORLD TO GOD
2 COR. 8:9	TO BECOME POOR SO THAT WE MIGHT BECOME RICH
GAL. 3:13	TO REDEEM US FROM THE CURSE OF THE LAW
GAL. 3:14	TO MAKE THE PROMISES GIVEN TO ABRAHAM AVAILABLE TO BELIEVING GENTILES
GAL. 3:26	TO MAKE THOSE WHO BELIEVE CHILDREN OF GOD
GAL. 3:28	TO MAKE IRRELEVANT THE DIFFERENCES THAT DIVIDE HUMANKIND
GAL. 5:1	TO SET US FREE
EPH. 1:3	TO BLESS US WITH ALL SPIRITUAL BLESSINGS
EPH. 1:5	TO BE THE AGENT OF OUR ADOPTION INTO GOD'S FAMILY
EPH. 1:10	TO BRING ALL THINGS TOGETHER UNDER HIS HEADSHIP
EPH. 2:5	TO MAKE THOSE WHO WERE DEAD IN SINS ALIVE IN HIM
EPH. 2:6	TO RAISE US UP AND SEAT US WITH HIMSELF IN THE HEAVENLY REALMS
EPH. 2:13	TO BRING US NEAR TO THE FATHER THROUGH THE SON'S SHED BLOOD
EPH. 2:20	TO BECOME THE CHIEF CORNERSTONE OF GOD'S REDEMPTIVE PLAN
EPH. 3:11	TO ACCOMPLISH GOD'S ETERNAL SAVING PURPOSE
EPH. 3:21	TO BRING GOD GLORY IN THE CHURCH
EPH. 4:32	TO BE AN EXAMPLE OF FORGIVENESS THAT WE ARE TO FOLLOW

EPH. 5:2	TO BE AN EXAMPLE OF THE LIFE OF LOVE WE ARE TO DEMONSTRATE
EPH. 5:23	TO BE THE HEAD AND SAVIOR OF HIS CHURCH
EPH. 5:25	TO BE AN EXAMPLE OF SELF-SACRIFICAL LOVE TO HUSBANDS
PHIL. 1:11	TO ENABLE US TO BE FILLED WITH THE FRUIT OF RIGHTEOUSNESS
PHIL. 2:5	TO BE AN EXAMPLE OF HUMILITY WE ARE TO FOLLOW
PHIL. 2:11	TO BE LORD, TO THE GLORY OF GOD THE FATHER
PHIL. 3:9	TO BE THE SOURCE OF A RIGHTEOUSNESS THAT IS RECEIVED THROUGH FAITH
COL. 1:27	TO DWELL WITHIN BELIEVERS AS OUR HOPE OF GLORY
COL. 2:9	THAT THE FULLNESS OF THE GODHEAD MIGHT BE EXPRESSED IN BODILY FORM
COL. 2:10	THAT HE MIGHT BE HEAD OVER EVERY AUTHORITY AND POWER
COL. 2:20	THAT WE MIGHT DIE WITH HIM TO THE ELEMENTARY PRINCIPLES OF THIS WORLD AND BE FREED FROM ITS RULES
COL. 3:4	THAT WHEN CHRIST RETURNS, WE MIGHT APPEAR WITH HIM IN GLORY
1 TIM. 1:15	TO SAVE SINNERS
1 TIM. 2:5	TO BECOME THE MEDIATOR BETWEEN GOD AND HUMANKIND
2 TIM. 1:10	TO BRING LIFE AND IMMORTALITY TO LIGHT
2 TIM. 4:1	TO JUDGE THE LIVING AND THE DEAD
HEB. 5:5	TO BECOME OUR HIGH PRIEST
HEB. 9:14	TO CLEANSE OUR CONSCIENCES SO THAT WE MAY SERVE THE LIVING GOD
HEB. 9:15	TO BE THE MEDIATOR OF THE NEW COVENANT
HEB. 9:15	TO DIE AS A RANSOM TO SET US FREE FROM SINS
HEB. 9:26	TO ONCE FOR ALL DO AWAY WITH SIN BY THE SACRIFICE OF HIMSELF
HEB. 9:28	TO APPEAR A SECOND TIME TO BRING SALVATION TO THOSE WAITING FOR HIS RETURN
HEB. 10:10	TO MAKE US SANCTIFIED, OR HOLY, THROUGH HIS SELF-SACRIFICE
1 PET. 1:19	TO REDEEM US WITH HIS PRECIOUS BLOOD
1 PET. 2:21	TO SUFFER FOR US, LEAVING US AN EXAMPLE TO FOLLOW
1 PET. 3:18	TO DIE FOR SINS ONCE FOR ALL IN ORDER TO BRING US TO GOD
2 PET. 2:20	TO ENABLE US TO ESCAPE THE DEFILEMENTS OF THE WORLD
1 JOHN 3:16	TO LAY DOWN HIS LIFE FOR US

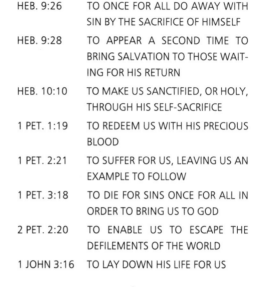

DELIVERER

It is significant that Jesus is referred to as the "Deliverer" in Romans 11:26. In chapters 9 through 11, Paul reviews human history. He emphasizes God's freedom to choose Israel and His right to open the door of faith to the Gentiles. Sadly, many first-century Jews viewed the gospel offer of salvation to all as an abandonment of Israel and a repudiation of the promises given to Israel by the prophets.

In chapter 11, Paul explains that God's decision to graft believing Gentiles into the tree of faith, which clearly has Jewish roots, was not a rejection of Israel. First, many Jews have become Christians. Second, God intends one day to graft the Jews as a people back into the tree of faith. "And so," Paul concludes, "all Israel will be saved, as it is written: 'The Deliverer will come out of Zion, and He will turn away ungodliness from Jacob; for this is My covenant with them, when I take away their sins'" (Rom. 11:26, 27).

Thus, the title "Deliverer," which holds out such promise in the Old Testament, is a reminder for us. Jesus came not only as our Savior, but also to fulfill the prophetic

The image in Revelation 3 of Jesus standing at the door knocking reminds us that the latch which opens the door is within us. We must choose to respond to Jesus' invitation.

❖

promises to Israel. (For further information, see the article on "God of my salvation," p. 54.)

DOOR

"Door" is a metaphor that Jesus applied to Himself in John 10:9. He said, "I am the door. If anyone enters by Me, he will be saved, and will go in and out and find pasture."

There is an interesting story associated with this verse. In the early days of the Reformation, Luther of Germany and Zwengli of Switzerland met, intending to present a unified front and work out any theological differences. The sticking point was over the Eucharist.

Luther believed in consubstantiation. In other words, while the bread of the communion table did not literally become the body of Christ, in some way Christ was really present *with* [*con*] the bread. In contrast, Zwengli held that the bread of the communion *represented* Christ, but that Christ's substance was not actually present with the substance of the bread.

As the argument became more heated, Luther insisted that when Jesus said "this *is* My body," He literally meant what He said. Finally, Zwengli, who was furious because Luther would not admit that Jesus' calling His body "bread" was a metaphor, countered, "Jesus also said 'I *am* the door!' But no one remembers Him with splinters!"

In point of fact, Zwengli misunderstood Jesus' metaphor. In John 10:7, Christ was not speaking about the wooden door of a home. Rather, He was speaking about a sheepfold. Sheepfolds were often caves or, when constructed on open ground, areas enclosed by brambles and other bushes that would prove to be barriers to wild animals who were eager to carry away sheep.

The "door" to such a sheepfold was an open space in the barrier, in which the shepherd himself slept at night. He slept there to provide protection for the sheep, for no wild animal could reach the sheep while the shepherd was there to ward it off. Also, no sheep could wander away into danger.

Thus, when Jesus said, "I am the door," He was reminding His listeners that He Himself was the One who guards and protects His own. It is no wonder that anyone who enters by Him "will be saved, and will go in and out and find pasture."

FORERUNNER

Hebrews 6:20 refers to Jesus as "the forerunner." (The NIV refers to Jesus as the One "who went before us.") The writer of Hebrews is explaining why we who have come to Jesus for refuge can have total confidence in our salvation. First, the promise of salvation rests not only on the promise of

God, but also on the fact that He confirmed His pledge with an oath. Verse 19 says, "This hope we have as an anchor of the soul, both sure and steadfast."

But as Christians we have even more! We have Jesus, who has entered the very presence of God as our High Priest. As the "forerunner" (v. 20), His presence before God the Father is a guarantee that we too will one day follow Him. Because Jesus is our Forerunner, we who follow Him will surely enter God's presence in eternity.

HEAD

"Head" is an important theological term. In the Old Testament, the Hebrew noun rendered "head," *ro'sh*, was a word that conveyed a number of ideas. It might mean "the beginning" or "the source"; "the top of a mount or building"; and "the chief of a family or clan," whether living or ancestral. *Ro'sh* also suggested primacy or importance (Deut. 28:13), as well as a position at the top of a bureaucracy, nation, or hierarchy.

There are three theologically significant uses of "head" in the New Testament, each of which rests on the fact that Jesus Christ is the One who bears the title "Head."

Christ as the head of the church. The New Testament portrays the church as a living organism and Jesus as the living head of His spiritual body (Eph. 1:22; 4:15; 5:23; Col. 1:18; 2:10, 19). As head of His body, the church, Jesus sustains, protects, guides, and is the source of the church's life.

In presenting Christ as the living head of the church, the New Testament sets aside those Old Testament aspects of headship that implied a hierarchical structure. In fact, Jesus made it very plain that there was to be no form of rank or hierarchy in His church (Matt. 20:25-28; 23:8-12; Rom. 12:3-8). Christ's headship over the church is to be reflected in the guidance exercised by the leaders in His church.

Christ as the head of every man (1 Cor. 11:3). In a much misunderstood passage, Jesus is presented as the "head of every man," man as "the head of woman," and God as the "head of Christ." This passage is covered thoroughly in a companion volume in this series, *Every Woman in the Bible*. Nevertheless, one section from its discussion of this passage is worth reproducing here:

> "The head of every man is Christ, the head of woman is man, and the head of Christ is God" (1 Cor. 11:3). Paul launched this teaching with a strong affirmation. Those who hold a hierarchical view of the relationship between the sexes view this as a statement about authority and subordination. They read it as if Paul had written, "Every man is under Christ's authority, woman is under man's authority, and Christ is under God's authority." This, however, is not what Paul wrote.
>
> While "head" in Greek may mean "leader" or "boss," this meaning is unusual. Even in the Greek translation of the Old Testament, in nine out of the ten cases where *ro'sh* ("head") is used in the sense of "leader," a different Greek word than *kephale* ("head") is chosen to translate it. Thus, the argument that "head" here must mean "authority over" is hardly compelling.
>
> Another problem exists with this interpretation. The second phrase in the Greek text is *de gunaikos ho aner kephale*. *Gunaikos* may mean either "woman" or "wife," and *aner* may mean either "man" or "husband." Here the definite article *ho* suggests that Paul means "the husband is head of the wife," rather than "man is the head of woman." If we take this phrase in the first sense, we see that Paul is making a distinct statement about three different relationships:
>
> • Christ is the "head" of "every man."
> • The husband is the "head" of the wife.
> • God is the "head" of Christ.
>
> "Head" in this passage cannot be used here to ascribe superiority or subordination; Christ is

not inferior to God the Father. "Head" cannot mean that men are the "source" of women, for husbands are not the source of wives. In what metaphorical sense can "head" be used to fit all three applications?

In the next chapter (1 Cor. 12), Paul again uses "head" to refer to Christ. Paul describes the relationship Christ has to the church that is His body. In chapter 12, Paul uses "head" and "body" to indicate that a true, organic relationship exists between Jesus and Jesus' people. If we take "head" to have a similar metaphorical meaning in 1 Corinthians 11 that it has in 1 Corinthians 12, what Paul says fits the rest of his argument beautifully. Every man has an organic relationship with Jesus—so that each man reflects glory or dishonor on Jesus (see 1 Cor. 11:7). Wives have an organic, one-flesh relationship with their husbands, so that what they do reflects glory or dishonor on their husbands. Jesus had an organic relationship with God the Father, and what He did reflected glory and honor on God.

Why then should women cover their heads when praying or prophesying in church? Because it is proper behavior, and when wives behave properly they reflect glory on their husbands. By behaving improperly, women would dishonor not only their husbands but also Christ (p. 222, 223).

The organic sense in which Christ is affirmed to be the head of the church is in most passages definitive of the use of "head" in Christian interpersonal relationships.

Head in Ephesians 5:21-33. This, too, is a passage in which Christ's headship over the church is associated with Christian interpersonal relationships, this time also involving that of a husband to his wife. In this passage, Paul holds up Christ's relationship with the church as a pattern to guide the relationship of a husband with his wife. Once again, it is important to remember that the New Testament replaces the hierarchical image of headship with an organic image of headship.

Furthermore, in Ephesians 5:21-33 the particular role of the "head" is carefully limited and defined. Husbands are the head of their wives as Christ is the head of the church. Christ, Paul tells us, exercised His headship by loving the church and giving Himself for her (v. 25) "that He might sanctify and cleanse her with the washing of water by the word, that He might present her to Himself a glorious church, not having spot or wrinkle or any such thing, but that she should be holy and without blemish" (vv. 26-27).

Paul then states that husbands are to love their wives just as Christ loved the church (v. 28). That is, in exercising their headship, husbands are to follow Christ's example of self-giving, seeking always to facilitate the growth of the wife spiritually and as a person. This surely is a far cry from the kind of subordination that some teach the husband's headship requires.

Implications of Christ's headship. If we look at each New Testament reference to Jesus as head of the church, we develop the following picture from this important title.

First Corinthians 11:3. Jesus has an organic relationship with every believer. Because of this, what we do reflects on Jesus and has the potential to glorify Him.

First Corinthians 12:12-31. As head of a spiritual body that is composed of all types of believers, Christ unites and directs Christians. He blends their spiritual gifts and links them with other believers into a harmonious whole.

Ephesians 1:22, 23. As head of the church and as Lord of the universe, Jesus not only protects His body but also guides and directs each individual member.

Ephesians 4:15. As head of the church, Jesus provides spiritual leaders who will help us grow and mature as members of His body.

Ephesians 5:22-24. As head of the church, Jesus not only sacrificed Himself for her in the past, but also remains actively involved in purifying believers and in nurturing their spiritual growth.

Colossians 2:19. As head of the church, Christ maintains the connections between members of His spiritual body and causes both individuals and the body to grow and mature.

Christ's position as head of His church is indeed a significant one. To acknowledge Jesus as our living Head is to look to Him for guidance, to gladly respond to His will, and to honor Him as the source of our life each day.

JESUS
SAVIOR

Jesus is specifically called "Savior" twenty-two times in the Gospels, Acts, and Epistles. And the very name "Jesus" is a constant reminder of Christ's work as Savior, for "Jesus" is the Greek form of the Hebrew name "Joshua," which means "God is salvation." In naming Mary's yet unborn child "Jesus," God was announcing that He would grow up to be the Savior (Matt. 1:21; Luke 1:31).

The Old Testament emphasis on salvation is explored in the article on the title, "God of My Salvation," which begins on page 54. The full doctrine of salvation is developed in the New Testament. Only when we understand salvation itself can we grasp what it means to acknowledge Jesus and name Him as our Savior.

Salvation in the New Testament. The basic concept established so firmly in the Old Testament is the foundation of our New Testament's teaching about salvation. Salvation is from God, who acts to deliver the spiritually helpless who trust in Him.

The primary Greek terms for salvation are *sozo* (a verb) and *soteria* (a noun). Numerous times "salvation" is used in the Old Testament sense of deliverance from some pressing physical danger (Matt. 24:13; Mark 13:13-20; Acts 27:20). Jesus' healing miracles saved the sick in the sense of restoring lost health and wholeness to them (Matt. 9:21, 22; Mark 5:23, 28, 34; Luke 7:50). But in most contexts salvation focuses on what God has done in Christ to deliver human beings from the powers of death, sin, and Satan. In the New Testament, the greatest enemies of humankind are spiritual, not physical, for spiritual terrors threaten people with eternal loss.

Past-tense salvation. New Testament salvation has three distinct aspects, reflected in our past, present, and future tenses. Jesus died for us in the past and accomplished all that was necessary for our salvation. When we trust in Jesus, the Father considers us as having died with the Son and been raised again with Him to new life (Rom. 6:3-5). Christians have been saved, for in God's sight the great transaction is complete. Thus, the Bible says, "according to His mercy He *saved* us" (Titus 3:5; italics mine) and He "*has saved us* and called us to a holy calling (2 Tim. 1:9; italics mine). Because of what Jesus has done, we who believe are saved and have already passed from death to life.

Present-tense salvation. It is also true that Jesus is currently saving us. Salvation has great impact on our present experience. We who have been reconciled to God by Christ's death are being saved through Jesus' life (Rom. 5:10). As 6:5-14 emphasizes, our union with Jesus in His death and resurrection brings release from our natural slavery to sin. We are freed to serve God and live righteous lives.

The title "lamb of God" recalled the sacrifice of lambs for the first Passover. Their blood on Jewish doorways signaled the death angel to pass over the homes of God's people.

---❖---

Future-tense salvation. Finally, the Bible assures us that we will be saved. In the Resurrection, Christians will be fully delivered from the last taint of sin, perfected at last, and made completely pure and holy. This certain future is beautifully described in Romans 8:18-39 and 1 Corinthians 15:12-58.

Jesus as Savior. The New Testament presents Jesus as Savior, and teaches that salvation is available only through faith in Him. Jesus, the eternal Son of God, entered our world to bring us salvation (John 3:17; 1 Tim. 1:15). His death won us forgiveness and new life, gifts guaranteed by His resurrection (2 Tim. 4:18; Heb. 7:25). Jesus saves us from wrath (Rom. 5:9), adopts us into God's family (Eph. 1:5), and assures us of resurrection to an eternity to be spent in fellowship with Him (1 Cor. 15:20-23).

In Jesus we see that God *has* acted. Salvation has been won for us. Now all that remains for us is to trust God, relying completely on Jesus and counting on the victory He already has won.

What then does it mean for us to name Jesus as Savior? First, it means that we confess our helplessness to combat sin and the spiritual forces that hold humanity captive. Second, it means that we trust in Jesus, who has acted in history to provide deliverance for us in His sacrificial death on the cross. Third, it means that we confess God's trustworthiness (especially as we abandon ourselves to Him) and rely on Him alone to bring us deliverance. It is no wonder that "Savior" is one of the most precious and surely one of the most significant names or titles of our Lord!

LAMB OF GOD
PASSOVER

It was John the Baptist who, recognizing who Jesus was after baptizing Him, announced to some of his own followers, "Behold! The Lamb of God who takes away the sins of the world!" (John 1:29). In 1 Corinthians 5:7, Paul expanded on the name "Lamb of God" by noting that "Christ, our Passover, was sacrificed for us."

The reference in each passage is to an historic event. The final plague God used to force the pharaoh of Egypt to release his Hebrew slaves was the death of the first-born in every Egyptian family. Moses had been told to instruct the Hebrews how to avoid this disastrous plague. Each family was to take a lamb into its home. Then, the night before death was to strike the land, the lamb was to be sacrificed. The lamb's blood was to be sprinkled on the door posts and lintels, and the lamb was to be eaten by the family. When the death angel saw the blood on the doorway, he would *pass over* that home, and everyone inside would be safe (Ex. 12:1-13).

The animal sacrifices of the Old Testament foreshadowed Jesus' sacrifice of Himself to pay for our sins.

After that first Passover, which took place around 1450 B.C., the Hebrew people were to reenact the event annually. They were to take a lamb, kill it and eat it, and remember how the death angel had passed over Hebrew homes when he saw the blood of the lamb (vv. 21-28).

The titles "Lamb of God" and "Passover" speak of a security that can be found only in the shed blood of a sacrifice offered on our behalf. Jesus, who shed His blood on the cross, was the One foreshadowed in the Passover Lamb. He is the One whose sacrifice cleanses and protects all who believe in Him.

BIBLE BACKGROUND:

BLOOD SACRIFICE

The idea of sacrifice isn't particularly popular with the critics of Christianity. Blood sacrifice has been dismissed as reflecting primitive superstition. But for Christians blood sacrifice is an honored concept.

Jesus is history's ultimate blood sacrifice. But the first sacrifice was offered in Eden, just after the Fall. There God killed animals to provide skin coverings for sinful Adam and Eve (Gen. 3:21).

The tradition of sacrifice is found in many ancient cultures whose people saw the flesh of the sacrificial animal as food for their idols. But in the Old Testament the blood is central. Leviticus 17:11 explains, "For the life of the flesh is in the blood, and I have given it to you upon the altar to make atonement for your souls; for it is the blood that makes atonement for the soul." The message of sacrifice in the Old Testament is that sin brings death, but that God will accept the death of a substitute in place of that of the sinner.

Noah, Abraham, and other ancient people of faith offered sacrifices. But it was not until the time of Moses that a thoroughgoing sacrificial system was established for God's people. Violations of the Law of Moses called for the making of sin offerings. Individuals who inadvertently committed sins brought sacrifices immediately. But there was also a central sacrifice, made once a year on the Day of Atonement, through which all the sins of God's entire people were covered. This sacrificial system provided a way in which God's sinning people could approach the Lord.

The Old Testament prophets often condemned their contemporaries for treating the sacrifices of their religion as mere ritual and for offering them to God while continuing their sinful ways. Sacrifice in the Old Testament was to be the expression of a repentant heart, and offerings were to express the worship of a morally pure people (Is. 1:13-17; Amos 5:21-27; Mic. 6:6-8).

Jesus, too, condemned a merely ritual faith. He challenged His critics to "go and learn what this means: 'I desire mercy and not sacrifice'" (Matt. 9:13; see 12:7). According to Jesus, love for God and neighbor is more important than all the burnt offerings and sacrifices we might offer, if for no other reason than that God calls us to live holy lives. Had Israel shown mercy, the people would not have committed the sins that required expiation by sacrifice.

The criticism of Israel's ritualistic faith was not a rejection of the principle of sacrifice. It was, instead, a rejection of Israel's mis-

interpretation of sacrifice. At the heart of the practice, sacrifice is an expression of faith, not a ritual. Sacrifices were to be offered by people who were not only aware of their sin but also confident that God was faithful to His promise and would accept them despite their failures. When Old Testament believers stood at the altar and watched a sacrificial animal die because of their sins, they acted out a reality ultimately expressed in Jesus' death on the cross. Sin brings death. But God will accept the life of a substitute and welcome the sinner into relationship with Him.

The New Testament interprets Christ's death on the cross as history's culminating sacrifice. "God presented him as a sacrifice of atonement, through faith in his blood" (Rom. 3:25 NIV). Jesus died for us and justified us by His blood (5:8, 9).

Three chapters of Hebrews explore the meaning of blood sacrifice (Heb. 8—10). The Old Testament sanctuary and sacrifices were "a copy and shadow of the heavenly things" (8:5), serving as illustrations for the present time (9:1-9). Christ, with His own blood, entered no earthly temple but rather entered heaven itself "once for all, having obtained eternal redemption" (9:12). Jesus' one sacrifice dealt fully and finally with sin and was enough to take away the sins of all who trust in Him (vv. 23-28).

Thus, the sacrifices of history were illustrations. They were God's way of instructing humanity so that the meaning of Jesus' death would be understood. The repeated sacrifices of the Old Testament were "only a shadow of the good things to come, and not the very image of the things" (10:1). Today repeated animal sacrifices are no longer necessary, for "we have been sanctified through the offering of the body of Jesus Christ once for all" (v. 10).

Yes, Christians believe in blood sacrifice. We are convinced that only the shed blood of Christ—only His life exchanged for ours—could have won forgiveness for sinners. Blood sacrifice is not "primitive." It is basic to the Christian faith.

MEDIATOR

The role of a mediator is described in Galatians 3:20. A mediator is a person who represents both parties in a transaction or dispute, not just one party. Israel viewed Moses as the mediator of the Law, with the angels (representing God) on one side and human beings on the other. Thus Paul states that the Law was "appointed through angels by the hand of a mediator" (namely, Moses; Gal. 3:19).

This statement makes Paul's affirmation in 1 Timothy 2:5 particularly important: "For there is one God and one Mediator between God and men, the Man Christ Jesus." The new covenant, unlike the old covenant, is administered by someone who is both God and man, while the old covenant (the Law of Moses) was administered by angels. (For a discussion of the role of angels in the Mosaic Law, see the companion volume *Every Angel in the Bible*.)

The writer of Hebrews focuses our attention on the fact that God Himself is the mediator of the new covenant. The writer maintains that the new covenant had to be superior to the old one and founded on better promises (Heb. 8:6). Because Christ died and rose again, the covenant He mediates ensures that we will receive the promised inherence of eternal life (9:15). (For a thorough discussion of the all the biblical covenants and an exploration of the relationship between what the Bible calls the old covenant and the new covenant, see the companion volume in this series, *Every Promise in the Bible*.)

MESSIAH

See the discussion of "Anointed One" (p. 94) and "Christ" (p. 176).

PHYSICIAN

It was Christ who called Himself "Physician" in Luke 4:23. Of course, He was quoting others at the time. Nevertheless, Christ's ministry of healing surely qualifies Him to be called the "great Physician." Jesus not only healed those with ordinary fevers, such as Peter's mother-in-law (Matt. 8:14, 15), but also miraculously restored sight to the blind (John 9) and strengthened withered limbs (Matt. 15:31). Most important of all, as the great Physician, Jesus is the Healer of souls. He restores life to those who are spiritually dead and transforms the corrupt, making them truly good.

BIBLE BACKGROUND:
HEALING

Christians believe that God wants us to have eternal life forever and an abundant life now. To some Christians it seems that abundant life must include health. They are convinced that when Isaiah writes, "by [Christ's] stripes we are healed" (Is. 53:5), he promises physical healing *now* for believers. These Christians teach that all a believer has to do is to claim the promise of healing by faith, and then healing will surely come.

Other Christians disagree. They point out that all believers surely will be healed of every physical infirmity, but that such healing is only assured in our resurrection. Also, they argue that the "abundant life" cannot be summed up in one's physical condition or economic state. Abundant life is found in intimate relationship with Jesus. Moreover, the sick may have an especially close relationship with the Lord.

While these views differ significantly, they also hold common ground. Christians all believe in a God who is able to heal. We may differ in our understanding of when and how He chooses to act, but none of us doubts that Jesus can act in our here and now. We all pray about our needs, sure that the Lord who hears us really does care.

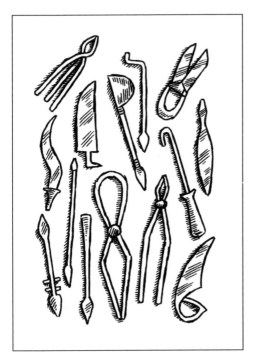

Many physicians in biblical times were skilled in surgery, as indicated by this sample of the equipment used by Egyptian physicians.

Given the common ground, what does the Bible say about healing? In the Old Testament, sickness and disease are often used as pictures of sin (Is. 1:4-6). Healing is thus related to forgiveness and to relationship with the Lord (2 Chron. 7:14; Hos. 6:1). It is true, too, that sickness at times is a punishment for sin, so that healing comes with forgiveness (Ex. 15:26).

Still, sickness is not always a punishment, and while physical health comes from God, His Old Testament people saw nothing inappropriate in the use of medication (Is. 1:6; 38:21; Jer. 51:8). What the Old Testament does criticize is King Asa (for example), who sought help only from physicians and not from the Lord (2 Chron. 16:12).

Healing was a very significant part of Jesus' ministry, and it also played a part in the early ministry of the apostles. In the Gospels, healing is often associated with the sick per-

son's faith (Matt. 8:1-3; 9:20-22; Acts 5:16; 14:9). Yet other miracles of healing never mention faith (Matt. 9:23-26; Mark 6:5; Acts 3:1-10; 8:7; 28:8).

Surprisingly, we find very little about healing in the New Testament Epistles. Nevertheless, Hebrews 12:13 speaks about healing in an inner, spiritual sense. Also, James calls on the sick to let the elders pray over them (James 5:14, 15). Moreover, in 1 Corinthians 12:28-30, Paul lists healing as one of the spiritual gifts. But the idea that Christians can claim physical healing as a right is never taught explicitly in the New Testament.

Isaiah 53:4 and 5 speak of healing by Jesus' wounds, and Matthew 8:17 says this was fulfilled in Jesus' acts of healing while on earth. While the primary focus in Isaiah is clearly on spiritual healing, the Matthew reference does indicate that physical and spiritual healing are linked. Does this pair of verses, then, indicate that physical healing is promised to God's people today as a right won by the shed blood of Jesus? If so, it is hard to explain what happened when New Testament believers became ill.

Paul suffered from a serious disease (probably affecting his eyes). He pleaded with the Lord to take it away (2 Cor. 12:8). But God did not. Instead, Paul was given grace to enable him to live with his malady. Timothy had chronic stomach trouble. Paul advised him to drink a little wine in addition to water (1 Tim. 5:23). Epaphroditus, after coming to Paul from Philippi, became severely ill and almost died. After the recovery of Epaphroditus, Paul wrote, "For indeed he was sick almost to death; but God had mercy on him, and not only on him but on me also, lest I should have sorrow upon sorrow" (Phil. 2:27).

What can we conclude from the above? We see Jesus as the great Physician, and we depend on the Lord when we become ill. We bring this need to the Lord and pray with confidence. We know that God hears and that, in His love, He will do what is best for us. Nevertheless, we pray realizing that we have no guarantee of healing in this world. All that

Jesus guarantees is that there is healing in eternity, and that in this world God will act in our lives for our good.

PROPHET

In Deuteronomy 18:18 and 19, God told Moses,

> I will raise up for [Israel] a Prophet like you from among their brethren, and will put My words in His mouth, and He shall speak to them all that I command Him. And it shall be that whoever will not hear My words, which He speaks in My name, I will require it of him.

This is one of those passages that is filled with special significance. It is a prophetic passage, indicating what God will do. Also, it shares with other prophetic passages what theologians call the "law of double reference." In other words, the prophecy has multiple application.

On the one hand, this passage was partially fulfilled in the many prophets that God raised up in Old Testament times to communicate His message to His people. On the other hand, this passage from the beginning was properly understood to indicate that one day God would send a premier Prophet, who would be like Moses. As Moses set history on a new course, not only freeing Israel from slavery in Egypt but also giving the nation a Law to live by, so also the promised Prophet would set a new direction for faith. He would make redemption available to all humankind, and He would replace law with grace as a way of relating to and living for God.

JESUS AS "THE PROPHET"

While the full significance of the ministry of the promised Prophet was not understood in Old Testament times, many Jews in the first century A.D. were aware that God

would one day send His people *the* Prophet. This truth is very clear from a challenge issued by the religious leaders to John the Baptist in which they demanded that he identify himself (John 1:19-24). John made it clear that he laid no claims to being the Christ (Messiah).

John then was asked whether he was the forerunner, Elijah. Again John said, "I am not." Finally the delegation of religious leaders demanded, "Are you the Prophet?" And again John said, "No." Clearly, "the Prophet" was someone whom the Pharisees and other religious leaders *expected to appear.*

Later, after seeing one of Jesus' miracles, the observers said, "This is truly the Prophet who is to come into the world" (6:14). In fact, one of the many rumors about who Jesus was (after He had begun His healing and teaching ministry) focused on this identity. It was assumed that Jesus was Elijah (the forerunner of the Messiah) or "the Prophet" (Mark 6:15). In fact, Jesus fulfilled all three lines of Old Testament prophecy. He was the Prophet (like Moses); He was the Priest (after the order of Melchizedek; Ps. 110:4); and He was the King from David's line, the Messiah (Luke 1:31-33).

JESUS' MISSION AS "THE PROPHET"

There are a number of parallels between the ministries of Moses and Jesus.

Each was appointed to be God's spokesperson. Moses spoke for God to Pharaoh and to Israel. Similarly, Jesus spoke to Israel.

Each was authenticated by miracles. The miraculous judgments that Moses announced against Pharaoh and Egypt made it clear that he represented the Lord. Likewise, the miraculous healings and exorcisms that Jesus performed made it clear that He also represented God. Even the Jewish Sanhedrin, according to Nicodemus (one of the supreme council's members), admitted, "Rabbi, we know that

Elijah, who confronted four hundred prophets of Baal at Mount Carmel, is one of the Old Testament's premier prophets.

You are a teacher come from God; for no one can do these signs that You do unless God is with him" (John 3:2).

Each introduced a new revelation of God. Through Moses, God showed Himself to be a God of power, who would kept His ancient covenant with Abraham and his descendants. Through Moses, too, the name "Yahweh" was revealed to the Israelites. And through Jesus, God showed Himself to be a God of love. Also, through the name "Immanuel" (which means "with us is God"), God the Son showed that He took on flesh to provide redemption for sinful humanity.

Each was mediator of a covenant. Moses was the mediator of the old covenant, which taught Israel how to live in fellowship with God. Similarly, Jesus is the Mediator of the new covenant, which establishes a new relationship with God for believing Jew and Gentile alike. This covenant replaces the lifestyle of legalism with one of grace (see Romans 6 and 7).

Having noted these similarities, it is important to recognize that the ministry of Jesus was far superior to that of Moses. Hebrews 3:2-6 points out:

> Moses . . . was faithful in all [God's] house. For this One has been counted worthy of more glory than Moses, inasmuch as He who built the house has more honor than the house. For every house is built by someone, but He who built all things is God. And Moses was indeed faithful in all His house as a servant, for a testimony of those things which would be spoken afterward, but Christ as a Son over His own house, whose house we are.

BIBLE BACKGROUND:
PROPHETS AND PROPHECY IN THE BIBLE

The basic Hebrew word for prophet means "spokesperson" or "speaker." A prophet essentially is a person authorized to speak for another, as Moses and the Old Testament prophets were authorized to speak in the name of the Lord (Ex. 7:1, 2; Num. 12:1-8). Prophets are also called "messengers," "seers," and "people of God" in the Old Testament. Their messages are called "prophecy," "visions," "oracles," "burdens," or simply "the word of the Lord."

The men and women who served as God's spokespersons had the primary task of providing supernatural guidance to God's people. These prophets came from every walk of life. Their ministries took them to kings and priests, to foreign lands, and to the common people. Most often the prophet's message was moral in nature; it confronted Israel with sin and called her back to the holy ways revealed in God's Law. In addition, prophets gave military advice, made promises to Israel about her future, and warned the people against various courses of political action.

The prophet's mission was, first of all, to the people of his or her own time. The predictive gift exercised by many prophets was focused primarily on near events. By identifying correctly what would happen in the near future, the prophet's claim to be God's spokesperson was authenticated. God alone can make known the "end from the beginning" (Is. 46:10) and bring about what He has planned. Foretelling future events without mistake was compelling evidence of the prophet's call to be God's spokesperson. And, when the events predicted were distant in time, the fulfillment of nearer events guaranteed that the distant forecasts would also be fulfilled.

The New Testament likewise contains predictions about the future. In addition, it describes prophets and prophecy in the early church. People who were moved by the Holy Spirit gave special, inspired messages to local congregations (Acts 11:27-30; 21:10, 11).

Prophecy is named as a spiritual gift in 1 Corinthians 12:10. But what is the prophetic gift? Some Christians believe this indicates a continuation of the Old Testament prophetic ministry, and that today some believers can give special, inspired guidance from God to congregations and individuals.

Other Christians take the New Testament reference to prophets in a slightly different sense. They believe that prophets are still God's spokespersons, but that they now speak for Him by teaching and preaching what has been already been revealed in the Old and New Testaments. Thus these prophets are not channels through which God provides new revelation. Both they and their audiences are guided internally by the Holy Spirit.

Still others believe that, like the Old Testament prophets, some believers today are specially called to confront their fellow Christians and unbelievers in society at large. In their confrontational role, these prophets among us are God's spokespersons, calling us to live by His standards of justice and mercy.

RESURRECTION AND THE LIFE

It was Jesus who said, "I am the resurrection and the life" (John 11:25). The New Testament mentions resurrection some 40 times, and develops a theology of resurrection in 1 Corinthians 15. Yet the context in which Jesus identified Himself as "the resurrection and the life" is especially significant.

Jesus' enemies were actively seeking Him. This prompted Him to leave the area around Jerusalem. In the small town of Bethany, just about two miles from Jerusalem, there lived three of Christ's closest friends—Lazarus and his two sisters, Mary and Martha.

When Lazarus became seriously ill, the two sisters sent immediately for Jesus. The messengers found Jesus, but curiously He decided not to hurry back to Bethany with them. Instead, Jesus waited. Only after Lazarus had died did Jesus go to Bethany with His disciples.

Lazarus had been dead for four days when Jesus arrived and was met by one of the tearful sisters. The period of time was important. Jewish custom required the immediate burial of a person who died. Then for four days relatives visited the tomb, on the unlikely possibility that the person had fallen into a coma rather than died. After four days, all were sure that Lazarus was dead.

When Jesus came to Bethany, Martha met Him and expressed her conviction that if He had arrived sooner, He could have prevented Lazarus' death. It was at this point

The empty tomb of Jesus reminds us that Christ was "declared to be the Son of God with power" by His resurrection from the dead (Romans 1:4).

that Jesus identified Himself as "the resurrection and the life." Jesus then went to the tomb and there restored Lazarus to life. Jesus did not resurrect Lazarus; rather, the Son of God resuscitated Lazarus. We know this because the resurrected do not die again. In contrast, those called back to this earthly life will die again biologically.

Interestingly, Jesus linked the two titles, "the resurrection and the life." As "the life," Jesus is the One who gives and sustains biological life. And as "the resurrection," Jesus can take a fallen human being and so transform him or her through resurrection that every mark of sin is lost. Consequently, that person will exist in an absolutely perfect state for all eternity.

The resuscitation of Lazarus—his recall by Jesus to earthly life—was proof of Jesus' power over death and of His right to be called "the resurrection." It was, of course, Christ's own resurrection after three days in a borrowed tomb that, in the words of Romans 1:4, "declared [Him] to be the Son of God with power." It is this same power that He will exercise when He resurrects all His saints.

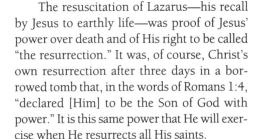

BIBLE BACKGROUND:

RESURRECTION

Resurrection in the Old Testament.
Although resurrection is suggested in the Old

Testament, it does not seem to be a major element in Old Testament faith. Old Testament saints looked beyond this life, but for the most part they trusted in God without clear information about His ultimate plan for them. Thirteen hundred years after Abraham, Isaiah revealed that God would "swallow up death forever" (Is. 25:8). Also, in the future, "your dead shall live; . . . [their bodies] shall rise" (26:19). The clearest statement about resurrection is found in Daniel 12:2,

And many of those who sleep
in the dust shall awake,
Some to everlasting life,
Some to shame and everlasting contempt.

Thus, death was not thought of as an end. Nevertheless, the doctrine of the resurrection, while taught, is not developed fully in the Old Testament.

The resurrection of Jesus. It was only with Jesus' resurrection that we catch a glimpse of the glory awaiting us. The fact of Jesus' resurrection is central to our faith. Every claim Jesus made during His life is confirmed by His resurrection. Jesus is also called the "firstfruits of those who have fallen asleep" (1 Cor. 15:20). His resurrection is the guarantee that death has been conquered and that eternal life is now our destiny.

The resurrection of the believer. All the dead will one day appear before God to be judged (Rev. 20:11-15). This recall, though, is not what the Bible means by resurrection. Resurrection is a transformation to a new state of being, and it is reserved for believers. We find more details in 1 Corinthians 15. Our resurrected bodies will correspond to our present bodies but will be imperishable, glorious, and infused with power. They will be spiritual rather than natural in makeup (1 Cor. 15:42-44). Those bodies will be "in the likeness of the man from heaven" (v. 49 NIV).

It is fascinating to learn that our resurrected bodies will be like Jesus' own glorified body. For instance, Jesus' raised body was "flesh and bones" (Luke 24:39) rather than flesh and blood (Lev. 17:11). Jesus could appear at will among the disciples despite the fact that they were in a locked room (John 20:19, 26). This suggests that when we are resurrected, unimaginable powers will be ours!

TEACHER

See the article entitled "Rabbi" on page 171.

SHEPHERD AND OVERSEER
GOOD SHEPHERD
GREAT SHEPHERD
CHIEF SHEPHERD

The New Testament frequently portrays Jesus as our Shepherd, adding either an adjective or another title to that name. While from the Old Testament we understand the basic ministry of God as the Shepherd of His people (see p. 85), the fact that Christ's ministries are further defined in this way is significant.

Jesus as the Good Shepherd (John 10:1-18). In this passage, Jesus draws a contrast between a hired man who is employed to look after the sheep and a good shepherd. The hired man is working, not because he loves the sheep, but rather because he wants to get paid. When the sheep are endangered by the appearance of a wild animal, the hired man flees. But the good shepherd, who genuinely cares for the sheep, is willing to lay down his life for them. It was as the Good Shepherd that Jesus died for us, His sheep, proving once and for all that the Lord falls into the category of "good Shepherd" (v. 11).

Jesus as the Great Shepherd (Heb. 13:20, 21). Jesus is the "great Shepherd" in view of what His death for us has accomplished. He did more than just die so that His sheep might continue to have earthly life. More importantly, "through the blood of the everlasting covenant," Jesus has made us "complete in every good work to do His will, working in you what is well pleasing in His sight." Thus, as the "great Shepherd," Jesus has enabled us to live in harmony with God here and now, and also to do His will daily.

Jesus as the Chief Shepherd (1 Pet. 5:4). In verses 2 and three, Peter encouraged human leaders of Christ's church to minister eagerly and to be servants and examples to God's flock. Then in verse 4, the apostle reminds these leaders that "when the Chief Shepherd appears, you will receive the crown of glory that does not fade away."

The context makes it clear that while God gives human leaders to shepherd His people, Jesus is the Chief Shepherd. He is actively involved in caring for us. It is because of His active involvement that He will reward His under-shepherds appropriately. Jesus not only is involved with us, but also He actively supervises, guides, and works through the men and women assigned to lead us.

Jesus as the Shepherd and Overseer (1 Pet. 2:24, 25). Peter reminds us that Christ bore our sins in His own body on the cross for a specific purpose. It was God's intent that we, "having died to sins, might live for righteousness" (v. 24). This is the reason that believers can return to "the Shepherd and Overseer of [their] souls" (v. 25).

What an exciting message of hope this is! We know that Jesus personally shepherds us. He does so by leading us to green pastures, enabling us to rest beside the still waters, and protecting us from the enemies of our souls. Because Jesus is our Shepherd and Overseer, we need not fear these dangers. All we should do is remain attuned and responsive to His guidance. We can be sure that wherever He leads us, He will be there for us, night and day.

WAY

Christians in the early church were often called "followers of the Way." This reminds us that Christianity is an exclusive faith. Unlike many mere religions, Christians take seriously Jesus' claim to be the only way—the only highway or road—to God. When Jesus said "I am the way, the truth, and the life. No one comes to the Father except through Me" (John 14:6), He made it clear that only through faith in Him can anyone establish a personal relationship with God.

Thus the many names and titles of God that refer to Jesus' mission here on earth are summed up in this last title. Christ is the only One through whom we can come to God. Jesus is the one Advocate, the one Mediator between God and humankind. Jesus is the person whom God anointed to make salvation available to all who believe. Jesus is the Door to heaven, the Head of the church, and our one and only Shepherd. Yes, the work that Jesus did here on earth—and the work that He now does in human lives—is utterly necessary if any human being is to find forgiveness and establish a family relationship with God.

NAMES AND TITLES OF THE HOLY SPIRIT

Older translations of Scripture made reference to the "Holy Ghost," while modern translations refer to the "Holy Spirit." The reason, of course, is that in ancient times a "spirit" was often synonymous with a "ghost," that is, a disembodied spirit. In Greek, *pneuma* is the noun for both "spirit" and "ghost" and can also be translated as "wind." The *pneuma* was that element of a person that was real and yet was as immaterial and difficult to grasp as the wind that blows through the treetops.

There is nothing ephemeral, however, about the Holy Spirit. While the third Person of the Trinity is spirit in His essential being, and thus cannot be seen by human eyes, the Bible makes it clear that He is both real and active in our world. Before we look at the various names and titles of the Holy Spirit, it is helpful to summarize what Scripture teaches about Him.

THE HOLY SPIRIT

The Spirit is a divine Person. Some people have suggested that the Holy Spirit should be viewed as the "divine influence" or as God's "animating power." Such attempts to rob the Holy Spirit of personhood and deity fail, simply because they are clearly contradicted by Scripture.

When Jesus spoke about the Holy Spirit, our Lord chose the personal pronoun "He," even though "spirit" in Greek is a neuter word (John 14:17, 26; 16:13-15). Christ promised to send His disciples "another Helper" (14:16) when He returned to heaven, and Jesus identified the Spirit as the promised One. The Greek word translated "another" is *allos*, a term that means "another *of the same kind.*" It is to be distinguished from *heteros*, a Greek word that means "another of a different kind." Christ, the second Person of the Godhead, would be sending the Spirit, who is equally God, to live within those who believe.

There are many other indications that the Spirit is a Person and not a force or influence. The Spirit knows and understands (Rom. 8:27; 1 Cor. 2:11). He communicates in words (v.13). He acts and chooses (12:11). The Spirit loves (Rom. 15:30), can

The writers of Scripture were "carried along" by the Holy Spirit as a sailing ship is carried along by the wind in its sails.

be insulted (Heb. 10:29), can be lied to (Acts 5:3), can be resisted (7:51), and can be grieved (Eph. 4:30). The Spirit teaches (John 14:26), intercedes (Rom. 8:26), convicts (John 16:7, 8), bears witness (15:26), and guides (16:13). Each of these activities testifies to the fact that the Spirit is a real, sentient Person, not an impersonal influence.

The Spirit is also a divine Person. The Bible clearly identifies the Spirit as God by the titles it gives Him. He is the eternal Spirit (Heb. 9:14), the Spirit of Christ (1 Peter 1:11), the Spirit of the Lord (Is. 11:2), the Spirit of the Lord God (61:1), and the Spirit of the Son (Gal. 4:6). Only someone who is truly and fully God bears such divine titles.

The deity of the Spirit can be shown in other ways. He is omnipresent, as only God can be (Ps. 139:7; 1 Cor. 12:13). The Spirit is all-powerful (Luke 1:35; Rom. 8:11). He was an agent in Creation (Gen. 1:2; Ps. 104:30) and has power to work miracles (Matt. 12:28; 1 Cor. 12:9-11). The Spirit is the One who brings us new birth (John 3:6; Titus 3:5). It was the Spirit who raised Jesus from the dead and who brings God's resur-

rection life to believers (Rom. 8:11). The biblical testimony is clear. The Holy Spirit is not only a real Person but also God.

NAMES ESTABLISHING THE SPIRIT'S IDENTITY

ETERNAL SPIRIT

The Holy Spirit is called the "eternal Spirit" in Hebrews 9:14. The scriptural meaning of the Greek word, *aionios*, is related to the Hebrew word *olam* in the Old Testament, which carries the connotation of unlimited continuance into the future. That which is eternal stands outside of and is not limited by time. This is true only of God. In calling the third Person of the Trinity the "eternal Spirit," the writer of Hebrews is clearly affirming the deity of the Holy Spirit.

GOD

In the Old Testament the Spirit is linked with various names of God. He is the

Spirit of *Elohim* (Gen. 1:2), the Spirit of *Yahweh* (Is. 40:7), and the Spirit of the Almighty (Job 32:8).

One incident recorded in Acts makes it absolutely clear that the Spirit is God. In the early days of the church in Jerusalem, Christians were cut off from the distribution of food to widows, which was organized through the temple. So the church set up its own distribution system for believing widows and orphans. This took money, and the funds came from people who gave generously. They often sold property and turned over the entire proceeds to the apostles to meet the needs of fellow believers in poverty.

One Christian couple sold property and, wishing to be thought of as generous but not willing to give the entire purchase price, *pretended* to give the whole amount. The husband and wife separately lied about the transaction, and both were separately struck dead!

Peter's words to the husband, Ananias, made it clear that there was nothing wrong with keeping back part of the price for themselves; it was, after all, their property (Acts 5:1, 2). The issue was the hypocrisy of the action. Ananias had pledged one thing but done another. Peter asked him, "Ananias, why has Satan filled your heart to lie to the Holy Spirit and keep back part of the price of the land for yourself? While it remained, was it not your own? And after it was sold, was it not in your own control? Why have you conceived this thing in your heart? You have not lied to men but to God" (vv. 3, 4).

Thus Peter makes it clear that "Holy Spirit" and "God" can be used interchangeably, establishing the fact that the early church recognized the deity of the Holy Spirit.

LORD

The title "Lord" is one that the New Testament generally reserves for the resurrected Jesus. Nevertheless, the Holy Spirit is called the "Spirit of the Lord" four times in

the New Testament (Luke 4:18; Acts 5:9; 8:39; 2 Cor. 3:17). In the last of these passages, the Spirit is called "Lord" in His own right.

In 2 Corinthians 3:7-18, Paul contrasts Moses and believers. When Moses had met with God, Moses' face had been transformed and became radiant. It was his practice after leaving the Lord's presence to put a veil over his face, concealing the brightness. Paul tells us that this was "to keep the Israelites from gazing at [Moses' face] *while the radiance was fading away*" (3:13 NIV; italics mine). Moses didn't want the Israelites to be reminded that he was essentially an ordinary man.

Paul writes concerning believers, "we use great boldness of speech—unlike Moses" (vv. 12, 13). In other words, we take the veil off (so to speak) and let others see us in our humanness—flaws and all. Then Paul explains why we do this. It is because we, "with unveiled face, beholding as in a mirror the glory of the Lord, are being transformed into the same image from glory to glory, just as by the Spirit of the Lord" (v. 18).

Others see Jesus in us not because we are perfect, but because *we are being perfected*. When we live open and honest lives with others, they see the Spirit working His changes in our lives. It is the changes others witness over time that reveal the reality of Jesus and the Spirit's work in our lives. While distinct as two Persons of the Trinity, both Jesus and the Spirit are the Lord our God. "Now the Lord is the Spirit; and where the Spirit of the Lord is, there is liberty" (v. 17).

POWER OF THE HIGHEST

This title of the Holy Spirit is revealed by the archangel Gabriel in his explanation to Mary concerning the virgin birth. The angel told her, "The Holy Spirit will come upon you, and the power of the Highest will overshadow you" (Luke 1:35).

The New Testament associates the Holy Spirit with power no less than ten times. Not only was the impregnation of Mary performed by means of the Spirit's power, but also Jesus ministered in the power of the Spirit (Luke 4:14; Acts 10:38). It was an exercise of the Spirit's power that raised Jesus from the dead (Rom. 1:4), and it is the Spirit's power that infuses the gospel message when it is shared with people (1 Thess. 1:5).

Especially significant for us is Jesus' promise that when the Holy Spirit is given, believers receive power (Acts 1:8). It is the Spirit who not only gives us power to witness, but also who strengthens us in our "inner being" (Eph. 3:16 NIV). How encouraging it is to remember always that the Holy Spirit in us is the source of all the power we will ever require to do God's will daily.

SPIRIT OF CHRIST
SPIRIT OF GOD
SPIRIT OF JESUS
SPIRIT OF THE LIVING GOD
SPIRIT OF THE LORD

Each of these names of the Holy Spirit associates Him with God the Father or God the Son. Elmer Towns, in *The Names of the Holy Spirit*, suggests that the expression "spirit of" is used in the Bible to express similarity of nature.

When Jesus is called the Son of God, this title implies He is by nature God. When the Holy Spirit is described as "the Spirit of His Son" (Gal. 4:6), the title implies that the Holy Spirit has the same nature as the Son, who has the same nature as the Father. This is the most trinitarian name of God in Scripture applied to any individual person of the Godhead. This title summarizes the teaching of Scripture on the equality and unity of nature of God (p. 104).

Aside from this implication of the associative names of the Spirit is the fact that these names also indicate that the Holy Spirit acts *on behalf of* the Father and the Son. The Spirit is the Person of the Godhead who is presently active in our world, the agent carrying out the plans of God the Father and the agent of God the Son in things pertaining to believers and the church. The nature of the Spirit's ministries is something we will examine in another section of this chapter.

NAMES DEFINING THE CHARACTER OF THE HOLY SPIRIT

The New Testament—when speaking about the Spirit apart from His relationship with another Person of the Godhead—typically calls Him the "Holy" Spirit. This and several other names emphasize the character of the third Person of the Trinity.

HOLY SPIRIT
HOLY ONE

The most common name for the third Person of the Trinity is "Holy Spirit." Holiness is an important concept in both the Old and New Testaments. Accordingly, to understand the significance of this name of the Spirit we need to understand the underlying concept of holiness. See also the following articles: "The Holy One of Israel" (p. 49), "Holy One" (p. 105), and "Holy One of God" (p. 147).

Holiness in the Old Testament. The underlying concepts of the Hebrew words translated "holy" are dedication and consecration. That which is holy is removed from the realm of the ordinary and dedicated to the sacred.

The underlying concept. Many passages make it clear that ultimately it is God Himself who is holy and the source of all that is holy. God is Israel's Holy One (Ps. 16:10; Is. 5:19, 24). One aspect of God's holiness is His essential power and splendor. When Isaiah saw the Lord in a vision, the prophet was stunned by the splendor that emanated from God's throne. Isaiah witnessed angelic

Isaiah heard God's angels crying endlessly, "Holy, holy, holy, is the Lord God Almighty."

beings who cried out endlessly, "Holy, holy, holy is the LORD of hosts" (Is. 6:3).

In the Old Testament "holy" also served as a technical religious term that was extended to persons, places, times, and things that were sacred because they were associated with God. For instance, the seventh day was holy (Ex. 20:8-11) and Israel's priesthood was holy (Lev. 21:7). The Old Testament places great stress on maintaining the distinction between the secular and the sacred, that is, between what is commonplace and what is intimately associated with God, the Holy One. This was true of both ritual practices with no essential moral aspect and also of matters that were moral in nature.

Moral holiness. God is holy not only in the sense of awe-inspiring splendor, but also in a moral sense. This moral dimension of holiness is seen in Leviticus 19:2, "Speak to all the congregation of the children of Israel, and say to them, 'You shall be holy, for I the LORD your God am holy.'" The commands that follow deal with such moral issues as theft, lying, and revenge. Here, as in many other Old Testament passages, God's holiness is displayed in His moral perfection as well as His power. From this we can conclude that in calling the third Person of the Trinity the "Holy" Spirit, Scripture intended to emphasize both His power as God and the essential morality of all He says and does.

Holiness in the New Testament. In the New Testament there is a shift in the emphasis on holiness. In the Old Testament holiness was maintained by carefully separating the sacred from the profane. This included the separation of the Israelites, whom God set apart from all other nations, to be a holy people dedicated to His name. In Old Testament times an Israelite lived a holy life by following the Mosaic Law, which called for individuals to be distinctly different from pagans in practices, diet, and other aspects of daily life.

In the New Testament era God's people live among unbelievers, following the same social customs, but distinguished by a dynamic inner transformation that is expressed by a loving concern for others and a commitment to do what is right and good.

Peter describes New Testament holiness, as do other Epistles. For instance, in 1 Peter 1:13-16 and 2:9-12 the apostle urges believers to

> Therefore gird up the loins of your mind, be sober, and rest your hope fully upon the grace that is to be brought to you at the revelation of Jesus Christ; as obedient children, not conforming yourselves to the former lusts, as in your ignorance; but as He who called you is holy, you also be holy in all your conduct, because it is written, "Be holy, for I am holy." . . .
>
> But you are a chosen generation, a royal priesthood, a holy nation, His own special people, that you may proclaim the praises of Him who called you out of darkness into His marvelous light; who once were not a people but are now the people of God, who had not obtained mercy but now have obtained mercy. Beloved, I beg you as sojourners and pilgrims, abstain from fleshly lusts which war against the soul, having your conduct honorable among the Gentiles, that when they speak against you as evildoers they may, by your good works which they observe, glorify God in the day of visitation.

Here we see something of the significance of calling the third Person of the Trinity the "Holy Spirit." The Spirit is the One whose power brings about the transformation of believers and who enables them to live holy and moral lives even though they sojourn in unholy and immoral societies (2 Cor. 3:18). In this, often called the "sanctifying" (or "making holy") work of the Spirit of God, the title "Holy" Spirit is especially appropriate.

Testament we read of Jesus praying for the sanctification of His followers and appealing to the Father to sanctify them through His Word so that they might glorify God in the world (John 17:17-19).

Various New Testament passages make it clear that we need to look at sanctification from two perspectives. In one sense every believer in Jesus *is already sanctified*. In other words, believers are set apart for God by virtue of what Jesus has done for them on the cross. This is sometimes called *positional sanctification*, and it reflects the fact that ultimately our holiness in God's sight rests entirely on Jesus' atoning work for us.

Thus Paul writes to believers in Corinth, "But you were washed, but you were sanctified, but you were justified in the name of the Lord Jesus and by the Spirit of our God" (1 Cor. 6:11). In this sense the phrase "were sanctified" does not indicate any special holiness, but rather means simply "the saved" (as in Acts 20:32; 26:18; Rom. 15:16; and 1 Cor. 1:2).

In another sense there is also a *practical* sanctification. Christians are called not only to be holy in God's sight but also to be holy in all they say and do. The transformation of believers into the likeness of Jesus is not an abstract concept. Rather, we who belong to Jesus truly are "being transformed" (2 Cor. 3:18) into His likeness. The Father and the Son have tasked the Holy Spirit to bring this about. The Spirit and the Word of God are agents the triune God uses to "sanctify [us] completely" (1 Thess. 5:23), so that we may increasingly reflect the reality of Jesus as we live holy lives here and now.

SPIRIT OF TRUTH

The third Person of the Trinity is called "the Spirit of truth" in John 14:17, 15:26, 16:13, and 1 John 4:6. John 14—16 contains Jesus' teachings that He gave to His disciples during the Last Supper. Jesus indicated that

BIBLE BACKGROUND:
SANCTIFICATION

Christians believe that faith in Christ produces a true change in life and character. This is what is meant by "sanctification." In the New the world of fallen humanity couldn't accept the Spirit of truth. Nevertheless, because He dwells in believers, He would testify to them concerning Jesus and "guide [them] into all truth" (16:13).

It is important to make a clear distinction here between "truth" as intellectual convictions and "truth" as the revelation of realities that believers are to experience. When Jesus told His disciples, "You shall know the truth, and the truth shall make you free" (8:32), He was not suggesting that doctrinal purity was the key to freedom from sin. Rather, what Jesus was saying is made clear in verse 31: "If you abide in My word, you are My disciples indeed." This could be paraphrased, "If you continue practicing my word, you are My disciples, and you will know by experience the truth, and the truth will set you free."

In Scripture truth is that which corresponds to reality. Something is true because that is the way things really are. Jesus' statements are truth (17:17) not simply because He spoke them but also because all that He said is in total harmony with reality.

Suppose you are far underground in a complex of caves and are threatened by gas seeping into the labyrinth. Someone might say, "There is a door at the end of this tunnel. Run down to it and you will be safe." What that person says is true if and only if there really is a door at the end of the tunnel. But that truth can set you free only if you hurry down the tunnel, find the door, open it, and step out into safety.

It is the same way with what the Bible calls "truth." God's Word is truth, for it reveals what is real and reliable. But that truth will benefit us only if we put what is revealed into practice by acting on it. When Jesus said that the Holy Spirit would guide us into all truth (16:13), Jesus did not mean that all Christians would agree on every detail of doctrine. Rather, what He meant was that the Spirit would be available to us and guide us concerning how to follow God's Word in our daily lives. And this is just what the third Person of the Trinity does for us as the Spirit of truth.

Another reference to the Spirit of truth is found in 1 John 4:6. There the apostle deals with the question of how we recognize the guidance provided by the Spirit of truth. We need to understand that there are also spirits of falsehood who would lead us astray. John plainly says, "We are of God. He who knows God hears us; he who is not of God does not hear us. By this we know the spirit of truth and the spirit of error." The "us" in this passage is best understood as the apostles, through whom the New Testament was given to the world.

This verse establishes a vital point. The Holy Spirit, who spoke through those who wrote Scripture, will never guide us to act in a way that is contrary to the written Word (1 Pet. 1:11). No person can truthfully say that he or she was guided by the Holy Spirit to steal, commit adultery, gossip, or behave in any other way that is contrary to the moral vision and teachings of Scripture. God the Spirit is truly holy, and His leading is always consistent with truth as it is revealed in God's Word.

NAMES AND TITLES INDICATING THE SPIRIT'S MINISTRIES

The New Testament reveals much about the various ministries of the Spirit. Some of these are seen in activities of the Spirit that are specifically identified, and others are seen in activities of the Spirit that are simply described. As background against which to better understand the names and titles associated with the ministries of the Spirit, it's helpful for us to preview His named and described activities.

THE IDENTIFIED WORKS OF THE HOLY SPIRIT

The following works of the Holy Spirit are specifically named in Scripture.

Water baptism is often confused with the baptizing work of the Holy Spirit, by which He unites believers with Jesus and one another.

❖

Baptism. The baptism of (or by) the Spirit is mentioned in a number of passages in the Gospels and Acts. While the Acts passages *describe* what the baptism of the Spirit is, they do not *define* it. Some have made the mistake of assuming that because certain events took place at the same time (namely, the coming of the Spirit, speaking in tongues, flames of fire resting on the heads of the believers, and the sound of a rushing wind) that the coming of the Spirit on Pentecost is the baptism of the Spirit and that speaking in tongues is the sign of the baptism of the Spirit.

It is, of course, hard to explain why the flames of fire and sound of a mighty wind are ignored in this interpretation. Nevertheless, the baptism of the Spirit is *defined* in 1 Corinthians 12:13; thus, we are not left in doubt or forced to attempt to draw our doctrine from mere description. Also, in this

verse, Scripture states that "by one Spirit we were all baptized into one body."

The baptism of the Spirit, then, is that action by which the third Person of the Trinity bonds a believer to Christ and to other believers as members of His body. This happens to all who trust in Christ at the moment of faith. It is true that Pentecost was the first occasion of the Spirit's exercise of this ministry. But it does not follow that the other events that took place at the same time either *were* the baptism or signs of it.

Filling. Acts 2:4 tells us that when the third Person of the Trinity came upon the believers in Jerusalem in fulfillment of Jesus' promise (1:8), all there were "filled with the Holy Spirit" (2:4). The Old Testament speaks of the Spirit coming upon believers who were called to perform special tasks (Judg. 6:34; 11:29). The Spirit was thus seen as necessary to enable the individual to complete the task successfully, for it was the Spirit who empowered him or her.

When the New Testament speaks of believers being filled with the Spirit, it does so in the passive voice. We are filled, but we do not fill ourselves. Filling is a work of God. Also, filling is viewed as essential for ministry. Being filled with the Spirit was a qualification of the first deacons (Acts 6:1-6), and it is also related to character, for these early deacons were known for their wisdom (v. 3) and faith (v. 6). The relationship of being filled with the Spirit to inner transformation is especially clear in Galatians 5:22 and 23, where the fruit produced by the Spirit in the lives of believers is described as "love, joy, peace, longsuffering, kindness, goodness, faithfulness, gentleness, self control."

Sealing. Ephesians 1:13 and 14 state that when we believed in Jesus, we "were sealed with the Holy Spirit of promise, who is the guarantee of our inheritance until the redemption of the purchased possession, to the praise of His glory." In this passage the Spirit is likened to the seal stamped on goods that had been purchased. The seal marked the goods as the possession of the owner, and also served as a guarantee that the owner would collect his goods one day. In this passage the "inheritance" is not ours; rather, it is us! We are God's inheritance; thus, we are precious to Him. The Spirit marks us as God's own and keeps us safe until the day of redemption.

Indwelling. Jesus told His disciples that the Spirit who had been with them would one day be in them (John 14:17). It is this reality that is expressed in the theological term "indwelling." While "indwelling" is not a term found in the Bible, the reality it expresses is taught unmistakably.

Several verses in Romans 8 use this language, emphasizing the fact that the Spirit has established a home in the hearts and lives of those who know Jesus. Thus, "You are not in the flesh but in the Spirit, if indeed the Spirit of God dwells in you. Now if anyone does not have the Spirit of Christ, he is not His" (v. 9). And, "If the Spirit of Him who raised Jesus from the dead dwells in you, He who raised Christ from the dead will also give life to your mortal bodies through His Spirit who dwells in you" (v. 11). From these verses we see that it is the Spirit in us who gives us the ability to live truly Christian lives.

Gifts. Another ministry of the third Person of the Trinity stated explicitly in Scripture is that of giving spiritual gifts to believers. This, too, is an enabling work of the Spirit. In other words, His presence enables us to make our own unique contribution to the health and well-being of the members of the Christian community.

BIBLE BACKGROUND:

SPIRITUAL GIFTS

Spiritual gifts in the Old Testament. Although the reality of spiritual gifts is present in the Old Testament, the words "spiritual gifts" are not mentioned there. We see that reality in God's words to Moses about a man named Bezalel: "I have filled him with the Spirit of God, in wisdom, in understanding, in knowledge, and in all manner of workmanship" (Ex. 31:3) to shape articles for the tabernacle where God's Old Testament people worshiped. And God adds, "I have put wisdom in the hearts of all the gifted artisans, that they may make all that I have commanded you" (v. 6). In the same way, the Spirit of God enabled Othniel to judge Israel (Judg. 3:10) and gave Samson strength (14:6). Throughout the Old Testament, God is seen as the source of the gifts and abilities that enabled people to serve Him and the Israelites.

The Holy Spirit gives believers gifts that enable them to minister to each other and nurture spiritual growth.

Foundational New Testament principles. The Greek word for spiritual gifts is *charisma*, which means "grace gift." A spiritual gift is a special endowment that equips a believer to serve others in the community of faith. At times Christians use "spiritual gift" in the sense of any divine enabling for any kind of ministry.

Four passages in the New Testament focus on spiritual gifts, but the two major passages are Romans 12:3-8 and 1 Corinthians 12:1-30. In each passage we are called to see ourselves as members of Christ's body, a living organism. In the organism each of us has a special role, a special way that we contribute to the well-being of the whole. There are different gifts (1 Cor. 12:14), which God distributes sovereignly as He chooses (v. 6). Each believer has at least one such gift (v. 7). These gifts are exercised when Christians live together in love, seeking to serve and help each other. As 1 Peter 4:10 says, "As each one has received a gift, minister it to one another, as good stewards of the manifold grace of God."

In the New Testament passages on gifts, the focus is always on the Christian community. Gifts are used for the common good and function to build up the body of Christ (1 Cor. 12:7). They help individuals and the congregation to become spiritually mature (Eph. 4:12-16). Also, these gifts come from God the Spirit, who not only gives them but who also then enables us as we use them in ministry.

Beside the activities of the Spirit that are given specific names (such as those listed previously), there are also other activities of the Spirit that are described but not named. It was the Spirit who enabled the first disciples to speak in tongues. (Tongues is identified as a spiritual gift in 1 Corinthians 12:28.) The Spirit's activity in leading and guiding individuals is illustrated in the life of Paul (Acts 11:12, 28; 16:6, 7; 20:22, 23, 28; 21:11) and affirmed in his letters (Rom. 8:14).

We have already noted that the Spirit is the One who effects our gradual transformation toward the likeness of Jesus (2 Cor. 3:17, 18; Gal. 5:22, 23). It is patently true that the Spirit's active presence is the key to growth in righteousness, a goal established in the Old Testament, but which the Law could not achieve (Gal. 3:19-25). In all these things the Spirit's presence and power are utterly essential to us. These are provided by our good and loving God, through the Spirit, whose ministry names we now explore.

COMFORTER
COUNSELOR
HELPER
PARACLETE

There is some confusion concerning the significance of one name given the Spirit. In Greek, Jesus called Him *"allos parakletos."* The Greek can be translated either "another Comforter" or "another Counselor." Or, as in some English versions, it may simply be transliterated as another "Paraclete." Essentially, these three names are one.

The confusion is caused by the fact that in the Greek, *parakletos* has many shades of meaning. The basic image is that of one who "comes along side" to help. For instance, the Spirit helps by bringing to mind Jesus' teachings (John 14:26) and also by revealing new truths (16:12-14). The emphasis in these passages seems to be on the Spirit's work of helping believers understand the significance of Scripture for their own lives and decisions. The Spirit is with us to help in every way and in every need. He is our Comforter, Helper, Counselor all in one.

SPIRIT OF ADOPTION

When used in a phrase with another person of the Godhead, "Spirit of" indicates both the Spirit's identity with that Person as God and also the fact that the Spirit is acting for the other Person of the Godhead. In some cases where "Holy Spirit of promise" appears in some versions, the Greek might be better rendered "the promised Holy Spirit" (Acts 2:33; Eph. 1:13).

Frequently the Spirit's name is found in phrases such as "Spirit of adoption," "Spirit of life," "Spirit of wisdom," and so on. Such phrases generally indicate a ministry or activity of the Spirit. Thus, when in Romans 8:15 the Spirit is called the "Spirit of adoption," we are informed that the Spirit is the One who adopted us into the family of God so that we might cry out to God "Abba, Father." (See the article on "Abba," p. 123.)

Adoption is mentioned several times in Paul's letters. He refers to this practice, which was well established in Roman law, in Romans 8:15, 23; 9:4; Galatians 4:5; and Ephesians 1:5. In ancient times, it was not at all unusual for adults to be adopted by a Roman *pater familias*. When the adoption took place, the adoptee changed families in a significant way.

In the Roman system, a son was responsible to his father as long as the father lived. But when an adult son was adopted into another family, the old family ties were completely severed. The adopted child was fully and completely a member of his new family. He owed no allegiance to the head of his old family, but rather owed total allegiance to the head of the new family. In fact, all that he possessed was now under the control of his new father, and all that he did reflected not on his birth parents but rather on the adoptive parent.

In return, the father owed allegiance to his adopted son. In a very real way, the estate of the father became the estate and inheritance of the adoptee. The new relationship called for commitment by the new father and new son to each other.

Paul uses the image of adoption to help us understand what happened when we became Christians. God the Spirit transferred us by adopting us into God's family. As God's adopted children, we owe no allegiance to our old father, Satan, or to his evil ways. While as sinners we were spiritually

Satan's offspring, in Christ we have become children of God. Our allegiance now is owed to God alone, and our choices reflect glory or shame on the Lord.

As members of God's family, we have His resources available to us. We no longer need to be slaves to sin, but rather can choose to live our lives for the Lord. And, as the Spirit of adoption, God the Holy Spirit stays with us to give us access to the very power of God, which will transform our lives so that we might bear His family likeness.

SPIRIT OF WISDOM AND UNDERSTANDING

SPIRIT OF COUNSEL AND MIGHT

SPIRIT OF KNOWLEDGE AND THE FEAR OF THE LORD

Each of these titles of the Holy Spirit occurs in Isaiah 11:2, and each describes a ministry of the Spirit to the promised Messiah (Christ). It was the Spirit who constantly supplied Jesus with counsel, might, wisdom, understanding, knowledge, and respect for the Lord. Hebrew poetry (Isaiah 11 is a poetic passage) utilizes parallelism, frequently repeating the same idea in similar or synonymous words. It is thus a mistake, then, to draw too careful distinctions between the meaning of the words used in poetic contexts. Given this there is still value in looking at each of these descriptive words.

Counsel. The Hebrew word here means "advice," "counsel," "purpose," or "plan." However, when the one giving the counsel is God, more than advice is implied. Advice implies that one has options. God's counsels are His purposes, which He intended to see carried out. As the Spirit of counsel, the Holy Spirit communicates God's will, marking out the path we are to follow so that we will fulfill God's purposes in our lives.

Might. The Hebrew has a variety of words that can be translated "strength," "power," or "might." The use of these words in the Old Testament reminds us that while human beings have limited physical prowess, God is unlimited in how He exercises His power. As the Spirit of might, the Holy Spirit is portrayed as the One who makes the resources of God's strength available. As the psalmist cried, "The Lord is my strength and my shield; my heart trusted in Him, and I am helped" (Ps. 28:7).

Wisdom and understanding. These two words are often found together. In the Hebrew, "wisdom" has to do with a person's basic approach to life. The wise person looks at life with full awareness that God is present and active not only in the world but also in one's experience. Because of that, the wise person makes choices that are both good and right. Wisdom, then, is a practical quality, having to do with life and the choices one makes daily.

The Hebrew word for "understanding" emphasizes good judgment and the ability to evaluate available choices. Given enough information, the person with understanding will make the appropriate choice. Here again the emphasis is on the practical. An individual with wisdom and understanding approaches life in view of the living presence of God. He or she is able to distinguish between available choices to determine what is right and good and then make the right choice.

Knowledge. The Hebrew concept of knowledge clearly overlaps the notions of wisdom and understanding. To "know" something is far different from having mastered ideas and concepts. "Knowledge" relates to experience. It is the ability to organize our experiences and grasp their significance so that we are able to come to right conclusions concerning moral and practical matters. Like wisdom and understanding, knowledge is both practical and moral in character. The Spirit is portrayed as the source of the wisdom, knowledge, and understanding that will mark the life of the Messiah.

The fear of the Lord. This is a familiar and significant biblical phrase. It occurs 22 times in the Bible. The Book of Proverbs portrays the fear of the Lord as the beginning of knowledge (1:7) and as the beginning of wisdom (9:10; see also Ps. 111:10). In other words, the fear of the Lord is the source of these vital qualities. *The New International Encyclopedia of Bible Words* explains the nature of this religious "fear" (p. 273):

> Such fear is reverence for God. We who fear God recognize him as the ultimate reality, and we respond to him. Fear of God is called the "beginning of knowledge" (Pr 1:7), meaning that taking God into account is the foundation of a disciplined and holy life (Pr 1:3; cf. Ge 20:11; Ps 36:1-4). To fear God means to reject every deity and to serve him only (Dt 6:13). Fear of the Lord is expressed by walking in all his ways, by loving him, and by serving him with all our heart and soul (Dt 10:12; Job 1:1; Ps 128:1).

It is exciting to realize that the Spirit who supplied Jesus with these gifts during His life on earth is with us now and ready to enrich us with the same benefits. How much better it is to look to the Spirit for counsel, might, wisdom, understanding, knowledge, and the fear of the Lord, than to rely on any other source for the direction of our daily lives.

SPIRIT OF LIFE IN CHRIST JESUS

Romans 8 is one of the most important chapters in the New Testament. And verse 2 is where we find the Holy Spirit titled the "Spirit of life in Christ Jesus."

The theme of Romans in righteousness, and Paul carefully develops his teaching on this vital biblical theme. In chapters 1—3, Paul demonstrates that "there is none righteous, no, not one" (3:10). Thus, it was necessary for Jesus to die for our sins if a righteous God would be free to forgive sinners. In chapters 4 and 5, Paul shows that

God graciously acquits sinners who believe in Jesus and gives them a righteous standing in His sight.

In chapters 6—8, Paul shows that God's gift of righteousness is more than a legal fiction. God intends to actually make us righteous. In chapter 6, Paul shows that righteous living is made possible by our union with Christ. Then, in chapter 7, Paul reveals that this is a struggle, especially given the fact that believers retain their sin nature until the Resurrection.

Clearly, righteous living is not something that is possible for us without divine help. Thus, in chapter 8, Paul presents the solution. He explains, "For the law of the Spirit of life in Christ Jesus has made me free form the law of sin and death" (v. 2). In this passage, "law" is used in the sense of "operating principle," just as we call gravity a "law of nature." Sin and death are active in us until the Resurrection. But the Holy Spirit is also active in us! And the Spirit is stronger than the sin within us!

Paul goes on in this vital chapter of Romans to encourage us. We can actually be the kind of person that God wants us to be, not because we have the strength in ourselves, but rather because we rely on the Lord to enable us. "He who raised Christ from the dead will also give life to your mortal bodies through His Spirit who dwells in you" (v. 11). Thus, the title "the Spirit of Life in Christ Jesus" is one of the most precious and certainly most enabling of Scripture's titles of the Holy Spirit.

BIBLE BACKGROUND:
RIGHTEOUSNESS

We believe in a righteous God, and we also believe that God calls us to live righteous lives. But the righteousness we believe in isn't some drab existence of following endless sets of rules. Instead, righteousness is a

Giving alms to the needy is still considered in contemporary Judaism to be a significant "righteous act."

❖

dynamic, positive, and exciting way of life. Our understanding of righteousness and how to become righteous is found in Scripture. In fact, righteousness is a theme that echoes through both the Old and New Testaments.

Righteousness in the Old Testament. The Hebrew words translated "righteous" are also rendered "just" and "justice" in our English versions. The underlying idea is that of conformity to a norm. A person is "righteous" when his or her actions are in harmony with established moral standards. The only valid standard by which righteousness can be measured is the revealed will of God, and in the Old Testament that will is most clearly expressed in the Law of Moses.

In a deeper sense, the Old Testament often calls God righteous (Ps. 4:1; Is. 45:21). What God does is always righteous (Ps. 71:24), for all His actions are in harmony with His character. In fact it is the character of

God, expressed in His revealed will, that is the ultimate standard of righteousness.

Despite the fact that "in [God's] sight no one living is righteous" (Ps. 143:2), the Old Testament does speak of righteous men and women. The apparent conflict is resolved when we understand that such references are not to righteousness in an absolute sense, but rather in a comparative sense. These are people who lived in closer conformity to God's will than others. For these individuals God promised blessings and rewards (Pss. 5:12; 112:6; 34:19; 119:121). But this comparative righteousness neither earned God's favor nor His salvation. Rather, in the Old Testament era (as in the New Testament era) it was faith in God that led to righteousness and salvation (Gen. 15:6).

Righteousness in the New Testament. Some New Testament passages use "righteous" in the Old Testament sense of behavior that conforms to the Law (Matt. 1:19; 5:45; Mark 6:20). Nevertheless, the Old Testament concept of righteousness is transformed and enriched in the New Testament.

In Matthew 5:17-20, Jesus explores the relationship between the Law and righteousness. Christ assures His listeners that His teaching does not nullify the Law, but rather that their righteousness must exceed "the righteousness of the scribes and the Pharisees." This statement undoubtedly shocked Jesus' listeners, for the Pharisees were dedicated to keeping the most insignificant provisions of the Mosaic Law, as applied by the rabbis.

Jesus then went on to give a series of illustrations that showed that God's concern was not simply wrong action, but also the motives and passions behind them. When properly understood, the Law of Moses taught humankind that it was not enough for the actions of people to conform to the Law. Just as important was the necessity of people experiencing an inner transformation so that their heart and soul were in harmony with God.

In Romans 1:16 and 17, Paul explains that righteousness is a matter of faith, for the ultimate righteousness—that which God required—can only be imputed to those who by nature are sinners. In 3:21—4:25, Paul shows that God's call for righteousness has always been associated with faith. The Old Testament itself speaks of a righteousness that comes from God without reference to the Law (3:21), for Genesis 15:6 (NIV) tells us that God "credited" Abraham's faith to him as a righteousness he did not have. In the same way, God today credits righteousness to the account of those who believe in Jesus. This is based on the sacrifice of Jesus, who died on the cross to pay for the sins of humankind.

But the Book of Romans goes beyond this issue of forensic, or legal, righteousness. God not only declares those who believe in Jesus to be righteous in His sight, but also so works in the lives of believers that they actually *become* righteous in their thoughts, actions, and words. This *becoming righteous* is the theme of chapters 6—8.

Believers are united by faith to Jesus, and in this union share in both His death and resurrection. Because of His gift of new life, our bodies can now become instruments of righteousness (ch. 6). While we cannot become righteous by our own effort or by trying to keep God's Law (ch. 7), the Spirit can and will release us from our bondage to sin. Through an inner transformation, He enables us to live godly and righteous lives (ch. 8).

These things are possible, not because we force our actions to conform to an external standard, but rather because our actions flow from a character that is becoming more and more like God's own holy nature. Assuredly, making us righteous is one of the most wonderful and awe-inspiring works of the Spirit of God!

Nevertheless, the Spirit's work is a quiet one, and for us, Jesus is the key to making it a reality. We have forgiveness through faith in Him. Because of Jesus' atoning sacrifice and subsequent resurrection from the dead, we are righteous in God's sight. And through our union by faith with Jesus, we also have the promise of inner transformation. As we grow in our Christian life, we will actually become more and more righteous, for we will truly be like our Lord in what we think, say, and do.

SPIRIT OF WISDOM
SPIRIT OF WISDOM AND REVELATION

We have previously seen that the Spirit ministered to Jesus as the Spirit of wisdom and understanding (p. 206). Deuteronomy 34:9 tells us that the Spirit performed a similar ministry for Joshua (and undoubtedly for other Old Testament saints). Also, in Ephesians 1:17, Paul prays that the believers at Ephesus might be given the "spirit of wisdom and revelation in the knowledge of Him."

It might be argued here that the "spirit" is not the Holy Spirit but rather a reference to a basic attitude toward God that enables believers to maintain their perspective on the significance of their relationship with God. Nevertheless, it is compelling to remember that the Holy Spirit opens our eyes to truth, enabling us to see and experience reality. The reality here is that God exercises His power for us, in us, and through us, for the Spirit's power is resurrection power, "which He worked in Christ when He raised Him from the dead" (v. 20).

IMAGES OF THE HOLY SPIRIT

Just as simile and metaphor are used in the Bible to enrich our understanding of God the Father and God the Son, so also they are used to enhance our awareness of God the Holy Spirit. The eight metaphors of the Spirit are the dove, earnest, fire, oil, seal, water, wind, and wine.

DOVE

It's not unusual these days to see a dove on an automobile license plate or on a lapel

The dove is probably the best-known symbol of the Holy Spirit and His works.

❖

pin. Christians immediately recognize this as a symbol of the Holy Spirit.

The dove is mentioned some twenty-four times in the Old and New Testaments. It was a dove that Noah sent out from the ark to see whether the waters of the Flood had dried up and the land was inhabitable (Gen. 8:8-12). In the Song of Songs, the lover calls his bride "my dove, my perfect one" (5:2; see also 2:14; 6:9). Also, in the Old Testament Law, those who were too poor to bring a lamb as an offering to God were permitted to bring a young pigeon or a dove (Lev. 12:6-8).

The source of the dove as a symbol of the Spirit is an event associated with the baptism of Jesus by John, just before Christ began His public ministry. Jesus had insisted that John baptize Him, so that Jesus might affirm John's call to the Jews to repent. When Jesus was coming up out of the waters of the Jordan River (where John was baptizing people), the Holy Spirit descended on Jesus in "bodily form like a dove" (Luke 3:22). This event is also mentioned in the other three Gospels (Matt. 3:16; Mark 1:10; John 1:32). The descent of the Spirit, along with a voice from heaven, confirmed Jesus as the Son of God. John 1:32 also tells us that the dove remained on Jesus, perhaps indicating a special continuing empowerment for the ministry the Savior was about to begin.

It would be wrong to read too much into the image of a dove; nevertheless, it is thought-provoking to consider that in Genesis the dove was the creature that brought Noah news about the fresh new world that awaited him outside the ark. Also, the dove is considered an appropriate symbol of love. Moreover, the dove, as a sacrificial bird, made it possible for even the poorest Israelites to worship God.

EARNEST

This image is used in Ephesians 1:13 and 14. W. E. Vine comments on the use of the Greek word translated "guarantee" in the NKJV, but which can also be rendered "earnest," "down payment," or "pledge."

Arrabon, originally meant "earnest"—money deposited by the purchaser and forfeited if the purchase was not completed. In general usage it came to denote a pledge or earnest of any sort. In the N.T., it is used only of that which is assured by God to believers; it is said of the Holy Spirit as the Divine pledge of all their future blessedness, particularly of their eternal inheritance.

In the presence of the Holy Spirit we have God's personal and ever-present guarantee that we are His and that He will surely claim us as His own.

FIRE

The image of the Spirit as fire is rooted in one of the signs given at Pentecost of His coming. Acts 2:1-4 says that flames of fire rested on the heads of the first Christians as the Spirit filled them and enabled them to speak in foreign languages. In the New Testament fire has three primary associations.

Fire is associated with God's glory. Fire serves as a sign of God's essential glory (Acts 7:30: Rev. 1:14), an image that is developed in Hebrews 12:18, 29. God appeared to Moses in the burning bush and shrouded Himself in flames at the top of Mount Sinai. The flames that stood above the first Christians on Pentecost symbolized both God's presence and His power.

Fire is associated with judgment. The image of fire is frequently found in passages that portray God's judgment on sinners (2 Thess. 1:6-10; Rev. 20:11-15). Even eternal judgment is portrayed as a lake of fire (Rev. 20:14).

Fire is associated with purification. This is seen clearly in 1 Peter 1:7 and Revelation 3:18. The experiences through which we go that are intended to cleanse and purify us are compared to the fire used by metalworkers to refine silver or gold. Two of these associations are implied in the image of the Holy Spirit as fire. It is His presence in us that reflects the glory of God. And it is the Spirit's work in our lives that purifies and cleanses our hearts.

OIL

Acts 10:38 speaks of Jesus being anointed by the Holy Spirit. The significance of anointing is discussed in the article on Christ as the Anointed One (p. 94). The normal substance used in anointing a person in biblical times was pure olive oil.

Illumination is one use of oil in biblical times that is linked with a ministry of the Holy Spirit. The small, open lamps of Palestine were filled with olive oil. Then a flax wick was dropped into the pool of oil and lit to give light to those who held the lamps.

First Corinthians 2:6-16 is the primary passage that discusses the Spirit's work of illumination. The Spirit knows the mind of God and has expressed His thoughts in the words of Scripture. Nevertheless, those words must be interpreted by the Spirit for those who have the Spirit. In the work of illumination, the Spirit uses the Word to communicate the will of God to each of us in our particular situation.

BIBLE BACKGROUND:
ILLUMINATION

Paul explains illumination quite simply in 1 Corinthians 2:6-16. He writes that the Spirit has unveiled even the deep things of God in human speech, in "words taught by the Spirit" (v. 13 NIV). The person who does not possess the Spirit does not accept or understand these words, for they are spiritually discerned.

This special work of the Spirit is not just for theologians struggling to master some abstract concept. Illumination is most often linked to what we might call "heart understanding." Jonathan Edwards, an early American preacher, linked illumination with the application of God's Word to our lives. He wrote, "This light and this only has its fruit in a universal holiness of life. No merely notional or speculative understanding of the doctrine of religion will ever bring us to this. But this light, as it reaches the bottom of the heart, changes the nature, so it will effectually dispose to a universal holiness" (Sermon on "Divine and Supernatural Life").

We, too, can open the Bible, commit ourselves to do what we discover there, and be sure of God's inner guidance in our lives. As Paul closes his thoughts, he gives us a unique assurance. The person with the Spirit can make evaluations about all things, for in the Word of God (especially as it is unveiled by the Spirit) "we have the mind of Christ" (v. 16). As Saint Augustine wrote, "Behold, brethren, this great mystery: the sound of our words strike the ear, but the teacher is within."

SEAL

The primary reference to the Spirit as a seal is in Ephesians 1:3. Herbert Lockyer, in *All the Divine Names and Titles in the Bible*, comments as follows (pp. 328, 329):

> Under ancient Jewish law, the seal was a token of the completion of a transaction; and when the agreement was concluded, the act passed and the price paid, the seal was appended to the contract to make it definite and binding (Jeremiah 32:9, 10). The moment a person is born anew by the Spirit, he is sealed with the Spirit, and because *He* is the seal, He cannot be broken. Sealed thus, we are no longer our own, for the Spirit, as the divine stamp upon us, marks us out as divine property until the day of final redemption, the redemption of the body (Romans 8:23).

WATER

Jesus introduced this metaphor as He spoke to the crowds in Jerusalem. John 7:37-39 records Jesus' words:

> On the last day, that great day of the feast, Jesus stood and cried out, saying, "If anyone thirsts, let him come to Me and drink. He who believes in Me, as the Scripture has said, out of his heart will flow rivers of living water." But this He spoke concerning the Spirit, whom those believing in Him would receive; for the Holy Spirit was not yet given, because Jesus was not yet glorified.

On the last day of the Feast of Tabernacles, the priests marched from the Pool of Siloam to the temple, and there they poured out water from the pool at the base of the temple. This ritual was associated with readings from Zechariah 14 and Ezekiel 47. These passages envisioned a day when rivers of water would flow from the temple, bringing life to the whole earth. Jesus' announcement on that particular day was a promise to those who yearned to see God act. Such thirsty persons should come to Jesus and drink, for life-giving waters would soon overflow from believers to bring life to a spiritually parched earth.

John explains that Jesus, in speaking of life-giving water, was referring to the Holy Spirit. He would dwell, not in Judaism's temple, but rather in the hearts of those who trusted in Christ for salvation. The Spirit Himself was the water that brings life, and He would bring life to all who believe.

WIND

It was Jesus who also used the metaphor of wind to describe the Spirit. This is a very natural metaphor, for the Greek noun translated "spirit," *pneuma*, also means "breath" or "wind."

Jesus used the metaphor in speaking with an influential religious leader named Nicodemus (John 3:1-21). When Jesus confronted Nicodemus with the necessity of spiritual rebirth, Nicodemus was confused by the idea of being "born again." Was Jesus speaking literally?

Christ explained that He was contrasting physical birth with spiritual birth, the latter calling for a work of the Spirit of God (v. 6). Jesus then observed that "the wind blows where it wishes, and you hear the sound of it, but cannot tell where it comes from and where it goes. So is everyone who is born of the Spirit" (v. 8). Like the wind, the Spirit is invisible and beyond humankind's ability to track. Nevertheless, just as the sound of the wind can be heard, so too the work of the Spirit in effecting the new birth will be visible in believers.

The ways of the Spirit are a mystery, and mere human beings cannot trace His course. But like the wind, He is very real. In fact, there is evidence of His passing in the life of everyone whom He has touched.

WINE

This metaphor is implicit in Ephesians 5:18, although it is never stated explicitly. Paul urges believers not to be drunk with wine, but rather to be filled with the Spirit. The analogy is that as wine frees people from their inhibitions and causes them to act spontaneously, so too the Spirit frees believers to act spontaneously for God.

Some have seen this imagery reflected in Acts 2:1-13, where the enthusiasm and energy of Jesus' followers as they spoke in other languages made some think that the disciples were drunk. It is sad when a person does become drunk, for his or her spontaneous actions will show a lack of judgment and an unfortunate lack of inhibitions. But it is wonderful when the Christian forgets himself or herself and spontaneously, without self-consciousness, worships or witnesses to God.

WE BELIEVE

Each name and title of God adds to our knowledge of Him and His purposes. In this appendix we bring together and summarize what we can know and believe about God through His special revelation of Himself in the Scriptures.

WE BELIEVE IN GOD

We believe God is the creative source of our universe. The material universe is no accident. The vast, empty reaches of space, scattered with myriads of stars, and the rich environment of planet earth are all the handiwork of the being we call "God." Everything that exists testifies to the complex mind and majestic power of the Creator. His inventiveness and infinite attention to detail are revealed in the design of living creatures, from the tiniest cell to the most complex systems that enable human beings to see, taste, smell, think, feel, and choose. No random mating of lifeless atoms in some ancient sea can adequately account for life as we know it in all its varied forms. No unexplained explosion billions of years ago can account for the order exhibited in the heavens or the friendly features of this planet. No, in all that is, we see the hand of God. And in reasoned faith, we understand with all God's people that "the universe was formed at God's command, so that what is seen was not made out of what was visible" (Heb. 11:3).

We believe God is a loving, personal being. God is a person, not some impersonal force. His personhood shines through His creation and is fully unveiled in Scripture. It is also reflected in our own personal attributes. We reason and we recognize the vast wisdom displayed in all God has made. We see beauty and we wonder at the One who designed delight for every sense as He shaped this world to be a home for humankind. We love, and caught in wonder, we pause to realize that the One who gave us the capacity to care loves us supremely. Because God is a person, we can have a personal relationship to Him on every level of our being. Our deepest yearnings to know and be known, to love and be loved, can be fully satisfied only in a personal relationship with the One who made us like Himself. God is a person, and we are destined for endless fellowship with our God.

We believe God is a moral, responsible being. The pain and the ugliness that mar our lives are evidence of human failure, not of divine indifference. Our own sense of justice is but a distorted echo of God's total commitment to all that is good. Because human beings, too, are moral beings, our consciences judge our thoughts and actions, and we condemn the wrong actions of others. But One greater than the human conscience is judge of the universe. God's judgments can be traced in the rise and fall of empires and in the consequences of our individual moral choices. However, the full revelation of God's moral nature awaits the judgment to come at history's end. Until then, judgment withheld demonstrates the richness of God's kindness, tolerance, and patience as He continues to hold open the door of repentance and moral reform for all humankind.

We believe God is active in our world. We affirm a hidden God, not directly accessible to the senses. But though God remains hidden, He has acted in this world of space and time, and God is at work among us today. Evidence of God's involvement is found in history past, culminating in the man, Christ Jesus, who bridged the gap between the invisible and the visible to reveal in human flesh the true nature of deity. Evidence of God's active involvement can also be found in life's present moments. His handiwork is recognized by the eyes of faith and is visible to all human beings who trust themselves to Jesus. They, through His transforming touch, reflect Jesus' own love and compassion for others.

We do believe in God. And the God we believe in is powerful, loving, personal, moral, and is at work in our world.

WE BELIEVE THAT GOD HAS SPOKEN

We believe God has spoken at many times and in many ways. God has spoken wordlessly in heavens that declare His glory, and He has established in human nature mute testimony to His existence. Through the ages, nature's silent witness has been supplemented by special gracious acts of self-revelation. God whispered to the ancients in dreams and visions, thundered from cloud-shrouded Sinai, and uttered calls for holiness through Israel's bold prophets. God confounded disbelief with mighty acts of power, enriched the worship of Israel with symbolic ritual, and patterned life for His people with a law that speaks compellingly of His own concern for the poor, for the oppressed, and for healthy relationships in the community of faith. Ultimately, God's self-disclosure culminated in the incarnation of His Son, Who is the full and exact representation of His being. In Jesus, God made flesh, God speaks in unmistakable human terms, inviting us to hear, see, and touch the Word of life. God has spoken at many times and in many ways; the ear of faith knows and acknowledges His voice.

We believe God has spoken in a reliable and relevant written word. The Scriptures, both Old and New Testament, are a unique treasure, filled with words breathed by God through writers He inspired. Reality, which no eye can see, no ear can hear, and no human mind can conceive, has been revealed to us in words taught by the Spirit of God. The Bible alone, of all books, blends, as does the person of Jesus Christ, the human and divine, so that it is rightly called the Word of God. Relying fully on its trustworthy nature, we look to the Bible confidently, submitting to its teaching, rebuke, correction, and training in righteousness. Looking into Scripture, we hear and recognize God's contemporary voice. Responding, we grow in our personal relationship to the Lord. We believe with the saints of all the ages that God has spoken to humankind. We recognize His voice, and we joyfully obey His living and His written Word, which speak together in fullest harmony.

WE BELIEVE IN GOD THE FATHER

We believe in God the Father, who planned the ages. God, though existing in three distinct persons, is the Father. From eternity past, before the first creative word was spoken, God the Father designed the ages, shaping all that is and will be, to display His attributes and to express His love. In the outworking of God's great and multifaceted plan, His sovereignty, holiness, mercy, justice, grace, and every other quality that makes Him so worthy of our worship will ultimately be known. Because God the Father has brought the whole creation into full submission to His will, history moves inevitably toward His intended end, and human existence is infused with purpose.

We believe in God the Father, who guards the present. God, the Father of our Lord Jesus Christ, is Father to Jesus' people. Assured of the Father's constant love, we come to Him freely, sharing every need. We rejoice in Jesus' reminder that we are truly valuable to our heavenly Father, and thus, released from anxiety, we seek first His kingdom and His righteousness, knowing that the Father will provide. Acknowledging God as Father, we take our place as obedient children, fully aware that we are to love our enemies and seek a perfection that mirrors His own.

We believe in God the Father, who guarantees the future. God the Father has committed Himself to covenants that establish the shape of the future. His ancient covenants with Israel and the new covenant He has established in Jesus stand as His unbreakable oath. The details of the future God intends, although enriched by the prophets' visions of tomorrow, may not be clear. But the bold outlines of God's plan for time and for eternity continue to provide a sure and certain hope. In God's good time, Jesus will return, hurts will be healed, and the sweet scent of justice and peace will fill the valleys and hover over every hill. Then, in that end which is a beginning, a worn universe will be replaced with one that is vital, holy, fresh, and new. With judgment past, God's people of every age and nation will join in endless celebration of eternal life in the presence of the Lord.

Yes, we believe in God the Father, who planned the ages, guards the present, and guarantees that future which His covenants with us proclaim.

WE BELIEVE IN JESUS

We believe in Jesus, who existed from the beginning. We believe that God, though One and indivisible, existing in three distinct persons, is Jesus Christ the Son. With God, as God, God from the beginning, Himself uncreated, the Son was the active agent in the Creation and even today sustains all things by the power of His being. All things visible and invisible owe their existence to the Son, and He is the One who is the source of all life. The unique person we meet in Jesus of Nazareth is truly God the Son.

We believe in Jesus, who lived and died on earth as a real human being. Jesus, though truly God, is also fully human. In history's ultimate miracle, God the Holy Spirit bonded the human to the divine. And so the Virgin Mary gave birth to her Son, and in Him, God the Son entered time and space to live as one of us. Jesus never surrendered His nature as God but shrouded His splendor in flesh and submitted to the limitations that human nature imposed: so the eternal Son humbled Himself. He became obedient to death, even the shameful death of the Cross, that through His suffering Jesus might win for His human brothers and sisters a salvation that, apart from Him, no one could earn. God the Son was made like us in every way that, stooping a little lower than the angels, He might taste death for every person and so bring us back with Him to glory. The unique person we meet in Jesus of Nazareth is in the fullest sense a human being, as well as truly God.

We believe in Jesus, who lives today in resurrection. Jesus of Nazareth hung on a criminal's cross, suffered death, and was buried in a rich man's tomb. Yet after three days, in a burst of divine power, the God/Man, Jesus, was raised to life again, His flesh transformed and energized by the Spirit. Jesus, forever liberated from bondage to decay, is seated today at the right hand of God the Father. There He intercedes for us and carries out His role as the living Head of the church that is His body. In His resurrected body Jesus will come again. And in His resurrected form Jesus will exist eternally, the source and model of a resurrection that awaits all the saved.

We believe in Jesus, who lives within us.
Today the living Jesus takes up residence in those who believe in Him. Through a mystical but real union, our personalities are linked with His. As branches draw strength and life from the vine and so are enabled to bear fruit, you and I draw from Jesus. Living close to Him, dependent on Him, obedient to Him, we experience the reality of Jesus' living presence within.

Yes, we do believe in Jesus. We acknowledge Him as the eternal God. We stand amazed before the cradle of His Incarnation, kneel beneath His cross, rejoice at His Resurrection, rely on His guidance and intercession, and depend on His living presence within us for strength to live our daily lives.

WE BELIEVE IN THE HOLY SPIRIT

We believe in the Holy Spirit, who strengthened Jesus. We believe that God, though One and indivisible, existing in three distinct persons, is the Holy Spirit. The Holy Spirit, eternally existing with the Father and the Son, supported and sustained Jesus in His mission to earth. From the moment of Jesus' conception to the unleashing of resurrection power, the Spirit ministered to and through Jesus. The Spirit's breath accompanied each miracle and shared each whispered prayer, infusing Jesus' touch and teaching with added power. One with the Father as with the Son, the Spirit served Jesus, even as today the Spirit does not speak of Himself but points the believing heart to Christ.

We believe in the Holy Spirit, who energizes us today. The Spirit continues to be active in our world today. He convicts those who do not yet believe, binds to Jesus those who trust in Him, and by His presence serves as God's own seal and guarantee of our full redemption. That matchless power exhibited in the resurrection of Jesus flows from the Spirit into the believer, bringing life to mortal bodies and enabling us to live a life that pleases God. The Holy Spirit is the source of the fruit of divine transformation—love, joy, peace, patience, goodness, and all that marks us as Jesus' own. The Holy Spirit is the One who manifests Himself in varied gifts that enable us to contribute to the common good, and who, as God, remains unlimited despite our theologies.

Yes, we do believe in the Holy Spirit. We see Him in all Jesus' words and works, and we are awed to realize that this same Spirit now infuses us.

WE BELIEVE IN A REDEEMABLE HUMANITY

We believe humanity was created by and is loved by God. We believe human beings are unique in all creation. Alone among the living creatures that share our planet, humankind has been endowed with the image and likeness of God. Crowned with that glory and honor by God's personal creative act, human beings are also entrusted with dominion over the works of God's hands. But mankind's special place in the Creation, evidenced by God's rich endowment of personhood, is seen most clearly in the constant love God bears for us. Human beings were created for fellowship with God, and history is but the stage on which the Lord's unquenchable love for men and women has been dramatized. Because human beings are special to God, each individual is of ultimate worth and value, to be loved and cherished, and to be aided toward the fullest possible development of every potential—especially the potential for knowing and loving God.

We believe humanity is trapped in and twisted by sin. By an act of disobedience that took place in space and time, the original humans, Adam and Eve, disobeyed God. This Fall drained them of innocence and wrenched their very nature out of shape, so that the imprint of the eternal was distorted.

In the Fall, mankind's original capacity for righteousness and for actual fellowship with God was lost. That distorted nature, not the original sinlessness, has been passed on to all of Adam's children but one, and so the human family has found itself trapped in, and twisted by, sin. All our misery, all our failures, all our hateful and criminal acts can be traced directly or indirectly to the sin that now infects the race. War, injustice, and oppression are evidence that the disease of sin has warped human society. Although endowed with a moral sense and still able to do limited good, human beings all fall short of the glory of God and even of the demands of their own consciences. We live with the reality of sin. No heartfelt desire or determined act of will can release us from our tragic bondage. Wars and fightings without, like selfish cravings within, bear constant testimony to the reality of the Fall and its tragic consequences. Similarly a sense of inescapable guilt and shame provide compelling evidence that sin has alienated us from God and has made us objects of His necessary wrath.

We believe in the unseen universe and in the personality of Satan and the angels. God's creative work is not summed up in the visible. Beyond the spectrum that our eyes can see lies a universe filled with spiritual beings who have an impact on our lives. The source of evil in our universe is rooted there in Satan, who rebelled against the divine order, carrying with him other spiritual beings who have arrayed themselves against God and His beloved. The influence of the evil one, resonating in harmony with the sinful nature of humankind, warps our society and holds people captive.

Yet other beings, faithful to their Creator, continue to obey His will and act as ministering spirits who serve His saints.

We believe humanity is redeemed by God's action in Jesus. A sinning humanity is both condemned and loved by God, the object of both His wrath and His mercy. The stern warnings of Scripture tell us that God must, and surely will, judge. But the dominant theme of God's message to us is this: Because of His great love for us, God, who is rich in mercy, has acted in Jesus to provide redemption and release.

God in Jesus slipped into our race to bend His shoulders under the weight of our burdens and to hang lifeless on Calvary's cross, so that His own blood's flow might wash away our sins. God's action in Jesus dealt decisively with human sin, providing a basis on which we can be forgiven, offering to all who believe a life of renewed righteousness.

We believe humanity is invited to experience an abundant life of true goodness. With forgiveness, God offers human beings an abundant life, rich in all those qualities that bring inner satisfaction even as they overflow in Christlike love to family and neighbor alike. Made alive in Christ, God's restored humanity leaves behind those desires and thoughts that mark the stunting grip of sin. We, His new creation, are renewed by Jesus' touch and reach toward those good works that God has prepared in advance for us to do. Human beings were created to know and love God and to express their relationship to Him through caring acts. A dynamic righteousness is the mark of the redeemed, and through that righteousness, which mirrors the beauty of the Lord, God's people can be fulfilled.

We believe humanity will experience ultimate transformation. Every individual human being is destined for endless, conscious, personal existence. Physical death is a transition, not an end. In Christ, God has acted to make it possible for us to experience an ultimate transformation, a resurrection into Jesus' full likeness and a full restoration of all that was lost in Adam's Fall. Humankind's destiny is to be lifted up above the angels, swept into the most intimate fellowship with God.

All who trust in Jesus and accept God's offer of eternal life will know that final transformation. Humanity will be redeemed.

We acknowledge human beings as unique in our universe, shaped in God's own image and likeness. We admit that a tragic Fall has warped every person. Yet we live in hope because mankind is redeemed through Jesus. Accepting God's gift of life in Jesus, we stretch out toward the good we are now able to do, and we yearn for the ultimate transformation that we know will come.

WE BELIEVE IN SALVATION

We believe in a salvation illustrated in God's mighty acts in history. God visited His people as they lay helpless in Egypt. In majestic acts of power, God reshaped His people's history, winning their release from bondage and leading them in triumph to the promised land. God stretched out His hand for individuals, too, working awesome wonders as He miraculously intervened in space and time on their behalf. In the signs and wonders God worked in history, we catch a glimpse of the meaning of salvation. God finds us helpless and, moved by love alone, He intervenes. What we could never do, God does, and those who are the recipients of His grace can only acknowledge His work and give Him praise.

We believe in a salvation won for us by Jesus' self-sacrifice. History's wonders culminate in Jesus. In Jesus, God's greatest act of intervention for a helpless humanity was accomplished; Jesus' self-sacrificial death met humankind's greatest need. No physical peril can compare to the eternal peril that endangers every human being. All who share in physical life are spiritually dead in trespasses and sins, unwilling and unable to reach out to God. All human beings stand condemned before the bar of God's justice. Yet in Jesus, God stripped off His judicial robes, and taking on our nature, He took the penalty of our sins as well. Dying for us, rais-

ing us through His resurrection, Jesus won us a deliverance that discharges us from sin's penalty, frees us from sin's power, and ultimately will release us from the very presence of evil within. Salvation is found in no one else, for "there is no other name under heaven given to men by which we must be saved" (Acts 4.12).

We believe in a salvation that is experienced in forgiveness. Jesus stands as the focal point of history, the One by whom time itself is reckoned. We look to Him as the focal point of our lives, the One by whom we reckon our passage from death to life. And the great invitation stands. Salvation, the free gift of God, is received by faith, and all who put their trust in Jesus are forgiven of all their sins. Thereafter, we are at peace with God. The source of our guilt is removed, and God Himself is satisfied. Forgiven, we know the meaning of grace and freely enter the presence of the Holy, knowing that in Jesus our welcome is guaranteed.

We believe in a salvation that is expressed in love and justice. We believe in a dynamic salvation. Forgiveness from past sins propels us into a life of active righteousness because God is intent on restoring human beings to His full likeness. The law's stern expression of righteousness is summed up in love, and salvation creates in human hearts a capacity to love others and to love God. This love must find expression both in simple acts of kindness to the needy neighbor and in commitment to that which is just and best for all of humanity. A zeal for good works that benefit people and bring glory to God is a natural and necessary expression of a salvation wrought by God.

We believe in a salvation to be enjoyed forever in God's presence. That salvation, experienced and expressed here and now, will be enjoyed forever. Long after this universe has been discarded and a new creation, vital and vibrant with holiness, has come, we who believe will experience the joy of our salvation in the presence of our Lord. In Jesus, the threat of eternal condemnation is replaced by the promise of perfected life, and we are destined to worship God and enjoy Him forever. Yes, we do believe in salvation, for we have a God who acts to aid the helpless. We see His power in history's mighty acts, and we discover His love in the self-sacrifice of Jesus, who through His death won us a salvation so great.

That salvation becomes ours through faith, bringing with it forgiveness and a commitment to love and justice. That salvation will ultimately issue in an endless life of joy lived in the very presence of the Lord.

WE BELIEVE IN A REDEEMED COMMUNITY

We believe in a redeemed community, called to live together in love and in unity. God's people are not called to live alone. Instead God has always placed His people in community. Surrounded by love, we are to live together as family and body, supporting and encouraging each other in good works and growth in godliness. All who acknowledge Jesus are to be welcomed and accepted as brothers or sisters in one holy community. Our differences are of less concern than the fact that, as children of one Father, we owe each other the debt of love. The redeemed community, affirming its mystical unity and acting ever in heartfelt love, gives compelling testimony to the reality and the presence of the Lord.

We believe in the redeemed community that celebrates its relationship to God in worship, baptism, and the Lord's Supper. The redeemed community shares not only in the life of its members but also in worship and remembrance. We come together as a people not only to hear God's Word, but also to offer Him our prayers, our praise, and our worship. In rituals long established, we act out the great realities of our faith: our union

with Jesus in death and resurrection and our participation in His broken body and shed blood. In all we do together, we affirm Him, confess Him, and testify of Him until Jesus comes.

We believe in the redeemed community that gives spiritual significance to each person. No person is unimportant in the body of Christ. Along with new spiritual life, each believer is given capacities that make him or her spiritually significant. Each person in the community of faith has the capacity to glorify God, reflecting the Lord in a transformed Christian character and in moral and loving daily choices. Each person in the community is given gifts by the Holy Spirit, special abilities that enable him or her to minister to others in ways that contribute to their good and to the vitality of the whole community.

Although each individual has a different role to play, as God sovereignly determines, each person is a full participant in the ministry and mission of the church. The commitment of each to his or her calling is vital if the body of Christ is to function as Christ intends.

We believe in the redeemed community that recognizes and responds to servant leaders. Christ is the living Head of His church. God has placed human leaders in the community of faith, not to lord it over His people, but to equip His people for ministry and to encourage their growth as believing persons. God's servant leaders live among His people, both demonstrating the Christian qualities Christ intends to work in every believer and sharing their understanding of His written Word as a guide to faith and life. Deserving of respect and material support, leaders of the community of faith are brothers and sisters who are among, not above, the other members of the body.

Yes, we do believe in a redeemed community that works out a common faith in loving unity, celebrates its relationship to

God in worship, affirms each person as a spiritually significant participant in the church's ministry, and responds to leaders who live among us as our servants for Jesus' sake.

WE BELIEVE IN THE FUTURE

We believe in the future of life on earth as meaningful and worthwhile. God's kingdom is now, as well as future, and life on earth has significance. The present time is of the utmost significance because our todays, as well as our tomorrows, give us the opportunity to glorify God. The sorrows that cause us to cry out to God and the joys that move our hearts to praise are woven into the tapestry of our lives, designed alike for good. By our touch, we can enrich others. By our responses to the challenges of life, we can offer others hope in God. Our involvement can better our society, relieve injustice, and offer hope to the helpless. Because all that we do shapes our own character, affects society, and reflects glory on God, this life we know on earth is both meaningful and worthwhile.

We believe in the future of Jesus' return. History moves beyond our individual tomorrows toward a grand culmination. In God's good time, the Jesus of history will return to execute God's final judgment and to bring in His realm of eternal righteousness. We look forward, not to the cooling of our sun or the dissolution of all things, but to God's grand denouement. Then, visible to all, Christ will receive the voluntary or forced worship of every bended knee, and time will give way to eternity.

We believe in the endless existence of every person. The brief time we know in our life on earth is not the end of any human being's self-conscious existence. Each of us is stamped by God's gift of life with the mark of the eternal; we are destined forever to be, and to be aware. For those who respond to God's invitation to life in Jesus, death is merely a transition to a new and fuller experience of joy.

For those who failed to respond, physical death is a transition, too, but it is a transition from present alienation to endless alienation—the unutterable tragedy of condemnation to what the believers have long called "hell."

Yes, we do believe in the future. We believe in the future of life here on earth, the future of Jesus' return, and the future that stretches on endlessly after what we call "time" has passed away.

❖

SPECIAL ISSUES IN THEOLOGY

Each name and title of God unveils more about who God is and His relationships with His creatures. It is often helpful to summarize this information by drawing it together under the heading of specific themes or topics. In this appendix we look at several such themes, and draw together truths unveiled in God's names and titles, and in the biblical context in which these names and titles appear.

In this appendix we look at the following special issues:

Attributes of God
The Body of Christ
Covenant Relationship with God
Creation
Eternity
Evil
The Existence of God
Forgiveness
The Holy Spirit
Incarnation
Jesus Christ
Revelation
Trinity
The Word of God
The Wrath of God

ATTRIBUTES OF GOD

Christians have a particular view of what God is like. The main qualities or characteristics we ascribe to God are called His attributes. God's attributes aren't of concern to theologians alone. Every person's concept of God is bound to influence his or her life

and decisions. For instance, if you are completely convinced that God is omniscient (knows all things perfectly), then you're more likely to follow scriptural guidelines for living than if you thought that God was wise, but limited, and therefore human beings must decide moral issues as best they can.

In every way, what you and I think of God is going to shape the way we live our daily lives. While some of God's qualities are similar to human qualities (God has emotions, thinks, decides, and acts), other qualities have no analogy in the human personality (God is sovereign). Yet each of the major characteristics of God does have practical implications for you and me.

What are the major characteristics? The lists that we find in Christian writing through the ages differ, but most Christians would include qualities like the following:

God is personal. God thinks, chooses, loves, and hates. We, too, have the capacity of thought, will, and emotions, and so we have a basis for understanding some things about the nature of God. But while God shares personhood with us, His thoughts, His will, His love, and His hatred are not exactly like ours. Through Isaiah, God reminds His people: "For My thoughts are not your thoughts, nor are My ways your ways. . . . For as the heavens are higher than the earth, so are My ways higher than your ways, and My thoughts than your thoughts (Is. 55:8).

Yet the fact that God is a person reassures us. God is no impersonal force, no abstract architect, no logical first cause so vastly different from us that we have no basis for any relationship. No, God is a person who understands our thoughts, feelings, and struggles to choose; He can relate to us on every level of our own personalities. But we must always remember that God remains the standard against which to judge our thoughts, emotions, and choices; we must resist the temptation to judge God by human thoughts and ways.

God is moral. God possesses all the moral virtues. At times, some of the virtues that mark His character are listed as separate attributes by theologians. However we list them, we can't think correctly about God unless we accept the Bible's description of Him: loving, good, holy, righteous, forgiving, truthful, and faithful. While you and I can be merciful, truthful, and compassionate, for example, only God is perfectly good, and only God's actions are untarnished by sin. Unlike our love, God's love never fails. Unlike our forgiveness, God's forgiveness erases even the remembrance of sin. While God's holiness generates a wrath that focuses on sin and sinner, His anger is never spiteful or arbitrary, and in wrath God always remembers mercy. Only God, who is perfect, can be both wholly loving and angry at the same moment. Each of these qualities is central to our Christian understanding of both God and morality. Each is deeply imbedded in God's revelation of His will for His people. Each is reflected in our convictions about how human beings ought to live with one another. Because God is truly moral, we can confidently trust ourselves to Him. And because God is truly moral, we who are His children can "be imitators of God ... and walk in love, as Christ also has loved us and has given Himself up for us" (Eph. 5: 1).

God is sovereign. To acknowledge God as sovereign is to recognize Him as supreme ruler of the universe. Ephesians 1:11 puts it powerfully: God is the One who "works all things according to the counsel of His will."

To affirm God's sovereignty is to acknowledge that our universe and our individual lives have meaning and purpose. While God does not act arbitrarily to exert His control of events, we believe that through the outworking of the physical and moral laws God designed, as well as by supernatural interventions, God is working out His entire complex plan in history. A passage that exalts God as sovereign helps us sense how wonderful it is to have a relationship to One who is truly in control of all things. Isaiah cries out to Judah, encouraging God's people not to be afraid but to catch a vision of God: "Behold, the LORD God shall come with a strong hand, and His arm shall rule for Him; Behold, His reward is with Him, and His work before Him. He will feed His flock like a shepherd; He will gather the lambs with His arm, and carry them in His bosom, and gently lead those who are with young" (Is. 40:10-11).

How wonderful to realize that the God who is the actual ruler of our universe stoops to use His power to care for His beloved own.

God is unlimited. Many of God's attributes have no corollary in human experience. We can only begin to grasp their meaning by contrast. We human beings are finite, limited to a single place and time, limited in our knowledge and our power. But God is unlimited in all these dimensions. Theologians speak of God as omniscient, omnipresent, and omnipotent.

God is omniscient; He knows everything. He knows every fact, every thought and every motive in every human heart. God knows the past and the future as well as He knows the present. There are no limitations to God's full knowledge of all things.

God is omnipresent; He is present everywhere. God's presence cannot be localized as ours necessarily is. Pantheism assumes that part of God is in every material thing—rocks, trees, people. But the Christian knows a God who is above nature, yet fully present at every location in the physical universe. David, filled with wonder at the unlimited nature of God, pauses to express his thoughts: "Where can I go from Your Spirit? Where can I flee from Your presence? If I ascend into heaven, You are there; If I make my bed in hell, behold, You are there. If I take the wings of the morning, and dwell in the uttermost part of the sea, even there Your hand will lead me, and Your right hand shall hold me" (Ps. 139:7-10).

Because God is everywhere present, He is with you and me always, whether our moments are dark or light.

God is omnipotent; He is all-powerful. God's power and ability to act are limited only by His own character. No one and nothing outside Himself can place limits on the Lord; He is able to do whatever He pleases. But it is important to realize that God limits Himself by His moral character; He pleases to do only what is good and right. God cannot sin, because His character is so perfectly holy that He would never choose to sin. But whatever God might choose to do, He can do.

Isaiah puts into beautiful perspective the meaning of this quality:

The everlasting God, the LORD,
The Creator of the ends of the earth,
Neither faints nor is weary.
His understanding is unsearchable.
He gives power to the weak,
And to those who have no might He increases strength.
Even the youths shall faint and be weary,
And the young men shall utterly fall,
But those who wait on the LORD
Shall renew their strength;
They shall mount up with wings like eagles,
They shall run and not be weary,
They shall walk and not faint.
Isaiah 40:28-31

God is eternal. God is independent of time. A psalm of Moses puts it this way: "Before the mountains were brought forth, or ever You had formed the earth and the world, even from everlasting to everlasting, You are God" (Ps. 90:2).

The eternity of God affirms that God has always existed and always will exist. While He is the source of all things, He Himself has no source. The eternity of God holds an exciting promise for us. When God offers us eternal life in Jesus, He holds out the promise of an endless existence rich with those same qualities that make His own life so rich and full.

God is free. God's freedom is seen in that He acts spontaneously, unrestricted by any consideration other than His own character and will. God's decision to save is a free choice, which does not grow out of any obligation to humanity. As a free choice, God's willingness to aid human beings who have become enemies is a demonstration of pure grace. All He has done for us is done out of His love and compassion.

Closely associated with this concept is the traditional idea of God's immutability. God does not change, and His essential character is not affected by events in this world of time and space. We can count on God to continue forever to be the kind of person that He is.

How are we so sure that God has these attributes? Basically because we are convinced that God has spoken and that He has revealed Himself to us. It is by God's initiative and not through speculative imagination that our concept of God has grown and taken clearer form. The God of the Bible is the one true God, and this God is personal, moral, sovereign, eternal, unlimited, and free.

THE BODY OF CHRIST

One of the most significant of Jesus' titles is that of Head of a living body, the church. In different eras, different theological questions have drawn the attention of believers. In the second century, Christians' attention was focused on the Trinity and on understanding the nature and person of Jesus. In the Reformation of the sixteenth century, the primary concern was salvation and the role of faith. In our time, the focus of many has been drawn to the church. Believers are looking anew at the biblical images and teachings about the community of those who believe.

The church has existed through all the centuries of church history, but not enough attention has been paid to issues raised in Scripture. One of the prime images in Scripture that is being taken more seriously today is the teaching that church is the body of Christ. The church is a living organism, not simply a human institution. We, who are Jesus' people, are linked so intimately and uniquely to one another and to Jesus, and together we constitute a unified and organic whole.

The image of a body of which Christ is the head emphasizes relationships. Note that Scripture does not suggest that the church is *like* a body: the Bible says we *are* a body. Our identity as God's people is deeply rooted in our organic relationship with each other and with Jesus.

Jesus is Head of the body. In the New Testament the term "head" is never applied to the human leaders of the visible church. Instead, the church is everywhere viewed as an organism, and Jesus is presented as the sole and living Head. You and I, as members of the body, are so linked with Jesus that He is able to guide, direct, and strengthen us.

A number of New Testament passages help us sense the importance of recognizing Jesus as our living Head. Ephesians presents Jesus as supreme, "far above all principality and power and might and dominion, and every name that is named, not only in this age but also in the age that is to come" (Eph. 1:21). This is the person that God has given us to be "head over all things to the church, which is His body" (Eph. 1:22).

Believers are growing parts of the body. Through our personal relationship to Jesus, we have a source of unimaginable power. We are invited to realize and to experience "the exceeding greatness of His power toward us who believe, according to the working of His mighty power which He worked in Christ when He raised Him from the dead" (Eph. 1:19-20). In our organic relationship to Jesus, the very power of God is made available to us, and all that cripples us can be overcome through His inner strength.

Ephesians 4 focuses our attention on growth. Our relationship to Jesus is the secret of individual and congregational spiritual growth. From Jesus, "the whole body" is involved in the process that "causes growth of the body for the edifying of itself in love" (Eph. 4:16).

Colossians 1 lifts Jesus up, showing His supremacy over the visible and invisible creation. He is also supreme over the church; He has priority in our thinking and in our lives (Col. 1:18). Colossians 2 warns believers that the key to our spiritual vitality and growth is found in our relationship to Jesus. We hold fast to the Head, not looking for spiritual fulfillment in ritual or religious practices (Col. 2:19). "For in Him dwells all the fullness of the Godhead bodily; and you are complete in Him, who is the head of all principality and power " (Col. 2:9-10).

These passages have implications for individuals and congregations. We must learn to look expectantly to Jesus for His guidance, confident that whatever our Head directs, He will also enable us to accomplish. Believers who view themselves as members of a living organism can never discount the supernatural. Human schemes of organization can never adequately capture this reality.

Another exciting implication of Scripture's teaching that Jesus is the living Head of the church is that we are to be the living incarnation of Jesus in the world. While Christ is in heaven, Jesus' people are on earth. Through His link with believers, Jesus, even now, is vitally present on the earth. He touches others through the living people who are His body. As we live in responsive obedience to our Lord, all His good purposes for humanity will be accomplished. How important, then, that Christians recognize the headship of the living Christ and look to Him for guidance, acting in total confidence in His ability to do through us what He directs us to do.

A COVENANT RELATIONSHIP WITH GOD

The term "covenant" is a vital one in the vocabulary of faith. Through the covenants God made with human beings as recorded in Scripture, we learn vital truths about who He is.

Christianity affirms that not only is God personal, He is also the all-powerful ruler of our universe. This God has chosen to reveal Himself to human beings. In doing so, God has shown us that He invites us to have a personal relationship with Him. Nothing more clearly underlines this truth than the biblical covenants.

In Scripture and in various Christian theological systems, covenants are basic, for they establish the basis on which personal relationships between God and humanity are possible. To understand the meaning of this important biblical and theological word, we need to look at relevant Hebrew and Greek words, at the theological covenants suggested by the Reformers, at three specific Old Testament covenants, and at the new covenant explained in both testaments.

The Hebrew and Greek words translated "covenant." In Old Testament times, ancient cultures adopted the concept of a covenant (*berit*) to express a range of interpersonal and social relationships. A covenant between nations was a treaty (Gen. 14:13; 31:44-55). Between persons, a covenant might express a business contract or a pledge of friendship (1 Sam. 18:3; 23:18). A covenant between a ruler and the subjects

served as the constitution of states, spelling out the responsibilities of both the ruler and the ruled (2 Sam. 3:21; 5:3). This fundamental relational concept was adopted by God to express truths about His relationship with human beings.

While the concept of covenant was familiar to the Old Testament people, the covenants between God and humanity have unique elements. The word covenant has different shades of meaning: "contract," "constitution," and "pledge of friendship." We shouldn't be surprised if there are distinctive aspects to the word covenant when it is applied to relationships between God and humanity.

The distinctives are captured in this definition of a biblical (divine/human) covenant: A biblical covenant is a clear statement by God of His purposes and intentions, expressed in terms that bind God by solemn oath to perform what He has promised.

The Bible identifies four major covenants. In each of them, the Lord states what He intends to, and most certainly will do. It is through these great covenant promises that we learn who God is and what His plans and purposes for us are. God's commitment to do as He has promised provides a firm basis for our faith.

Covenant has the same meaning in the New Testament. There the Greek word *diatheke* is used. The Greeks used this word in the sense of a will, in which a person chose how to dispose of property. That decision, put into effect when a person died, could not be changed by anyone else. Jesus' death put into effect what both testaments call a "new covenant." In Hebrews, another Greek word is used: God's Old Testament covenant is called an *orkos* (Heb. 6:17). This word meant "a legally binding guarantee." Hebrews says that "God, determining to show more abundantly to the heirs of promise the immutability of His counsel, confirmed it by an oath."

The emphasis in both testaments, then, is on the fact that God has expressed His purposes and announced His plans in the form of covenant promises. These covenant promises provide a firm basis for our faith and enable us to define our relationship with the Lord.

The theological covenants. The Reformers of the sixteenth century were well aware of the significance of the covenants. They expressed their understanding of what the Bible teaches about relationships between God and human beings by summing up that teaching in two basic covenants: a covenant of works and a covenant of grace. These theological covenants are not the same as the biblical covenants. But the Reformers believed that their statement of the theological covenants effectively and accurately summed up what the Bible teaches about salvation. What are the theological covenants?

The covenant of works, the Reformers taught, was a conditional promise made by God to Adam, who was a free moral agent. In effect, this covenant was a contract that included conditions. God promised eternal life and endless fellowship with Him on the condition that Adam would be obedient and not eat the fruit of a particular tree that was planted in the Garden of Eden (Gen. 2—3). If Adam violated the condition, the consequences would be his death, with all that "death" in Scripture implies. The Reformers taught that, as far as the unsaved are concerned, this covenant of works is still in force, with all its binding conditions. Disobedience and unrighteousness still bring God's condemnation. But the situation has changed for the saved. The Reformers realized that Jesus came to earth and lived a perfect life, fulfilling by His obedience every condition of the covenant of works. Then Jesus died for the sins of humankind, not only taking our sins on Himself but also offering His own righteousness to us. Believers, who through faith are united to Christ, are released from the covenant of works. That covenant of works is abrogated by the gospel.

To explain what Jesus has done, the Reformers thought in terms of a covenant of grace. This covenant relates specifically to God's plan of redemption. The Reformers saw this covenant as a contract concluded between God the Father (representing the Godhead) and God the Son (representing all the redeemed). Jesus covenanted to fulfill all the obligations of the covenant of works on behalf of His people. Jesus took on all our responsibilities, satisfied all God's conditions (including the condition that sin must be punished by death), and thus won eternal life for His own.

Nearly all aspects of Reformed theology grow out of the way that the Reformers organized their teaching about salvation under these two theological covenants. For instance, infant baptism is practiced as the visible sign and seal of the covenant of grace, just as circumcision functioned in Old Testament times as a sign that the child was a member of Israel's covenant community. The conviction that a covenant exists between God and humanity is basic in every Christian theological system. But differences about the nature of that covenant (or those covenants) have led to many differences in specifics of Christian beliefs and convictions.

The Old Testament covenants. When we hear Christians speak about covenants, it is important to know whether they are speaking of the theological covenants, described above, or of biblical covenants. The theological covenants sum up much biblical truth in a significant, systematic way. But the theological covenants are not the same as the biblical covenants, although they are modeled on them. What are the biblical covenants, and what do we need to know to understand each of them?

The Abrahamic covenant. This is the first of the biblical covenants. God appeared to pagan Abraham, who worshiped the moon god in his native Ur. God told Abraham to leave his homeland and travel to "a land I will show you." At that first contact, God made promises to Abraham that were later confirmed, following human custom to make a binding oath (Gen. 12:2-3; 15:1-21). Still later, God instructed Abraham to circumcise all male offspring as a sign that they belonged to the family line to which the covenant promises were given (Gen. 17:1-22).

The promises given to Abraham will be fulfilled at history's end. They tell what God intends to do for the Jewish people then. They also show blessings God offered to Abraham and Jewish generations between Abraham and history's end. What are the promises given in the Abrahamic covenant? "I will make you a great nation; I will bless you and make your name great, and you shall be a blessing. I will bless those who bless you, and I will curse him who curses you, and in you all the families of the earth will be blessed" (Gen. 12:2-3). One other clause is added to the covenant and is also confirmed by covenant oath: "To your descendants I will give this land" (Gen. 12:7).

The firm conviction that God spoke to Abraham and made promises to him about his offspring has given the Jewish people a sense of identity that has preserved God's Old Testament people as a faith and as a race to this day. Also, this covenant is the key to our understanding of the Old Testament, that story of how God has been working out His promises to Israel in history. Stories telling of God's covenant with Abraham are also our key to understanding personal relationship with God. Abraham heard God announce His purposes and state His promises. The Bible tells us that Abraham responded with faith. "And he believed in the LORD, and He accounted it to him for righteousness" (Gen. 15:6). Thus God showed Himself willing to accept faith in His promises instead of a righteousness that Abraham did not possess. In Romans, Paul teaches that "it was not written for his [Abraham's] sake alone that it was imputed to him, but also for us. It shall be imputed to us

who believe in Him who raised up Jesus from the dead" (Rom. 4:23, 24). Faith in God's promise is the key to salvation.

The Mosaic or Law covenant. This covenant is distinctive in several ways. After four hundred years in Egypt, Abraham's descendants were led out to freedom by Moses. God intended to bring them to the land that He promised to Abraham centuries before. On the way, God gave this people a law patterned after the suzerainty treaties of the ancient Middle East. Such treaties [covenants] were developed between rulers (called suzerains or sovereigns) and subjects. They spelled out the obligations of each party and defined what would happen if subjects kept or violated covenant conditions.

The Law covenant, Israel's national constitution, was between God and Israel. It regulated the personal, social, and civil life of Israel, as well as defining religious duties. But this covenant was both different from, and similar to, God's covenant with Abraham. Like the other biblical covenants, the Mosaic covenant includes an announcement by God of what He intends to do. This statement of God's intentions in the Law is unconditional. God will do what He states He will do. Unlike other biblical covenants, the Law covenant focused on the present experience of each Israeli generation. The other covenants announce what God will do at history's end. This covenant explains what God will do in history, as succeeding generations are either obedient to, or disobedient to, His law.

Unlike other biblical covenants, the Law covenant was ratified (renewed or confirmed) by the people. Each generation was to choose to commit itself to live by the Sinai Law (Ex. 24; Deut. 29; Josh. 24). Today in Jewish society, a child who is twelve years old makes a similar choice and becomes "bar mitzvah," a son of the commandment.

Law, then, defined how Israel was to live as a nation under God. It provided a full set of laws and regulations to govern every aspect of national and personal life. It was a covenant in the sense of a national constitution, and God, the ruler of Israel, specified not only how His subjects were to live but also committed Himself to bless the obedient and punish the disobedient. Unlike every other biblical covenant, the Old Testament views the Law covenant was temporary, to be replaced by a new covenant (Jer. 31: 31-32). The Mosaic covenant was designed to function during Israel's centuries as a nation until the Savior would come to introduce a new and better basis for a person's daily relationship with the Lord.

The Davidic covenant. The third biblical covenant is the Davidic covenant. David was Israel's ideal or model king. Under David the tiny country expanded tenfold to become a powerful state. David's faithfulness to God and his love for the Lord was the key to his effectiveness as a monarch. The Bible tells us that the prophet Nathan was sent by God to David with a special promise: "Your house and your kingdom shall be established forever before Me. Your throne shall be established forever" (2 Sam. 7:16).

This commitment is celebrated in the Psalms as a covenant promise (Ps. 89:2-4; 105:8-10). On the basis of this covenant promise, the Jewish people believed firmly that their Messiah (God's anointed deliverer) would be a ruler from David's line and would establish a kingdom ruled personally by God. The genealogies of Jesus contained in Matthew and Luke are there in part to establish Jesus' descent from King David and thus establish Jesus' hereditary right to the throne of the Old Testament's promised kingdom.

Like the Abrahamic covenant, this covenant is God's promise about His plans and His purposes to human beings. Like the Abrahamic covenant also, the Davidic covenant will find its complete fulfillment only when Jesus returns to actually take the throne of the kingdom He alone is qualified to rule.

The new covenant. The new covenant is the most significant of the biblical covenants for believers today. The new covenant was promised by the Old Testament prophet Jeremiah at a critical time in Israel's history. Mosaic Law was given about 1450 B.C., but the people of Israel were constantly unfaithful to their obligations under that covenant. Their disobedience led to national judgments. The culminating judgments were military defeats and exile from the promised land.

Part of the nation was deported by the Assyrians in 722 B.C., while the remaining Jews continued to plunge into idolatry, immorality, and injustice. Finally in the days of Jeremiah, the remaining Jews were crushed by Babylon. The great Jerusalem temple was destroyed, and in 586 B.C. the last of God's people were carried into captivity. For the first time in nearly a thousand years, the Jews no longer lived in the promised land so intimately associated with God's covenant promises to Abraham and David. The exiles must have wondered, "How could this happen?" Had their disobedience caused God to change His plan and withdraw His promises?

God used the prophet Jeremiah to answer this pressing question. First, God's people had broken His covenant and must be punished. But God's promises and His purposes still stood: "{Only} If heaven above can be measured and the foundations of the earth searched out beneath, I will also cast off all the seed of Israel for all that they have done" (Jer. 31:37).

But God has another, surprising word for Israel. He promises, through the prophet, that "the days are coming, says the LORD, when I will make a new covenant with the house of Israel" (Jer. 31:31). The law, under which blessing in this life depended on human performance, has not produced a righteous people. God will replace the Mosaic covenant with a more effective approach. Like other covenants, the new covenant states plainly what God intends to do. Jeremiah emphasizes God's work in the life of people: "I will put My law in their minds, and write it on their hearts; and I will be their God, and they shall be My people. No more shall every man teach his neighbor, and every man his brother, saying, 'Know the LORD,' for they all shall know Me, from the least of them to the greatest of them, says the LORD. For I will forgive their iniquity, and their sin I will remember no more" (Jer. 31:33-34).

It is not until the New Testament that we read of this new covenant actually being made. There we hear Jesus, on the night before His crucifixion, explain to His followers as He held up the communion cup, "This is My blood of the new covenant, which is shed for many for the remission of sins" (Matt. 26:28; Mark 14:24; Luke 22:20; 1 Cor. 11:25).

Like the Abrahamic covenant, this new covenant was initiated by a sacrifice (Gen. 15). But this time the sacrificial blood which seated the divine promise was that of God's own Son. On the basis of that sacrifice, the promised forgiveness was won for humanity, to be appropriated by faith, just as Abraham had believed God and was credited with righteousness.

The new covenant, then, replaces the Mosaic Law. That Law, carved in stone tablets, expressed objectively the righteousness that God's holiness requires. But the Law's statement of external standards was unable to produce righteousness in human beings. The new covenant takes a radically different approach. It takes the righteousness that was expressed in law, and it supernaturally infuses that righteousness into the very character of the believer.

The Book of Hebrews sums up the new covenant's key provisions: "I will put My laws in their hearts, and in their minds I will write them.... Their sins and lawless deeds I will remember no more" (Heb. 10:16-17). Rather than the Law's word—"do this, and live"—the new covenant majestically states God's intention: "I will write righteousness on their hearts!"

God has promised that He will work within the lives of His new covenant people to transform us from within. It is important to remember that the appropriate response to all God's covenant promises is faith. God has announced what He will do. We human beings can only take Him at His word. It is not surprising, then, that in both Romans 4 and Galatians 3, the New Testament argues that since the essence of covenant is promise, all that human beings can possibly do is believe.

Through Jesus, God provides forgiveness and an inner dynamic that will actually make human beings righteous. While the ultimate fulfillment of that promise awaits Jesus' return and our resurrection, faith wins the believer a present experience of new covenant blessings. When you and I believe God's promise in Jesus, the benefits won by His death and resurrection become our own.

The covenants in summary. Biblical covenants are statements of God's purposes, which are expressed as promises, often associated with binding oaths. The Abrahamic, Davidic, and new covenants look forward to history's end for their fulfillment.

But faith brings a person into covenant relationship with the Lord today! God graciously makes available now to those who believe in Him many of the benefits intended for a redeemed mankind when Jesus returns. The Mosaic covenant was temporary, designed to serve as Israel's constitution as a nation until Christ should come. It was different from the others in that, according to the New Testament, it was not based on promise. Instead of stating what God intends to do in the form of a promise, it stated what God would do in response to specified human behaviors. While people who had a faith relationship with God (like David) did seek to be obedient, the Old Testament system had to include sacrifices that could be made when they failed. Faith led a person to obey, and faith led that same person to bring the required sacrifices when he or she failed. Thus faith was critical in the age of Law, even as it has been in every age.

Faith alone, then, is the response that human beings can make when God speaks in promise. Faith alone can bring us into personal relationship with God. Faith alone enables us to experience in our present life those benefits and blessings that God has promised to bring to humankind.

While the theological covenants developed by the Reformers are not the same as the covenants spoken of in the Bible, they do express vital truths about personal relationship with God. They capture the basic Bible teaching that relationship with God must depend on faith and faith alone. The salvation that we can know as individuals flows from a faith appropriation of that commitment God has chosen to make to humankind in Jesus Christ.

CREATION

One of the major themes of Scripture casts God as Creator and Maker of all that exists. And across the millennia, believers have sensed God through His creation. With the psalmist, we have felt the wonder and awe often expressed in praise. "O LORD my God, You are very great." The psalmist goes on to honor God, "You who laid the foundations of the earth, so that it should not be moved forever, You covered it with the deep as with a garment; the waters stood above the mountains" (Ps.104:1, 5-6). When troubles came, the prophets of Israel often called on their people to remember that their God was the Creator, that all that exists demonstrates His power. How confident the believer can be, for we rely on One who holds all power in His hands.

Lift your eyes on high,
And see who has created these things,
Who brings out their host by number;
He calls them all by name,
By the greatness of His might

And the strength of His power;
Not one is missing.

Have you not known?
Have you not heard?
The everlasting God, the LORD,
The Creator of the ends of the earth,
Neither faints nor is weary.
His understanding is unsearchable.
He gives power to the weak,
And to those who have no might He
   increases strength.
                Isaiah 40:26, 28

The conviction that our God is Creator of the material universe, and remains its governor, is basic to Christian faith. Looking back to the beginning and looking at the world around us, we gain a fresh appreciation for the awesome power of the One we know and worship in Jesus Christ.

Creation and the Old Testament. People of every age have developed theories to explain the origin of the world and of life. In the ancient Near East, the world in which the Old Testament originated, the commonly accepted theory bore a close resemblance to the modern theory of evolution. Near Eastern myths and creation tales began with preexisting matter. This matter surged and writhed with energy (chaos), finally generating the gods, whose activity led to the emergence of human beings and the orderly universe we now know.

Old Testament teaching is a dramatic contrast. In simple words the Old Testament states, "In the beginning God created" (Gen. 1:1). Before time began, before the stars flared, before the planets swung in their courses, there was God. All the energy that infuses existence was His energy, not energy inherent in matter. Even after God first spoke and matter flashed into existence, it lay inert and unmoving, formless and empty and dark until God's Spirit molded it and set what we know as natural laws in motion (Gen. 1:1-2).

Christians have disagreed over certain details. How long did the creation take? Was the universe ordered in seven literal days or over long ages? Yet these differences of opinion about the when and how of creation do not shake Christians' common conviction that God did create. We believe with the Scriptures that everything owes its existence to God, and to God alone. In the words of the psalmist, "By the word of the LORD the heavens were made, and all the host of them by the breath of His mouth. . . . Let all the earth fear the LORD; let all the inhabitants of the world stand in awe of Him. For He spoke, and it was done; He commanded, and it stood fast (Ps. 33:6, 8-9).

Creation and the New Testament. While Christians have presented arguments showing that belief in a Creator is reasonable, the New Testament teaches that belief in the creation is a matter for faith. It is "by faith we understand that the worlds were framed by the word of God, so that the things which are seen were not made of things which are visible" (Heb. 11:3). Faith is essential because human beings, despite plain evidence in the creation of the Creator (Rom. 1:18-20), "did not like to retain God in their knowledge" (Rom. 1:28). In this critical passage Paul argues that humanity has been so warped by sin that societies and cultures willfully seek reasons to ignore the creation's testimony to God and thus "exchanged the truth of God for the lie" (Rom. 1:25). Faith, however, recognizes and affirms God as the invisible cause of the visible universe. And the New Testament goes on to teach us more about God's creative work than was revealed in the Old Testament.

The Gospel of John, like Genesis, looks back beyond the beginning, teaching us that God the Son, the eternal Word, was (along with God the Father) the source of creation. "All things were made through Him, and without Him nothing was made that was made" (John 1:3). Colossians picks up the same theme, saying of Jesus that "by Him all things were created that are in heaven and that are on earth, visible and invisible, whether thrones or dominions or principalities or powers. All things were created through Him and for Him" (Col. 1:16).

When we look at the total testimony of Scripture, we realize that each person of the Godhead was involved in the creation (the Father, 1 Cor. 8:6; the Son, John 1:3 and Col. 1:16-17; the Spirit, Gen. 1:2 along with Job 26:13 and Ps. 104:30). Theologians have summed up the Scripture's teaching by affirming that God created the material universe *ex nihilo*, from nothing. This Latin phrase emphasizes the difference between biblical and alternate views of the universe. God created the universe from nothing, without the use of previously existing materials. Every thing, material and immaterial, has its ultimate origin in God.

Christian attitudes toward the creation. We have in the Old Testament, and especially in the Psalms, a model for an appropriate attitude toward God's creation. There we see, again and again, expressions of wonder, awe, and celebration. The elemental power of the storm reminds the believer of the far greater powers of God. The vastness and beauty of the wilderness, the majesty of towering mountains, and the surging seas turn the eyes of faith to the Lord.

> O LORD, how manifest are Your works!
> In wisdom You have made them all.
> The earth is full of your possessions—
> This great and wide sea,
> In which are innumerable teeming things,
> Living things both great and small.
> Psalm 104:24-25

The sense of wonder generated by the creation helped to form in the Old Testament believer a healthy attitude toward life in this world. That attitude can be characterized as one of joy and celebration. As the psalmist says, "The works of the LORD are great, studied by all who have pleasure in them" (Ps. 111:2).

While at times Christians have adopted a gloomy attitude or a moody asceticism toward life in this world, recognition of God's good hand in shaping our world as a home for mankind has more often opened the way to a positive and joyful view of our present life. Our days must have significance since God has so carefully designed the stage on which we each play our part. Pleasure must be God's good will, since our bodies have been shaped to enjoy the tastes and to thrill to the beauty God has planned. No wonder, then, the New Testament affirms God as the One "who gives us richly all things to enjoy" (1 Tim. 6:17).

The beauty and harmony of the creation have been distorted by sin. The New Testament pictures creation as frustrated, awaiting liberation from its bondage to decay (Rom. 8:19-21). The message that creation gives is mixed, evidence of both God's goodness and of the existence of evil. Yet the basic message of creation remains clear. God exists, and He is the source of all that is. God exists, and because He is loving and good, filled with a love of beauty and the joy of life, the world that He shaped is also good, a fitting setting for rejoicing in His works and celebrating the life we have here and now.

God's new creation. The Bible looks back to the beginning and presents God as the creative force bringing existence and vitality to all that is. God spoke, and the material universe burst into existence. God spoke, and living creatures populated the earth and skies and seas. God stooped, and in a special creative act, he shaped mankind. God, thus, is the source of all that is fresh and new and good. It is not surprising then, in view of the impact of sin on this creation, to discover that the Bible promises a new creation. By another exercise of divine power, all that is warped and twisted will be set aside, and God will speak again, bringing a fresh newness to the universe.

The fact that God is, and remains, the Creator is one source of an optimism and hope that stays vital despite the corruption and pain so visible in nature and society. The Old Testament tells of a day when God will speak again and create a new heaven and a new earth. In that new creation, every cause of sorrow and sadness will be removed. "For behold, I create new heavens and a new earth; and the former shall not be remembered or come to mind. But be glad and rejoice forever in what I create; for behold, I create Jerusalem as a rejoicing, and her people as a joy" (Is. 65:17-18).

The New Testament adds its testimony to the Old Testament vision. Peter reminds his readers that the Lord will keep His promises in His own time. Then "the heavens will pass away with a great noise, and the elements will melt with fervent heat; both the earth and the works that are in it will be burned up" (2 Pet. 3:10). While the old creation will be destroyed, we, "according to His promise, look for new heavens and a new earth in which righteousness dwells" (2 Pet. 3:13). In that day, toward which all history moves, we will hear God announce, "I am making everything new" (Rev. 21:5).

The doctrine of creation, then, is not limited to beliefs about the origin of the universe and of life. We believe in a Creator God, whose limitless power has been, and will be, exercised to give vitality and shape to existence now and in eternity. Strikingly, the Bible and our experience teach us that God's work of re-creation has already begun. We see that work not in the world around us but within the hearts of believers. The Scriptures teach that when a person puts his or her trust in Jesus, that person is given new life by God. One image used in speaking of this new life is the image of creation. "If anyone is in Christ," the Bible says, "he is a new creation; old things have passed away; behold, all things have become new" (2 Cor. 5:17). The new self we are given by God has been "created according to God, in true righteousness and holiness" (Eph. 4:24). Because God has acted to create a fresh newness within us, we can now be "transformed into the same image [Jesus'] from glory to glory, just as by the Spirit of the Lord " (2 Cor. 3:18). God's power, exercised in the creation of our universe, is exercised today as He creates new life in those who come to Jesus. And God's power will be exercised in the future, shaping a new universe, the place of righteousness, to be our home through all eternity.

ETERNITY

The Bible nowhere explains eternity. It simply affirms that God existed before the Creation, before time began. And it affirms that God will exist endlessly after this universe has been folded up, like a worn-out tent, and put away. The psalmist finds a great sense of security in knowing that God inhabits eternity, unmoved by the changes taking place in time: "LORD, You have been our dwelling place throughout all generations. Before the mountains were brought forth, or ever You had formed the earth and world, even from everlasting to everlasting You are God" (Ps. 90:1-2; see also Is. 57:15).

God out of time. A number of concepts are linked with the concept of time and eternity. Scripture does not look at either in a philosophical way. But what the Bible does say about God, time, and eternity has great practical importance to the Christian. Paul carefully explains God's intention to transform Christians to be like Jesus. The process may be painful and slow, and it may be easy to become discouraged. So, Paul says, "We do not look at the things which are seen, but at the things which are not seen. For the things which are seen are temporary; but the things which are not seen are eternal" (2 Cor. 4.18).

Anything that exists in this world of space and time is caught up in processes of change. This means that anything we can touch or see or experience is necessarily temporary. But God and those unseen spiritual realities that participate in His nature are not subject to change. They are eternal. So God stands outside of time, and thus is unchangeable.

This conviction is important to our faith. You and I are constantly changing. Our bodies, our experiences, and our feelings are affected by the passage of time. But God is immutable: He never changes. He is outside of time and unaffected by its flow. Since God never changes, we can be sure that He who has loved us in Jesus will never change His mind or withdraw His promises. The writer of Hebrews builds on this fact when he reminds us that God has said, "I will never leave you nor forsake you." The writer then tells us how we can be so sure: "Jesus Christ is the same yesterday, and today, and forever" (Heb. 13:6, 8).

The eternity of God, His immutability as One standing outside of time and unaffected by it, means that you and I can have complete confidence in His endless love.

A new kind of life. This particular view of eternity helps us understand the implications of God's gift of eternal life. God has given those who believe in Him a new kind of life, a life that is untouched by time or the course of events. This is, in fact, the basis of Paul's argument in 2 Corinthians 4. Later Paul contrasts what is seen in a person's life with "what is in the heart" (2 Cor. 5:12). "If anyone is in Christ," the passage says, "he is a new creation; old things have passed away; behold, all things have become new" (2 Cor. 5:17).

God has changed you and me by giving us a new life that is unaffected by events in this world and that must grow stronger and stronger, enabling us to reflect Jesus. Peter picks up the same theme and expresses it this way: "having been born again, not of corruptible seed but incorruptible, through the word of God which lives and abides forever" (1 Pet. 1:23). God has taken something of His own enduring life, something imperishable, and has given it to you and me through the new birth. Somehow we have eternity in our hearts, and we know that we will never perish but live endlessly with our God.

Eternal life, then, isn't something that starts when a person dies or that begins after God's final judgment on humanity. Eternal life begins at the new birth, as God plants something of Jesus in our personalities, something that cannot be destroyed or changed by our experiences in time.

To have eternal life means that our present relationship to God cannot be affected by the circumstances of our lives. Because we have this kind of permanent relationship to the Lord, we have confidence and hope, no matter what our days in time may bring.

To survey what the Bible says about eternal life, see Matthew 19:16, 29; 25:46; Mark 10:17, 30; Luke 10:25; 18:18, 30; John 3:15, 16, 36; 4:14, 36; 5:24, 39; 6:27, 40, 47, 54, 68; 10:28; 12:25, 50; 17:2, 3; Acts 13:46, 48; Romans 2:7; 5:21; 6:22, 23; Galatians 6:8; 1 Timothy 1:16; 6:12, 19; Timothy 1:2; 3:7; 1 John 1:2; 2:25; 3:15; 5:11, 13, 20; and Jude 21.

EVIL

The relationship of God to evil is one of the most significant themes of Scripture. In part, this is because the reality of evil in our world has spawned one of the classical arguments against the existence of God. It is a simple yet seemingly compelling argument. If God is both good and all-powerful, He would not permit evil. But evil does exist in the universe. Therefore, the good and all-powerful God the Bible presents cannot exist.

It is an interesting argument, but it has problems. The first is that it makes God a two-dimensional caricature. The Bible presents a God of infinite wisdom. Simply because something may appear to be a contradiction to limited, finite human beings doesn't mean that it is a contradiction to God. In talking about God, we can never limit ourselves to a two-dimensional caricature.

The other problem with the argument lies in the meaning of the word "evil." In this argument it is used in a slippery way. Often when we speak of evil, we are really talking about evils: about sickness and sorrow, about pain and tragedy, and about distress and death. At other times when we speak of evil, we mean things like jealousy and injustice, hatred and anger, murder and theft. On the one hand, evil includes all those ills and troubles to which human beings are subject. On the other hand, evil involves all those wicked acts of which human beings are capable.

It is important when we discuss evil to be clear what we are talking about. Of course, evil in both senses does exist. To some extent every philosophy and every religion must face that fact and deal with it. Every system of thought must provide some answer to the question, "Why evil?" Every system must provide some answer to the person who cries out, "How do I deal with the evil and the evils that plague me?"

The answer to these questions is never simple. But we are convinced that our faith provides the best answers possible. Our answers square with what we know about evil. And our answers satisfy the hearts of those caught in the web that evil of both types spins to trap everyone who comes into our less-than-perfect world.

To catch a glimpse of a biblical perspective on evil, we need to look at several issues: What is the nature of evil? What is the origin of evil? What is the impact of evil on humanity? How does the Bible use words related to evil? And, What is God's solution to the problem of evil?

The nature of evil. Many people have struggled to define evil. To some, evil seems best understood as the absence or the lack of good. Bad fishing is simply the lack of good fishing (of catching fish). Similarly, in this view, bad behavior would simply be the lack of good behavior. In this framework, evil actions grow out of human limitations and finitude, from the fact that we are becoming, and have not yet arrived at, the divine perfection.

But evil cannot be so easily explained. If the argument were valid, we would call a fetus and a three-year-old child evil because they have not yet reached their adult potential. Instead we can speak of a good (healthy) fetus and even of a (morally) good three-year-old child, meaning that each functions appropriately at the level currently attained. Looking at the innocent Adam, who like us was finite and imperfect, God did not call His creation evil. Instead God called it "very good" (Gen. 1:14). Whatever evil may be, we cannot explain it merely as a lack or an absence of good.

Another ancient tradition views evil as a principle inherent in matter, while the immaterial or spiritual is good. In such dualistic systems, God is not viewed as the direct Creator of the material universe. Instead He is distanced from His creation; the "good" spiritual principle is viewed as repelled by the "evil" material world. In such systems, human beings are viewed as good spirits trapped in evil physical bodies. One either denies bodily needs and desires to gain mastery over evil (asceticism), or else one permits any physical excess because the "real" immaterial person within isn't affected by what the body does (libertarianism).

But this view, too, is inadequate. It is clear that the immaterial part of humanity, if we can use this language, is moral arbiter of the material. That is, when tempted by some passion rooted in the physical nature, one does not have to give in. The "inner me" rules the body and decides whether or not to respond to the body's urgings. Thus we choose to do good with our bodies, or we can choose to do evil with them. To say that evil resides in the material and good resides in the immaterial fails to reckon with the fact that we exercise an immaterial moral judgment and that our immaterial will makes choices about what the body does. The notion that evil is intrinsic in the material universe, while good is intrinsic to the non-material, simply cannot be upheld.

Others have presented a variation of the first argument, that evil should be viewed as the absence or lack of good. They have said that evil is moral ignorance or the absence of adequate experience. Plato, the classic proponent of this view, argued that if only human beings knew the good, they would choose it. But this concept also fails to fit the facts. Many people who know that smoking cigarettes shortens life continue to smoke, and all the oversized warnings from the Surgeon General placed on cigarette packages will not deter them. Somehow knowing what is good or what is best never succeeds in bringing Utopia. Despite our knowledge, human beings still choose to do things they know are wrong and harmful.

Another popular notion is that evil in human beings is the residue of the evolutionary process. Evil is the relic of the animal, not yet outgrown by a human race moving toward biological perfection. This is an attractive option because it excuses humanity from moral responsibility. It is not really our fault; evil is just a remnant of the savage. But this view is hardly sustainable or relevant. What the animals do, they do by instinct. What human beings do, they do with a knowledge of moral implications. We can hardly argue that human beings received their moral sense from animals that have no such sense. We cannot argue that our choices to do what we recognize as evil are made under the influence of uncontrollable instinct. Instead all human law and custom is based on the idea that the individual is responsible for what he or she does, unless insanity removes the burden of responsibility. Human evil is not done by instinct at all; it is done responsibly, with and in spite of all our uniquely human capacities.

Other people have offered views about the nature of evil. Rousseau felt that evil was a creation of culture; that left alone, living in a primitive state, humans would not be warped by evil. But no culture, however primitive, has ever been void of evil. Marx argued that evil was an economic creation:

Capitalism created inequities, leading to social injustice and all kinds of social and personal evils. If only human beings would turn to communism, where no issue of personal property could be raised, evil would be put aside and a golden age would emerge. Soviet Russia gave dark testimony to the folly of that view.

These and other attempts to explain the nature of evil all prove inadequate. While each approach recognizes the existence of evil, none is willing to go beyond the limits of the material universe in an effort to understand it. But the fact is, only when we take the God of the Bible and His revelation seriously can we begin to understand evil and see how we must deal with it.

The origin of evil. The Bible does not provide any philosophical or theoretical treatise on evil. Instead it speaks of God, who is perfectly good and who created a good and beautiful universe. Evil is an intruder in this universe, a distortion introduced by creatures and not by God.

On a cosmic scale, evil was introduced into the universe by Satan. Many people take Isaiah 14 as a description of Satan's self-transformation from a powerful angel (Lucifer) into God's implacable enemy.

> How you are fallen from heaven,
> O Lucifer, son of the morning!
> How you are cut down to the ground,
> You who weakened the nations!
> For you have said in your heart:
> "I will ascend into heaven,
> I will exalt my throne above the stars of
>   God;
> I will also sit on the mount of the congre-
>   gation
> On the farthest sides of the north;
> I will ascend above the heights of the
>   clouds,
> I will be like the Most High."
> Yet you shall be brought down to Sheol,
> To the lowest depths of the Pit.
>   Isaiah 14:12-14

If this description is of Satan's fall, then we see evil spring into being in the heart of a living creature. Evil, like creation itself and like good, has a personal origin. Evil has nothing to do with any inherent qualities residing in matter. What's more, evil is defined in this passage of "I wills." Evil is the creature demanding the place of the Creator. Evil is the will of the creature substituting for the will of the Creator. Evil is the shattering of the divine order, as contrary wills emerge to warp and distort the original harmony.

In this view, evil is an active rather than a passive force; it is rebellion against God's will and desires. The pattern, set on a cosmic scale in Satan's rebellion, is duplicated in the events reported in Genesis 1—3. God had shaped the material creation into perfect form. He has hung earth in space and molded the planet into friendly form. He populated it with animal life, and as a culminating act, He formed Adam and later Eve to share His image. God placed the happy pair in a beautiful garden; He gave them responsibility for the earth and the opportunity to live in obedient relationship with Him and so preserve their innocence and the harmony of this fresh creation. But Satan slipped into the garden, and Adam and Eve made a tragic choice. Like Satan before them, they chose to rebel against the will of God. Their act, like Satan's, shattered the harmony of their universe and introduced discord and pain. Their act, like Satan's first sin, warped the nature of the sinner and led to continuing rebellion against God's will and purposes.

In the cosmic and the experiential realm, evil is intimately linked with sin. By nature, evil acts are sin, and evil itself is the rebellious insistence on exercising the will of the creature against that of the Creator.

Evils, those tragedies and pains that plague humankind, result directly or indirectly from evil acts and especially from that first sin, which introduced discord into the original creation. Adam's Fall affected all the world, even as the misjudgment of a sea captain brings his ship to a watery grave.

This sketch of the biblical view of the nature and origin of evil makes several important points. First, we see both evil and evils as rooted in sin. The evil that we do is done because we refuse to subject our will to the good will of God. The evils that befall us can be traced directly to some person's evil acts or indirectly to the warping of nature that resulted from Adam's sin. To understand evil, a person must study and come to understand sin.

Second, the Bible affirms a personal universe. That is, reality cannot be explained in terms of impersonal or "natural" processes. When we seek to understand the nature and origin of the universe, we are forced back to God. When we seek to understand the nature and origin of good and evil, we are also forced back, to examine the relationship of God's creatures with the Lord.

Third, in seeking to come to grips with evil and with evils, Scripture asserts personal responsibility. We are not to blame some savage remnant, or to attempt to excuse ourselves as good but helpless creatures trapped in a material tomb. We understand the sinful nature of the evil urges that we feel, and we know that we must be responsible for our choices. Most of all, we must rely on God to break the bonds that evil has forged.

The impact of evil. Evil shrouds every corner of our universe. Everything that we know or experience has been distorted by evil; sin has torn our world from its moorings and has twisted it out of shape. The beauty and harmony of the original creation is gone, and we can hardly imagine Eden. The purity of a humankind fresh from the Creator's hand is lost, and we can hardly imagine innocence. Bluntly put, nothing in our experience or in our nature is free of the taint of evil; everything in human life is flawed and marred. Evil appears in the passions that tug at us, tempting us away from good. Evil appears in the hidden motives that lie behind our actions. Evil appears in the choices that hurt others or that selfishly set our own desires above the desires of God. Evil appears in the hurts we suffer at the hands of others, and in the injustices that social systems perpetuate. Evil lies within us and around us, expressing itself as sin.

When evil is seen as sin and when evils are seen to be rooted in sin, then we begin to understand the nature of evil and begin to realize how desperately we need Christ to rescue us.

The Bible's words for evil. In the Old Testament one family of Hebrew words expresses the notion of evil. The same root indicates both wickedness and misery or distress that are the consequences of wicked actions. The physical and emotional pains that we experience are evils in this derivative sense, and are viewed in the Old Testament as a consequence of doing evil.

Everywhere in the Old Testament, doing evil is defined in a simple way. Certain acts are wrong because they are evil "in the eyes of the Lord" (Num. 32:13; Deut. 4:25; 2 Sam. 3:39). God and His will are the standard of good; evil is any departure from that standard or any violation of that will. Moral evil, then, is whatever God views as wrong.

The Old Testament clearly links evils with evil. It shows that evil (moral) choices ultimately have evil (painful) consequences. Both physical and psychological disasters result from abandoning God's way. The interplay of these two meanings of the word evil explains puzzling statements in the Old Testament about God's involvement with evil. For instance, some versions of the Old Testament read, "I form the light and create darkness; I bring prosperity and create evil: I the LORD do all these things" (Is. 45:7 KJV) and, "When evil comes to a city, has the LORD not caused it?" (Amos 3:6 KJV). Statements like these reflect the conviction that God is moral judge of His universe. He is not only the standard of good but also the One who will punish evil. God takes responsibility for ordering a universe in which evil acts invariably result in evil consequences of some sort. God does not act wickedly. But God does bring upon a sinning humanity the evils that are the result of humankind's sin.

Two Greek word groups are used in the New Testament to express the idea of evil. While they can be used synonymously, the two have different shades of meaning. The *kakos* group looks at a thing's nature and evaluates it as damaged. According to Romans 7:7-25, human beings are evil in that they are damaged—damaged to the extent that they are flawed and unable to do even the good they wish to do. From humankind's flawed nature flow the acts of wickedness and malice that harm others. The *poneros* group is stronger and more active, portraying hostility. Not only are human beings flawed, they are also in active rebellion against God. Wickedness is rooted in our evil will, as well as in our flawed nature.

Once again, we are forced to face the personal nature of evil. Evil is not some impersonal thing, some irresistible force, some characteristic of matter, or some natural consequence of incomplete evolution. Evil is rooted in the creature's rebellion against the Creator. Evil is rebellion against the standards of God, a shattering of the harmony of original creation. And evil in this active, personal sense is the cause of all the pain and evils to which mankind is subject.

God's solution to the problem of evil. Proposed solutions to the problem of evil are directly related to one's theory of its nature. The evolutionist suggests that we must wait until moral development catches up with us. The communist calls for economic reform. But the Christian, who understands evil as rooted in the creature's relationship with the Creator, calls for radical individual conversion from hostility toward God to a love for Him.

Actually, evil must be dealt with on both the cosmic and the experiential levels. On the cosmic level, God will one day exercise His power and judge all sin. Every contrary will shall be forced to submit to God's will, and every rebellious creature will be bound and isolated forever in what the Bible calls the "lake of fire." Then God will create a new universe to be the home of righteousness, where every evil will be a stranger (Is. 65:17-25).

On the experiential level, God has acted to make reconciliation possible. In Jesus, God has punished sin and has established the basis for restored personal relationship with Him. Our hostile, evil will can be changed by conversion. When we put our faith in Jesus, God begins an inner process of transformation to be completed at the resurrection. We come to love God, and we want to please Him. With rebelliousness replaced by love for God (2 Cor. 5:11-12) and with our human inadequacy overcome by the power of the indwelling Spirit of God (Rom. 8:1-11), we can actually begin to do good.

Even though the believer is made new and the power of the evil that distorts human personality is withdrawn, Christians still live in an evil world. Life still holds its tragedies. Every relationship has its pain. Sickness and death are still with us. But personal relationship with God even provides an answer to the hurts that flow from evil. Christians are not immune to evils. Instead we are told that God will sovereignly use even such evils to work His good (Rom. 8:28-29). God will so weave the experiences that come to us in our life that His good purpose for us and in us will be achieved.

To transform evils into good stands forever as one of the great triumphs of our God.

In summary, then, the Bible acknowledges the reality of evil and is fully aware of the evils to which humankind is subject. But God is God, and evil can never triumph. The cosmos will be purified of evil by a cataclysmic final judgment, and evil beings will be isolated in the lake of fire. Until then, humanity can find release from evil within through a faith relationship with God. In Jesus, we have the offer of forgiveness and re-creation, the promise of a changed heart and of a divine enablement that releases us to do good.

Is the existence of evil, then, a compelling argument against the existence of God? Hardly. The opposite is true. Only when we meet the God of the Bible and sense the personal origin of all things can we begin to understand the nature of evil and its workings. Only in God do we find an end to the philosophers' quest and also relief for the hurting heart. In God we find the message of love and salvation that can free us from the evil we sense within ourselves. In God we find the calm assurance that the evils we experience in this life will be transformed by our Lord into gifts that bring us good.

THE EXISTENCE OF GOD

The Bible doesn't argue the existence of God. Scripture simply states, "God is." Beyond the beginning, the cause of all, there looms the image of a God who later breaks through all the barriers between time and eternity to reveal Himself to the human beings He created.

Scripture assumes that creation itself gives compelling evidence that God is. This theme is found in passages like Psalm 19 and Romans 1. The psalmist says, "The heavens declare the glory of God; and the firmament shows His handiwork. Day unto day utters speech, and night unto night reveals knowledge. There is no speech nor language where their voice is not heard. Their line has gone out through all the earth, and their words to the end of the world (Ps. 19:1-4). And Paul argues that "what may be known of God is manifest in them, for God has shown it to them. For since the creation of the world His invisible attributes are clearly seen, being understood by the things that are made, even His eternal power and Godhead " (Rom. 1:19-20).

The classic arguments. Three different kinds of arguments have been advanced to "prove" the existence of God. One rests on a kind of logic, and the other two rely on arguments drawn from experience.

The ontological argument, presented first in the eleventh century by Anselm, goes like this: "We can conceive of a perfect being, one who is so great and perfect that there could be none greater. Such a being must have existence as one characteristic. Therefore such a being must exist." This argument is abstract and hard to grasp. Unlike the other arguments for God's existence, this one has only tenuous roots in Scripture. Anselm thought that his argument was implied by Scripture's comment that "the fool has said in his heart, 'There is no God'" (Ps. 14:1). How clear it seemed to Anselm: Only a fool could conceive of God and then deny Him. Only a fool would fail to realize that the being he denied must in fact exist, for the very concept of such a being demonstrates His existence.

Cosmological and teleological arguments appeal to the order observable in the universe. The cosmological arguments observe the orderliness of events and note that cause and effect rule. Moderns note the first law of thermodynamics and observe that energy is lost in each transaction so that the universe is, in essence, running down. Somehow, then, there must have been a first cause of the cause/effect chain we see in our universe; somehow there must have been a first burst of energy to explain the existence of that receding flow of energy we now observe. Whatever one wants to call that first cause, the believer is convinced that the self-existent Creator our universe calls for is, in fact, the God who has revealed Himself to us in Scripture.

The teleological arguments note orderliness and its testimony to a mind that shaped things as they are to fulfill their purpose in His scheme of things. This argument is often put in simple forms. "You can no more explain the design of the stars and the structure of living beings by chance than you could expect a tornado to hit a junkyard and put together a new car." Or "If you walk through a field and find a clod of dirt, you suspect nothing special. But if you find a ticking watch, you know it didn't just happen. There must have been a watchmaker." In its most modern expression, this argument is expressed by scientists in what is called the Intelligent Design movement. While Intelligent Design proponents do not argue for the existence of "God," this fresh expression of the classic argument insists that the complex design and order exhibited in living creatures requires a designer who purposefully shaped things for the purpose they fulfill.

Still another argument rests on observance of human beliefs and behavior. The human race exhibits a sense of morality, an awareness of right and wrong. This moral sense implies the existence of a moral source, and thus human nature itself testifies to the necessity of a personal and moral Creator.

The value of the arguments. Christians have disagreed over the value of these arguments for the existence of God. Some insist that they effectively prove that God must exist. The problem is that proof does not compel belief. It is still the "fool" (our translation of a Hebrew word indicating a person who is morally and spiritually though not necessarily mentally deficient) who refuses to accept the evidence inherent in creation. As Hebrews asserts, "By faith we understand that the worlds were framed by the word of God, so that the things which are seen were not made of things which are visible" (Heb. 11:3).

A faith response to God so changes our perspective that we can at last see clearly what was obvious all along. At the same time, the arguments for God's existence do have value in pre-evangelism. They can help us show that Christian faith is reasonable and defensible; we can show that the world we live in is best understood by considering the existence of God. The modern is likely to dismiss the idea of God as old and discredited by "science." Taking the arguments for God's existence seriously, and presenting

them to young people or old, may open minds that have been closed to the gospel message.

The believer also finds value in these arguments. The arguments confirm the confidence that we already have in God. Reasonable arguments for God's existence will never replace Scripture's revelation as a basis for our faith. But such arguments remind us that our faith is more reasonable than all the scornful world's confidence in disbelief.

FORGIVENESS

God is consistently portrayed in Scripture as a forgiving God. This quality of God is all too easily misunderstood. Biblically, forgiveness is not passing offenses off with an "Oh, it doesn't matter." In fact the sins and offenses for which we need forgiveness do count. Only when we understand both our need for forgiveness and God's commitment to forgive us in Christ will we be able to develop an appropriate concept of God.

God's forgiveness in the Old Testament. In the Old Testament God is known as a forgiving person. Moses, begging God to forgive straying Israel, based his appeal on God's character as a loving person. "Pardon the iniquity of this people, I pray, according to the greatness of Your mercy, just as You have forgiven this people, from Egypt even until now" (Num. 14:19).

This vision of a God who recognizes human fault and yet forgives is basic to the Old Testament concept of God. No wonder the psalmists celebrate Him, praising, "If You, LORD, should mark iniquities, O Lord, who could stand? But there is forgiveness with You, that You may be feared . . . O Israel, hope in the LORD; For with the LORD there is mercy, and with Him is abundant redemption. And He shall redeem Israel from all his iniquities" (Ps. 130:3, 4, 7, 8).

Along with this picture of a loving God, the Old Testament presents the portrait of a penitent believer. Psalm 32 celebrates God's forgiveness and reveals the attitude of the psalmist. Burdened by a sense of guilt and an awareness that he had offended God, David resisted until finally he could say, "I acknowledged my sin to You and my iniquity I have not hidden. I said, 'I will confess my transgressions to the LORD,' and You forgave the iniquity of my sin" (Ps. 32:5). God's forgiveness was experienced only by those who acknowledged their sin and humbly came to Him to receive forgiveness.

Forgiveness is offered freely by God. But forgiveness must be accepted by human beings who acknowledge their failures and openly confess their sins to the Lord.

The Old Testament does not fully explain how it is possible for a holy God to lovingly forgive His sinning creatures. But it does affirm that God is forgiving. And it celebrates the joys of those who are willing to abandon pride and beg, "According to the multitude of Your tender mercies, blot out my transgressions. Wash me thoroughly from my iniquity, and cleanse me from my sin" (Ps. 51:1, 2).

Forgiveness in the New Testament. The Old Testament presents God as a forgiving person and relates forgiveness to the sacrifices of atonement that Old Testament law established. To receive forgiveness, sinners must humble themselves, admit their sin, and demonstrate faith by bringing the appropriate sacrifice. Those who refused to admit their sins, or who rebelliously refused to approach God, could not receive the forgiveness God yearns to extend.

This same pattern is seen in the New Testament, but here the great mystery of how God can forgive is solved. God is a moral person. He is holy and just, as well as loving. God can't just pass sin off as unimportant, for He has a moral obligation as judge of His universe to punish sin. So throughout the ages it remained a mystery how God could offer sinful human beings forgiveness of sins. That mystery was solved in the death and resurrection of Jesus Christ.

Romans puts it this way: "All have sinned and fall short of the glory of God, being justified freely by His grace through the redemption that is in Christ Jesus, who God set forth as a propitiation by His blood, through faith, to demonstrate His righteousness, because in His forbearance God had passed over the sins that were previously committed, to demonstrate at the present time His righteousness, that He might be just and the justifier of the one who has faith in Jesus" (Rom. 3:23-26).

God extended forgiveness to Old Testament saints, even though no one could see justice in His offer of pardon. Then Jesus came and in His death offered Himself as our substitute. The Bible says Jesus "bore our sins in His own body on the tree, that we, having died to sins, might live for righteousness" (1 Pet. 2:24). A holy God demands that sin be punished. But a loving God entered history to take that punishment on Himself so that He might be free to forgive.

Jesus not only resolves the mystery of how God can forgive us and retain His moral integrity, but Jesus is also the object of our faith. Like the Old Testament saints, we hear the offer of forgiveness. Like them, we humble ourselves. We admit our moral failure and desperate need. Stripped of pride, we throw ourselves on God's mercy, believing that He will forgive us for Jesus' sake. Then, joyfully we rise again, aware that we have been accepted and forgiven by our God.

Experiencing forgiveness. Christians are a people called to enjoy forgiveness and live daily with its benefits. God's forgiveness is far more than a legal judgment of pardon and acquittal. Forgiveness is linked with love and freedom.

One day Jesus was eating at the home of a Pharisee who did not want to accept Jesus as God's messenger. As they ate, a local prostitute slipped into the home, and weeping, poured perfume over His feet. The Pharisee thought, "If this man were a prophet, he would know the kind of woman she is" (Luke 7:39). Jesus answered the Pharisee's unspoken criticism with a story about two debtors. One owed fifty denarii and the other owed five hundred denarii. If the lender canceled the debt, Jesus asked, which creditor would love him more? The Pharisee responded, "I suppose the one who had the bigger debt canceled." Jesus looked toward the weeping prostitute and nodded agreement. The woman, whose sins were many, had recognized the wonder of forgiveness and had responded to Jesus with love. Similarly, as you and I remember how much we have been forgiven, our love for God deepens and grows.

Awareness of forgiveness is also freeing. The letter to the Hebrews looks at the impact of Jesus' self-sacrifice. There the writer calls the Old Testament sacrifices a shadowy illustration of the sacrifice that Jesus made for us. While those Old Testament sacrifices spoke of God's promise, they were unable to clear the conscience of worshipers (Heb. 9:9). Each repetition of those sacrifices reminded the worshipers that that they remained sinners in continual need. But, the writer goes on, the blood of Christ cleanses consciences (Heb. 9:14). The wonderful result is that Jesus' "once for all" cleansing releases us from guilt (Heb. 10:10). We know that in Jesus our sins have been removed—removed so perfectly that God says, "Their sins and lawless acts I will remember no more" (Heb. 10:17).

Because we know our sins are forgiven, we can approach God with confidence (Heb. 10:22). We need never cringe from our Lord or try to hide from Him, for Jesus' death has won a full and complete forgiveness for us. We no longer need to carry the burden of our past failures, for in Jesus all our sins are forgiven and put away. Because of Jesus we can forget the past and look forward with hope to the future.

But true freedom is not found in removing the burdens of our past sins but

in transforming our future. This also is linked with our continuing experience of forgiveness. Through forgiveness God promises us the freedom to become new and different persons.

As we live humbly with God, acknowledging our failures and seeking His grace, we experience God's inner, transforming power.

The doctrine of forgiveness truly reveals much about God. It expresses both His commitment to judge sin and His commitment to love lost sinners. And it makes a powerful statement about God's determination to restore human beings to a personal relationship with Him based on grace rather than on human effort. In the Cross of Christ all of God's attributes meet, and in the Cross we discover what He is truly like.

THE HOLY SPIRIT

Christians honor and worship the Holy Spirit as God, the third Person of the Trinity. Christians differ in their understanding of some of the Holy Spirit's works, but we recognize Him as God and affirm His importance in Christian experience. While our differences tend to attract attention, areas of agreement are far greater and more significant.

The differences among us focus on two areas. One area is that of spiritual gifts. Some Christians believe that the visible gifts of the Spirit, such as tongues and healing, are given and operate today. Other Christians argue that the visible gifts were intended to authenticate early Christianity and ceased when the last book of our New Testament was written. The second area of difference relates to spirituality. Some Christians believe that after salvation the Holy Spirit performs a second, special work that is important for personal holiness. Other Christians believe that the Holy Spirit enters fully into the life of the believer at conversion and that spiritual growth and personal holiness are simply matters of learning to "walk in the Spirit."

This article, however, will focus on those things that Christians commonly understand about the unique and wonderful person, God's Holy Spirit.

The Holy Spirit, a divine person. Some people have suggested that the Holy Spirit should be understood simply as the "divine influence" or as God's "animating power." Such attempts to rob the Holy Spirit of personhood and deity fail, simply because they are so clearly contradicted by Scripture.

When Jesus spoke of the Holy Spirit, our Lord chose the personal pronoun "He," even though "spirit" in Greek is a neuter word (John 14:17, 26; 16:13-15). Christ promised to send His disciples "another Comforter" when He returned to heaven and He identified the Spirit as the promised One. The very word He chose to describe the Spirit in this passage is definitive. One word in Scripture translated "another" is *altos*, a Greek term meaning "another of the same kind." A different word, *heteros*, means another of a different kind. Christ chose the word *altos* when promising the disciples "another" Comforter. Christ, the second person of the Godhead, was to send the Spirit, equally God, to live within those who believe.

There are many other indications that the Spirit is a Person and not a force or influence. The Holy Spirit knows and understands (Rom. 8:27; 1 Cor. 2:11). The Holy Spirit communicates in words (1 Cor. 2:13). The Holy Spirit acts and chooses (1 Cor. 12:11). The Spirit loves (Rom. 15:30), can be insulted (Heb. 10:29), can be lied to (Acts 5:3), can be resisted (Acts 7:51), and can be grieved (Eph. 4:30). The Holy Spirit teaches (John 14:26), intercedes (Rom. 8:26), convicts (John 16:7-8), bears witness (John 15:26), and guides (John 16:13). Each of these activities testifies to the fact that the Spirit is a person, not an impersonal influence. Surely the Holy Spirit is a divine person.

The Bible also identifies the Spirit as God by the titles it gives Him. He is the eternal Spirit (Heb. 9:14), the Spirit of Christ (1 Pet. 1:11), the Spirit of the Lord (Is. 11:2), the Spirit of the Sovereign Lord (Is. 61:1), the Spirit of the Father (Matt. 10:20) and the Spirit of the Son (Gal. 4:6). No other being apart from God bears such divine titles.

The deity of the Spirit is shown in other ways as well. He is omnipresent, as only God can be (Ps. 139:7; 1 Cor. 12:13). He is all powerful (Luke 1:35; Rom. 8:11). He was an agent in Creation (Gen. 1:2; Ps. 104:30) and has power to work miracles (Matt. 12:28; 1 Cor. 12:9-11). The Spirit is the one who brings us new birth (John 3:6; Titus 3:5). It was the Spirit who raised Jesus from the dead and who brings God's resurrection life to you and me (Rom. 8:11). The Holy Spirit can be blasphemed (Matt. 12:31-32; Mark 3:28-29), and lying to the Holy Spirit is said to be lying to God (Acts 5:3-4). The biblical testimony is clear. The Holy Spirit is a person. And the Holy Spirit is God.

The cosmic role of the Holy Spirit. When we probe Scripture for the nature of the Holy Spirit's activities, we discover a complex and multifaceted ministry. While there are many ways these might be organized, we will simply consider both the Spirit's cosmic ministries as they relate to the God's plan and His personal ministries as they relate to human beings.

The Spirit's cosmic ministries focus on creation, revelation, and on the Incarnation. Genesis 1 suggests that both Jesus and the Spirit were active in creation. Other passages link the Spirit to the origin of life (Job 33:4; Ps. 104:30) and to preservation of the created order (Ps. 104:29-30). The Spirit often is linked to revelation. Old Testament passages such as 2 Samuel 23:2 and Micah 3:8 link the prophet's ministry as divine spokesperson to the Spirit of the Lord. The New Testament attributes a number of Old Testament verses to the Spirit (Matt. 22:43; Acts 1:16; 4:25), and Peter writes that "for prophecy never came by the will of man, but holy men of God spoke as they were moved by the Holy Spirit" (2 Pet. 1:21). Those who preached the New Testament gospel likewise did so "by the Holy Spirit sent from heaven" (1 Pet. 1:12).

The Spirit was intimately involved in the incarnation of Jesus and in the events of Christ's life. Mary conceived by the Holy Spirit (Luke 1:35). The Spirit filled and led Jesus during His life on earth (Luke 4:1; John 3:34), and the Spirit's power was expressed in Christ's miracles (Matt. 12:28). Christ's death was a sacrifice offered to God by the Spirit (Heb. 9:14), and His resurrection was effected by the Spirit's power (Rom. 1-4; 8-11; 1 Pet. 3:18).

As an active agent in creation, revelation, and the Incarnation, the Holy Spirit has had an active role in carrying out the cosmic plans and purposes of the Father.

The interpersonal role of the Holy Spirit. The ministries of the Spirit that have rightly drawn the most attention are interpersonal. The New Testament, and to some extent the Old Testament, shows the Spirit to be intimately involved in activities that vitally affect human beings. We can sum up these ministries under three headings. The Holy Spirit has ministries that (1) relate to the unsaved, (2) are associated with initial salvation, and (3) affect the experience of believers.

Some ministries of the Holy Spirit relate to the unsaved. Both testaments seem to suggest that the Holy Spirit operates to restrain the full expression of sin (Gen. 6:3; 2 Thess. 2:6). Most important, however, is the work of the Spirit in convicting those who do not yet believe. Jesus defined this work in John 16:8-11, and it seems to involve driving home certain essential truths basic to the gospel. Whether or not people choose to believe, the Spirit confronts the unsaved with the truth about sin, about righteousness, and about judgment.

Some ministries of the Spirit are linked with our initial salvation experience. The Holy Spirit is the One who regenerates us (brings us new birth). While the Word of

God provides the content of the message (James 1:18; 1 Pet. 1:23), it is the Spirit who gives life (Titus 3:5). At conversion, we are also baptized by the Spirit, as that term is defined in 1 Corinthians 12:13. While the word *baptize* is given a different meaning in some traditions, the apostle Paul uses it to define that act by which the Spirit of God unites believers to Jesus and to one another in Christ's mystical body.

A number of passages speak of believers as sealed by the Spirit (2 Cor. 1:22; Eph. 1:13; 4:30). As seal, the Holy Spirit serves as a mark of divine ownership and suggests preservation and security. Thus the Holy Spirit is the One who supervises our entrance into eternal life and who effects our union with Jesus.

Most of the personal ministries of the Holy Spirit focus on His work in the lives of believers. And, as *A Contemporary Wesleyan Theology* says, "It is evident in the teachings of Paul that the Holy Spirit is now present in every believer" (p. 427). Romans 8:9 and 1 Corinthians 6:19 make it plain that even unspiritual believers are no exception. The presence of the Spirit means that the power and enablement are now available to us. The Old Testament speaks of the Spirit operating within believers (Gen. 41:38; Num. 27:18; Dan. 1:8) and falling upon them to provide special enablement (Judg. 3:10; 1 Sam. 10:9-10; Judg. 14:6; 1 Sam. 16:13). But Jesus suggests that today our relationship with the Spirit is new and different (John 14:17; 7:39). Today the Spirit is with us as the source of overflowing spiritual life and joy (John 7:37-38) and to be our helper in every need (John 14:15-17, 25-26; 15:26-27; 16:7-15). The Spirit opens our eyes to the meaning of what Jesus taught, and He leads us into truth (John 14:25-26; 16:12-13; 1 Cor. 2:10, 12-14). The Spirit guides our steps (Rom. 8:4-5), assists in prayer (Rom. 8:26), and is the One who transforms us toward Christlikeness (2 Cor. 3:18).

A number of biblical terms are associated with the overflowing presence and power of the Holy Spirit in the Christian. Some people take these terms as equivalent, and some argue for distinctions. But all of these terms (baptism, filling, receiving, anointing, and pouring out of the Spirit) communicate the exciting reality. God the Holy Spirit is present within us that He might be active in and through our personalities. It is our responsibility and opportunity to rely on the Holy Spirit, walking in step with Him and responding to His prompting (Rom. 8:3-11; Gal. 5:16-18).

Fruit and gifts. Two biblical themes emphasize what the Spirit does in us, and what He does through us. The fruit of the Spirit (Gal. 5:22-23) represents the transformation of the human personality in such qualities as love, peace, patience, and the like. We who are at birth corrupted by sin are progressively transformed as we remain close to Jesus and responsive to God's Spirit (John 15; 2 Cor. 3:18). The moral qualities and virtues indicated by fruit are the primary evidence of the influence and power of the Holy Spirit within us.

What the Holy Spirit does through us is expressed in the concept of spiritual gifts. The Spirit equips each believer with special endowments, which the New Testament calls "gifts." Not only do these various endowments make it possible for us to contribute to the spiritual welfare of others, they also may relate to our witness to non-Christians.

The Bible teaches that it is the Spirit who both produces the fruit of goodness in our lives and who enables us to serve God and others. Because we rely on the Spirit to enable us, we understand God's commands as invitations to experience the Spirit's power, never as threatening demands. Because we know the Spirit is present to empower us, we respond to God's call to holiness with joy, sure that the Lord Himself will lift us beyond our inadequacies.

Scripture thus presents the Holy Spirit as one of three persons of the Trinity. The Spirit

had a role in those cosmic events represented by creation and the Incarnation, and had a critical role in revelation. But most of what we know of the Spirit's work focuses on His interpersonal ministries. The Spirit restrains evil and enlightens everyone about basic gospel elements. The Spirit is the One who brings us God's new life and unites us to Jesus. And the Spirit is the one who ministers continually to believers. God's Spirit leads, guides, and empowers. God's Spirit works the inner transformation that produces moral fruit. And God's Spirit gifts believers with those endowments that make it possible for us to minister to one another. Because the Spirit is with us, you and I can live vital, victorious life. Because the Spirit is present we can face our future with hope and confidence. The Spirit will lift us as we rely on Him, and He will help us reach our full potential in Jesus.

INCARNATION

The Old Testament foretold the Incarnation in a name. The Messiah/deliverer of the Jewish people was to be called Immanuel. That name, capturing the emphasis of the Hebrew, means "With us is God."

This was hard even for some early Christians to grasp, and the notion that God would become a human being has been ridiculed by ancient and modern skeptics. Yet this wonder is clearly taught in the Bible and is basic to our faith. In the person of Jesus Christ, God has come to us in the flesh. This is the Christian doctrine of incarnation. We believe that God has pierced the barrier between the seen and the unseen, and in history's greatest miracle, God became a true human being.

Four aspects of the Incarnation. Scripture does not attempt to explain, but it clearly and forcefully teaches the Incarnation. We can look, for instance, at four New Testament passages. John's Gospel begins by identifying Jesus as the Word who "was with God" and who "was God" (John 1:1). This

Word "became flesh and dwelt among us, and we beheld His glory, the glory as of the only begotten of the Father" (John 1:14). The eternally existing Word took on flesh, becoming a true human being, who for a few brief years lived among other human beings on planet earth. Galatians 4:4-5 picks up the theme of preexistence—the fact that the One who came was God the Son with the Father from eternity. "When the fullness of time had come," the Bible says, "God sent forth his Son, born of a woman, born under the law, to redeem those who were under law, that we might receive the adoption as sons." Philippians 2 is one of the clearest and most powerful biblical expressions of incarnation. It presents Jesus Christ "who, being in very nature of God" [NIV] yet "made Himself of no reputation, taking the form of a manservant, and coming in the likeness of men." As a human being the Son of God "humbled Himself and became obedient to the point of death, even the death of the Cross." Exalted now, Jesus has been given "the name which is above every name" and will hear "every tongue...confess that Jesus Christ is Lord" (Phil. 2:5-11).

A fourth passage is found in Colossians. There Jesus is described as the "image [the exact representation] of the invisible God." It was "by Him all things were created that are in heaven and on earth, visible and invisible.... He is before all things, and in Him all things consist," for "it pleased the Father that in Him all the fullness [of God] should dwell" (Col. 1:15-19).

It was Jesus Christ whom God invested with humanity and Who is the agent of salvation. Through Jesus, God chose to reconcile all things to Himself by making peace through His blood, shed on the Cross (Col. 1:20). This same passage emphasizes the fact that the Incarnation was no mere illusion: God has reconciled us "by Christ's physical body through death" (Col. 1:22 NIV).

Significance of the Incarnation. Given the fact that the Bible teaches the Incarnation,

why make an issue of it? Why view the incarnation of Christ as central to Christian faith? Simply because so much hinges on it. Before the first century A.D., philosophers despaired of ever really knowing God. He was so wholly "other." Whoever or whatever "God" might be, whether Aristotle's "unmoved mover" or Neoplatonism's "pure spirit," God was so removed from mankind's universe that he was deemed unknowable. And then, in an obscure little country on the fringe of the mighty Roman Empire, this unknowable God arrived. He came not in majesty but as an infant. He lived as a real human being, not among the political movers but among the common people. And He died, not as victim but as Victor. Because God the Creator entered His own universe, the hidden God that humanity despaired of knowing was fully unveiled. And because in Him God acted to free humanity from bondage to sin, the distant God that humanity feared was discovered to be lovingly near, inviting each of us to truly know Him in an intimate, personal relationship.

This is, of course, the real reason for and necessity of the Incarnation. Sin's ruin had devastated our whole race, alienating us from God, and so warping our outlook that we were actually God's enemies (see Colossians 1:21). Only God's personal intervention could deal finally with sin, reveal the full extent of His love for us, and transform us from enemies into children. No one could do for us what Jesus did, and so Jesus had to come, impelled by the necessity imposed by God's deep love.

JESUS CHRIST

Commenting on the *Earliest Christian Creeds*, Martin Luther expressed the common conviction of all Christians. "He who steadfastly holds to the doctrine that Jesus Christ is true God and true man, who died and rose again for us, will acquiesce in and heartily assent to the other articles of the Christian faith." Paul's saying in Ephesians

1:22 is true: Jesus Christ is the chief treasure, the basis, the foundation, the sum total to whom all are drawn and under whom all are gathered. In Him are hidden all the treasures of wisdom and knowledge.

Jesus is central. He is the heart, the soul, the beauty, and the being of our faith.

Who is Jesus? It is important that when we speak of Jesus, we mean the real Jesus. Some theologians, in attempting to discover what they call a "historical Jesus," have challenged the Bible's statements about Him. They have assumed that after Jesus' death His followers gradually ascribed deity to the simple carpenter of Nazareth. Jesus, the Jewish prophet whose moral and spiritual vision was so exalted, is to be honored, they say, but simply as a man.

These scholars have taught that even though Jesus was the best of men, He was never any more than what any of us can aspire to become. The Jesus of the critics, stripped of majesty and robbed of essential deity, is not the Jesus of Christian faith. The Jesus of faith is the Jesus the Bible proclaims, the Jesus whom Luther identifies as "true God, and true man, who died and rose again for us."

Rather than mimic the uncounted books that have been written on the Bible's picture of Jesus, I want to simply list key passages and the central truths they teach. And then I want to share something of who Jesus is *for us.* This is what is so exciting about our Lord. He is God, but He is God bent low, stooping to bond Himself to you and me, that in Him we might be lifted high. Only the Jesus of the Bible, He who is God and man in one, could be everything for us that He is.

Who is the Jesus of the Bible? In a helpful *Handbook of Basic Bible Texts* (Zondervan), John Jefferson Davis lists the following key passages that identify the biblical Jesus. According to Scripture, Jesus is:

Co-equal with God, the second Person of the Trinity, who existed from all eternity

Is. 9:6; Mic. 5:2; John 1:1-3; 6:38; 6:56-58; 17:4-5; Gal. 4:4-5; Phil. 2:5-7; Rev. 22:12-13

Virgin born, conceived by the Holy Spirit

Is. 7:14; Matt. 1:18-26; Luke 1:26-38

Without a sinful nature, free from acts of sin

Luke 1:35; John 8:29,46; 14:30-32; Heb. 4:15, 26-28; 9:14; 1 Pet. 1:18-19; 2:22-23

Truly and fully human

Matt. 4:1-2; 8:23-24; Luke 2:52; John 1:14; 4:5-6; 11:35;Rom. 1:2-3; Heb. 2:14, 17-18; 4:15

Truly and fully God, the possessor of divine titles:

Is. 9:6; Matt. 26:63-66; Mark 1:2-3; Luke 1:17; 3:1; Acts 2:21

possessor of divine attributes:

Matt. 28:20; John 1:1; 17:5; Eph. 1:22-23; Phil. 2:5-7

possessor of divine power:

John 1:3,14; 5:21,26; 11:25; Col. 1:16, 17; Heb. 1:2

possessor of divine prerogatives:

Matt. 25:31-32; Mark 2:5-7; John 5:22,27; Acts 7:59

Equal in every way to the Father:

John 1:1; 20:28; Titus 2:13; Heb. 1:8; 1 Pet. 1:1

Christians joyfully confess that Jesus is who the Bible states He is, and this Jesus of Scripture is the focus of our worship and our hope.

Who Jesus is for us. *Jesus is our prophet.* A prophet speaks for God. Jesus is the ultimate spokesperson, the ultimate revealer of the Father and of His will. We pay careful attention to all that Jesus taught, confident that His words are completely trustworthy. We acknowledge the miracles that authenticated His message, but most important we rely on the Spirit's inner testimony, which enables us to recognize His voice. We trust Jesus' portrait of the Father, we rely on His promises, and we respond obediently to His commands. We yearn to experience the kingdom of heaven He described, and we expect to experience the perfect love and holiness He promises. Jesus is our prophet, the source of truth about God, the trustworthy spokesperson, Whose words guide and shape our lives (see Matt. 5:1-7,29; John 10:1-4; 14:15-22; Heb. 1:1-3; 2:1-4).

Jesus is our high priest. A priest is a mediator, representing God to the people and the people to God. Jesus, our high priest, offered Himself as the perfect sacrifice to God. That one sacrifice made us perfect forever.

As our high priest, the living Jesus stands today by the Father's throne. He represents us there, praying for us and hearing our petitions. His intercession guarantees continuing forgiveness when we fall short of God's will or stray from His paths.

Jesus understands and sympathizes with our weaknesses. His presence in heaven gives us the confidence to freely approach God's throne whenever we need mercy or help (Heb. 3:1-4.16; 1 John 1:8—2:2).

Jesus is our coming king. We recognize Jesus as the ultimate authority and power in the universe. He, the source of all, is also ruler of all. The kingship of Jesus is real in our lives, for we acknowledge Him as Lord and obey Him. But we look forward to Jesus' return. Then He will exercise His power openly, and then every knee will bow to Jesus. In the age to come, Jesus will be acknowledged by the universe as King of kings and Lord of lords. He will rule over all, instituting His golden age of righteousness and peace (Rev. 11:15-19; 19:11-16).

Jesus is our example. We view the life that Jesus lived on earth as the perfect life. His lifestyle reveals true spirituality, that close fellowship with and obedience to God that finds expression in compassion for human beings. Jesus' walk on earth expresses the values that we profess. His outlook on what is important in life is the outlook we struggle to share. We look to Jesus to learn how to respond to hurts and injustice, to opposition and hatred. We look to Jesus to see how we are to react to suffering. From Jesus we learn how to trust ourselves to the Father, whatever the circumstances.

We see in Jesus the perfect love that He commands in His disciples. In confessing Jesus to be our model, we agree with the apostles that we who claim Him are to love as He loved, to walk as He walked. Jesus is our example, and we delight to walk in His steps (Matt. 5:43-48; Luke 6.40; 1 John 2:6; 3:16).

Jesus is our life. Jesus is the source of all that is good in us. The new life that God gave us when we trusted Christ as Savior is His. He is the vine, and all the power to produce fruit comes from His vitality flowing into us. The life we live on earth now is in the most significant sense His life—eternal and enriching, expressing itself in love, joy, peace, patience, kindness, goodness, faithfulness, gentleness, and self-control. All that is good and beautiful in our lives is an expression of Jesus, springing directly from our relationship with Him.

Because Jesus lives in us, our bodies can become instruments of righteousness, and our hearts the home of love. We depend on Jesus not only for forgiveness but also for everything. He truly is the food we eat, the air we breathe, the life we live (John 15:1-8; Gal. 2:20; 5:22-25; Eph. 2:4-10; 2 Cor. 12:9-10).

Jesus is our risen Lord. In His resurrection, Jesus was given the name above every name: Lord. His is the authority, His the power, His the right to rule. He is head over the church, His body, and He is Lord of every person. Acknowledging the lordship of Jesus means that we confess His right to set our standards, establish our priorities, and guide our choices. We respond to Jesus as He speaks to us in His written Word, and we open our lives to His special, supernatural guidance. We acknowledge Jesus' lordship over other Christians and extend them the freedom to follow their own convictions, fully responsible to Christ.

We pray to our Lord about our decisions, and we depend on Him to shape our circumstances. Because we believe that Jesus, as Lord, has all power in heaven and on earth, we face even suffering with hope, sure that in all things God works for the good of those who love Him. Because Jesus is Lord, He merits our total allegiance, and we commit ourselves fully to Him and to His will (Matt. 28:18; Rom. 8:28-29; 14:1-13; Eph. 1:18-23; Phil. 2:9-11; 1 Pet. 3:14-15).

In every way Jesus truly is the heart, the center, the beauty, and the glory of our faith. Christianity is no mere philosophy. It is not simply a higher ethical vision. Christianity is Jesus Christ, foretold in the Old Testament, unveiled in the New Testament. Christianity rests entirely on the conviction that in Jesus of Nazareth, God became flesh to dwell among us. Jesus lived, taught, died, was raised again, and even now is at the Father's right hand, ready at any moment to return. But Christianity offers more than God enfleshed. Christianity offers us a transforming, personal relationship with this God. Through faith Jesus becomes ours: our savior, our prophet, our high priest, our coming king, our example, our life, our risen Lord. Everything that we have and are is ours through Jesus Christ alone.

Christianity is Christ. We rejoice, for we are His and He is ours.

REVELATION

The Scriptures make it clear that only God can make God known, and that God has acted to reveal Himself.

The word revelation simply means "to unveil something hidden; to make something known for what it is." Some people sum up revelation by saying it is knowledge about God that comes from God. The Bible identifies two avenues of revelation. The first is usually called general revelation. General revelation includes all those wordless ways God expresses truth about Himself to all humanity. The second is special revelation. Special revelation includes God's acts of unveiling of Himself to individuals or groups. Our Bible comes to us by special revelation, and Jesus Himself is the ultimate special unveiling of the person of God.

General revelation. Most Christians see two primary avenues of general revelation. The first is the creation itself. The psalmist says, "The heavens declare the glory of God; and the firmament shows His handiwork. Day unto day utters speech, and night unto night reveals knowledge. There is no speech nor language where their voice is not heard. Their line has gone out throughout all the earth, and their words to the end of the world" (Ps. 19:1-4). The apostle Paul says of creation's silent witness, "What may be known about God is manifest in them, for God has shown it to them. For since the creation of the world His invisible attributes are clearly seen, being understood by the things that are made" (Rom. 1:19, 20).

Paul argues elsewhere in Romans that God has implanted another witness to Himself in human nature. This witness is conscience, which bears witness that we live in a moral universe. While the specific acts that different cultures define as wrong may differ, every culture identifies some actions as morally right and others as wrong. And everywhere there is the inner judge, conscience, expressed as we condemn or excuse ourselves for actions that make us feel guilty.

What can human beings know about God from general revelation? We can know that God exists. We can know the Creator is not only greater than His creation but also distinct from it. We can know something of his intelligence. We can also sense His moral nature and realize that He will judge human actions. Because so much knowledge about God is accessible to us in general revelation, Paul concludes that we humans are without excuse for our failure to acknowledge God and respond to Him with praise and thanks.

What may be most striking in the New Testament's treatment of general revelation is this fact: human beings meet and come to know truth about God in general revelation. But humanity has always reacted negatively to this knowledge. Warped by sin, our race has failed to glorify or thank the God we meet in nature; instead humans have foolishly "changed the glory of the incorruptible God into an image made like corruptible man—and birds and four-footed animals and creeping things" (Rom. 1:23).

More than information about God is needed. There must be an inner transformation of humanity's attitude toward God. There must be faith, which historically has been stimulated only by special revelation from God.

Special revelation. The Book of Hebrews begins, "God, who at various times and in various ways spoke in time past to the fathers by the prophets, has in these last days spoken to us by His Son" (Heb. 1:1-2). Special revelation has come through dreams, waking visions, and by "face-to-face" communication with God.

This revelation has been shared in stories passed down verbally, expressed in ritual and sacrifice, and recorded in Scripture. Separate revelations, unfolding over the centuries, have been gathered into a harmonious whole, together giving us in our Scriptures a clear portrait of God and His purposes.

What is so exciting about special revelation is that it does more than show us God from a distance. Special revelation takes us inside the heart and mind of God, showing us His deepest motives and purposes. In special revelation, the meaning of His actions in our world is explained. Why did God create? Who are human beings? What is God's attitude toward sin and sinners? Why did God choose Israel as His people and miraculously free this people from slavery in Egypt? As God reveals more and more of Himself and His purposes, we come to realize that all special revelation is gospel; all is good news, for all portrays a God Who cares deeply about human beings and Who reaches out to establish a personal relationship with any who will trust Him.

Through general revelation we know that God is. Through special revelation we know *who* He is and *what* He is like. Scripture is the repository of special revelation, a reliable record of all that God intends to unveil to us until Jesus returns. But we also recognize Jesus Himself as the ultimate unveiling of God. In the words, actions, and character of Jesus Christ, we have the exact representation of God's being" (cf. Heb. 1:3). As Jesus said, "He who has seen Me has seen the Father" (John 14:9).

Special revelation takes us beyond the evidence that God exists to help us know God as a person. We trace His thoughts as they are unveiled in Scripture, and in Jesus we sense the fervor of His love and the depth of His commitment to us. As we come to know the God who unveils Himself so fully, our fears dissolve, and we joyfully respond by trusting Him with everything we have and are.

TRINITY

Christians have never been able to explain the Trinity or even to understand how one God exists as three persons. When we've tried to explain the Trinity, we've usually worked with analogy. We've noted that one egg is composed of three substances: shell, white, and yoke. Augustine used a tree's root, trunk, and branches. The shamrock, with its three petals, and a triangle have also been used. At times some people have pointed to water to explain the Trinity, for water can be ice, liquid, or a vapor. But somehow none of these analogies have satisfied Christians, much less outsiders. We are driven back to a simple position. The Bible clearly teaches that God the Father, God the Son, and God the Holy Spirit are each divine, each distinct, and yet there is just one God. Augustine, writing in the fifth century, sums up our conviction: "The Father and the Son and the Holy Spirit, each of these by Himself is God, and at the same time they are all one God; and each of them by Himself is a complete substance, and yet they are all one substance."

While we soon become confused when we try to conceptualize the Trinity, and while our analogies break down, we really aren't troubled by so-called logical contradictions. After all, there are many things in the material universe that human beings don't understand. Why should we expect to be able to comprehend God?

Yet the reason we are not troubled by our failure to understand the Trinity is that God's threeness and oneness both are taught in Scripture.

God is three. Plural language is found even in the Old Testament. The name of God used in Genesis 1:1, *Elohim*, is plural, and in making human beings God uses plural language: "Let *us* make man in *our* image" (Gen. 1:26, italics added). Even the Hebrew word in Israel's great affirmation, "the LORD our God is one LORD" (Deut. 6:4, *italics* added), uses a Hebrew term that emphasizes plurality in unity. Beyond this, we look back and see an Old Testament filled with references to God's Spirit, and we suspect that in many instances the "angel of the Lord" was a preincarnate appearance of Jesus.

We see these hints of plurality in the Old Testament because we look back with a perspective given by the New Testament revelation, where we find bold statements. We see Jesus presented as One who was with God and was God from eternity (John 1:1-3). We hear Jesus speak of the Father as "the only true God" and yet affirm that "I and the Father are one" (John 10:30; 17:5). In towering statements the Bible speaks of Jesus as God incarnate, one with and yet distinct from the Father (Phil. 2:5-11; Col. 1:15-20). In the same way Jesus identifies the Holy Spirit as One like Himself (John 14:15-17). The Spirit is given divine attributes (1 Cor. 2:1-11; Heb. 9:14) and is identified with God in His acts (1 Cor. 12:4-6). In Ephesians 1, we see the roles of Father, Son, and Spirit in salvation spelled out for us, with each person acknowledged as God. We may not understand how it can be, but we are comfortable in the knowledge that the Bible presents one God who exists eternally as three: Father, Son, and Holy Spirit.

God is one. While the New Testament calls for us to acknowledge Father, Son, and Holy Spirit as God, the Old Testament undergirds the conviction that there remains only one God. Of course the New Testament teaches it too in words like "I and the Father are one" (John 10:30).

The unity of God was especially important in Old Testament times, for ancient cultures multiplied gods and goddesses. Against this background Israel's Jahweh stands out as unique, author of creation, life, and redemption. Only Israel among all the ancient cultures never differentiated the deity sexually and so protected the people against the moral abuses of surrounding nations.

Not only is the substance of God in the Old Testament one substance, but He is one in the total unity of His character and purpose. The Old Testament's call to Israel, "The Lord our God, the Lord is one" is followed by an exhortation to love the Lord completely, with all one's heart and soul and strength. The God Israel was to love is one God, even as the God we love and worship in Father, Son, and Spirit remains one.

Thus we are convinced. We do not really understand the Trinity, and no analogies seem capable of symbolizing the three-in-oneness of God. We do not understand, but we hear the testimony of Scripture and we believe. We believe and we worship. We worship the Father. We worship the Son. And we worship the Spirit. For these three are God, and these three are One.

THE WORD OF GOD

Christians are convinced that ours is a revealed religion: God has spoken to us. Our beliefs are truths unveiled by God, not the best guesses or highest thoughts of mere human beings. This conviction is expressed in a number of biblical concepts, such as truth, revelation, and inspiration. Taken together they affirm that God has communicated to us in words, and that that His words are recorded in the Scriptures, our Bible.

We are confident that our Bible is both reliable and relevant, a clear and understandable message from the Lord, our authority in faith and morals. As theologian Emil Brunner states in *Faith and Reason*, "The church has always called the Scriptures of the Old and New Testaments the 'word of God.' In so doing, the church expresses the fundamental truth of the Christian faith, namely, that in these books the historical self-manifestation of God is offered to faith in an incomparable, decisive, and unique manner; this means that no Christian faith can either rise or be preserved which ignores the 'Holy Scripture.'"

By studying the writings of the early church fathers, we know that the same books of the Old Testament and New Testament that we accept as authoritative today were recognized as authoritative from the beginning. Christians have always relied on the Scriptures for our knowledge of who God is and what His plans and purposes are. As we study the Bible, we seek to know Him and to trace His thoughts, willingly submit-

ting our notions about reality to the reality which God's Word reveals.

The Bible as the inspired Word of God. This conviction is especially expressed in the Bible's own teaching of inspiration. This doctrine answers the question of whether the Bible is a record of human speculation and experience, or a revelation given to us by God Himself. Inspiration makes it clear that the Bible is special, an unveiling of truth by God.

What is inspiration? When speaking of their message, the Old Testament prophets often identified it as the "word of God." The words they spoke could be counted on to accurately convey God's intention. As David affirmed, "The Spirit of the LORD spoke by me; His word was on my tongue" (2 Sam. 23:2). The New Testament describes the process, stating that "all Scripture is given by inspiration of God" (2 Tim. 3:16). Here the word translated "inspiration" is "God-breathed," picturing the breath or wind of God filling the writer and carrying him or her along so that the product, the words, convey just what God intends.

From the beginning the Christian community has agreed that the Bible is inspired, its words the trustworthy expression of God's thoughts. Clement of Alexandria called the Scripture "true, given through the Holy Ghost; and you know that there is nothing unrighteous or counterfeit in them." Justin Martyr, another early church father, spoke of the Scriptures as the product of the "energy of the Divine Spirit . . . using men as an instrument like a harp or lyre" to "reveal to us the knowledge of things divine and heavenly."

Irenaeus called the Scripture "perfect, since they were spoken by the Word of God and His Spirit." Origen writes that "the sacred books are not the compositions of men, but they were composed by inspiration of the Holy Spirit." Even those who challenge the doctrine today admit that from the beginning of time to the eighteenth century,

Christians remained convinced that God exercised a supernatural influence on the writers of the Scripture, enabling them to communicate His truth without error, giving us a trustworthy and authoritative Word on which we can rely.

The Bible as divine revelation. Truly, if we are to know God He must take the initiative and reveal Himself to us. By the time Jesus was born, the most astute philosophers had agreed there was no way to know God. He was too distant, too different, too divorced from the material universe. Most doubted that a God really existed, but if one did, there was no way for humans to know him. Those same philosophers had long ago despaired of gaining knowledge of reality. Empedocles, who lived in the fifth century B.C., writes: "Weak and narrow are the powers implanted in the limbs of man; many the woes that fall on them and blunt the edges of thought; short is the measure of the life in death through which they toil. Then are they borne away; like smoke they vanish into air; and what they dream they know is but the little that each hath stumbled upon in wandering about the world. Yet boast they all that they have learned the whole. Vain fools! For what that is, no eye hath seen, no ear hath heard, nor can it be conceived by the mind of man."

The apostle Paul picks up Empedocles' words as he speaks of the necessity of a divine revelation. "'Eye has not seen, nor ear heard, nor have entered into the hearts of man, the things which God has prepared for those who love Him.' But God has revealed them to us through His Spirit" (1 Cor. 2:9-10). Paul goes on to point out that only the spirit of a person knows his or her inmost thoughts. Only the Spirit of God knows the thoughts of God. Weak and narrow as our powers are, we could never penetrate the thoughts of God or discover the nature of reality unless God communicated it to us. And so we have the wonder unveiled. God has chosen to communicate, speaking to us through the prophets and apostles, "not in

words which man's wisdom teaches but which the Holy Spirit teaches" (1 Cor. 2:13).

So we not only believe in Scripture, we risk everything on its trustworthiness. Through the Bible we come to understand and to know God. Through the Bible we learn how to live godly lives. While there may be some passages and sections in Scripture which are difficult to understand, all the major teachings are undoubtedly clear. When we take the Bible seriously and take its words in their plain sense, we do know truth about God, and we do know how to live to be pleasing to the Lord.

THE WRATH OF GOD

It seems like a grim item with which to close a book on the names and titles of God. But the wrath of God is, in more than one sense, a message of hope. It seems strange, because Scripture warns us against anger. Although anger may be justified, it too easily leads us to sin. The Old Testament calls it a cause of strife (Prov. 30:33) and something cruel (Prov. 22:24) to be avoided (Prov. 29:8). The New Testament bluntly commands us to "let all bitterness, wrath, anger, clamor and evil speaking be put away from you, with all malice" and to "be kind to one another, tenderhearted, forgiving one another, even as God in Christ has forgiven you" (Eph. 4:31-32).

Some have argued that it is inconsistent for God to tell us to forego anger and be compassionate and yet be angry Himself. But both testaments speak of the wrath of God, and they use the same Hebrew and Greek terms that are used to identify human anger. But there are vast differences between God's anger and our own.

God's anger in the Old Testament. God's anger is never capricious and is never expressed in uncontrollable tantrums. God's anger is a righteous anger, provoked only by sin. What God becomes angry about is injustice. Exodus 22:22-24 says, "You shall not afflict any widow or fatherless child. If you afflict them in any way, and they cry at all to Me, I will surely hear their cry; and My wrath will become hot." This and other violations of relationship are pictured in the Old Testament as the cause of divine wrath (Deut. 4:23-26; 29:23-28).

God's anger is kindled when He is not trusted (Ex. 4:14), when He is disobeyed (Num. 21:6), and when He is spurned for false deities (Fx. 32:10-12). It would be totally wrong to see God as some unemotional, uninvolved force Who is unaffected by the doings of humanity. The God we worship cares intensely. And that caring is expressed both in the anger that moves Him to punish and in the compassion that leads Him to forgive. Yet always God's wrath is tempered, and while His anger is momentary, His favor lasts a lifetime (Ps. 30:5).

The stereotype of an angry Old Testament God is inaccurate, for it suggests an uncontrollable wrath aroused by trifles. On the contrary, the Old Testament pictures a loving God Who is moved by righteous anger, whose wrath is exercised in necessary punishment of sin. Even then God's wrath is ultimately for our good. Disciplinary punishments may bring reform, and the destruction of the evil may free us to enjoy a life of peace. However angry God becomes, His wrath is never the controlling factor in His choices.

We human beings, falling so short of perfection, can never know a truly righteous anger. Only the Lord can remain compassionate and gracious while executing necessary judgments (Ex. 34:6).

So Christians do not apologize for the Old Testament's angry God. We see justice in the Flood as He judged a wicked world (Gen. 6:1-7). We honor God's anger at Egypt's persecution of His people as He punished Egypt with plagues (Ex. 15:7). We respect His right to use the pagan armies with which He punished His idolatrous people, Israel (Is.10:5). God's anger and God's acts of judgment are both justified, and the anger of God, aroused by sin, is rightly to be feared by people and nations who stray from righteousness.

God's anger in the New Testament. The New Testament emphasizes the love of God, but even Jesus continues to warn us against God's anger. Wrath in the New Testament is focused on those who refuse to respond to the offer of a salvation purchased by the death of God's own Son (John 3:36; Rom. 3:5; Eph. 2:3). That wrath is never directed at us, because Jesus has paid fully for the sins of all who believe in Him.

Everything that arouses God's anger is forgiven for Jesus' sake. But the unsaved, who still bear the guilt of their own sins, remain in the court of a God Who must, and Who will judge sin.

There is another striking feature of the New Testament's teaching on the wrath of God. God's wrath is not treated as something that people need to fear now, except as it might be exercised indirectly through government or natural consequences. When the New Testament speaks of God's wrath, it speaks of history's end, when Christ will return, "in flaming fire taking vengeance on those who do not know God, and on those who do not obey the gospel of our Lord Jesus Christ" (2 Thess. 1:7-8). Only at history's end, but surely then, God's wrath will be unleashed (Luke 21:23; Rom. 2:5-8; 9:22; 1 Thess. 1:10; 2:16).

Why this delay? Romans 2:4 tells us that it is because God is rich in kindness, tolerance, and patience. God is holding back in order to provide people with an opportunity to repent. The withholding of God's wrath is a hallmark of today's day of forgiveness and grace. Those who stubbornly resist and reject His grace store up for themselves "wrath in the day of wrath and revelation of the righteous judgement of God" (Rom. 2:5).

Our God is no stranger to anger. His wrath is not to be dismissed lightly as if love rules out righteous anger and compassion drains sin of its evil. God remains God, and human sin arouses His wrath and merits His punishment.

Christians see the ultimate expression of God's wrath in His greatest act of love. On Calvary Jesus died because of sins, bearing the punishment that we deserve. And yet that terrible act of judgment opens the door to forgiveness for all who accept it as Christ's gift. Only the punishment of sin by our righteous God could clear the way for Him to welcome us in love.

Anger and hope. So how does word of the wrath of God become a message of hope? In many ways. In God's wrath, we see God as a person who cares deeply and is fully involved. A force or thing could never heed our cries, but a person with the emotional capacity to care deeply may.

Word of the wrath of God is a message of hope for another reason, too. We see the things that arouse God's anger, and we sense His commitment to the good and right. We take hope from the fact that there is morality rooted in the universe, that mere might does not make right, and the strong will not overcome the weak.

Word of the wrath of God is a message of hope because it helps us understand the death of Jesus. God unleashed wrath's destroying bolt, crushing the One who hung there on the Cross. And then the good word comes: It was the punishment for our sins He suffered, for He had none of His own. The Cross exhausted the wrath of God as sin's full penalty was paid, and from that same Cross there now flows forgiving love.

Word of the wrath of God is a message of hope for us who believe, because we know that Jesus died to deliver us from the wrath to come (1 Thess. 5:9).

Finally, word of God's wrath is a message of hope even for the unsaved. It is a word of wrath withheld, a promise of a day of grace when salvation can still be found. Yet it is also a warning most stern. If the Son of God, who died for sinners, seems unworthy of trust, then wrath will surely come when He returns.

Wrath has its honored place in the vocabulary of our faith and in the character of our God. Even the wrath of God reminds us of His love. And even fear of punishment to come is intended to turn our eyes to Jesus and His forgiving love.

EXPOSITORY INDEX

An expository index organizes information by topic and guides the reader to Bible verses and book pages which are critical to understanding the subject. It does not list every verse referred to in the book, but seeks to identify key verses. It does not list every mention of a topic in the book, but directs the reader to pages where a topic is discussed in some depth. Thus an expository index helps the reader avoid the frustration of looking up verses in the Bible or the book, only to discover that they contribute in only a small way to one's understanding of the subject.

This expository index organizes references to names and titles of God by topic. Topics and sub-topics are identified in the left-hand column. Key Bible verses and passages are listed in the center column under "Scriptures." The far right column identifies pages in this book where the topic is covered.

In most instances, several of the key verses in the "Scriptures" column will be discussed on the book pages referred to. Very often additional verses will be referred to on the pages where the topic is covered. Our goal is to help you keep in focus the critical Bible verses and passages. Similarly, the book pages referred to are only those which make a significant contribution to understanding a topic, not every page on which a topic may be mentioned.

Please note that material under sub-topics is sometimes organized chronologically by the sequence of appearance in Scripture, and sometimes alphabetically, depending upon which organization will be most helpful in understanding and locating information.

NAMES AND TITLES OF GOD IN THE NEW TESTAMENT

Names and Titles of God the Father in the Gospels

Names and Titles of God the Father in the Epistles

TOPIC	SCRIPTURE	PAGES
Father of Mercies	2 Corinthians 1:3	125
Father of Lights	James 1:17	125-126
Father of Spirits	Hebrews 12:9	126-127
God of All Grace	1 Peter 5:10	127-130
God of All Comfort	2 Corinthians 1:3	130
God of Love and Peace	2 Corinthians 13:11	130-131
God Our Savior	1 Timothy 1:1	131-132
God Who Gives Life to the Dead	Romans 4:17	132
God Who Calls Those Things Which Do Not Exist as Though They Did	Roman 4:17	132
Holy One	1 John 2:20	132-133
The King Eternal, Immortal, Invisible	1 Timothy 1:17	133
Lawgiver	James 4:12	134-135
Light	John 8:12; 1 John 1:5-10	135-136
Lord Almighty	2 Corinthians 6:18	136
Lord God	1 Peter 3:15	136
Lord of Peace	2 Thessalonians 3:16	137
Majesty [in the heavens, on high]	Hebrews 8:1	137
Most High God	Hebrews 7:1	137
Savior		137

Names and Titles of God the Father in Revelation

God of the Earth [of the Heaven]	Revelation 11:4	138
He Who Is and Who Was and Who is to Come	Revelation 1:4	138
King of the Saints	Revelation 15:3	138
Lord God Omnipotent	Revelation 19:6	139
Lord God Almighty	Revelation 4:8	138
Great God, The	Revelation 19:17	139

QUALITIES OF GOD

Authority	31-32, 45, 64-67, 105, 133, 136, 137, 142, 151-153, 156, 157
Avenging	56, 57, 59
Comforting	62
Eternity	42, 101, 133, 138, 141, 196
Faithfulness	81, 85
Forgiveness	58-61
Glory	43, 125

NAME AND TITLES OF THE HOLY SPIRIT

SIMILES AND METAPHORS FOR GOD IN THE OLD TESTAMENT

SCRIPTURE INDEX

(Bible references are in boldface type, followed by the pages on which they appear in this book.)

THE EVERYTHING IN THE BIBLE SERIES

EVERY ANGEL IN THE BIBLE (ISBN: 0-7852-4533-2)

Explore an unseen world inhabited by agents of God and Satan.

The most complete contemporary exploration of every angelic appearance from Genesis to Revelation. More than 100 drawings, charts, and maps, along with comprehensive Expository and Scripture Indexes, focus on specific instances of angelic appearances and what the Bible teaches through them.

EVERY MAN IN THE BIBLE (ISBN: 0-7852-1439-9)

Share the lives of the men who shaped our faith and our world.

Meet the men God used to tell His story. The significant contributions of patriarchs, prophets, and kings, as well as the men around Jesus, are explored and explained. Even more, the men of the Bible are portrayed as real people whose flaws often betrayed them, yet who found in their personal relation-ship with God the strength to achieve great things.

EVERY MIRACLE IN THE BIBLE (ISBN: 0-7852-4531-6)

Examine the mighty works of God in time and space.

Richards takes you on a grand tour of all the Bible's truly "extra-ordinary events caused by God." This book will help you understand the amazing miracles and wonders of the Bible and strengthen your faith in a God who cannot be bound by time and space. Richards explains each miracle's significance in God's unfolding revelation.

EVERY NAME OF GOD IN THE BIBLE (ISBN: 0-7852-0702-3)

Understand who God is through His names, titles, and images.

Humanity has come to understand God more fully by way of the names, titles, and images used to identify Him in the Bible.

- *Names* – Yahweh, Sovereign Lord, Eternal God
- *Titles* – Creator of heaven, God of truth, God of justice
- *Images* – Fortress, Potter, Father

Richards expands our view of Jesus and the Holy Spirit by examining terms applied to them in both the Old and New Testaments.

EVERY PRAYER IN THE BIBLE (ISBN: 0-7852-4534-0)

Learn to follow God's patterns for confession, petition, and intercession.

An in-depth examination of prayer throughout the Scriptures. Journey through the Old and New Testament to strengthen and empower your times of communion with God as you learn to appropriate His promises and follow His biblical patterns for worship, confession, petition, and intercession.

EVERY PROMISE IN THE BIBLE (ISBN: 0-7852-4532-4)

Find comfort and strength in God's unshakable commitments.

Richards demonstrates that God is a keeper of His word, trustworthy and dependable to fulfill everything He has promised. A helpful compilation of "Words to Count On" provides hundred of beloved expressions of faith and confidence in God as recorded by the biblical writers.

EVERY WOMAN IN THE BIBLE (ISBN: 0-7852-1441-0)

Discover all the women of the Bible and how they lived.

This comprehensive reference book explores the individual life and contribution of each woman who appears in Scripture. Building upon the most up-to-date scholarship, it provides powerful vignettes exploring the character of Bible women and draws healing and helpful lessons for today.

COMING SOON:

EVERY TEACHING OF JESUS IN THE BIBLE (ISBN: 0-7852-0703-1)